Fodor's

COSTA RICA

FODOR'S TRAVEL PUBLICATIONS

NEW YORK • TORONTO
LONDON • SYDNEY • AUCKLAND

WWW.FODORS.COM

CONTENTS

KEY TO SYMBOLS

- Map reference
- Address
- Telephone number
- Opening times
- Admission prices
- Underground station
- Bus number
- Train station
- Ferry/boat
- Driving directions
- Tourist office
- Tours
- Guidebook
- Restaurant
- Cafe
- Bar
- Shop
- Number of rooms
- Air conditioning
- Swimming pool
- Gym
- Other useful information
- ▷ Cross reference
- ★ Walk/drive start point

140

70

88

110

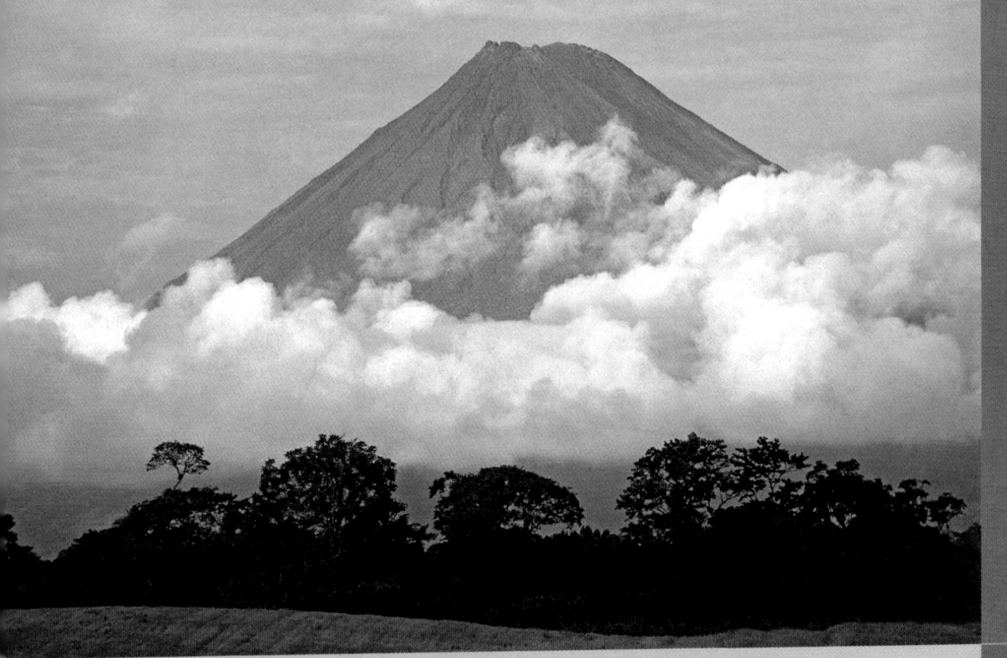

UNDERSTANDING COSTA RICA

Understanding Costa Rica is an introduction to the country, its geography, economy, history and its people, giving a real insight into the nation. Living Costa Rica gets under the skin of Costa Rica today, while The Story of Costa Rica takes you through the country's past.

Costa Rica's headline act is its incomparable natural diversity. The country might be small—less than
(180 miles) wide and 400km (250 miles) north to south—but it is home to twice as many bird species as
America and more species of butterfly than all of Africa. One quarter of it is protected land, ranging from c
covered mountains to steamy rain forests pulsating with vitality. But this peaceable Central American nation
one-hit wonder. Further down the bill, a trio of live volcanoes provide consistently fiery entertainment. And vi
are drawn to Costa Rica's jungle-backed beaches: You can find surf and sunshine on both coasts. Costa R
country that pioneered ecotourism, is now also a thrilling adventure travel destination. Gold-seeking conquist
largely bypassed this gem of a country. Don't make the same mistake.

GEOGRAPHY

Costa Rica owes at least part of its biological variety to its position in the narrow isthmus linking North and South America. Flora and fauna from both continents meet and flourish in the country's exceptionally varied habitats. Visitors will find chilly cloud forests, sultry lowland jungle and highland plains. Volcanoes are thrust skyward as tectonic plates beneath Costa Rica crumple together: The country has seven active volcanoes in three cordilleras (ranges). You can even get a crater-side view at Volcán Poás and Volcán Irazú.

The highest ground in Costa Rica is the Talamanca mountain range in the south of the country. The highest peak here, Cerro Chirripó, is 3,820m (12,533ft) and swathed in impenetrable forest. But most of Costa Rica's population lives at the more moderate altitude of 1,525m (5,000ft) in the Central Highlands. The capital, San José, sprawls across a fertile, temperate valley, the Meseta Central, with beaches, rain forests and volcanoes no more than a couple of hours' drive away. To the east, the Caribbean lowlands are a mix of forest and fruit plantations. Jungle also extends to the Pacific coast, but towards the northwest of the country, the Guanacaste region, the landscape changes to a hot, dry savanna.

Travel south down the Pacific coast and the climate
becomes progressively wetter until you reach the re
Osa Peninsula, a challenging environment for huma
and a sanctuary for jaguars and rare macaws.

SOCIETY

Ticos (the name Costa Ricans give to themselves) a
Central America's best-educated, wealthiest people
Education is free and compulsory up to the age of
with the result that the literacy rate tops 95 percent
Three state universities produce 18,000 graduates
year. Costa Rica's comprehensive social security sy
also provides effective health care to 95 percent of
the population. Infant mortality and population grow
rates—at 8.7 and 1.4 per thousand a year, respectiv
are among the lowest in the region, and life expecta
is 78, as opposed to a Latin American average of 7
the best education and health service in the region
money and many Costa Ricans see the current wel
system as unsustainable. Nonetheless, the welfare
system is a cherished element of Costa Rican socie
and the government's proposals to fund reforms by
privatizing some state-owned organizations face sti
highly vocal opposition.

Left *Waves lap a rocky beach at Dominical*

PEOPLE

Costa Rican people may seem enviably egalitarian on the surface, but they are as divided as any other society. The principal divisions are racial and regional. The 94 percent majority of Costa Rica's population of about 4.25 million are considered to be white of mixed Spanish descent. The next largest single group is Afro-Caribbeans, representing 3 percent, followed by Amerindians, Chinese and others at 1 percent each. There are also as many as 400,000 refugees and economic migrants from Nicaragua in Costa Rica. Following Hurricane Mitch in 1998, the Costa Rican government announced a one-year amnesty to all illegal Central American immigrants living in the country. By June of 2000, 156,000 people had qualified for legal residency papers, the majority of them from Nicaragua. Fair-skinned Costa Ricans of Spanish descent tend to look down upon dark-skinned Costa Ricans of African descent and the indigenous tribal peoples. There are eight indigenous tribes in Costa Rica: Huetar, Bribrí, Cabécar, Guaymí, Chorotega, Boruca, Guatuso and Térraba, with land protected in 22 reserves. It was only in 1994 that tribal people were granted the vote and often they feel marginalized, while the Comisión Nacional de Asuntos Indígenas (National Commission for Indigenous Affairs; CONAI) is considered ineffective. Most tribal groups have opened up to ecotourism in recent years.

POLITICS

Power alternates between the two main national parties, the left-wing National Liberation Party (PLN) and the right-leaning Social Christian Unity Party (PUSC). Elections are often close-run events and bribery, corruption and cronyism are major concerns. In 2006 Oscar Arias Sánchez, of the PLN, became the first president elected for a second term after he initiated a constitutional amendment permitting multiple terms.

The 57 members of the Legislative Assembly, based in a Moorish building in San José's Plaza de la Democracía, represent Costa Rica's seven provinces: Alajuela, Cartago, Guanacaste, Heredia, Limón, Puntarenas and San José. Since the creation of Costa Rica's Constitution in 1949, the country has had no standing army, hence its reputation as "the Switzerland of Central America." The nation's neutrality has enabled it to take a prominent role in negotiating for peace in turbulent Central America.

ECONOMY

The single largest factor affecting Costa Rica's economy is its colossal national debt. In 1981 the country was the first in the world to default on its loans. Following a period of austerity, in 2007 the country had its first budget surplus in 50 years, although the national debt had risen to $9.2 billion in 2009. Economically, the country has been undergoing a slow revolution, with every year bringing a shift away from traditional agricultural production and growth in manufacturing, the service sector and tourism, the country's largest source of foreign income. The economy experienced strong growth in the late 1990s and early 2000s, with gross domestic product (GDP) averaging a 5 percent year on year increase. However, two of Costa Rica's most important crops, bananas and coffee beans, are suffering, respectively, from falling quotas and plummeting prices, and inflation, at approximately 13 percent, is also hurting economic forecasts. Still, unemployment—just 4.9 percent in 2008—is low by the standards of the region.

LANGUAGE

Costa Ricans speak Spanish, with a Tico twist. It's based on Castilian Spanish but there are several minor differences; there are no soft "*c*"s or "*z*"s, for example, and Costa Ricans use the more formal versions of "you," "*vos*" and "*usted*." Local slang is easy to pick up and includes such common words and phrases as "*tico*" and "*pura vida*." The suffix "*tico*," used to indicate something in the diminutive, has been adopted by Costa Ricans as a self-deprecating way of referring to themselves. "*Pura vida*" means "pure life," a prized Costa Rican concept often used as a salutation. An influx of Westerners means that increasing numbers of people speak or understand English outside the capital, but in rural areas don't expect to find many English-speakers, except in Puerto Limón, where settlers from Jamaica prefer English.

Below *Children playing outside a small home in Tortuguero*

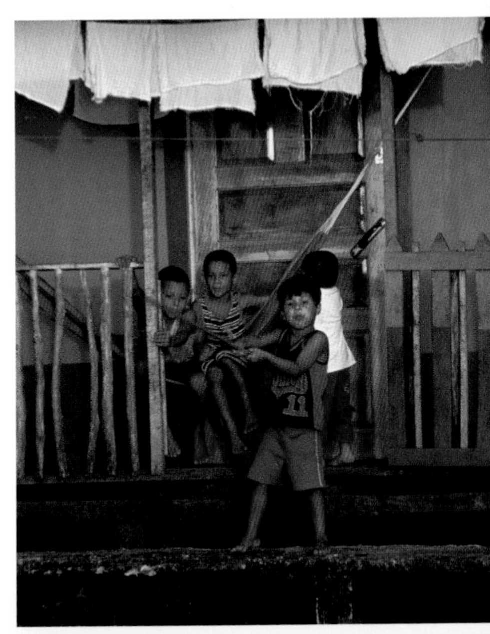

COSTA RICA'S REGIONS AT A GLANCE

San José The Costa Rican capital is not one of the world's great cities, but it benefits from a provincial scale, a compact downtown easily explored on foot, and a mild climate. If you spend a day or two here, the Mercado Central and the Museo de Oro Precolombino make good diversions.

Central Highlands You don't have to go far from San José to arrive in some spectacular scenery. The Central Highlands surround the capital, with the colossal crater Volcán Poás to the north and Costa Rica's highest volcano, Irazú, to the east. Tapirs and jaguars reside in the primary forest of Parque Nacional Braulio Carrillo, while Heredia is the coffee-growing heartland.

Northern Region The Cordillera de Tilarán mountain range sweeps north through this region, where dairy farmers have carved out settlements among the mountains, lakes and wildlife parks. Volcán Arenal is a classically conical volcano and may be either spitting lava, fuming quietly or shrouded in cloud. Monteverde is a world-renowned nature reserve.

Guanacaste This is ranching country, with a rugged but welcoming regional identity. There's little rainfall here, offering a respite from the humid forests and insect-infested jungles farther south, but tracts of tropical dry forest survive in national parks and white-sand beaches line the Pacific shores.

Central Pacific and Nicoya Head west to the remote and relatively undeveloped Nicoya Peninsula and you will find some of Costa Rica's finest beaches and bays, with Pacific swells attracting surfers from around the world. The low-lying Central Pacific region continues the sun, sand and surf theme and is the principal region for sportfishing.

Southern Region As the Central Pacific coast heads south, it gets steadily more tropical and humid, until conditions become extremely demanding in the steamy rain forest of the Osa Peninsula. Inland, the Southern Region claims Costa Rica's highest point, Cerro Chirripó, and some of the country's remaining indigenous communities.

The Caribbean Lowlands The culturally diverse Caribbean coastline stretches from the sea turtle breeding grounds and lagoons of Tortuguero, past banana plantations to the laid-back charms of Puerto Limón and the beautiful beaches farther south.

TOP EXPERIENCES

Learn to surf (▷ 165–166) at a surf camp at one of Costa Rica's world-class west coast beaches, but leave the big waves to the experts.

Watch turtles hatch at Parque Nacional Tortuguero (▷ 199) the most important breeding site for green turtles in the Caribbean.

Hike Cerro Chirripó (▷ 178–180); the country's highest point is in the Cordillera de Talamanca.

Go sportfishing (▷ 147, 164–166) for marlin, dorado, tuna and sailfish in the Pacific and snook, tarpon or hard-fighting bonefish in the Caribbean.

Witness a night-time eruption at Volcán Arenal (▷ 111–113)—if your timing is good, you might catch Arenal throwing glowing lava into the night skies.

Walk to the Blue Lagoon in Parque Nacional Rincón de la Vieja (▷ 136)—and wallow in the hot springs.

Hike to the Montezuma Falls (▷ 156). There are waterfalls throughout Costa Rica, but those on the Montezuma River are among the most impressive.

Take a yoga class (▷ 169–171) at one of the New Age lodges in the Central Pacific and Nicoya region.

Watch the macaws fly home to roost in Parque Nacional Carara (▷ 156)—in late afternoon it's time for the noisy macaws to fly back to their trees for the night.

Track a jaguar in Parque Nacional Corcovado (▷ 181–184). During the turtle breeding season the big cats venture onto the beach to hunt turtles.

String up a hammock on a beach. Pick a beach (Manuel Antonio is a good choice, ▷ 160–161). Find two trees about 2.5m (8ft) apart. Attach hammock. Relax.

Go white-water rafting (▷ 189) through virgin rain forest on the Pacuare River. Other rivers, such as the Sarapiquí, are less turbulent.

Take a canopy tour (▷ 165–166). Several are offered and help to understand the rain forest ecosystem.

Rent a mountain bike (▷ 56) because there's no better way of experiencing Costa Rica's countryside than cycling through it on jungle trails and rough tracks.

Go scuba diving among hammerhead sharks at Parque Nacional Isla del Coco (▷ 157, 164) where great concentrations of the predators feed on smaller fish. Experienced divers only.

Start the day with a coffee, Costa Rica's finest commodity. Café Britt (▷ 85), an excellent, nationally available brand, is made from 100 percent arabica beans.

Finish the day with a local beer. Imperial is the most widespread brand, while Bavaria Gold is equally popular.

Watch the sunset from a Pacific-facing restaurant (▷ 167–168) for one of the most romantic sights of all, but reserve early because the best restaurants fill up fast in the high season.

Rent a four-wheel drive and explore the hill country (▷ 49–50). A rugged four-wheel-drive vehicle is the only way to travel in some of the remote regions and every trip has the potential to become an adventure.

Take a day-trip to Granada. It's a short hop from Daniel Oduber Quirós airport (▷ 45) to Central America's grandest and oldest colonial city in Nicaragua.

Above *Relaxing with a book on a hammock on an idyllic beach at Punta Leona as the sun sets*

SAN JOSÉ

Galería Namú (▷ 76) Get your gifts at the best souvenir shop in San José.

Grano de Oro (▷ 79) Treat yourself to a meal at one of San José's top eateries, and rest your head in the city's best digs.

Mercado Central (▷ 76) Bargain hunt or just browse the stands at the biggest market in the country.

Museo de Oro Precolumbino (▷ 69) Contain your avarice at this astounding display of gold artifacts dating from AD500.

Museo del Jade (▷ 68) Don't miss this fascinating collection of hundreds of jade artifacts, the best to be found in Latin America.

Teatro Nacional (▷ 71) The most handsome and interesting building in the Costa Rican capital is the National Theater in the Plaza de la Cultura.

CENTRAL HIGHLANDS

Barry Biesanz (▷ 102) Wood-carver Barry Biesanz is Costa Rica's top craftsman, designing furniture and other items at his workshop in Escazú.

Botanical Orchid Garden (▷ 103) A visual delight, this garden at La Garita has been decades in the making.

Fábrica de Chaverri (▷ 103) Buy your Sarchí oxcart here and they'll mail it home for you.

Finca Rosa Blanca Coffee Plantation & Inn (107) Go horseback riding and tour the coffee estate that surrounds this architecturally superb boutique hotel outside Heredia.

La Luz (▷ 105) Treat yourself at one of the best restaurants in Costa Rica, in Escazú.

Parque Nacional Braulio Carrillo (▷ 90–91) A highway runs straight through this relatively unexplored park.

Volcán Irazú (▷ 93) Arrive early at the country's tallest volcano to avoid clouds and crowds.

Volcán Poás (▷ 92) Close to San José, this colossal crater attracts plenty of visitors hoping for a glimpse of it through the clouds.

NORTHERN REGION

Kite-surfing at Lake Arenal (▷ 112) Don a wetsuit for kite-surfing at this wind-whipped lake in a mountain saddle.

Monteverde (▷ 116–121) Renowned for its diversity, this compact cloud forest reserve is right at the top of most sightseers' lists.

Pizzeria de Johnny (▷ 127) The best restaurant in the region? Pizza lovers think so.

Volcán Arenal (▷ 111–113) Brooding over the surrounding area, Arenal is a classically conical volcano, prone to fiery eruptions.

GUANACASTE

Playa Grande (▷ 140) Watch the surfers catch the rolling waves by day, then return to watch leatherback turtles nest by night at this magnificent beach location.

Above *Palm trees on a beach in the Refugio Nacional de Vida Silvestre Gandoca-Manzanillo*

Parque Nacional Rincón de la Vieja (▷ 136) As well as hot springs, turquoise bathing pools and waterfalls, verdant Rincón de la Vieja offers a challenging hike to the summit.
Sueño del Mar (▷ 151) Stay at this charming bed-and-breakfast on Playa Langosta.

CENTRAL PACIFIC AND NICOYA

Barba Roja (▷ 167) Watch the sunset from the popular cocktail bar at this hilltop restaurant overlooking Manuel Antonio.
Festival of the Virgin of the Sea (▷ 166) A parade of brightly painted boats sails out from Puntarenas during this festival.
Flying Crocodile Lodge (▷ 171) This imaginatively decorated hotel offers ultra-light flying lessons.
Jungle Crocodile Safari (▷ 166) A boat trip on the Río Tárcoles in search of giant American crocodiles is an "Indiana Jones" adventure you'll aways remember.
Del Mar Surf Camp (▷ 165) Beginners can learn to surf at this popular women-only camp at Playa Hermosa.
Parque Nacional Carara (▷ 156) If you can't wait to get to the forest, this is the closest park to San José.
Parque Nacional Isla del Coco (▷ 157) An uninhabited desert island and a UNESCO World Heritage Site famous for shoals of hammerhead sharks.
Parque Nacional Manuel Antonio (▷ 160–161) String up a hammock at the beach or take a walk along the popular trails.

SOUTHERN REGION

Casa Orquídeas (▷ 188) Admire the orchids and hundreds of other specie of flora at this lovingly crafted tropical garden.

Above *Flowers on the edge of the crater of Volcán Irazú*
Below left *Walkers negotiate a bridge in the wooded Osa Peninsula*

Finca Eddie Serrano (▷ 189) Haven't seen a quetzal yet? Visit this reserve for an almost guaranteed sighting.
Lapa Ríos Lodge (▷ 192–193) Chill out at this highly rated eco-lodge in Matapalo.
Parque Nacional Chirripó (▷ 178–180) Costa Rica's second-largest park is home to its highest mountain and high-altitude plains called the *páramo*.
Parque Nacional Corcovado (▷ 181–184) Sweltering in the southwest corner, Corcovado repays the hardiness of its visitors with extraordinary wildlife-spotting opportunities.
Pavones (▷ 176) This surf spot has one of the world's longest waves.

THE CARIBBEAN LOWLANDS

Miss Edith's (▷ 209) A legend in Cahuita, Miss Edith's restaurant serves good, inexpensive Caribbean food to queues of eager diners.
Parque Nacional Cahuita (196–197) Follow the coast trail through this easily accessible national park teeming with exotic wildlife.
Parque Nacional Tortuguero (▷ 198–200) Watch turtles laying their eggs on the beaches of this national park, where boat trips along the canals and lagoons offer spectacular wildlife encounters.
Puerto Limón Carnaval (▷ 208) It's noisy, chaotic and even edgy, but Costa Rica's biggest street party is also a lot of fun.
Tortuga Lodge and Gardens (▷ 212) Splash the cash at this fashionable resort in Tortuguero, with economical package deals also available.

The relationship between temperature, altitude and rainfall creates Costa Rica's variety of ecosystems. National parks may cover one or more category, depending on location. Find out whether you're standing in tropical lowland, tropical premontane, lower montane or dry forest, with this brief guide.

LOWLAND WET FORESTS

Lowland wet forest is found in the northern and southern Caribbean lowlands and in the southern Pacific lowlands. Protected areas containing this forest include La Selva Biological Reserve, Cahuita National Park, Manuel Antonio National Park and Corcovado National Park.

These are the classical tropical forests. Tall, semi-deciduous and evergreen trees reach to a height of 40–55m (130–180ft) and even taller, emergent evergreen trees soar above this canopy. A subcanopy of lower trees is often present, while the ground may be bare or have a sparse shrub layer. While walking through the forest, some of the most commonly seen plants in the understory and shrub layer are members of the genus ***piper***. There are more than 90 species in this genus within Costa Rica. All are small trees or shrubs characterized by their erect, candle-like flowering structures, which are generally pollinated by bats. Buttress and stilt roots are common features in these forests. Buttress roots appear as broad ridges attached to the side of a tree trunk and act as support for the tree, accounting for the minimal subsurface root system. Stilt roots come off the side of a tree trunk, growing down and entering the earth some distance from the trunk to anchor the tree more firmly in the soil.

Palms are common in this type of forest and one species you may well see is *Welfia georgii*, which bears its fruit on its trunk. Vines are also numerous; quite common is the **passion flower** *(Passiflora foetida)*, with bright red flowers, and the **Swiss cheese plant** *(Monstera deliciosa)*, a large-leafed climber in these wet forests and commonly seen as a house plant in European and North American homes. **Epiphytes**, plants that grow on other plants, are frequent in the lowland wet forests, and large trees such as the **kapok** *(Ceiba pentandra)* are often heavily laden with them. This tree is massive, often emerging above the surrounding canopy, with a broad, flat crown and a seed that produces a fibrous material often used to stuff cushions and furniture. Epiphytes include mosses, ferns, orchids and bromeliads. The orchids, with more than 1,000 species in Costa Rica, can be spectacular when in flower—indeed Costa Rica's national flower is an orchid, the **guaria morada** *(Cattleya skinneri)*. **Bromeliads** typically have fleshy, often spiky, leaves formed into a rosette with a central "well" that holds water, which is often used as a small pond by a host of animals including snails, worms, insects and even frogs and tadpoles.

The driving force for change in the lowland wet forest is forest gaps. Clearings created by a tree fall produce a sudden availability of light and various plant species rush to colonize the area, before being gradually replaced by more mature, slower-growing species. Within the lowland forest, pioneer species such as the **balsa tree** *(Ochroma lagopus)*, grow rapidly in these gaps to reach a height of 30m (98ft). Its light, soft wood is used for making many of the wooden souvenirs available to tourists in Costa Rica. *Cercropia obtusifolia* is another

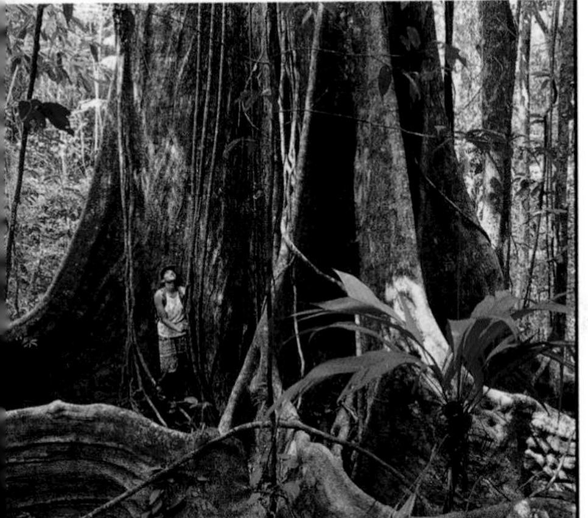

Left *A goat enjoys the shade of a spreading tree in Guanacaste*
Above *Standing beside a towering* ceiba *tree*

pioneer species, frequently found in lowland forests. Thriving on the light of forest gaps, it has large, umbrella-like leaves, which sloths love to eat.

Also found in disturbed areas of the forest, in clearings and along streams are species of *Heliconia*, which have large leaves and red, orange and yellow flowers, shaped rather like lobster claws, pollinated by hummingbirds. Banana plants belong to this family.

LOWLAND DRY FOREST

This type of forest once covered extensive areas of Costa Rica's northern Pacific coastal plain, but most has been cleared for agriculture. The rainy season here only lasts six months (May to October). By comparison, rain falls year-round in the Caribbean lowlands, hence the difference in forest type. The dry forest is semi-deciduous, with a canopy at 20–30m (65–100ft), an understory of trees 10–20m (33–65ft) tall and a 2–5m (6.5–16ft) high, dense shrub layer. Vines are present, but epiphytes are generally rare. Common or conspicuous plants include the **gumbo limbo tree** *(Bursera simaruba)*, which is recognizable by its smooth, red/orange bark. The *Crescentia alata*, a fairly common large, shrub-like tree, has hard fruits or gourds growing from its trunk which are eaten by rodents and also used for decoration. *Corteza* trees, in the genus *tabebuia*, are commonly seen but stand out when in flower, as all members of a species flower simultaneously towards the end of the dry season, though for only four days. The flowers are yellow, pink or purple. **Palms** are not as frequent in the dry forests as they are in the wetland forest, but one palm, *Acrocomia vinifera*, is fairly common; it has long, sharp spines on its lower trunk and occurs particularly in swampy areas and along roads.

Wildlife is often easier to see in these more open, less dense forests than in the thicker, wetter forests, though biodiversity is lower.

PREMONTANE AND MONTANE FOREST

In the forests at higher elevations, the hot stickiness of the lowland forest areas is replaced by a cooler dampness. The cooler climate is due to the temperature dropping, on average, by 0.5°C (0.9°F) for every 100m (330ft) gained in altitude. Mists of cloud or fog enshroud the forest canopy for much of the time, hence the name "cloud forest," which is often used to describe them. Light levels tend to be reduced at higher elevations and the foliage drips with water that condenses out of the atmosphere. These forests are less diverse than those in the lowlands, but they are often home to species that are found nowhere else in the world. These forests occur on the slopes of Costa Rica's mountains. In the lower areas the cloud forest is mixed deciduous and evergreen, while at higher elevations it is uniformly evergreen. There are frequent strong winds in the higher forests so the tops of the trees become flatter than those of lowland trees. In addition, the trees tend to become gnarled, twisted and multistemmed and the leaves are much smaller, narrower and leathery. Canopy height at lower levels is around 30–40m (100–130ft), declining as elevation increases. There is usually a subcanopy and dense undergrowth. **Vines** and **epiphytes** grow profusely, especially in the evergreen cloud forests; indeed **lichens** can be seen hanging in curtains from trees. Though also found at lower elevations, **tree ferns** are especially common in the higher forests. Quite a number of the trees and shrubs at these higher elevations may be found in temperate regions, such as **oaks** *(Quercus)*, **buddleia** *(Buddleja)* and **magnolia** *(Magnolia)*. Also found in these high forests is the **Winter's bark** *(Drimys winteri)*. Growing to about 15m (50ft) in height, it has aromatic bark, large, leathery, oval yellow-green leaves and clusters of fragrant, small, white flowers and purple berries.

PÁRAMO

This treeless, subalpine habitat predominates at the highest elevations in Costa Rica. Only grasses and shrubs are found in these areas. Chirripó National Park contains some areas of *páramo*.

Below *Coffee beans, freshly picked from a Costa Rican plantation*

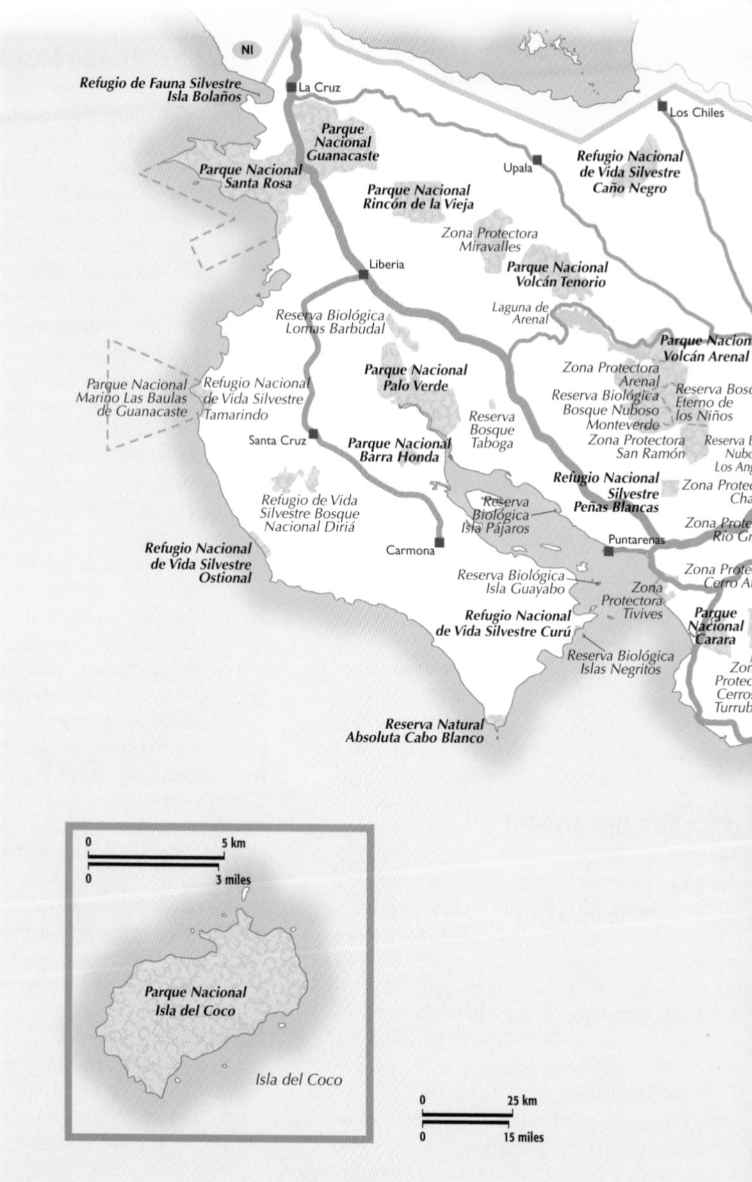

NATIONAL PARKS

Costa Rica is promoted as a model of conservation with national parks protecting 12 percent of the country and just over one quarter of the national territory falling within a protected status category of some kind.

The country has undergone a dramatic turnaround in recent decades. From the 1940s to the 1970s the country had some of the highest rates of deforestation in the world, clearing at a rate that would have stripped the entire country by the 21st century. Fortunately, the efforts of a dozen or so national and international individuals and groups—among them such guiding lights as Mario Boza, Archie Carr, Leslie R. Holdridge and the Organization for Tropical Studies (OTS)—have been successful in highlighting Costa Rica's extraordinary flora and fauna. Coupled with timely falls in commodity prices, the government moved away from state-sponsored land clearance for ranching and agriculture, preferring instead the creation of the national parks system.

The evolution of protected parks began in 1970 with the creation of the National Parks Service (SPN). The latest reorganization completed in 1995 divided the entire country into 11 regions, creating a National System of Protected Areas (SINAC—Sistema Nacional

de Areas de Conservación), which is administered as part of the Ministry for the Environment and Energy (MINAE—Ministerio del Ambiente y Energía).

In addition to national parks, the National System protects land within categories that include biological and forest reserves, wildlife refuges. Its goals are to consolidate and guarantee the conservation of the protected areas and the national biodiversity, and to manage their sustainable use. Many national parks have a combined purpose of protecting watersheds which feed the country's essential hydroelectric power system and protecting areas of particular biological interest.

The tourist boom of the past decade has helped foster an appreciation for the environment and has given natural ecosystems an economic value they previously lacked. Principled foreign landowners—many of them hoteliers—have led the way in private efforts to protect primary forest or to reforest denuded land. As a result, the amount of forested land now approaches 50 percent of Costa Rica's total land area. Many of these private resources have been incorporated into the National Parks and Wildlife Refuge System, often with the purpose of linking contiguous units to form (or protect) migratory corridors for mammalian fauna.

Costa Rica, for its size, contains more species of plants and animals than any other country in the world, with around 10,000 plant species, 875 bird species, 205 species of mammals, 215 reptiles, 160 amphibians and some 360,000 insects. It is home to around five percent of the world's terrestrial species.

Costa Rica's amazing biodiversity is partly due to its geographical situation linking two huge continental masses, the fact that it is a barrier between two oceans, and to its wide variety of landscapes, including mountains, valleys, coastal plains and prairies. In addition, though wholly within the tropics, Costa Rica has numerous miroclimates.

Much of the country's wildlife remains only in the small, but numerous, national parks and reserves which protect 25 percent of the country. Elsewhere, most of the forest, home to the majority of the animals, has been cut down and replaced by farmland.

PRIMATES

Costa Rica has four of the 70 or so species of New World monkey. The three larger ones are common in many protected areas, while the squirrel monkey is found in only a few lowland wet forests of the southern Pacific slope of the country.

Red-backed squirrel monkeys *(Saimiri oerstedii)* are small monkeys, with a golden orange back, hands and feet, a black crown and muzzle and white mask. Moving in groups of 10 to 20 individuals, they run and jump through the trees feeding on fruits, seeds, leaves and insects. The groups contain several adult females and males, with juveniles and infants. This species is only found in Panama and Costa Rica and is considered to be in danger of extinction.

White-faced capuchin monkeys *(Cebus capucinus)*, are medium-sized monkeys with a white throat, head and shoulders, while their back and prehensile tail are black. They forage in wet forests, including mangroves, and may even be seen on the ground. Their diet is mostly fruit, but also includes leaves, nuts, flowers, insects, small birds, reptiles and young mammals. Group size is around 10 to 20, consisting of males and females. These monkeys are probably the most commonly seen in Costa Rica as they occur in dry and wet forests and are active and noisy during the day; their threat display involves jumping up and down and shaking branches.

Geoffroy's spider monkeys *(Ateles geoffroyi)* are the most endangered Costa Rican primates. Their coat varies from light buff to black, with black hands and feet. They use their prehensile tail as a fifth limb, swinging, climbing and hanging in the upper canopy, preferring the wet, evergreen forests to the dry forests. They eat mainly fruit, but add seeds, flowers, leaves and insects to their diet. Groups usually have twice as many females as males, though the number moving together is variable as the troop divides into small foraging parties. Spider monkeys are active during the day.

Mantled howler monkeys *(Alouatta palliata)* are black except for a fringe of long gold hairs on their sides. Even if not seen, these large monkeys will certainly be heard by anyone visiting lowland evergreen forests or the dry forests, though they are also present in montane forests. The males, in particular, give loud roaring vocalizations at dawn and in the late afternoon. Howlers move slowly and deliberately high in the forest and may well be passed by unnoticed. Leaves are the main component of their diet, along with flowers and fruits. Group size is usually 10 to 20, made up of adult males and females and offspring.

OPOSSUMS

There are nine species of these marsupials in Costa Rica, occupying most habitats. The **common possum** *(Didelphis marsupialis)* resembles a large rat with yellowish face, gray-black body, black ears and a long, hairless, prehensile tail. They are nocturnal, but may be seen during the day foraging on the ground for fruits, eggs, invertebrates and small vertebrates. The smaller gray **four-eyed opossum** *(Philander opossum)* is found in rain forest regions; it has a black face mask with large white spots over its eyes. The **water opossum** *(Chironectes minimus)* is also seen quite commonly, often by or in water. This species has a gray body with broad black or brown stripes.

ANTEATERS

Costa Rica has three species of anteater. The most commonly seen is the **northern tamandua** *(Tamandua mexicana)*, which has a brown or yellowish head and legs with a black vest on its belly and back. It is found in trees and on the ground in wet and dry forests and in savanna habitats, feeding mainly on termites at night. The **giant anteater** *(Myrmecophaga tridactyla)* is up to 2m (6.5ft) long and extremely rare, while the tiny **silky anteater** *(Cyclopes didactylus)*, standing 17cm (6.5in) tall, is arboreal, nocturnal and unlikely to be spotted.

ARMADILLOS

Two of the world's 20 species of armadillo live in Costa Rica. The more common species is the **nine-banded armadillo** *(Dasypus novemcinctus)*. It has a gray to yellowish, armor-plated body, a long snout, large ears and scales on its head and legs, and is found on the ground in all but the most arid habitats. Its diet is variable, including insects and small vertebrates, fruit, fungi, tubers and carrion. It, and Costa Rica's other species, the **naked-tailed armadillo** *(Cabassous sp.)*, is nocturnal. Uniquely among mammals, the nine-banded and other armadillos may give birth to four genetically identical offspring.

SLOTHS

Costa Rica has two of these strange, slow-moving, upside-down creatures: **Hoffman's two-fingered sloth** *(Choloepus hoffmanni)* and the brown-throated **three-fingered sloth** *(Bradypus variegates)*. The former is generally a tan color and has no tail, while the latter is grayish brown with a distinctive gray and white mask and a small, stumpy tail. In moist conditions, the coats of both species may be suffused with green, the tint coming from the blue-green algae that live on their fur and help camouflage them in the trees. Both have three curved claws, or "toes," on their hind feet, while it is the claws on the forefeet that give them their common names. The three-fingered sloth is active day and night and may move through four or five trees in two days, whereas the two-fingered is nocturnal and is often in the same tree for two consecutive nights. Both species eat only leaves and it may take a month for a full meal to be completely digested. They average 18 hours a day sleeping in the sun to aid digestion. As a result, they need to descend to the base of a tree to defecate only once a week. Young are born throughout the year and are carried by their mother for six to nine months.

CATS

All six species of the cat family in Costa Rica are nocturnal and rare, which makes it unlikely that they will be seen. The smallest, spotted species is the **oncilla** or **trigrillo** *(Felis tigrinus)*, which is the size of a small domestic cat; next in size is the **margay** *(Felis wiedi)*, followed by the medium dog-sized **ocelot** *(Felis pardalis)*, and then the large **jaguar** *(Panthera onca)*. The two unspotted cats are the smaller **jaguarundi** *(Felis yagouaroundi)*, and the long, slender, tan-colored **puma** *(Felis concolor)*, which is almost the same size as a jaguar. All species are found in forest, though some also occur in scrubland and even savanna. The diet of the smallest, the oncilla, includes large insects, frogs, birds, lizards and small mammals, while even the largest, the jaguar, is not averse to small prey such as fish and frogs; it also takes deer, tapirs, monkeys and nesting turtles. Most climb trees as well as hunting on the ground and both the jaguar and ocelot are excellent swimmers. Nocturnal activity is most common, though the jaguar and jaguarundi may also be active during the day. Walking at night along trails cleared in the forest will give you the best chance of seeing one of these cats. Wear a headlamp, rather than carry a torch, as then their glowing eyeshine is reflected back to your eyes.

Opposite *A squirrel monkey, known as a red-backed monkey, feeding*
Below *This ocelot is sharpening its claws on a handy tree trunk*

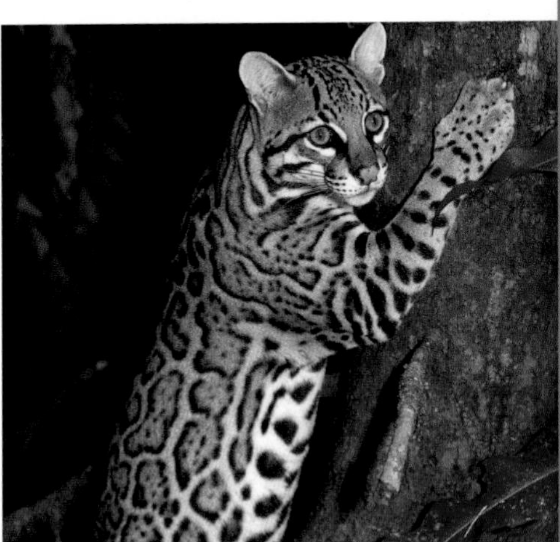

PECCARIES

The **collared peccary** *(Tayassu tajacu)* and the **white-lipped peccary** *(T. pecari)* both travel in groups of up to 50 individuals in the case of the collared peccary and 100 or more for the white-lipped. They tend to divide into smaller family groups of adult males, females and their offspring, and are pig-like, in both activity and appearance. With a diet of roots, seeds and fruit, signs of their rooting activities are often seen, as well as their dung piles, which are used as territory markers, and their mud wallows.

The collared peccary is black or gray with a band of lighter hair around its neck. It is the more widespread species, occurring in all forest types at low and mid elevations, in shrublands and agricultural areas, and it is active during the day. The white-lipped peccary lives in forests and is active day and night.

DEER

The **white-tailed deer** *(Odocoileus virginianus)* is the largest of Costa Rica's two deer species, standing 1m (3.3ft) high at the shoulder, and is seen more commonly. It is a light-, dark- or grayish-brown deer, with a white belly and white under the tail. Males over a year old have branched antlers, which are shed and regrown each year.

The smaller red **brocket deer** *(Mazama americana)* is reddish brown, with white under the tail. The males have small, straight antlers. The white-tailed deer lives in open drier forests and on forest edges, while the brocket deer tends to be in thicker, wet forests. Both are active day and night. The deer graze on grass and browse on leaves and twigs from trees and shrubs, with the brocket deer also eating fruit and flowers. Brocket deer live singly or in very small groups, while the white-tailed deer form larger, usually single-sex, groups. When alarmed, both species flee with their tail raised, displaying its white underside. A disappearing rump is the most frequent sighting of the deer.

TAPIRS

Baird's tapir *(Tapirus bairdii)* is related to the elephant. The coat of this large, stocky animal is sparsely furred with reddish brown hair and it has a short, bristly mane extending along the back of its neck. The tapir has a short, fleshy trunk, derived from the nose and upper lip, which is used to pull leaves and shoots into its mouth. Its sense of smell is excellent, its hearing is good, but its vision is poor. Found in wet forests and swampy areas, it is active mostly at night, feeding on leaves, twigs, fruit and grass. The most likely clue to its presence is its characteristic three-toed track, but tapirs are uncommon and rarely seen.

RACCOONS

Of the six species of raccoon found in Costa Rica, the **white-nosed coati** *(Nasua narica)* is most likely to be seen; also quite common are the **northern raccoon** *(Procyon loctor)* and the **kinkajou** *(Potus flavus)*. The **crab-eating raccoon** *(Procyon cancrivorous)*, the **olingo**, *(Bassaricyon gabbi)* and the **cacomistle** *(Bassariscus sumichrasti)* are also present. All but the coati are nocturnal and all are omnivorous. Generally, these species have pointed muzzles, short legs and long tails. The northern and crab-eating raccoons have a striped tail and a black face-mask; the coat of the former is grizzled gray, while that of the latter is brown. The northern raccoon is more widespread in Costa Rica, the crab-eater being confined to the Pacific lowlands. Both are seen mostly living near water. Unlike the other species, coatis are very sociable, with females and offspring living in groups; adult males are solitary. They have a long, ringed tail that is often held erect above the body, and a mobile, upturned and elongated snout.

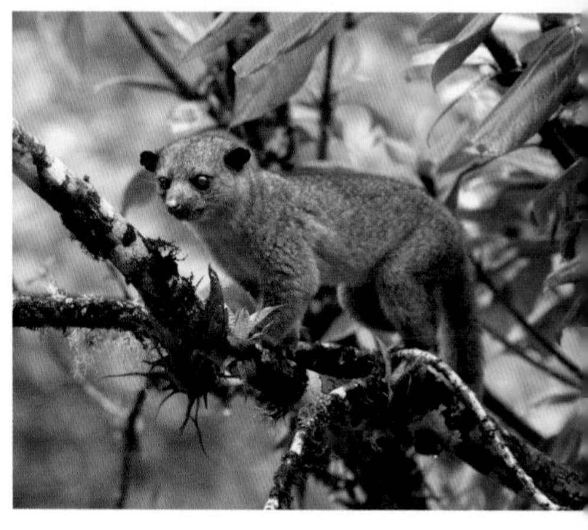

The kinkajou is uniformly grayish or reddish brown and without a ringed tail; it also has a shorter muzzle than the others. Its tail is prehensile, and it has a long tongue used for probing nectar from flowers and obtaining honey from bees' nests. The olingo is similar in behaviour, but is smaller with indistinct rings on its bushier (non-prehensile) tail and faint gray markings on its more pointed face; it is also rarer. The cacomistle, found in drier forests, has a fox-like face, larger ears than the other species in this group and a bushy, ringed tail.

DOGS

The **coyote** *(Canis latrans)* and the **gray fox** *(Urocyon cinereoargenteus)* are Costa Rica's two species from the dog family. The coat of the former, the larger species, varies from grizzled gray to brownish yellow, while that of the latter is silver gray with tawny legs, feet and ears. Both are active during the day and night and are found in forest or, more commonly, open areas of the northern Pacific lowlands. They tend to eat whatever is available, from fruit and insects to small mammals or even deer. The howl of the coyote—high-pitched staccato yelps followed by a long wail—is likely to be heard.

RABBITS

Two species are found in the country: the **eastern cottontail** *(Sylvilagus floridensis)* and the **forest rabbit** *(S. brasiliensis)*. The former is found on forest edges and in open areas, while, as you'd expect, the latter lives in forests.

RODENTS

There are about 50 rodent species in Costa Rica, including mice, rats, gophers, squirrels and others such as the **Mexican hairy porcupine** *(Coendou mexicanus)*, **paca** *(Agouti paca)* and **agout***i (Dasyprocta punctata)*. The agouti, a reddish brown creature resembling a large, long-legged guinea pig, searches the forest floor for fallen fruit and seeds. The paca is similar in shape, but twice the size and nocturnal. Mexican hairy porcupines spend most of their time in trees, using their prehensile tails to get around. Their diet consists of leaves, fruits, seeds, roots, insects and small vertebrates.

Of Costa Rica's five squirrel species, the **red-tailed** *(Sciurus granatensis)* and the **variegated squirrel** *(S. variegatoides)* are the ones most likely to be seen. The former tends to be in wet forests, while the latter is found in drier forests and more open areas. Both are diurnal, foraging for food in the trees.

WEASELS

Costa Rica's three species of skunk are more likely to be smelled than seen. The **striped hog-nosed skunk** *(Conepatus semistriatus)* is black, with a white stripe on its head and along its back and a white, bushy tail. The **spotted skunk** *(Spilogale putorius)* and the **hooded skunk** *(Mephitis macroura)* are less common. All three are nocturnal and omnivorous.

The **tayra** *(Eira barbara)* is a long, slender, badger-like animal with a black or brown body and a tan head. They are often seen in pairs, foraging for birds, small mammals and fruit.

Other species found in Costa Rica are the **grison** *(Galictis vittata)*, which has a gray back and tail, with black legs and face and a white stripe on its forehead; the **long-tailed weasel** *(Mustela frenata)*; and the **neotropical otter** *(Lutra longicaudis)*.

BATS

With more than 100 species in the country and all just glimpsed as they swoop past at night, it is often very difficult to identify the species seen. The smallest bat in Costa Rica, the **black myotis** *(Myotis nigricans)* has a wingspan of 5cm (2in), while the largest, the **bulldog fishing bat** *(Noctilio leporinus)*, has an 80cm (30in) wingspan. The latter eats fish, snatched from rivers with eagle-like talons. Other species eat pollen, nectar, fruit, insects, small vertebrates (such as fish, frogs, birds, rodents or other bats) and blood, depending on bat species. Daytime roosting sites are hollow trees, caves, tree branches, rock crevices, under bridges and in buildings, or even in rolled up plant leaves.

BIRDS

Though the mammals in Costa Rica might be elusive, you can guarantee that you will see birds, and lots of them. They vary from "little brown jobs" (LBJs for short) to comparatively massive, eye-catching macaws and toucans. For anyone with more than a superficial interest, a good bird book is a must.

SEA AND SHOREBIRDS

Very obvious by the sea is the magnificent **frigate bird** *(Fregata magnificens)*, a soaring, black bird with a 2m (7ft) wingspan and forked tail. Males have red throat pouches that they inflate during courtship displays. Seeing these frigate birds stealing fish from other seabirds and eating sea turtle hatchlings makes you realize that their habits do not live up to their elegant appearance. **Brown pelicans** *(Pelecanus occidentalis)* are sturdier birds, easily recognizable by their throat pouches, which they use as a net to scoop up fish underwater. Ungainly on the ground, a group of them flying slowly in formation is an impressive sight.

Clockwise from top left *A bushy-tailed olingo; white tent bats, roosting in a tent made of a leaf; the white-nosed coati is one of the six species of raccoon found in Costa Rica*

WATERBIRDS, HERONS AND EGRETS

Also seen by the sea, as well as in freshwater areas, are anhingas and cormorants—quite similar looking birds, very often observed standing with their wings spread out to dry in the sun. The **olivaceous cormorant** *(Phalacrocorax brasilianus)* is a black or brown bird with a wingspan of 1m (3.5ft), a long tail and a down-curved bill. The **anhinga** *(Anhinga anhinga)* has a longer neck and a long, pointed bill without a hook; the female has a brown neck. Many other birds, including storks, ibis, herons, egrets and spoonbills can be seen in aquatic habitats. The **roseate spoonbill** *(Ajaia ajaja)* is a large, pink wading bird with a white neck and distinctive spoon-shaped beak that it opens and swings about underwater, snapping it shut when it feels a frog, fish or other such prey. Also distinctive is the **jabirú stork** *(Jabiru mycteria)*, a very large, white wading bird standing 1.4m (4.5ft) high, with a huge black beak and a red area on its neck.

Snow-white **cattle egrets** *(Bubulcu ibis)* are ubiquitous in cattle pastures, where they feed on ticks drawn to the cattle. They often roost en masse in riverbank trees. The **bare-throated tiger-heron** *(Tigrisoma mexicanum)* is a far more impressive bird, standing 80cm (31in) tall. The juvenile has tiger-like stripes that blend perfectly against the alternating shade and sunlight, eventually growing out at adulthood.

MARSH AND STREAM BIRDS

Among Costa Rica's marsh and stream birds are such species as the jacana, several rails, crakes, gallinules, coots and the sunbittern. The **northern jacana** *(Jacana spinosa)* is often seen walking on top of lily pads or other floating vegetation, its long toes spreading its weight. It feeds on insects, snails, frogs, fish and vegetable matter. Adults have a black head, neck and chest with bright brown wings, belly and back and a yellow beak, forehead and unmistakable yellow under the wings. The **purple gallinule** *(Porphryula martinica)*, found in marshes and around lakeshores, has a purple head, neck and chest, green wings, red and yellow beak, light blue forehead and yellow legs.

DUCKS

Costa Rica's 15 or so species of duck includes the **muscovy** *(Cairina moschata)*; it is mostly greenish-black, with white patches on its wings and the male has a feathered crest and red warts on his face and beak. It is no longer very common due to hunting pressure and habitat destruction.

KINGFISHERS

There are six species of kingfisher in Costa Rica, often seen perching on branches while they scan the water beneath them for fish. All have large heads, with long, straight, sturdy bills and stubby bodies, but they vary in size. The bigger species eat larger prey to avoid competition with the smaller ones. They lay their eggs in burrows dug in the banks of rivers or streams. The **ringed kingfisher** *(Ceryle torquata)*, a blue-gray bird, with a brownish front, white neckband and throat, is the largest kingfisher in the country. The smallest is the **American pygmy kingfisher** *(Chloroceryle aene)*. It has a green back and head, a reddish brown neck-band and throat and chest with a white lower front. The female has a green bar across her chest.

MOTMOTS

The motmots, relatives of the kingfisher, are handsome birds, with distinctive, long narrow tails tipped by broad feathers. Perhaps the most attractive of the country's six species is the **turquoise-browed motmot *(Eumomota superciliosa)***, a brownish-green bird, with a black throat, a black mask around its eye, a turquoise bar above the eye, and turquoise tail and wings. Motmots are more common in low and mid-altitude forests, but they can also be seen in parks and orchards. They tend to sit and wait for their prey, mostly insects, then swoop down, grab it and return to their perch to beat it to death.

VULTURES

Not beautiful, but conspicuous and commonly seen, are Costa Rica's vultures. There are four species in the country. The more sociable **black vulture** *(Coragyps atratus)* and **turkey vulture** *(Cathartes aura)* are a frequent sight around towns and villages. Both are large black birds, the former with a bare, red head and neck and the latter with a featherless, black head and neck. Larger than either of these, with a wingspan of 2m (6.5ft), is the **king vulture** *(Sarcoramphus papa)*, which is white with black wings and tail and has a featherless, black, orange and yellow head. It usually hunts over forest and wooded areas. Least common and smallest is the **lesser yellow-headed vulture** *(Cathartes burrovianus)*. All are carrion eaters, though the king and black vulture do sometimes take live prey.

Below *An American purple gallinule resting on a leaf*

Above *A spectacled owl at Hacienda Baru National Wildlife Refuge*

RAPTORS

Also known as birds of prey, raptors hunt mostly living animals, usually other vertebrates. They include birds such as hawks, kites, eagles, falcons and caracaras; there are about 50 species in Costa Rica. Though often quite difficult to identify as they soar far overhead above all types of habitats, some more conspicuous ones can be picked out. The **osprey** *(Pandion haliaetus)* is unusual in that it feeds on fish, grabbing them with its sharp claws from fresh- or saltwater. White below and brown above, it is found more or less worldwide. The **American swallow-tailed hawk** *(Elanoides forficatus)* can be distinguished from other raptors by its deeply forked, long black tail. It feeds on the wing, grabbing flying insects and snatching small prey such as lizards from trees. The **harpy eagle** *(Harpia harpyja)* used to be widespread in Costa Rica, but is now very rare and seen only in Corcovado National Park and the Talamanca mountains. It is a spectacular bird—standing around 1m (3.5ft) tall—that can grab small monkeys and other mammals from the treetops as it flies above them. The **crested caracara** *(Polyborus plancus)* is a large black bird, with a barred black and white neck, a black, white and red head and yellow legs, that is found over open areas and quite commonly seen in groups eating carrion.

OWLS

You might be lucky and see one of Costa Rica's 15 species of owl during the day, especially if a local guide knows a roosting site that a particular owl regularly uses, however, as they are mostly nocturnal hunters, you are more likely just to hear them. Both the **spectacled owl** *(Pulsatrix perspicillata)* and the **ferruginous pygmy owl** *(Glaucidium brasilianum)* can sometimes be seen hunting in the day or at dusk. The former is large, 46cm (18in) tall, with a dark brown head and back with a lighter chest and, as its name indicates, white "spectacles" and white on its throat. It is found in forest and in more open areas. The diminutive **pygmy owl** is just 16cm (6in) tall and usually hunts during the day. It is a reddish or grayish brown with white streaks on its front.

GOATSUCKERS OR NIGHTJARS

Nine species of these nocturnal birds are found in Costa Rica, the most common being the **pauraque** *(Nyctidromus albicollis)*. They inhabit open areas such as farm- and parkland, thickets and forest edges, but are most commonly seen as they fly up directly in front of your car. Indeed, their Spanish name means "common road blocker." Their mottled brown, black and white color is an excellent camouflage, ensuring that they are almost impossible to spot roosting (on the ground or along tree branches) during the day. The **common potoo** *(Nyctibius griseus)*, unlike most other nightjars, adopts a vertical roosting posture, often perching during the day in the open on a dead tree stump, looking much like an extension of it.

SWIFTS AND SWALLOWS

There are 12 species of swallow and 11 swifts in Costa Rica. Though not closely related groups, they do superficially resemble each other being slender, streamlined birds. They can be seen swooping through the air catching insects while on the wing. This group will be familiar to most visitors, indeed the **barn swallow** *(Hirundo rustica)* is a common species more or less worldwide.

HUMMINGBIRDS

Hummingbirds are wonderful little creatures that are a delight to watch. Costa Rica has more than 50 species of them. Though easy to recognize as a group, they are actually quite difficult to identify as they dart past at high speed or hover briefly at a flower extracting its nectar. So tiny are some of the species, mostly weighing between 3–6g (0.12–0.24oz), that they can become entangled in spiders' webs or be eaten by praying mantises and frogs. The major part of their diet is nectar, but they also feed on insects to obtain protein. The largest hummingbird in Costa Rica is the **violet sabrewing** *(Campylopterus hemileucurus)*, which is 15cm (6in) in length with a down-curved bill and white patches at the end of its tail. The male has a violet head and front with a dark green back and wings, while the female has a violet throat but a gray front. Although the **long-tailed hermit** *(Phaethornis superciliosus)* also measures 15cm (6in) in length, much of this is, indeed, its tail. It is a greenish brown hummingbird, with a long white tipped tail, a down-curved bill, black and light colored eye stripes and a light brown front; it is found in forests and on forest edges. Most "hummers," including the **crowned woodnymph** *(Thalurania colombica)*, are less than 10cm (4in) long. The male of this species has a glossy green throat, chest and rump, with a purple head and belly and a dark forked tail and dark wings; the female is greenish with a light gray throat and chest. Both have a straight bill, only slightly curved at the tip. Many hummingbirds act as pollinators for flowers, the flowers generally being red, pink or orange, thereby indistinguishable to insects, and scentless so they don't attract nectar-feeding insects. The flowers also tend to be shaped into long thin tubes, adapted to fit the birds' beaks.

TROGONS

Of the 10 trogon species found in Costa Rica, the resplendent quetzal is the one most people want to see. However, all species are spectacular, particularly the males. They have metallic green, blue or violet heads and chests, with contrasting bright red, yellow or orange underparts. They usually sit erect in the forest with their distinctive tails (long, with horizontal black and white stripes on the underside and a squared off end) pointing downwards.

The impressive male **resplendent quetzal** *(Pharomachrus mocinno)* is a bird of the cloud forests, with an emerald green head, a crest of green feathers and long trailing green plumes extending 45cm (17.5in) or more beyond its white tail. In spite of their bright colors, trogons can be quite difficult to spot in forests as they blend into the dark green foliage and tend to sit silently waiting to catch passing insects. They also feed on small lizards and frogs, as well as fruit, especially figs. Other trogons found in Costa Rica are the **slaty-tailed trogon** *(Trogon massena)* and the **violaceous trogon** *(Trogon violaceus)*, the latter being found in dry as well as wet forests at low elevations.

TOUCANS

The toucans, all sporting large, bright bills, are an unmistakable group. There are six species in Costa Rica—two toucans, two aracaris and two toucanets. The **chestnut-mandibled toucan** *(Ramphastos swainsonii)* is the largest. Both it and the slightly smaller **keel-billed toucan** *(Ramphastos sulfuratus)* are mainly black with a yellow face and chest and red under the tail. The former has a bicolored bill, chestnut below and yellow above, while the latter has an amazing multicolored one, red, orange, green and blue. The **collared aracari** *(Pteroglossus torquatus)* and **fiery-billed aracari** *(Pteroglossus frantzii)* look somewhat alike, but the former is found on the Caribbean side of the country and in the Guanacaste region, and the latter on the south Pacific. Both have a black head and chest, a dark green back and a yellow belly with a central black spot; the bill in both is black below, but is bright orange red above in the fiery-billed and pale yellow in the collared. The **yellow-eared toucanet** *(Selenidera spectablis)* and **emerald toucanet** *(Aulacorhynchus prasinusare)* are smaller birds, the latter only 30cm (12in) in comparison with the 56cm (22in) of the chestnut-mandibled toucan. The emerald toucanet is mostly green, but has a blue throat and is chestnut below its tail. Its bill is black below and yellow above. All species are forest-dwelling, fruit eaters, and tend to be seen in small groups, high up in the canopy. Toucans nest in hollow trees, often using holes that have been made by woodpeckers.

PARROTS

Many of Costa Rica's 16 species are small and green and quite difficult to tell apart unless seen very clearly. Quite unmistakable and very spectacular is the **scarlet macaw** *(Ara macao)*. It is a large bird, 84cm (33in) long, with a bright red body, yellow and blue wings, a long red tail and a white face. This species became quite rare, devastated by habitat destruction and hunting for the pet trade, but it is making a comeback. It is found in pockets along the Pacific. The similarly sized **green macaw** *(Ara ambigua)* is found on the Caribbean side. It, too, is endangered in Costa Rica. Most parrots are noisy and sociable, feeding on fruits and seeds that they tear apart with short, powerful, hooked beaks. Breeding usually occurs in hollow trees, with the young of the large macaw species remaining in the nest for three to four months and those of smaller species for three to four weeks. They are vulnerable at this time as many nestlings are taken and sold as pets. Typical of the smaller species is the **white-fronted parrot** *(Amazona albifrons)*, a green bird with red around its eyes, a white forehead, blue on top of its head and red and blue patches on its wings.

WOODPECKERS

Two of Costa Rica's 16 woodpecker species, the **lineated woodpecker** *(Dryocopus lineatus)* and the **pale-billed woodpecker** *(Campephilus guatemalensis)*, have crested heads with red markings, large black bodies with white markings and banded, black and white fronts, but only the lineated has white on its head. Both are found in wet forests. Though insects make up most of the woodpeckers' diet, fruits, nuts and nectar are also eaten. The smallest of the woodpeckers in Costa Rica is the **olivaceous piculet** *(Picumnus olivaceus)*, which may be spotted in gardens as well as woodland. It has a dull green back and lighter front. The male has orange streaks on its head. Medium-sized members of the species, around 19cm (7.5in) in length, include **Hoffman's woodpecker** *(Melanerpes hoffmannii)* and the **red-crowned woodpecker** *(Melanerpes rubricapillus)*. Both have black and white bars on their backs and wings and light brown chests; the former has a yellowish belly and the latter a reddish one. The male Hoffman's has red on the top of his head, while both sexes of the red-crowned have red backs to their necks and the male has a red crown. Both species prefer open, wooded sites and are found on the Pacific slope, but Hoffman's occurs in the north and the red-crowned in the south.

CURASSOWS

This group of 13 species, related to partridges, contains the quans and chachalacas, as well as curassows, with the larger members weighing up to 4kg (9 lb). Unfortunately, they taste so good that several species, including the **black guan** *(Chamaepetes unicolor)*, **crested guan** *(Penelope purpurascens)* and the **great**

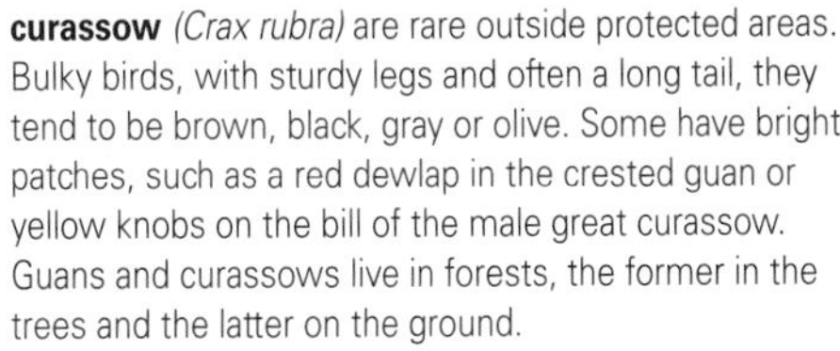

curassow *(Crax rubra)* are rare outside protected areas. Bulky birds, with sturdy legs and often a long tail, they tend to be brown, black, gray or olive. Some have bright patches, such as a red dewlap in the crested guan or yellow knobs on the bill of the male great curassow. Guans and curassows live in forests, the former in the trees and the latter on the ground.

TINAMOUS

The five species of **tinamou** look like partridges, with chunky bodies, short tails and legs and a small head. All are terrestrial, feeding and sleeping on the ground, except for the **great tinamou** *(Tinamus major)*, which roosts in trees. Their flight is clumsy and they are more likely to run than fly from danger. Tinamous are brown, gray or olive, with darker spots or bars, so they are well camouflaged as they forage in the forest for fruit and seeds. Females lay their eggs under a bush, but it is the male that incubates them and looks after the chicks. They feed themselves as soon as they hatch, but the male leads them around the forest and protects them from predators.

CUCKOOS AND ANIS

Most commonly seen among the 11 species in this group are the **squirrel cuckoo** *(Piaya cayana)*, the **smooth-billed ani** *(Crotophaga ani)* and the **groove-billed ani** *(Crotophaga sulcirostris)*. None of them lays their eggs in other species' nests. The secretive squirrel cuckoo, a large reddish brown bird, with a long tail with black and white stripes on its underside, is found in wooded areas. In contrast, the anis are noisy, gregarious birds.

Left *A male resplendent quetzal delivering food to nestlings*
Above *A keel-billed toucan at Pura Vida Gardens*

PASSERINES

The groups mentioned earlier include fewer than half of Costa Rica's birds. All the others are passerines, with feet specialized to grasp and perch on tree branches. They tend to be small land birds; many are LBJs ("little brown jobs") but some are very bright and conspicuous.

Included among them are 16 species of **woodcreeper**. These are slender brown birds, with longish beaks and stiff tails, most often seen moving up and down tree trunks. The **antbirds** (30 species) are not seen often as they are inclined to skulk in the forest shade. Their name comes from their habit of following marching columns of ants and eating insects disturbed by the ants.

The 22 species of **wren** are all small and mostly brown or reddish brown. Their distinguishing feature is their tail—usually held stiffly upright. They are found in forests, thickets, grassland and marshes.

Many of the 50 species of **warbler** are migrants from North America. These small birds are commonly found in gardens. They can be brightly colored, usually yellowish or greenish with amounts of black, gray and white, and patches of red, orange or blue.

The thrushes, 11 species breeding in Costa Rica, also tend to be rather drab, but you will see the **sooty robin** *(Turdus nigrescens)*, as it looks and acts much like Europe's blackbird. The **black-faced solitaire** *(Myadestes melanops)* is famed for its singing: Its numbers have declined as it is caught for the pet trade.

Another diverse group is the **blackbirds** and **orioles**, including **caciques**, **cowbirds**, **grackles**, **meadowlarks** and **orpendolas**. Around 20 species occur in Costa Rica, distributed through all elevations and most habitats. They vary in size, color, ecology and behaviour. The most spectacular is **Montezuma's orpendola** *(Psarocolius montezuma)*, which has a large brown body, with a black head and chest, a yellow-edged tail, an orange tip to its large black bill and a blue patch under its eye. Orpendolas breed in colonies, weaving large bag-like nests, which hang from tree branches. Montezuma's orpendola is unusual in that 3 to 10 males establish a colony in a single tree and then defend the 10 to 30 females that join them to mate and nest there.

Jays are some of the largest passerines. Most are brightly feathered, such as the **white-throated magpie-jay** *(Calocitta formosa)*, from the northern Pacific slope. This species is brilliant blue above and white below with a conspicuous crest and a long blue tail. Jays are omnivorous and eat eggs, nestlings, carrion, insects, fruit and nuts. They live in small groups and jointly defend a territory. The oldest pair mates; the others help to nest build and feed the young.

The American flycatchers number about 75 species in Costa Rica. Many of the small, drab varieties are difficult to identify, but the **scissor-tailed flycatcher** *(Tyrannus forficatus)* is handsome and easily seen as it adopts the typical flycatcher technique, perching motionless on a fence to dart out and grab a passing insect and then return to the same perch to eat it. This medium-sized flycatcher is found in open areas on the northern Pacific slope. It is a silver-gray bird with a long black, forked tail, black wings with reddish patches under them and a white chest.

Some of the gaudiest of Costa Rica's passerines are the 50 species of **tanager**, including **honeycreepers** and **euphonias**. They are found in shrubby areas over a wide range of elevations and are often seen feeding near human habitation. Most tanagers are arboreal and eat small fruits and berries. Honeycreepers eat nectar, making holes at the base of a flower and sucking out the liquid. The **blue-gray tanager** *(Thraupis episcopus)* is found in abundance over most of the country. As its name implies, it is a blue-gray bird, with a darker blue back and bright blue wings and tail. The male **scarlet-rumped tanager** *(Ramphocelus passerinii)* is black with a red rump and pale blue-gray beak. Many male honeycreepers are dressed in brilliant hues, such as the **red-legged honeycreeper** *(Cyanerpes cyaneus)*, a bright blue bird with a black back, wings, tail and eyestripe, a turquoise patch on its head and red legs.

Though they are small, stocky birds, male **manakins** are noted for their bright plumage and elaborate courtship diplays. They are active, forest-dwelling birds, foraging for fruits and insects. One attractive species is the **long-tailed manakin** *(Chiroxiphia linearis)*, which is found in forests on the northern Pacific slope. The male is black with a bright blue back, a red crest on his head and two long, black tail feathers. During the February to July breeding season, several manakin males display at special sites, trying to attract females with visual and vocal displays. In some species several males do a coordinated dance on the same perch; once the female has selected the most spectacular and has mated with him, she goes off to nest build and rear the young on her own.

Closely related to the manakins are the **cotingas**. This diverse group contains **bellbirds, umbrella birds**, **phias** and **fruitcrows**. The male **three-wattled bellbird** *(Procnias tricarunculata)* is a medium-sized, brown bird with a white head and three odd-looking appendages or wattles, hanging from its beak.

SNAKES

Costa Rica's reptiles include 138 snake species. The best place to see snakes is in a zoo or snake farm—they are not often seen in the wild. Indeed, there are some of them you will be very glad not to encounter. The **bushmaster** *(Lachesis muta)*, for instance, is the New World's largest venomous snake, reaching 3.5m (11.5ft) in length. It is an aggressive, slender, large-headed snake with a yellowish to tan body with black or brown blotches along it. Another large (up to 2.5m/ 8ft), venomous snake to be avoided is the agressive **fer-de-lance** *(Bothrops asper)*. It has a triangular head and a patterned olive, beige, black and brown body. Both this species and the bushmaster tend to be found on the ground, though young fer-de-lance may be found in trees. The **eyelash viper** *(Bothriechis schlegelii)* is much smaller, reaching only 75cm (30in) in length and is arboreal. It varies from gray, olive and reddish yellow, to bright golden yellow with or without markings on the body. Its name comes from the horny spine-like scales that jut out above each eye. Another eye-catching, venomous snake is the **Central American coral snake** *(Micrurus nigrocinctus)*, which may be found on the floor in forests, but also in more open areas. It is vividly patterned, with a small, black and yellow head and red and black rings along its body, which may or may not have narrower yellow rings as well. At a glance, it is easy to confuse the nonpoisonous **harlequin snake** *(Scolecophis atrocinctus)* and the **tropical kingsnake** *(Lampropeltis triangulum)* with the coral snake. Both have bodies with bands of yellow, red and black, mimicking the coral snake, perhaps in an attempt to deter predators. It should be noted that the majority of Costa Rica's snakes, such as the **green vine snake** *(Oxybelis aeneus)*, are harmless. Those that are venomous tend to be nocturnal and secretive. However, it is unwise to poke under rocks and logs or into bushes, and pay attention to where you are walking and putting your hands.

LIZARDS

Perhaps most conspicuous and certainly largest of Costa Rica's 68 lizard species are the **green iguana** *(Iguana iguana)* and **black iguana** *(Ctenosuara similes)*. The green iguana is more widespread, found in wet forests at low elevations and along streams and rivers in drier areas on both the Caribbean and Pacific slopes. It can often be seen sunbathing high in trees, especially early in the morning. The black iguana is found only on the Pacific slope, often in drier areas and in forests. Considerably smaller, but very commonly seen at night in houses are **geckos**, usually gray or brown with large eyes, and toes that appear to have little pads on them. Unlike most lizards, they make quite audible squeaks and can run upside-down along a ceiling.

Of the two crocodilians, the smaller **spectacled caiman** *(Caiman crocodiles)* is more common, but the **American crocodile** *(Crocodylus acutus)*, growing to 5m (16.5ft) is also found in the country. The crocodile has a longer and more pointed snout than the caiman and also, unlike the caiman, has a tooth on each side of its lower jaw, projecting upwards, visible when the mouth is closed.

TURTLES

Freshwater turtles (there are eight freshwater and six marine species), such as the **white-lipped mud turtle** *(Kinosternon leucostomum)* are quite a common sight, sunning themselves on logs along rivers. Six types of marine turtles nest on Costa Rican beaches, and with luck and planning you may get to see one or two come ashore to nest on either the Pacific or Caribbean beaches. The small **olive ridley turtle** *(Lepidochelys olivacea)* arrives at Playa Nancite and Playa Ostional in spectacular *arribadas* with many thousands nesting over

Clockwise from top left *The blue-gray tanager can be seen in most island areas; a bright yellow eyelash viper in mid-meal; the green vine snake is not venomous*

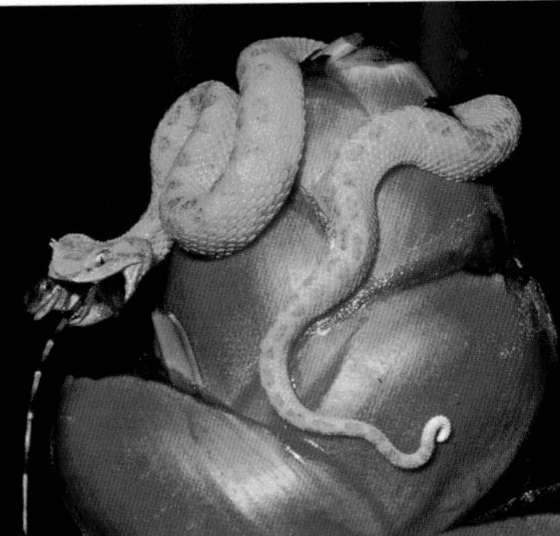

a few consecutive nights at certain times of the year. The hook beak of the **hawksbill turtle** *(Eretmochelys imbricata)* is a distinctive characteristic of the species, as is the treasured tortoise-shell carapace once prized for its subtle patterns. Green turtle soup is fortunately on fewer menus, improving the survival rates of the **green turtle** *(Chelonia mydas)*. The largest reptile in the world is the **leatherback turtle** *(Dermochelys coriacea)* which can grow to 2m (6.5ft) in length and weigh more than 500kg (1,100 lb). All marine turtles are endangered and protected, along with their nest sites and eggs, by international law.

AMPHIBIANS

Around 35 salamanders, 3 caecilians, 14 toads and some 105 species of frogs are found in Costa Rica. **Salamanders** look rather like wet lizards and tend to be nocturnal and secretive, hiding in damp places. **Caecilians**, which are legless and resemble earthworms, are even less commonly seen as they live underground mostly. The largest toad in the country is the huge **marine** or **cane toad** *(Bufo marinus)*, which reaches up to 20cm (8in) in length and 1.2kg (2.5 lb) in weight. These toads can be found in forests, in more open areas and in and around buildings. In contrast, Costa Rica's **golden toad** *(Bufo periglenes)* is only 6cm (2.3in) in size; the males are golden while the females are black with red spots ringed with yellow. These toads were found only in the Monteverde Cloud Forest Reserve, but the last sighting was in 1990 and they are now believed to be extinct (▷ 29). Their demise, and that of many other amphibian species in Costa Rica, is due principally to an infectious fungal disease. The amphibian that is probably the best known and most sought after by visitors is the beautiful **red-eyed leaf frog** *(Agalychnis callidryas)*. This is 5–7cm (2–3in) long with a pale or dark green back, blue-purple patches both on the underside of its limbs and vertical bars on its side, orange fore and hind feet and blood red eyes. When resting or dormant, only the green coloring shows, making the frog virtually invisible. The vivid poison-dart frogs are also much sought after. These include the **strawberry poison-dart frog** *(Dendrobates pumilio)*, which is bright red with varying quantities of black flecks on its body and with red, blue, green or black limbs; the **orange and black poison-dart frog** *(Phyllobates vittatus)*, which is small and black with a wide pair of orange stripes on its back and turquoise mottling on its limbs; and the **green poison-dart frog** *(Dendrobates auratus)*. This species can be up to 4cm (1.5in) in size and patterned in bright blue, turquoise, green or dark green with brownish or black patches. They are easily seen on the forest floor or in low vegetation, mostly in forests at lower elevations. While the vivid warning colours are sufficient to scare away predators, Costa Rica's species lack the extreme toxicity of the true poison-dart frogs of western Colombia and southern Panama, where Choco Indians use the secretions to tip their hunting darts.

INSECTS

There is no space in this guide to cover Costa Rica's inumerable invertebrates, but try, at least, to visit a butterfly farm and keep your eyes open to search out these smaller creatures in the forests. You might well, for instance, see long marching columns of **leaf-cutter ants** *(Atta spp)*, each carrying a piece of leaf back to the nest. These can be very large structures—a mound of leaf mulch surrounded by a considerable area of forest floor cleared of all green vegetation. Probably most impressive of the many butterfly species is the **morpho** *(Morpho peleides)*, which has a 15cm (6in) wingspan. The upper side of its wings are bright, shiny blue with a brown edge marked with white, but once it settles and closes its wings, the dull brown underside ensures that it is almost invisible.

Below *Green turtles were once popular for their meat*
Right *The morpho butterfly is blue until it closes it wings*

LIVING COSTA RICA

The isthmus of Costa Rica links North America and South America and separates the Caribbean and the Pacific ocean. As a result, the country has an unparalleled biodiversity: for its area, there are more species in Costa Rica than anywhere else in the world, living in a wide variety of landscapes, including mountains, valleys, coastal plains and prairies. In addition, the country has great climatic diversity, from the impossibly lush jungles of the Caribbean coast to the chilly, windswept reaches of its highest peaks. Today, Costa Rica is revered globally as a model for conservation, which is something of a dramatic turnaround following periods of widespread deforestation between 1940 and 1970. International and national figures, including Mario Boza and Leslie R. Holdridge, have been the great torchbearers for conservation initiatives, and the National Parks have achieved their intended goals of consolidating and protecting the area's biodiversity.

Clockwise from above *Mangrove trees fringe the water's edge near Playa Grande in Parque Nacional Marino las Baulas de Guanacaste; a male golden toad—the species is now believed to be extinct; the Cachí Dam in the Cartago region*

TURTLE TROUBLE

Time is running out for the leatherback and other turtles (▷ 140). Protection has reduced the poaching of eggs from Costa Rica's beaches, but the global picture does not bode well for these creatures. Causes of the decreasing numbers include modern fishing techniques, disorientation from lighting at beach resorts and discarded plastic bags, which they mistake for their principal food—jellyfish. In 2000, six nations, including Costa Rica, signed the Inter-American Convention for the Protection and Conservation of Sea Turtles.

One of the biggest problems in Costa Rica is unregulated and illegal trawling by shrimp vessels close to nesting beaches. Policing of nesting beaches, where turtles are harassed by hungry predators and ignorant humans is lax.

EDUCATION IN MANUEL ANTONIO

Finding a balance between rain forest conservation and economic growth is a complex task, but children will keep things simple. Kids Saving the Rainforest is a non-profit association founded by two schoolchildren, Janine Licare and Aislin Livingstone, in the town of Manuel Antonio, who want to protect the local jungle and save its remaining community of endangered squirrel monkeys. The leading causes of death of the squirrel monkeys are cars and electrocution. Funds they have raised have purchased 120 monkey bridges to help them cross the busy main road without dodging traffic on the ground or using the dangerous electric cables which straddle the road.

GOODBYE TO THE GOLDEN TOAD

They're just 6cm (2.3in) long, a bright orange-gold (or black with red spots if female) and have been described as jewels scattered on the forest floor. At least they were: Nobody has seen a golden toad *(Bufo periglenes)* since 1990. Their habitat was, remarkably, just a small area high in Monteverde's cloud forest. Each April, the rare toads would congregrate in pools of rainwater for a brief spell of mating. But suddenly the toads disappeared. In 2004, the World Conservation Union added them to its list of extinct species. Reasons for the toad's demise include climate change, with hotter, drier seasons at Monteverde, pollution and a deadly fungus.

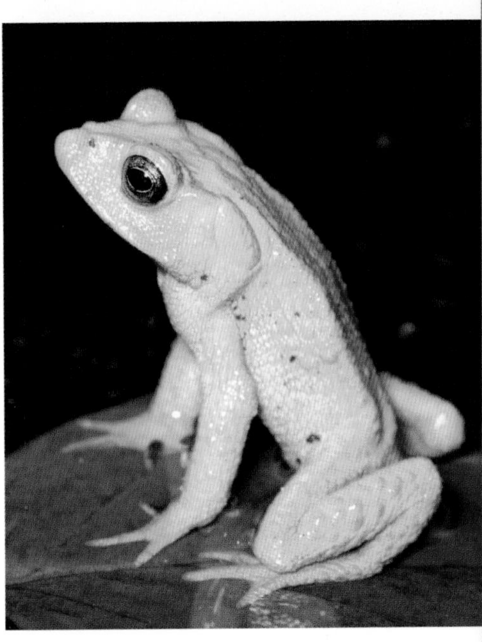

SUSTAINABLE TOURISM

What happens to the waste you flush down the toilet? Does your hotel treat the local community with respect? To inspire ecologically and culturally sustainable practices, in 1999 the Costa Rica Tourism Board initiated a program—the Certificate for Sustainable Tourism (CST)—to grade and certify tourism entities, such as hotels, according to their compliance with a model of sustainability. Independent reviewers categorize each establishment based on 150 variables. Depending on the tally, each establishment is awarded one to five "leafs." The most ecologically sensitive hotels recycle solid waste into composting systems, later to be used as organic fertilizer. "Graywater"—from showers, kitchens and laundry—goes through reed bed systems that remove the pollutants, enabling it to be used for irrigation.

LAGUNA ANGOSTURA —A NEW ARENAL?

Being self-sufficient in energy is the goal of most nations and Costa Rica is no different. Hydroelectric power has the greatest potential here. There are several large projects dotted around the country. South of Turrialba, Angostura Dam was completed in 2000, but not without controversy. Blocking the Río Reventazón, the dam has created the 256ha (632-acre) Lake Angostura and inundated farmland and world-class sections of white water that attracted international kayakers to Costa Rica. It has the country's largest hydroelectric generator, which produces 177 megawatt hours and has created local employment. Archaeological studies have revealed 42 new sites of pre-Columbian cultures that have now been flooded. Plans to drain the nearby Río Pacuaré have met with fierce opposition.

Costa Ricans, regardless of descent, use the self-deprecating term *tico* (*tica* for women) to describe themselves. It's thought to have its origin in the Costa Rican suffix "-tico" which changes a word into its diminutive form. Most Ticos are descended from Spanish settlers, but there are three other important groups: Afro-Caribbeans on the east coast; the Chinese, who migrated to Costa Rica to work; and indigenous peoples. Today, Costa Ricans have the highest literacy rate in Central America and the highest life expectancy. About 60 percent of the total population of 4.2 million live in the Central Valley, with ever-increasing numbers attracted to San José's suburban sprawl. But outside the capital there are distinctive regional differences. The cultural foundations of Guanacaste lie close to the land in ranching and rodeos. Take a short flight east to the Caribbean and the laid-back lifestyle is accompanied by calypso and reggae. Indigenous Indian communities are generally high in the Talamanca mountains or deep in the jungles of the south. A more pervasive influence on society comes from the large number of Western expatriates retiring or setting up businesses in the country.

Clockwise from above *Relaxing outside a house in Barra del Colorado in the northeast of the island; fans watch a soccer match in the Estadio Nacional in San José; children leading a Sunday procession on the Route of the Saints*

LA DANZA DE LOS DIABOLITOS

Each year on the last day of December and the first two days of January the hardships of agricultural life are discarded by the Boruca tribe in the celebrations of *La Danza de los Diabolitos:* the Dance of the Devils. Dosed with *chicha*, a traditional corn liquor, and dressed as devils, men come down from the hills to play an elaborate game of tag with a "bull," also a man in costume. Three days of fiestas culminate in the symbolic killing of the bull. The bull represents the colonization and persecution of the lands and indigenous people by the Spanish, and the centuries-old dance offers the hope that, one day, the Indian communities will be victorious. Each dancer wears a fearsome balsa-wood mask, which empowers the dancer to fight and conquer the evil Spanish conquistadors.

CARIBBEAN CHARM

In Costa Rica, the Afro-Caribbean population is concentrated on the Caribbean coast, in particular in Puerto Limón. Most Costa Rican Afro-Caribbeans are descended from people who arrived from Jamaica to build the Atlantic railroad in the 19th century and later found work on banana plantations. Subjected to social and political marginalization, they were granted citizenship only in the middle of the 20th century. Poor transportation links between the capital and the Caribbean region, caused underdevelopment, but it has preserved a rich Afro-Caribbean heritage, a world apart from the Latin culture in the rest of Costa Rica. The most exuberant expression of Caribbean culture is Carnaval, a parade of floats, dance groups and calypso bands, held to celebrate the arrival of Christopher Columbus.

SWITZERLAND OF CENTRAL AMERICA

By fortune or disinterest, Costa Ricans have never really got the hang of conflict. Instead, they have a strong pride in their democratic traditions, renowned health care and excellent education system. As far back as the 1930s one commentator named Costa Rica "The Switzerland of Central America." The lack of any army, which was abolished after the civil war in 1948, contrasts with the military factions in other Central American countries. The national character is passive: National hero and ex-president José Figueres famously likened the Ticos to sheep. But Costa Rica also resembles the neutral European nation in another respect: It has become a tax-free banking haven. The "Switzerland" moniker also seems appropriate given the alpine setting of the Costa Rican highlands, with their huts and Tyrolean lodges.

LA RUTA DE LOS CONQUISTADORES

With such a challenging climate and such difficult terrain, Costa Ricans have had to be adventurous; none more so, perhaps, than local athlete Roman Urbina. In 1991, retracing the steps of conquistador Juan de Caballón across Costa Rica, he realized that the route would be the world's toughest mountain bike race. *La Ruta de los Conquistadores* race was soon inaugurated and is now held annually in November. Racers face riding 483km (300 miles) from the Pacific Ocean to the Caribbean coast in four days, with 7,300m (24,000ft) of altitude gain in 90 percent humidity and sweltering temperatures. The 300 riders start in Jacó, with only a handful making it all the way across Costa Rica's volcanoes, jungles and rivers. If you're not that masochistic but would like an adventure, Urbina offers guided cycling tours along the route, taking 10 days instead of 3.

NATIVE PRIDE

Costa Rica's eight indigenous tribes have been marginalized since the early Spanish arrival. Today's 20,000 native peoples mostly live on 22 Indian reserves in relatively remote mountain regions, where they continue to face encroachment by banana, logging and mining companies and by land-grabbing squatters. Their traditional, animistic religions have been corroded by Christian missionaries. Nonetheless, relative isolation has enabled these communities to preserve the threads of their traditional language and cultural practices. Belgian human ecologist Jean Pierre Knockaert, founder of the Museum of Indigenous Culture, in Sarapiquí, has been at the forefront of inspiring respect for Costa Rica's native peoples. Native pride has soared. Many communities now welcome visitors, even overnight—a chance to buy native crafts and to experience a simple lifestyle in harmony with the environment.

Contemporary arts and crafts flourish in Costa Rica, particularly in the capital. The first Costa Rican sculptors emerged in the 19th century and, using wood, worked mainly on religious themes. Francisco Zuñiga (1912–98) was the best-known artist in this field. Painting blossomed from the 1930s and by the 1960s was influenced by Western abstract painters. Some painters, including Manuel de la Cruz González, Loda Fernández and Juan Luis Rodríquez, achieved international recognition. The Bocaraca school of painting, influenced by Francis Bacon and informal Catalan art, arrived in the 1980s. Literature in Costa Rica is still young and lacks the struggles that inspired many Latin American writers. A thriving theatrical and contemporary dance scene has much to offer visitors. Some of the best productions are performed by the Companía Nacional de Teatro, but smaller amateur productions tackle every subject. Theaters are required to perform at least two plays a year written by local playwrights. Costa Rica's distinctive handicraft tradition includes the pottery from Guaitíl produced by the Chorotega Indians, the balsa-wood masks of the Boruca tribes and the omnipresent oxcarts.

Clockwise from above *Pottery being fired in a kiln in Guaitíl; a Boruca woodcarver holding two masks he has crafted; hand-painted exotic birds decorating the side of a souvenir oxcart made in Sarchí*

SARCHÍ'S OXCARTS

Sarchí's (▷ 92) painted oxcarts, decorated with floral motifs, are not an old tradition. Wooden oxcarts were introduced from Nicaragua in the mid-1800s to haul coffee, but it was not until 1903 that an inspired *campesino* (farmer) decided to decorate the wheels. His idea caught on with other farmers. Soon after, metal axles and sectioned wheels led to even more elaborate designs, while preserving the original star-shaped motif. In 1915, painting spread to the body of the cart and colors evolved from grays and greens to today's orange, pink, blue and black. When motorized transportation took over in the 1960s, Sarchí's oxcart painters turned to the tourist trade, but some carts are still used in San Antonio de Escazú and other remote parts of the country.

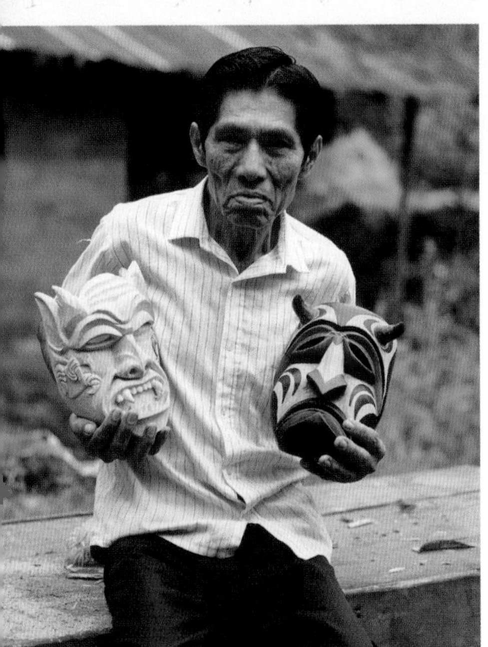

BARRY BIESANZ

Craft in Costa Rica reaches its peak in the expert work of Barry Biesanz (born 1948). Originally employed as a furniture designer, producing highly individualistic pieces, Biesanz has extended his repertoire to create a stunning array of decorative bowls and ornate boxes handcarved from Costa Rica's exotic woods, including rosewood, tigerwood, satinwood and purpleheart. With a conservationist philosophy, Biesanz works with the natural beauty of the wood: knots, grooves, stains and other perceived flaws become artful features of individual pieces. Biesanz has gained international fame, and visiting dignitaries often come to his Escazú studio, where he employs more than 20 people. Biesanz takes his inspiration from the harmonious and sensual qualities of traditional Japanese bowls.

CHOROTEGA POTTERY

The Chorotega Indians, one of eight indigenous groups in Costa Rica, are the flagbearers in a revival of pre-Columbian traditions. The dusty roads of Guaitíl are lined with urns, pots and vases in eye-catching black-and-white designs. In the pre-Columbian period, the distinctive Chorotega pottery was valued highly and it was often traded with the Zapotecs, Aztecs and Panam. Traditionally, the women of the town made and sold the pottery, which was originally more practical than ornamental in nature; pots to cook beans or to ferment *guaro*, the local alcohol. The old techniques are still used: First the clay is shaped then dried before being fired in large kilns. Traditional dyes are used to hand-paint each piece in stylized geometric and anthropomorphic motifs that hark back to the time of the Chorotegas' forebears.

JIMÉNEZ DEREDIA

Costa Rica has a heritage of producing world-class sculptors going back to Francisco Zuñiga. The current standard-bearer is Jiménez Deredia (born 1954), whose sculptures are displayed in the Vatican and throughout the world. In the 1970s he studied in Italy, and remained to devote himself entirely to sculpture. Gradually he evolved a unique and easily recognizable style, using organic and symbolic shapes heavily influenced by the theme of maternity and by Costa Rica's pre-Columbian spheres, in which Deredia gains a symbolic, global vision of the universe. Many of his works are massive: His 5.35m (17.5ft) tall Carrara white marble statue of San Marcellino, in St Peter's Basilica, weighs 20 tonnes. His many public sculptures in Costa Rica include that of Pope John Paul II, outside San José's Metropolitan Cathedral.

CORAZONES VALIENTES

The vibrant natural beauty of Costa Rica is expressed through *campesino* folk art. In 1994, the Peace Corps established a program in Costa Rica aimed at harnessing the talents of impoverished groups, ranging from street children to women in the countryside, who traditionally had no outlet for their creativity.

Corazones Valientes is one of several cooperative art groups in Costa Rica producing a kaleidoscopic array of art in a variety of different media from oil and canvas paintings to papier-mâché mirrors, picture frames and ornamental tiles. The women of Corazones Valientes range in age from 12 to 50 years, and live in a down-at-heel area close to Volcán Arenal. Idiosyncratic, evocative and unselfconscious, the paintings are very personal representations of the natural landscape around the artists.

Costa Rica is part of the Central American Free Trade Agreement (CAFTA), which Costa Rica approved in 2009 after contentious debate. Economically, the country has been undergoing a slow revolution, with every year bringing a steady shift away from traditional agriculture and towards manufacturing, the electronic services, economy and tourism. The national economy experienced strong growth in the last years of the 1990s, taking the average increase of gross domestic product (GDP) during the decade to a steady 5 percent a year. In 2008, GDP was US$11,500 per head.

Above *A banana-processing plant where the local fruits are prepared for distribution and export*

TOURISM IS TOP

In recent years tourism has superseded coffee and bananas as a source of foreign currency for Costa Rica. More than 2 million people visited the country in 2009, an increase of 5 percent on 2007. These visitors spent almost $2.2 million, compared to $1.9 million in 2007. This income accounted for 8.7 percent of the GDP and 23 percent of export revenue, more than three times the money earned from bananas and eight times the income from coffee. The sector directly employs more than 100,000 workers and up to 500,000 workers indirectly. Since the construction of the first private hotel in 1930, tourism has taken over the economy, but clearly it will need careful management if it is not to become a victim of its own success.

GOING BANANAS

Bananas are key to the Costa Rican economy. In 1994, Costa Rica signed up to the Banana Framework agreement which gave it a quota of 23.4 percent of all bananas imported to Europe from Latin America, but this expired in 2006. The certain losers in the global market for greater competition are the independent growers of Costa Rica, who sell to the multinational companies. Hard-won, and reluctantly given, concessions have slowly improved working conditions and job security for banana industry workers.

However, the industry is blamed for fouling rivers with plastic bags and for pollution with pesticides and fertilizer run-off.

In 2009, pineapples overtook bananas as the most valuable agricultural export of Costa Rica.

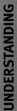

THE STORY OF COSTA RICA

Humankind first arrived in the Americas somewhere between 40,000 and 15,000 years ago, when people crossed the Bering Strait from Asia. A slow southerly migration steadily occupied the continent, and evidence suggests that humans first appeared in what is now Costa Rica roughly 10,000 years ago. Early human settlement developed in this intermediate zone without a single dominant cultural group. Each group was characterized by its own distinct craft traditions and by its trading with other Mesoamerican cultures. The region was at a north–south divide, influenced by both the Maya civilizations of modern-day Mexico and several smaller groups in South America. Farming began in earnest around 1000BC, and with increased food supplies, social organization and hierarchy developed to manage the larger populations. Population estimates prior to the arrival of the Spaniards in 1502 vary dramatically. Early studies put it as low as 27,000, but these are almost certainly estimates made after the first wave of imported diseases had ravaged the region. More recent studies put the figure somewhere between 250,000 and 400,000.

CHOROTEGA INDIANS

The Chorotega Indians arrived from Chiapas in southern Mexico early in the 14th century and settled on the Nicoya Peninsula, in present-day Guanacaste. As the largest and most advanced tribe in the country at the time, they cultivated beans and maize, and produced ceramics influenced by the Mesoamerican cultures of the Maya. Crops were traded and other foods were obtained by fishing and hunting. Evidence suggests that slaves were often sacrificed and war was common. In recent decades, tombs have been excavated to reveal valuable artifacts, and evidence of substantial urban centers with cobbled streets and plazas has been unearthed on the Narascolo Peninsula, in Nicoya. The Chorotega still make ceramics in traditional fashion.

Clockwise from above *Ceramics dating from between 800 and 1550, on display at the National Museum of Costa Rica in San José; a member of one ot the eight indigenous tribes, many of whom now live in reserves around Suretka; one of the mysterious Diquis stone spheres*

CACICAZGOS

Regions of Costa Rica were divided into *cacicazgos*, political units based on tribal kinship, which were the basis for exchange of goods. The political leader was the *cacique*, a chief who exerted absolute power through the supernatural beliefs of the social strata beneath him. War was commonplace and usually based on the expansion of the *cacique*, protection of trade routes or the acquisition of slaves.

Each *cacicazgo* was distinguished by its own language, culture, religious beliefs and political structures. Most *cacicazgos* were animistic and the shaman played a large role in communicating with supernatural entities. Following the conquest of Costa Rica and Central America, the Spaniards named many regions after the names of the ruling *caciques*.

MYSTERIOUS JADE

Inhabitants of Costa Rica were carving jade as far back as 500BC, but experts today are puzzled about the source of the jade. None has ever been found in the country, yet thousands of exquisite jade carvings have been discovered in Greater Nicoya and the Atlantic watershed.

One idea is that the stone could have been brought by the Mayas or the Olmecs, tribes native to Mexico and Guatemala to the north, or traded through intermediaries. Olmec influence has also been traced in "baby-face" sculptures that possibly followed the same route. Another theory is that the scant sources of jade could have been used up in prehistoric times.

Whatever the truth, it is clear that jade was highly prized at the time, more so even than gold.

GUAYABO NATIONAL MONUMENT

The largest single pre-Columbian site in the country is the Guayabo National Monument, close to Turrialba, which is believed to have been ruled by a *cacique* or shaman. Guayabo was inhabited from 1000BC to AD1400, flourishing around AD800, the period when many of the stone structures that remain were constructed. The economy of Guayabo was based on agriculture, hunting and fishing. Stone roads stretch for considerable distances with mounds of different sizes and heights thought to have been constructed as bases for housing. Petroglyphs have been etched on to many of the stones, their meaning undeciphered, and centuries-old aqueducts still carry water to the reservoirs. The reasons for abandoning the site remain a mystery.

THE DIQUIS STONE SPHERES

Found in the southern region, around Palmar Sur, Buenos Aires and Golfito, the Diquis stone spheres *(esferas piedras)* are one of Central America's most intriguing archaeological phenomena. Believed to be around 2,000 years old, thousands of stone spheres, from 10cm (4in) to 2.5m (8ft) in diameter, were uncovered in the 1940s. How they were created and what purpose they served is a mystery. Many of the stones were close to grave sites, aligned in straight and curved lines, triangles and parallelograms. Considerable mechanical and mathematical skill was required to produce such precise shapes. They were most likely constructed by the ancestors of the Boruca, Térraba and Guaymí. Were they ceremonial symbols or did they denote a chief's rank?

From the day Christopher Columbus (left) anchored off the Costa Rican coast in 1502, it took almost 60 years of half-hearted attempts on the part of the Spanish to settle the region. The conquest of Central America was launched from Panama to the south, and, following Cortés' successful defeat of the Aztecs, from Mexico to the north, but it was hampered by difficulties. Despite some successes, a pattern of exploration, settlement and desertion continued as Spanish attempts to colonize through coercion met with resistance. Not until 1561 was an attempt at conquest successful, when Juan de Cavallón moved through the territory from east to west for the first time. The relatively small indigenous population and the absence of mineral wealth in any substantial quantity denied the Spanish landholders many of the comforts afforded landlords in other parts of the Spanish empire. Most were simple farmers, forced to work the land themselves. For a brief time in 1709, money was so scarce that the cacao bean was temporarily used as currency. The growth in cacao production along the Caribbean coast brought a short-lived wave of Afro-Caribbean migration as slaves were imported from Jamaica. However, a plantation system never took hold in Costa Rica and slavery was short-lived, as blight decimated the cacao trees and the weak Spanish authorities abandoned the coast to pirates and smugglers.

Clockwise from above *An illustration of Spanish governor Diego Gutiérrez demanding gold in 1540, from* Girolamo Benzoni's Travels to America 1541/56 *by Theodor de Bry; Sir Henry Morgan, a well-known pirate; Christopher Columbus arrived at Costa Rica in 1502*

FOOLS' GOLD

The Genoese explorer Christopher Columbus introduced European influences to Costa Rica when he dropped anchor off the coast of Puerto Limón at Isla Uvita on September 18, 1502—his fourth voyage to the New World.

His initial intention was merely to repair his storm-ravaged vessels. After 17 days exploring the coastal area, teased by the prospect of welcoming Indians draped in glittering gold jewelry and ornamentation, Columbus and his men moved south, calling the section of coast Costa Rica de Veragua—the rich coast of Veragua.

"I saw more signs of gold in the first two days than I saw in Española during four years," he optimistically recorded in his diary, referring to the region as La Huerta (the Garden). But despite all that, the precious metal never materialized in significant quantities.

BRINGING DISEASE

The lack of workers in Costa Rica was partly the Spaniards' own doing. The indigenous population, with no immunity to diseases that had never previously affected the Americas, succumbed rapidly to smallpox, measles, influenza, typhoid and the bubonic plague introduced to the New World by the Europeans. Terrible epidemics swept the country in 1519, then again between 1545 and 1548, reducing an already small Indian population. Within a century of Columbus's arrival in Costa Rica, the tiny indigenous population had been severely depleted.

Modern estimates suggest that up to 400,000 native Costa Ricans were killed by smallpox, an extremely contagious virus. The decimation of the indigenous peoples was hastened by enslavement by the Spaniards, who forced native people to toil, while others were put to the sword without reason.

The global eradication of smallpox was finally confirmed in 1980.

JUAN VÁSQUEZ DE CORONADO

Spanish conquistador Juan Vásquez de Coronado established the first truly permanent settlement in Costa Rica. Forging temporary alliances and utilizing rivalries between different indigenous groups—a technique that proved successful for Cortés in Mexico and Pizarro in Peru—he founded Cartago in 1563. Here, in the Central Highlands, there was plenty of fresh water and fertile volcanic soils for agriculture.

Despite Vásquez de Coronado's less bellicose approach to settlement, he too faced problems of indigenous uprisings. The energy and resources of the governor were all but depleted and the city nearly abandoned in 1568, when the next governor, Perafán de Ribera, arrived with more supplies, manpower and enthusiasm for the conquest. Still searching for precious metals, Ribera attempted to pacify the Indians of the Talamanca region, but they resisted, and attempts at settling the region were quickly abandoned.

PIRATES OF THE CARIBBEAN COAST

During the 16th and 17th centuries, the Caribbean coast became the target of swashbuckling pirates and privateers of the Spanish Main: French and Dutch buccaneers, but, above all, the notorious English pirates, including Sir Henry Morgan and Sir Francis Drake. The Miskito Indians of the coast of Honduras and Nicaragua became allies with the English, looting various targets, including the cacao plantations of Limón. Raids were so successful that by 1779 the Miskitos were able to demand tribute from Costa Rica, a tradition that continued until 1841. During this time there was also a flourishing black market between the pirates and the settlers.

DIEGO DE NICUESA

Spanish conquistador Diego de Nicuesa was appointed governor of Veragua (the Caribbean coast of today's Panama and Costa Rica) by the Spanish Crown in 1508.

He founded the first colony in the region at Castillo de Oro in 1509. Soon after, he launched the first attempt to establish a settlement on Costa Rica's Caribbean coast, using Panama as a base. But his expedition foundered off the coast of Panama. Ground troops who attempted to march north endured sickness and hunger, and encountered hostile tribes who denied the Spaniards food and slaughtered the invaders when the opportunity allowed, eventually forcing them to retreat.

INDEPENDENCE AND DEMOCRACY

Independence for the nations of the Central American isthmus was granted on September 15 1821. Mexico declared independence a few weeks before the Central American provinces, and General Agustín de Iturbide invited the other nations to join a Mexican empire. Heredia and Cartago wanted to join with Mexico, but San José and Alajuela preferred the Central American Federation. With the collapse of the Mexican Empire in 1821, Costa Rica joined the Central American Federation. Conflicts ensued until the forceful leader Braulio Carrillo Colina established San José as the capital in 1837. When he declared himself dictator for life in 1841, his opponents sought out Honduran General Francisco Morazán Quesada. Morazán was briefly popular until he imposed direct taxes with the aim of funding a Costa Rican army and relaunching his ideal of the regional federation. He was overthrown and later executed in San José's Central Park. Economic hardship between the two world wars, culminating in the depression of the 1930s, led to social conflict as Costa Rican politics became ideological. The Communist Party was founded in 1931 and strikes paralyzed the banana plantations in 1934. Despite the problems, government continued to invest in health and education, while reforms in the 1940s drained power from social elites.

Clockwise from above *José Figueres Ferrer seized power after a short uprising in 1948; the statue of Juan Mora Fernandez, Costa Rica's first elected head of state, stands outside the Hotel Gran Costa Rica in San José; workers wait in line to weigh the coffee beans they have picked*

THE GOLDEN BEAN

Coffee was first introduced to Costa Rica at the end of the 18th century. Conditions were perfect for growth and by 1829 it had overtaken cacao, tobacco and sugar as the nation's major source of foreign revenue. When Braulio Carrillo Colina became head of state in 1835, he encouraged cultivation of coffee, donating publicly owned land to anyone who would plant it with coffee trees. He also built roads to bring the coffee to market. The breakthrough for Costa Rica occurred in 1843, when an English captain took sacks of coffee beans as ballast for his return journey back to Liverpool. The cargo was well received in England. The ripe beans—*grano de oro* (grain of gold)—are hand-picked in winter and sent to *beneficios* (mills) to be processed and roasted.

THE ATLANTIC RAILROAD

In 1870, when General Tomás Guardia Gutiérrez instigated the building of the railroad link from the Central Valley to the Atlantic coast, the logic was to facilitate the shipping of coffee to Europe's markets. Guardia contacted Henry Meiggs, who had experience in railroad building in Chile and Peru. The first tracks were laid in 1872, but mismanagement and corruption meant frequent delays. Meiggs's nephew, Minor Cooper Keith, completed the line in 1890, having managed to secure some generous concessions—a 99-year lease on the railroad, and land for banana cultivation alongside the track—in return for taking on the debts of the railroad. During construction more than 4,000 people died, and workers from China, Italy and Jamaica were recruited to finish the railroad.

THE WALKER AFFAIR

In 1855, American William Walker tried to reunite Central America and extend slavery to his new "empire." Arriving in Nicaragua, he declared himself President, and set about implementing his plans. News reached President Porras that Walker had taken La Casona ranch in Guanacaste and he gathered the army, swelled by volunteers. After a victorious battle in March 1856, the Costa Rican forces marched on to Rivas in Nicaragua where Walker's troops were defeated in a bloody battle which saw the young Alajuelan drummer boy Juan Santamaría become a national hero by torching the mercenary's headquarters. Walker was sentenced to death by firing squad in 1860 by the Honduran authorities. For Costa Rica, the Battle of Rivas kindled a sense of nationalism in what was a young state.

BRAULIO CARRILLO COLINA 1800–45

A legislator and judge at only 30 years old, Braulio Evaristo Carrillo Colina was also briefly President of Costa Rica's Legislative Assembly. In 1835, he was elected Head of State and led the forces that defeated the citizens of Alajuela, Cartago and Heredia in a brief civil war. After losing the 1837 election, he assumed absolute power again in a coup and a year later declared Costa Rica's independence from the Federal Republic of Central America. He established the nation's civil service and replaced archaic Spanish law with modern legal codes. Carrillo was deposed by Francisco Morazán Quesada and went into exile in El Salvador, where he was assassinated on March 15, 1845. Parque Nacional Braulio Carrillo is named for him.

DON PEPE'S DAY

The elections of 1940 were won by Rafael Angel Calderón Guardia of the Partido Republican Nacional (PRN). A vocal critic was José Figueres Ferrer who was exiled to Mexico. In 1944. Calderón lost the election, but next day the ballots were destroyed in a fire. Figueres returned from Mexico and called for a military uprising in support of democracy. The five-week civil war caused 2,000 deaths before government troops surrendered in April 1948. Don Pepe, as Figueres was known, became head of state. The Junta nationalized the banks, and created public health and utility bodies, and social security. The army was abolished and the constitution granted suffrage to women, Afro-Caribbeans and Indians. Figueres handed power peacefully to elected president Ulate in 1949.

The post-1949 era was defined by the acceptance of public involvement in the economy, centrist politics and the introduction of democratic elections. Through the 1960s and 1970s, despite economic growth, governments battled to balance the books that funded the welfare and social security system. Banana and coffee exports provided higher tax revenues. The oil crisis of 1973 deflated the economy. The drop in commodities' prices and the global recession exacerbated the shortfall in income. By 1987, the national debt had risen to US$4.7 billion—more than the gross domestic product. Governments in the 1990s had to reduce public spending and reschedule debt repayments while managing to hold on to the education, health and social security benefits that made Costa Rica stand out from most countries in Latin America.

Above *San José's cityscape is reflected in a modern office buiding*

THE NICARAGUAN BORDER DISPUTE

Relations between Costa Rica and her northern neighbor have periodically been difficult.

Prior to the 1979 revolution in Nicaragua, Sandinistas (a socialist political party) were alleged to be launching attacks from bases in Costa Rica. After the revolution, the region was used as a base by Contras, groups of rebels that combined to fight against the Sandinistas's government.

Tension mounted again in the late 1990s when Costa Rican police began patrolling the San Juan River, which Nicaragua claims in entirety. The situation was just short of outright conflict in 1998, when Nicaragua felt its sovereignty was threatened.

In 2009, the International Court of The Hague affirmed Nicaragua's claim but granted Costa Rica use of the river.

NOBEL PEACE PRIZE

Oscar Arias Sánchez was born in Heredia in 1941. After studying at the University of San José, in the United States and earning his doctorate in Great Britain, he entered the political arena. He was elected president in 1986, and gained a reputation as an idealistic and charismatic leader.

In a turbulent time in Central America, Sánchez negotiated a peace plan between Nicaragua, El Salvador, Guatemala, Honduras and Costa Rica. The plan made big steps towardw stability in the region, calling for an end to guerrilla war, amnesty between warring factions and the suspension of military aid. It seems appropriate for a country that disbanded its army almost 40 years before to be the seedbed for regional peace.

Sánchez received the Nobel Peace Prize in 1987. After campaigning successfully to lift a restriction limiting presidents to one term, he was reelected in 2006.

THE 2009 EARTHQUAKE

Costa Ricans are used to living in a tectonically unstable country, but the earthquake that struck the Cinchona region, on the east slopes of the Poás volcano, on the afternoon of January 8, 2009, was the most devastating in living memory. At least 34 people died and the entire village of Cinchona disappeared in huge landslides.

The situation was worsened by a lingering wet season that was the wettest—and longest—in recorded history, leaving the ground super-saturated and prone to movement with the least disturbance.

La Paz Waterfall Gardens, a popular tourist attraction, received significant damage but soon reopened after repairs. However, nine months later, the road between the saddle of the Poás and Barva volcanoes had still not been fully repaired.

ON THE MOVE

On the Move gives you detailed advice and information about the various options for traveling to Costa Rica before explaining the best ways to get around the country once you are there. Handy tips help you with everything from buying tickets to renting a car.

ARRIVING BY AIR

Most visitors will arrive by air at Juan Santamaría International Airport. The opening of Daniel Oduber Quirós Airport, outside Liberia, in Guanacaste, has led to competitively priced tickets from the US and direct flights now arrive from more than a dozen US cities.

AIRPORTS

Juan Santamaría International Airport (SJO), tel 506 2437 2626, is 16km (10 miles) northwest of San José on the outskirts of Alajuela.

For arrivals, the airport is laid out with immigration, baggage reclaim and customs following one after the other. After customs, but before leaving the customs hall, there is a tourist desk which can provide maps and information, as well as make hotel reservations and organize transportation to San José and other areas. In the same area is a branch of Banco Nacional, which opens to meet international flights, and the car rental desks.

For departures, you will find currency exchange, bank ATMs, a few shops, a restaurant and cafe close to check-in and the departure gates. Beyond passport control there are cafes, a newsagent and gift store, and perfume and liquor stores.

Confirm your flight details at least 24 hours in advance. The departure tax is US$26, payable in dollars, colones or a mixture. This must be paid at the desks immediately to the right as you enter the main terminal. You will need to show your receipt before you can check in.

Arrive at least two hours before the departure time.

GETTING TO THE CITY FROM THE AIRPORT

AIRPORT (CODE)	JUAN SANTAMARÍA (SJO)	DANIEL ODUBER QUIRÓS (LIR)
TAXI	Outside, the swarms of greeting taxis will compete for your business. A pre-pay, fixed-fare system operates at the booth to the right as you exit the terminal. The standard fare is US$23 to downtown San José, but outside the microcenter you may pay more; the fare to Alajuela is US$5.	A taxi from outside the terminal building to Liberia will cost approximately US$10.
BUS	The cheapest option for getting to downtown San José is by bus. Buses on the Alajuela to San José route stop to the right of the main exit. Services run between 5am and 11pm, every 10 minutes; fare: 250 colones (US$0.50).	Empreso Alfaro local buses heading in the direction of Nicoya or the northwestern Guanacaste beaches stop at the entrance road to the airport terminal, a 1.5km (1-mile) walk from the main terminal. Only recommended if you have very light luggage.
CAR	When you exit the airport, head east on the Pan-American Highway, and follow the signs for San José, 16km (10 miles).	The airport is 13km (8 miles) west of Liberia, along Highway 21.

Daniel Oduber Quirós International Airport (LIR), tel 506 2668 1032, in the northwest of the country, 13km (8 miles) from Liberia along Highway 21, is a smaller airport, but more convenient if you are heading for the Guanacaste beaches and national parks. Renovation and expansion continues, but the modern terminal, which reopened in 1995, has full customs and immigration services, a small cafe, bank and car rentals.

AIRLINES AND PRICE INFORMATION

From the US and Canada

Daily flights leave various cities in the United States and Canada for Costa Rica. There are direct daily flights from Atlanta, Charlotte, Chicago, Dallas, Fort Lauderdale, Fort Worth-Houston, Los Angeles, Miami, Newark, New York, Orlando, Philadelphia, Phoenix and Washington, D.C., with American Airlines, Continental, Delta, JetBlue, Spirit Airlines, United Airlines and US Airways. In addition, Martinair, a low-cost subsidiary of KLM, provides services from Orlando three times a week and Miami four times a week. Indirect flights offer a broader range of departure points, but normally stop in one or more Central American capitals en route. Flights from Los Angeles via Guatemala City and/or San Salvador are provided by United Airlines and Grupo Taca airline. From Chicago, United Airlines has a flight via Guatemala City, and Grupo Taca has flights via Guatemala City and/or San Salvador and Managua.

Scheduled flights from Canada leave Montreal and Toronto for San José. Air Canada and Grupo Taca offer direct flights from Toronto.

Prices vary, but start from as little as US$235. While they tend to be more expensive, there are direct flights to Daniel Oduber Quirós International Airport in Guanacaste with American Airlines (daily from Dallas and Miami), Continental (daily from Houston, once weekly from Newark), Delta (daily from Atlanta) and United (once weekly from Chicago). Prices start from $458.

From the UK and Ireland

There are no direct flights to Costa Rica from the United Kingdom or Ireland. You will have to make at least one stopover. American Airlines, Continental, Delta, United Airlines and Virgin Atlantic connect through Miami, or any of their direct services from the US. Alternatively, travel via Europe: Iberia flights connect in Madrid.

For a long trip you can go via Bogotá, Colombia, with Avianca.

Prices start from about €835 with Iberia via Madrid in the high season. The low season corresponds to winter in the northern hemisphere.

Direct options from Europe are limited and vary with the seasons. Iberia has direct flights from Madrid year-round. Martinair has direct flights from Amsterdam seasonally, as do Condor from Dusseldorf and Air Caraibes from Paris.

From Australia, New Zealand and South Africa

Routes from Australia and New Zealand go through Los Angeles and then south, picking up one of the North American airlines to Costa Rica. Expect to spend from US$2,685 flying via Los Angeles.

From South Africa, your best routes are to fly to Europe to connect with direct flights to Costa Rica, or to New York to reach San

WEB RESOURCES
www.expedia.com
www.travelocity.com
www.orbitz.com
www.opodo.com
www.priceline.com

AIRLINE CONTACT INFORMATION

AIRLINE	WEBSITE	TELEPHONE
Air France	www.airfrance.com	0820 320 820
Air Transat	www.airtransat.com	866 874 1112
American Airlines	www.aa.com	800 433 7300 (US)
Avianca	www.avianca.com	866 998 3357 (US)
British Airways	www.british-airways.com	0844 493 0787 (UK)
Continental Airlines	www.continental.com	800 523 3273 (US)
Delta Airlines	www.delta.com	800 221 1212 (US)
Grupo Taca	www.grupotaca.com	800 400 8222 (US)
Iberia	www.iberia.es	0870 609 0500 (UK)
Martinair	www.martinair.com	800 627 8462 (US)
United Airlines	www.united.com	800 864 8331 (US)

José. Prices between South Africa and the USA begin at around US$700.

From Latin America

Regular daily flights are available from Panama and Nicaragua and every Latin American capital city with Grupo Taca.

PRICES AND DISCOUNTS

Hard and fast rules are difficult to establish, but a few general guidelines can be helpful.

Fares vary seasonally and from destination to destination. If you have flexibility, check with a local agent for the cheapest time to travel. The high (popular) season in Costa Rica (December–April) does not correspond with the high (expensive) season for airline tickets (July–September) from the northern hemisphere. The busiest seasons are 7 December–15 January and 10 July–10 September.

There are generous discounts for students, the young (under-26s) and, increasingly, teachers.

Apex or excursion (return) fares purchased in advance normally provide a discount off the full economy fare. Flexibility is restricted, but you can change flights for a fee.

Discounted fares that come and go with the popularity of a particular flight are sold through discount firms or consolidators with the aim of filling up the plane, but restrictions normally apply. The internet offers opportunities to pick up a bargain with online auctions and sales.

Yearly fares are simply return tickets with a return date set to a year or several months from departure, or left open. You are required to fix the route in advance and are normally charged a fee to make changes.

BAGGAGE ALLOWANCE

European carriers usually restrict passengers to two bags of checked luggage weighing up to 20kg (44 lb) for economy class. One piece of hand luggage is permitted. If you are taking specialist equipment such as a surf board, confirm the cost of transportation in advance. Some airlines have greater allowances, so check before purchasing your ticket. Excess luggage is charged extra, and many airlines now charge for a second bag.

Below *San José airport*

ARRIVING OVERLAND AND BY SEA

BY CAR, BUS OR SHIP

Traveling overland to Costa Rica is possible from North America and all countries in Central America. Whether you travel by bus or private vehicle, allow plenty of time for the trip.

Many American cruise ships dock in Costa Rica, letting passengers disembark and spend a day ashore.

BY PRIVATE VEHICLE

Driving overland requires advance planning and a prepared vehicle. You will need vehicle registration documents, your driver's license, an international driver's license (not essential, but can be useful) and insurance. On entering Costa Rica you will be required to buy insurance (three months: US$30) and road tax (US$10 per month).

» Drive with caution: potholes, animals and people are some likely hazards. Avoid driving at night, and choose when and where to park very carefully.

» A detailed map is essential. International Travel Maps publish a good series on the region: Maps: (ITM), 12300 Bridgeport Road, Richmond BC, V6V IJ5, Canada, tel 604 273 1400; www.itmb.com

BY LONG-DISTANCE BUS

The most direct service to San José is with Tica Bus, starting in Tapachula, Mexico at 6am daily. The journey involves staying overnight in Managua, Nicaragua; book accommodation in advance and take a taxi to your hotel.

Contact details

Tica Bus, in Mexico: 17 Oriente y 3ra Norte, Col. Centro, Tapachula, tel 529 626 2880; www.ticabus.com
In Costa Rica: Avenida 3, Calle 26, tel 506 2248 9636.

BORDER POSTS

Peñas Blancas–Nicaragua

On the western side of the isthmus, Peñas Blancas is the only road crossing between Costa Rica and Nicaragua. It takes the traffic of the Pan-American Highway. There is a US$1 fee for entering the border crossing area, and a US$2 fee for having your passport checked.

After the formalities at the immigration office on the Nicaraguan border, head to the Costa Rican border post. The immigration office is open daily, 6am–8pm; allow at least an hour. Pedestrians will need to purchase a *cruz roja*; fill out an immigration card and get both stamped and checked. All cars are fumigated at a cost of US$4.

Paso Canoas–Panama

On the western side of Costa Rica, Paso Canoas marks the frontier with Panama and the Pan-American Highway. Immigration and customs are open 24 hours on the Panama side; Costa Rica provides services daily from 6am to 10pm.

CRUISE LINERS

Luxury cruise liners departing from Los Angeles and Fort Lauderdale stop at Puntarenas on the Pacific coast and Limón on the Caribbean coast. Excursions are offered on shore, ranging from visits to Manuel Antonio National Park, Cahuita National Park or white-water rafting on the Río Sarapiquí. Cruises from the US run from September to May. A better option is to explore Costa Rica by ship with Cruise West and National Geographic Expeditions. The companies use small ships, allowing for a more intimate experience on multi-day tours.

Contact details

Cruise West
2301 Fifth Avenue, Suite 401
Seattle. Tel 888 851 8133 (US); www.cruisewest.com/costarica
National Geographic Expeditions
1145 17th Street NW, Washington, D.C. 20036. Tel 888 966 8687; www.nationalgeographic expeditions.com

Transportation within Costa Rica is simple and straightforward by air or road, whether in a private or rented vehicle or on public buses. Judicious use of hotel-provided transportation to get to out-of-the-way places like Tortuguero or Corcovado National Park, combined with a rented vehicle, provides the freedom to explore a bit of the country at your own pace. An efficient and generally effective network of buses will get you to all major destinations and most smaller towns. You may find that occasionally you have to go via one town to make a connection for your destination, but the extra time taken is rarely excessive. Two national airlines, Sansa and Nature Air, provide scheduled services to numerous destinations across the country.

BY CAR

The road network throughout Costa Rica is generally good, with most destinations of interest accessible by paved road. As a whole the roads are better than most in Central America, but worse than those in North America and are still liberally sprinkled with potholes. The majority of roads in the Central Highlands are paved, creating a warren-like network that is poorly signposted and very confusing. Beyond the Highlands, paved roads link most regions, apart from the northeastern Caribbean lowlands.

Moving between major destinations is easy, but as soon as you want to deviate slightly, the roads deteriorate from hard-packed stony roads which allow a fair speed, if a somewhat juddering ride, to wash-board bone-shakers—loosely packed, rutted sandy shales which become quicksand in the rain—or rocky roads more like dry-stream beds. It may not be possible to assess the quality of a road when you start out, so the only solution is to take advice from locals and try to be flexible about your travel plans.

Renting a vehicle in Costa Rica provides the most freedom of movement. You choose when to start, stop, dally and deviate, but a four-wheel-drive is essential.

BRINGING YOUR OWN CAR

» Most vehicles from the United States arrive in Costa Rica by sea. The principal port is Puerto Limón on the Caribbean side.
» Import taxes are very high, and you will be charged CIF (cost, insurance and freight)
» Shipping time for a vehicle from the US varies from five to ten days.

» Tourists are legally permitted to drive their vehicles for three months, after which they will be required to pay road taxes of around US$90. The three months starts when you, and not your vehicle, arrive in Costa Rica.

CAR RENTAL

» Most international companies have an office in San José. Check opening hours to ensure you don't miss the drop-off time.

» If you do rent, make sure you are going to use the vehicle. In some locations you won't need it, and it is pointless to have a car sitting around doing nothing. You can get round this problem to a certain degree by arranging drop-offs and pick-ups from different locations around the country. There is normally a charge for this service, but it can work out cheaper than driving back to the original rental office.

» To drive in Costa Rica you have to be over 21 (although some rental companies insist that drivers are over 23) and have a full driving license from your home country. In order to rent a car you will need your passport and be able to pay a deposit, normally by credit card, of up to US$1,500 against any possible damage.

» Think about where you are likely to want to go; the general recommendation is to get a four-wheel drive with high clearance, but if you only intend to stay on good roads and visit the main areas then you'll be paying for more fuel and vehicle than you need. If you are thinking of moving around the quieter areas of the Nicoya Peninsula, heading for Santa Elena, Monteverde or the Osa Peninsula, driving in the rainy season, or just striking out to see where a road goes then four-wheel drive is a must.

» Vehicles available for rent are normally Japanese—mainly Toyotas, with some Suzukis and other makes, ranging from simple sedans like the Toyota Tercel, through mid-size four-wheel drives like the Suzuki Sidekick or Toyota Rav 4, up to the Toyota

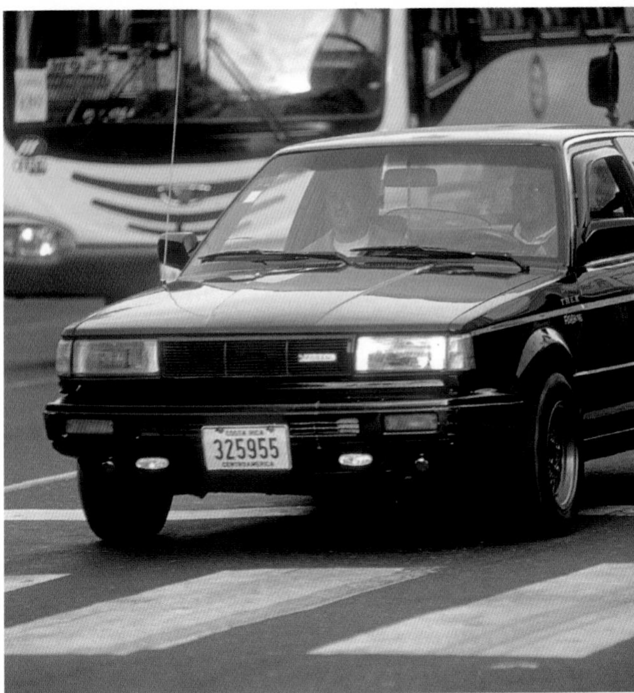

Land Cruisers. Most cars will have air-conditioning, a good radio and cassette and locking system.

» Prices vary from around US$40 a day for the cheapest cars. A Suzuki Sidekick is around US$65, a Rav 4 US$75 and a Toyota Land Cruiser between US$90 and US$120. The weekly rate is normally priced at seven days for the price of six. The monthly rate is the weekly rate times 3.5. To this you need to add insurance–from US$15 to US$25 a day.

» There are many car rental firms in San José. The main international companies have offices in the city and at the airport, or you can go with a local company, or companies that specialize in using lower quality vehicles. Beyond San José, all the rental companies are represented in Liberia (near Daniel Oduber Quirós airport), and all the main towns and

CAR RENTAL COMPANIES

COMPANY	WEBSITE	TELEPHONE
Adobe	www.adobecar.com	506 2258 4242
Avanti	www.avantirentacar.com	800 497 3659
Avis	www.avis.com	506 2293 2222
Budget	www.budget.co.cr	506 2436 2000
Dollar	www.dollar.com	506 2257 1585
Economy	www.economyrentacar.com	506 2299 2000
Europcar	www.europcar.com	506 2440 9990
Hertz	www.costaricarentacar.net	506 2221 1818
National	www.natcar.com	506 2242 7878)
Payless	www.paylesscr.com	506 2436 5401
Thrifty	www.thrifty.com	506 2257 3434
Toyota	www.toyotarent.com	506 2258 5797
Tricolor	www.tricolorcarrental.com	800 949 0234 (US)
U-Save	www.usavecostarica.com	506 2430 4647

beach resorts have one or more rental agencies.

» The level of integrity of many car rental companies is questionable. When checking out the vehicle, stay with the assistant and agree on paint chips, dents and damage. Check the amount of fuel in the tank. Likewise when returning it stay with the assistant and agree on any charges to be paid before you leave the office. If the car is very dirty, it may be worth getting it cleaned before returning it to the rental company.

» The *autopistas* (motorways), mainly in the Central Highlands, have road tolls with minimal charges.

DRIVING IN COSTA RICA

Costa Rican drivers, despite a propensity for tailgating and dangerous overtaking maneuvers, are generally observant, and this is the best advice for prospective drivers. Look out for other drivers, for potholes, poorly signposted roads and unmarked speed restrictions. Beyond that, here are a few tips:

» Signposting is generally appalling. Most people will start their journey in San José, and if you don;t know the city, you could end up driving around for a couple of hours before you get anywhere. Instinct is useful, a compass is better, local knowledge is best.

» Driving in the rain has an added danger, especially in torrential downpours. Be especially careful when roads are drying out. Overhanging trees mean the roads dry out in patches, particularly in and approaching the Central Highlands, where twisting roads make driving dangerous at the best of times.

» In less populated areas, be aware that some vehicles do not always put their lights on at night. It is safest not to drive at night unless it is essential.

» Gas stations in parts of the country are few and far between. Fill up when you get the chance.

» Driving off-road creates new

	Alajuela	Bribrí	Carmona	Ciudad Neily	Guácimo (Heredia)	Heredia	Jacó	Liberia	Los Chiles	Nicoya	Nosara	Palmar Norte	Puerto Limón	Puerto Viejo de Sarapiquí	Puntarenas	Quepos	San Isidro de El General	San José	San Rafael (Alajuela)	Tilarán
Bribrí	220																			
Carmona	297	498																		
Ciudad Neily	368	536	633																	
Guácimo (Heredia)	86	144	377	415																
Heredia	12	209	305	338	78															
Jacó	75	295	282	207	157	92														
Liberia	190	428	116	523	286	209	166													
Los Chiles	166	386	397	511	258	178	223	289												
Nicoya	260	461	37	596	340	268	245	79	360											
Nosara	295	496	72	631	375	303	280	114	395	35										
Palmar Norte	297	465	562	71	344	267	136	452	440	525	560									
Puerto Limón	156	64	434	472	80	145	237	364	322	397	432	401								
Puerto Viejo de Sarapiquí	93	201	390	422	57	66	168	293	151	353	388	351	137							
Puntarenas	98	298	243	416	181	90	68	133	200	206	241	345	234	191						
Quepos	138	358	345	150	220	155	63	229	286	308	343	79	300	231	131					
San Isidro de El General	153	321	418	215	200	123	109	308	296	381	416	144	257	207	201	52				
San José	20	210	311	349	66	12	91	220	192	274	309	278	146	73	115	154	134			
San Rafael (Alajuela)	139	365	217	504	221	146	214	101	122	180	215	433	295	125	142	277	289	155		
Tilarán	156	367	181	521	238	163	139	65	158	144	179	450	312	161	106	202	306	172	36	
Upala	175	401	253	540	257	182	183	95	158	174	209	469	331	161	150	246	325	191	36	82

Chart showing distances in kilometers of a car journey between major towns in Costa Rica

hazards, apart from the fact that your rental company may stipulate you are not allowed to do so. If you've ended up in difficulty unintentionally, retrace your route and find another way through. If you come across a landslide, mudpools or a ford, get out and walk the route first: If you can't walk through, round or over the obstacle it's unlikely the vehicle will make it.

THE LAW

» On highways and secondary roads the speed limit is 80kph (50mph). In urban areas the limit is 40kph (25mph). Around schools, hospitals and clinics the limit is 25kph (15mph).

» Driving under the influence of alcohol and/or drugs is prohibited.

» Wearing a seatbelt is a legal requirement.

» You must pull over if requested to do so by a police officer. Your personal documents and the vehicle registration are private property and may not be retained by a police officer for any reason. If the police officer insists on retaining your documents ask him to escort you to the nearest police station to clear up the problem. If you believe a police officer has acted inappropriately tel 506 295 3273.

» If you are involved in an accident, do not move your vehicle until a police officer has arrived and prepared a report. The accident can be reported on 911 or direct to the transport police on 117. You should also call the car rental company.

» If you are fined for an infringement of the law, do not give money directly to the police. Car rental agencies will handle the fine, which is added to your rental bill.

» Driving on beaches is prohibited across Costa Rica, except when there is no other route connecting two towns.

PARKING

» Parking in San José is not that difficult, with several *parqueos* (parking lots) dotted around the city.

» 24-hour parking is available but may be harder to find. Reserve a space in a secure parking area and never leave your personal belongings inside your vehicle.

» For early starts ensure access to the parking area is 24 hours.

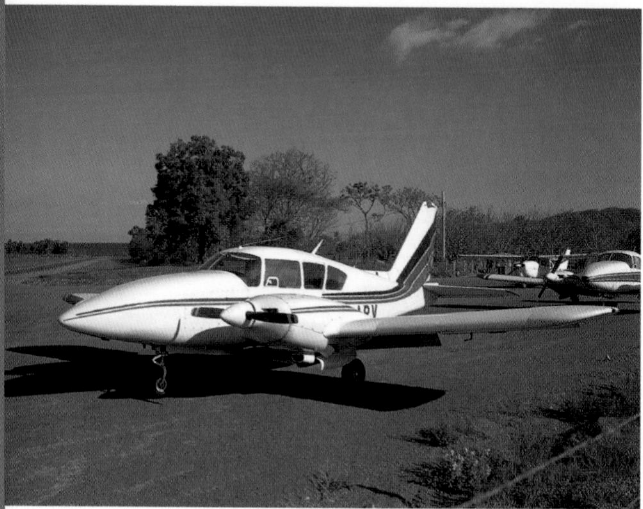

BY AIR

Two companies provide a scheduled service to destinations throughout the country: Sansa and Nature Air. If you have limited time and tolerance for bone-shaking bus and car journeys, go by air; services are regular and cost-effective, especially if you are visiting the more remote parts of Costa Rica. It is worth bearing in mind that packages offered by agencies in San José may well work out to be even more economical. Lodges in the Southern Region often have their own landing strips and will arrange flights. Charter flights also operate out of Tobías Bolaños Airport, in Pavas, 5km (3 miles) west of San José, and helicopter charters are available.

AIRLINES

» Sansa (tel 506 2229 4100 and 877 767 2672; www.flysansa.com) flies out of the domestic terminal at Juan Santamaría International Airport near Alajuela. Flights are in 14-passenger Cessna Caravans and have a reputation for being late, frequently cancelled or overbooked. Sansa has free airport shuttles from downtown San José. It also flies to David, Panama.

» Nature Air (tel 506 2299 6000 and 800 235 9272 (US); www.natureair.com) operates out of Tobías Bolaños Airport. It uses twin-engine DeHavilland Dash 6 Twin Otters. In addition to internal destinations, Nature Air flies to Bocas del Toro in Panama from San José. Nature Air also provides a charter service to all its scheduled destinations from Tobías Bolaños Airport. Reservations can be made in advance and Nature Air has its own package tours and travel agency.

» Aerobell has a fleet of single-engine Cessnas and twin-engine Cessnas and Pipers operating out of Tobías Bolaños Airport (tel 506 2290 0000; www.aerobell.com).

» Paradise Air utilizes Gippsland Airvans from both Tobías Bolaños airport and Juan Santamariá International Airport (tel 506 2231 0938; www.flywithparadise.com).

» Working out of Tobías Bolaños is Alfa Romeo Aero Taxi (tel 506 2733 5353; www.alfaromeoair.com), which operates mainly between the capital and the southwest.

» Aerodiva offers sky tours and air charters using helicopters (tel 506 2296 7241; www.aerodiva.com).

» You can charter a helicopter with Helisa (tel 506 2231 6867) from Tobías Bolaños Airport.

TICKETS AND FARES

» Children under two years old travel free, from two to twelve, there is a 25 percent discount.

» Weight allowances are minimal at 12kg (25 lb) with a US$0.45 surcharge for every pound.

» Flights must be paid for when you make the reservation, which can be done online, and tickets are non-refundable.

» Always confirm that the flight is direct.

» Services are less frequent in the low season.

FLYING WITHIN COSTA RICA

DESTINATION	NATURE AIR FREQUENCY (EACH WAY)	PRICE (US$)	SANSA FREQUENCY (EACH WAY)	PRICE (US$)
Arenal	1 per day	59		
Barra del Colorado			1 per day	79
Dominical	1 per day	55		
Drake Bay	2 per day	71	2 per day	97
Golfito	2 per day	61	4 per day	95
Liberia	3 per day	62	4 per day	95
Nosara	2 per day	61	1 per day	95
Palmar Sur	1 per day	55	3 per day	87
Puerto Jiminez	5 per day	61	6 per day	95
Punta Islita	1 per day	65	1 per day	95
Quepos	3 per day	34	9 per day	56
Sámara			1 per day	98
Tamarindo	3 per day	60	6 per day	95
Tambor	2 per day	45	4 per day	75
Tortuguero	1 per day	50	1 per day	79
Toro (Panama)	5 per week	138		

DOMESTIC AIR, BUS AND FERRY ROUTES

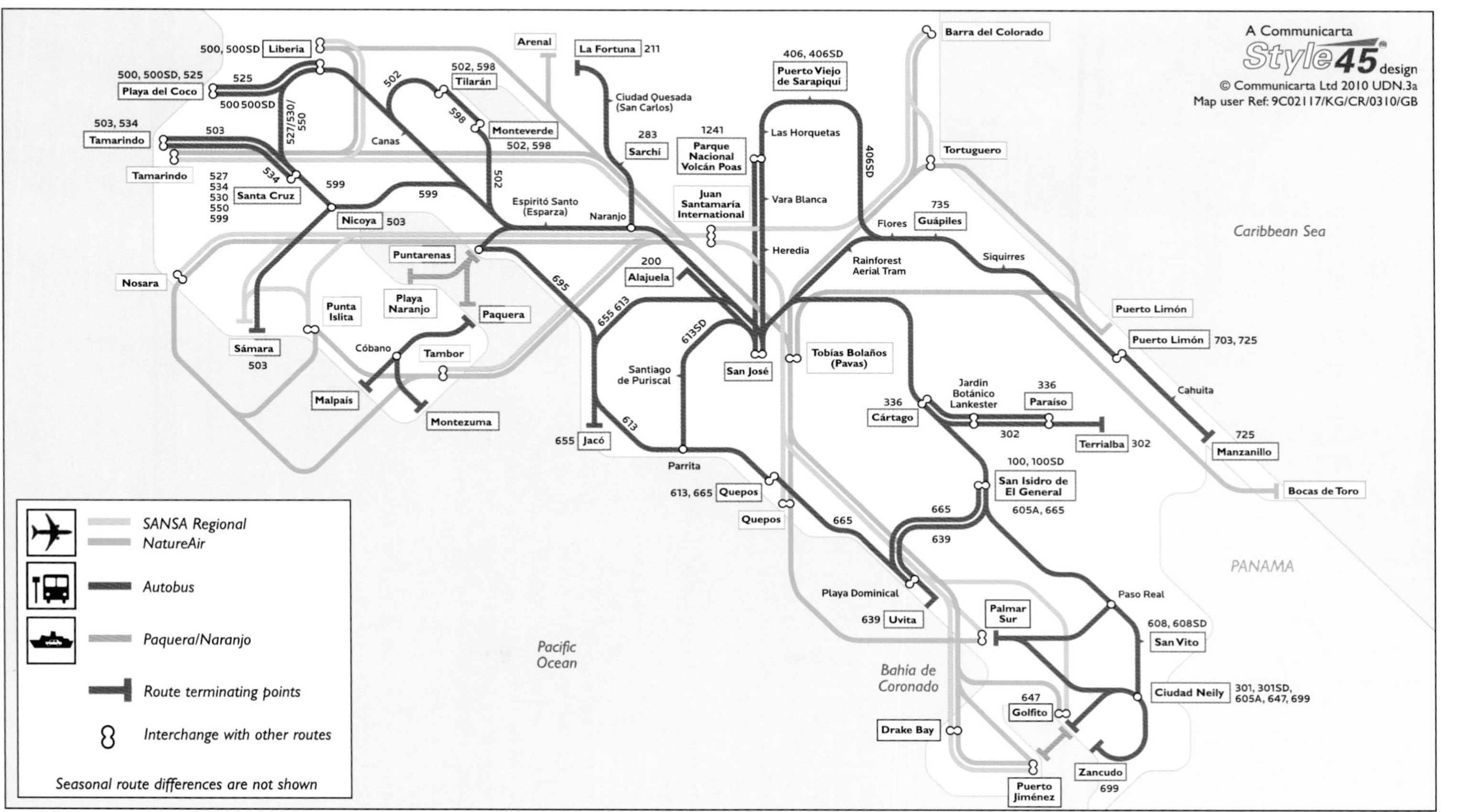

BY BUS

Buses serve even the most remote destinations. Nationwide services are provided by about 20 private companies, which are dotted around San José in clusters. Most companies operate from streets in the Coca-Cola district. All Caribbean destinations are neatly served from the Gran Terminal del Caribe. Beyond the capital, a few towns act as regional hubs.

There are alternatives to public buses. Comfortable, air-conditioned, private shuttle buses run by Interbus and Grayline will collect you from your hotel and drop you at your destination. You can also rent a bus from Coach Costa Rica if you are traveling in a group (up to 22 people).

PUBLIC BUSES

» Buses tend to depart promptly, so arrive on time.
» If your bus is scheduled to arrive late in the day, particularly in popular areas such as Montezuma and Tamarindo, it is always advisable to reserve your tickets in advance.
» Buses are prone to break down, which means sending a replacement bus from San José, adding several hours to the journey time.
» On services longer than five hours, there will invariably be a 15-minute stop midway. Always take your carry-on bags off the bus with you.
» Services tend to be reliable if the weather and conditions have been kind to the road.
» The cost of travel is cheap, working out at roughly between US$1 and US$2 an hour.
» The longest journey in Costa Rica is currently from San José to Puerto Jiménez on the Osa Peninsula (eight hours), and will cost you about US$7.
» Local buses exist in the larger towns, but tend to be of limited use to the passing visitor outside San José.
» Always keepan eye on your belongings, both in the bus terminals (especially Coca-Cola in San José) and inside the bus.

TRANSPORTATION HUBS

» To the west, Puntarenas is a good stop-off point, negating the need to return to the Highlands and linking to services down the Pacific coast and up to Santa Elena and Monteverde.
» Farther north, Cañas is the point to break from the Pan-American Highway and head inland to Tilarán and from there to La Fortuna or Monteverde.
» Liberia offers similar, but lesser opportunities with links to the Nicoya Peninsula.
» Heading south, San Isidro de El General is a useful place to change buses, as is Palmar Norte, where you can link with the southern section of the coast road *(costanera)* and travel north to Dominical, Quepos and Manuel Antonio.
» On the Caribbean, Limón is the main transportation hub, but it is possible to get buses traveling all the way down the coast from San José, so you don't have to change, unless you're stopping over in Limón.

PRIVATE BUSES

» The Fantasy Bus by Grayline operates hundreds of services connecting most towns, cities and tourist attractions. Prices range from US$27 to US$45; call or check the website for full details of the schedule.
» Interbus offers a similar service with hundreds of daily trips on 44 established routes from San José. Prices range from US$29 to US$45; or see the website for the full schedule
» Montezuma Expeditions provide bus services from San José to Montezuma, connecting with the Paquera ferry, and to other locations on the Nicoya Peninsula from Montezuma.
» Always reserve seats at least 24 hours in advance, especially for services to the northwestern Guanacaste beaches and the Nicoya Peninsula.
» Many services pick up passengers from several hotels, and if you are picked up first and dropped off last you are unlikely to gain much time.

COACH HIRE

» Coach Costa Rica's rates are for each destination on a daily basis, or for US$125 a day with a chauffeur, if rented for more than three days.

BUS AND COACH CONTACT INFORMATION

COMPANY	WEBSITE	TELEPHONE
Coach Costa Rica	www.coachcostarica.com	506 2229 4192
Fantasy Bus Grayline	www.graylinecostarica.com	506 2220 2126
Interbus	www.interbusonline.com	506 2283 5573
Montezuma Expeditions	www.montezumaexpeditions.com	506 2642 0919

GETTING AROUND COSTA RICA BY BUS

COMPANY	PICK-UP POINT	TELEPHONE	ROUTE
CENTRAL HIGHLANDS			
TUASA	Ave. 2, Calle 12–14, San José	506 2222 5325	San José to Alajuela, airport, Heredia, Volcán Poás
Busetas Heredianos	Calle1, Ave. 7–9, San José	506 2261 7171	San José to Heredia
Lumaca	Calle 3, Ave. 4, San José	506 2537 2320	San José to Cartago
Auto Transportes Mata	Behind Cartago convent	506 2533 1916	Cartago to Orosi Valley
Transportes Grecia	Ave. 3, Calle 16–18, San José	506 2258 2004	San José to Grecia, Sarchí; Alajuela to Naranjo
Transportes Palmarenos	Calle 16, Ave. 1–3, San José	506 2256 8445	San José to Palmares
Empresarios Unidos	Calle 16, Ave. 10–12, San José	506 2222 0064	San José to San Ramón
Coopacaraigres	Calle 8, Ave. 10–12, San José	506 2410 0015	San José to San Ignacio de Acosta
Transtuasa	Calle 13, Ave. 6–8, San José	506 2222 4464	San José to Turrialba
Buses Metropoli	Ave. 2, Calle 1–3, San José	506 2536 7003	San José to Volcán Irazú
Transportes San Carlos	Calle 16, Ave.1–3, San José	506 2255 4300	San José to Zarcero
NORTHERN REGION			
Pulmitan	Calle 12, Ave. 7–9, San José	506 2256 9552	San José to Ciudad Quesada, La Fortuna, Pital, La Guatuso
Transportes Pital	Plaza San Carlos, Ciudad Quesada	506 2460 2596	Ciudad Quesada to Pital
Transpisa	Ciudad Quesada bus terminal	506 2460 1886	Ciudad Quesada to La Fortuna
Transportes Linaco	Ciudad Quesada bus terminal	506 2710 7780	Ciudad Quesada, San José to Puerto Viejo de Sarapiquí
Transportes Upala	Calle 12, Ave. 3–5, San José	506 2221 3318	San José to Bagaces, La Fortuna, Guayabo, Aguas Claras, Upala
Transportes San Carlos	Calle 12, Ave. 7–9, San José	506 2255 4300	San José to Los Chiles
GUANACASTE			
Pulmitan	Calle 10–12, Ave. 5–7, San José	506 2256 9552	San José to Liberia, Playas del Coco
Alfaro-Tracopa	Calle 14, Ave. 5, San José	506 2222 2666	San José to Santa Cruz, Tamarindo
TUASA	Calle 20, Ave. 3, San José	506 2222 5325	San José to Brasilito, Playa Flamingo, Panama
Transportes Tilaran	Calle 20, Ave. 3, San José	506 2256 0105	San José to Tilarán
Transportes Deldin	Calle 18, Ave. 1, San José	506 2256 9072	San José to La Cruz, Peñas Blancas
CENTRAL PACIFIC AND NICOYA			
Alfaro-Tracopa	Calle 14, Ave. 5, San José	506 2222 2666	San José to Nicoya, Sámara, Nosara
Trajol	Nicoya bus terminal	506 2685 5352	Nicoya to Sámara, Carrillo, Nosara, Garza, Guiones
Empresarios Unidos	Calle 16, Ave. 10–12, San José	506 2222 8231	San José to Puntarenas
Transportes Delio Morales	Calle 16, Ave 1–3, San José	506 2223 5567	San José to Quepos, Manuel Antonio
Transportes Blanco	Perez Zeledon, Quepos	506 2771 4744	San Isidro to Dominical
Transportes Morales	Calle 16, Ave. 1–3, San José	506 2223 5567	San José to Jacó
SOUTHERN REGION			
Empresa Los Santos	Ave. 16, Calle 19–21, San José	506 2221 7070	San José to Los Santos
MUSOC	Calle Central, Ave. 22–24, San José	506 2222 2422	San José to San Isidro de El General, Chirripó
Transportes Blanco	San Isidro de El General	506 2771 4744	San Isidro to Uvita, Dominical
Transportes Blanco	Calle 12, Ave. 7–9, San José	506 2735 5189	San José to Puerto Jiménez
Tracopa-Alfaro	Ave. 5, Calle 14, San José	506 2221 4214	San José to Ciudad Cortes, Palmar Norte, Paso Canoas, Golfito, San Vito
THE CARIBBEAN LOWLANDS			
Autotransportes Caribeños	Calle Central, Ave. 13, San José	506 2222 0610	San José to Cariari, Tortuguero, Guápiles, Braulio Carrillo, Puerto Limón, Siquirres
Boats Ruben Bananeros	Calle Central, Ave. 13, San José	506 2709 8005	San José to Moín; boat to Tortuguero
Transportes Mepe	Calle Central, Ave. 13, San José	506 2257 8129	San José to Cahuita, Puerto Viejo de Talamanca, Sixaola

CHILDREN

On long-distance buses children generally pay half or reduced fares. For shorter trips it is cheaper, if less comfortable, to seat small children on your knee. Often there are spare seats, which they can occupy after tickets have been collected. On city and local excursion buses, small children do not generally pay a fare, but are not entitled to a seat when paying customers are standing.

On sightseeing tours always bargain for a family rate—often children can go free. Note that a child being carried free on a long excursion is not always covered by the operator's travel insurance; it is advisable to pay a small premium to arrange cover.

Airlines charge a reduced price for children under 12 and less for children under 2. Check the child's baggage allowance; some are as low as 7kg (15.5 lb).

TAXIS

Taxis offer an alternative way of exploring San José and the Central Highlands. A realistic price for a trip in a cab to Volcán Irazú is 20,000 colones (US$40). With a group of four, this becomes a remarkably affordable way to travel without the trouble of driving yourself. If taking a long-distance ride, you may have to pay part of the fare in advance. Most red cab drivers have a list of recommended prices for various destinations.

BICYCLING

Costa Rica is generally bicycle friendly, with less traffic than many other nearby countries. However, thin paving on roads soon deteriorates, especially at the shoulders, so look out for cracks and potholes, which bring traffic to a crawl. Paved highways are also narrow and winding and pose many hazards. Many bicycle routes require negotiating unpaved roads. Much of the terrain is exceedingly hilly, although following the coast roads is flatter.

The prevailing wind is from the northeast, so if you plan a long tour, going from Nicaragua to Panama is slightly easier.

The Nicoya Peninsula is particularly good for bicycling; a mountain bike is essential for the terrain and the state of the unpaved roads (dusty in dry season; muddy in wet season).

VISITORS WITH A DISABILITY

Costa Rica could be much more accessible to the visitor with a disability, but progress is being made. New hotels are now fitted with wheelchair ramps, and most have rooms for handicapped travelers.

Vaya con Silla de Ruedas (Go With Wheelchairs) is a specialist organization with vehicles for disabled travelers. Its specially equipped vehicles are available for 24-hour service, and the company offers day excursions and multi-day tours (tel 506 2454 2810; www.gowithwheelchairs.com). The Association of Costa Rican Special Taxis, tel 506 2296 6443, also has specially equipped taxis and vans.

Flying Wheels Travel, 143 W. Bridge Street., Owatanna, MN 55060, USA, tel 507 451 5005; www.flyingwheelstravel.com, is a travel company specializing in making arrangements for people with disabilities.

SAN JOSÉ CITY TRANSPORTATION

WALKING

Central San José is easy to explore on foot—most places of interest are close to downtown. Joining the general mêlée, you can struggle your way through the chaos or stroll at leisure, stopping at will for caffeine fixes and nibbles. With the simplicity of the street layout, if you're lost just head back towards the lower numbered streets and you end up in the center.

But hazards do exist. The streets of capital cities are rarely paved with gold, but in parts of San José they are barely paved at all. This is not a warning to watch out for the occasional raised or cracked paving slab; it is serious advice to look where you are walking. Slabs stick up at shin-cracking angles and in some places they're missing completely, revealing precipitous drops to the drainage system below. Keep your eyes down while walking; stop when you want to look around.

A second hazard is the traffic. Crossing the roads is safest at pedestrian crossings, which conform to the standard green light code. You'll be pushing your luck if you leave the curb on anything but green. A complicated one-way system adds to the confusion.

BUS

An extensive service covers the surrounding districts and suburbs of the city. Once you get the hang of a few basic routes, judicious use of buses can be very convenient.

One benefit of catching a bus is to share the experience of commuting, San José-style. All but the very wealthiest travel by bus and you'll be elbow-to-elbow with a broad cross-section of Joséfinos. As ever, warnings related to busy places hold true. Pickpockets and bag-snatchers love crowded settings, so take extra care.

The urban bus system is extensive and efficient enough, traffic congestion permitting. Buses run from around 5am until 11pm or so at night. Urban buses cost 250 colones (US$0.50) payable to the driver on boarding. It's a little more (300 colones, US$0.60) for towns on the outskirts, such as Escazú, Alajuela and Heredia. Buses get very crowded at rush hours, and luggage space is limited at the best of times.

Destinations are marked on the front of the bus. Officially, buses stop only for passengers to board and alight at official stops. Far from obvious, the cunningly disguised metal posts doubling up as stops are found through chance not design. Labelled on one side with the destination, the bus stop blends in perfectly with the sidewalk furniture. The clearest indication is a neat line of people patiently waiting.

A few general routes may be of interest to visitors. Heading west towards Parque Sabana down Paseo Colón from the middle of town, buses leave from along Avenida 3. Returning from Parque Sabana buses travel down Paseo Colón before joining Avenida 2. With these two routes you can move through the heart of the city.

An inexpensive tour of San José can be made on the bus marked "periférico" from Paseo Colón in front of the Cine Colón, a 45-minute circle of the city. A smaller circle is made by the "Sabana/Cementerio" bus going along Paseo Colón out to Parque Sabana and then returning along Avenida 10. Pick it up on Avenida 2, at Parque Morazán or on Avenida 3.

A few starting points for stops and destinations: Desmaparados, Avenida 4, Calle 5–7; Escazú, Avenida Central–1, Calle 16; Moravia, Avenida 3, Calle 3–5; Sabana Cementerio, Avenida 2, Calle 8–10; Sabana Estadio, Avenida 2, Calle 2–4; San Pedro, Avenida Central, Calle 9–11.

INCOFER (Instituto Costarricense de Ferrrocarriles) operates the *tren urbano*, a commuter train that runs east–west across San José, between Pavas and San Pedro, 5am–7.30pm on weekdays. Fares are 150 colones (US$0.30) to downtown, and 300 colones (US$0.60) across town.

DRIVING

Few would advise driving in San José as a way of seeing the city, but given that most car rental journeys will start and end in the capital, you may have little choice.

The combination of an unfamiliar vehicle, new road layouts, street signs and traffic-flow systems, and uncertainty about where you may be going and how to get there, make driving in Costa Rica a challenge. Add heavy traffic loads and the urgency found in capitals throughout the world, and the best advice is simply to be cautious. One-way systems are poorly signposted, lane discipline is nonexistent and pedestrians appear from nowhere. Stay alert; a helpful passenger can be a godsend. Parking in the day is not that difficult, with several *parqueos* dotted around the city; 24-hour parking is available but may be more difficult to find. If you are planning an early start make sure access is 24-hour. One specific word of warning. Most car rental firms have offices along Paseo Colón, one of the busiest and fastest stretches of San José, and it is a test to start your driving career in the city here. Added to that, traffic flows change at rush hour when the road becomes one-way, eastbound, heading into the middle of town, on weekdays between 6.30am and 8.30am.

TAXIS

With more than 7,000 cabs cruising the streets, taxis are a quick and efficient way of moving around the city. The official red cabs are marked with a yellow triangle on the side and they are equipped with meters or *marías* that should be used for all journeys within the metropolitan district.

Although meters are generally used if you're traveling with a Tico, visitors often find them "broken," which does little to dispel the universal suspicion that taxi drivers rip you off given half the chance. But the other universal truth holds true: Taxi drivers know their patch and once you've made friends, they're an invaluable asset.

On the whole, drivers are fair, but you should get a rough idea of the cost before setting off. The meter starts at 405 colones and advances 38 colones every 100m (110 yards) or so. A cross-town journey will cost in the region of 1,500–2,500 colones (US$3–US$5).

REGIONS

This chapter is divided into seven regions of Costa Rica (▷ 8). Region names are for the purposes of this book only and places of interest are listed alphabetically in each region.

Costa Rica's Regions 59–212

Delta

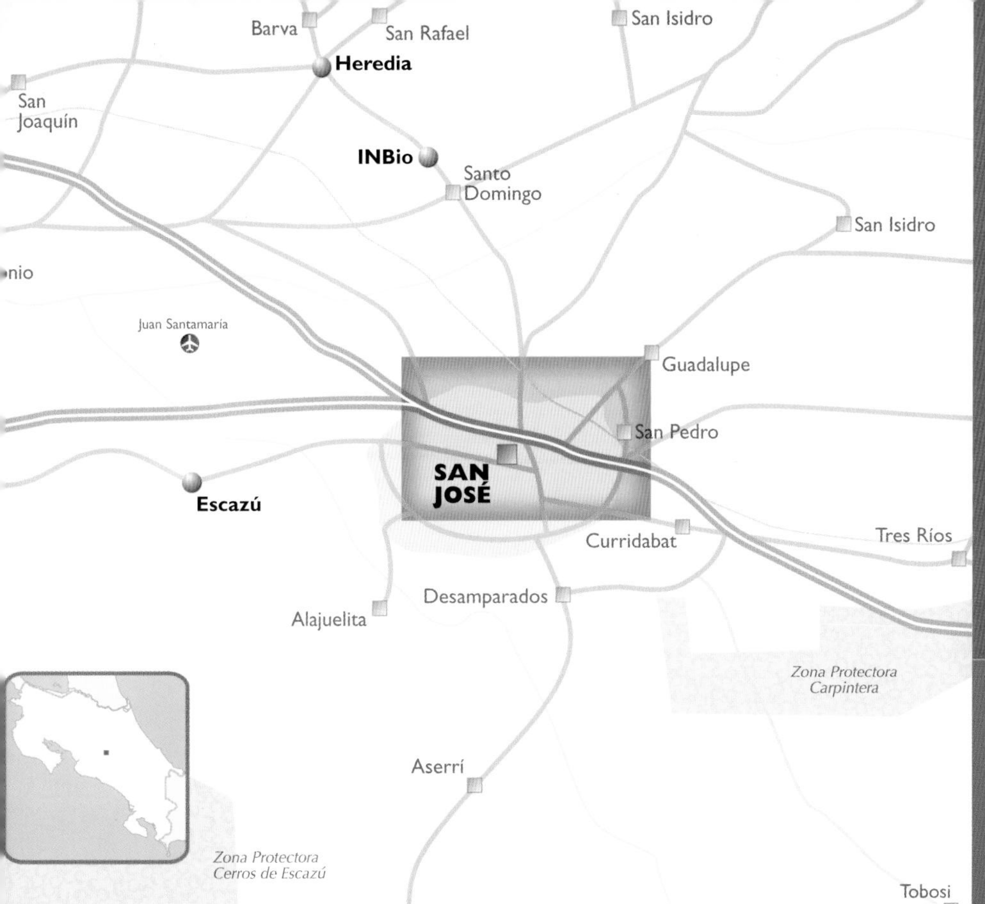

SAN JOSÉ

Although frequently bypassed in favor of other parts of the country, Costa Rica's compact capital city offers a medley of superb museums and art galleries, first-rate restaurants and a vivacious nightlife. Blessed with an idyllic ever-springlike climate, it spreads across a fertile plateau cusped dramatically on all sides by mountains. The city's principal sites are concentrated downtown, arrayed around tree-shaded plazas within easy walking distance of one another. Despite a paucity of colonial buildings, San José's history comes alive while strolling the sloping streets of the Barrio Amón and Otoya districts, with their quaint 19th-century clapboard mansions. The city's pride and joy is the Teatro Nacional, a neoclassical stunner rising over Plaza de la Cultura, the major square. Beneath the plaza, the Museo de Oro Procolombino (Museum of Precolumbian Gold) literally shines, while nearby, the Museo del Jade boasts Latin America's largest collection of ancient jade ornaments and artifacts.

Endearingly referred to as *"chepe"*—the nickname for José—by locals, San José is not a large city, and one of its greatest pleasures is to sit at a sidewalk cafe overlooking a pedestrian boulevard, savoring delicious coffee and pastries between bouts of exploring and shopping. Those in search of high culture will be joyed by San José's classical repertoire, while young and young-at-heart hipsters can thrill to trendy jazz clubs and discos that permit night owls to dance until dawn. The city is also blessed with great hotels, which, combined with its location at the very heart of the country, make San José perfect for touring by bicycle.

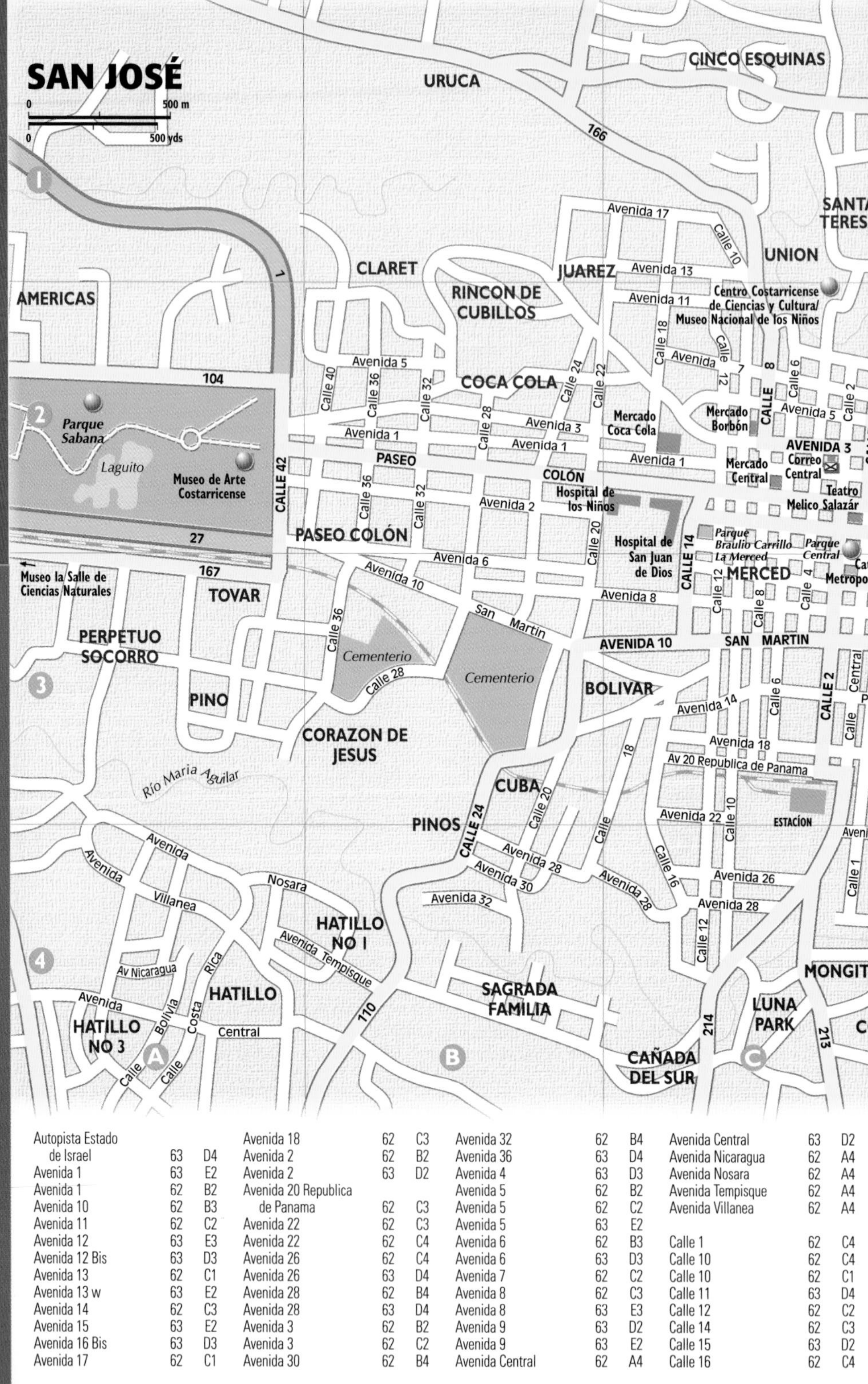
SAN JOSÉ
0 500 m
0 500 yds
URUCA
CINCO ESQUINAS
166
SANTA TERESA
UNION
Avenida 17
Calle 10
CLARET
RINCON DE CUBILLOS
JUAREZ
Avenida 13
Avenida 11
Centro Costarricense de Ciencias y Cultura/ Museo Nacional de los Niños
AMERICAS
1
Avenida 5
104
COCA COLA
Calle 40
Calle 36
Calle 32
Calle 24
Calle 22
Calle 18
Avenida 7
Calle 12
Calle 8
Calle 6
Calle 2
Parque Sabana
Laguito
Museo de Arte Costarricense
Avenida 1
Avenida 3
Calle 28
Mercado Coca Cola
Mercado Borbón
Avenida 5
AVENIDA 3
Correo Central
Mercado Central
PASEO
COLÓN
CALLE 42
Hospital de los Niños
Avenida 2
Teatro Melico Salazár
27
PASEO COLÓN
Calle 20
Hospital de San Juan de Dios
CALLE 14
Parque Braulio Carrillo La Merced
Parque Central
Catedral Metropolitana
Avenida 6
MERCED
Museo la Salle de Ciencias Naturales
167
TOVAR
Avenida 10
Avenida 8
San Martin
PERPETUO SOCORRO
Cementerio
AVENIDA 10
SAN MARTIN
Calle 28
BOLIVAR
Avenida 14
CALLE 2
PINO
CORAZON DE JESUS
Avenida 18
Av 20 Republica de Panama
Río Maria Aguilar
CUBA
Avenida 22
ESTACÍON
PINOS
CALLE 24
Avenida 28
Avenida 30
Avenida 26
Calle 16
Calle 1
Avenida
Villanea
Nosara
Avenida 32
HATILLO NO 1
Avenida 28
Avenida Tempisque
Av Nicaragua
Costa Rica
HATILLO
SAGRADA FAMILIA
MONGITO
Bolivia
Central
HATILLO NO 3
110
LUNA PARK
214
213
CAÑADA DEL SUR
A
B
C
1
2
3
4

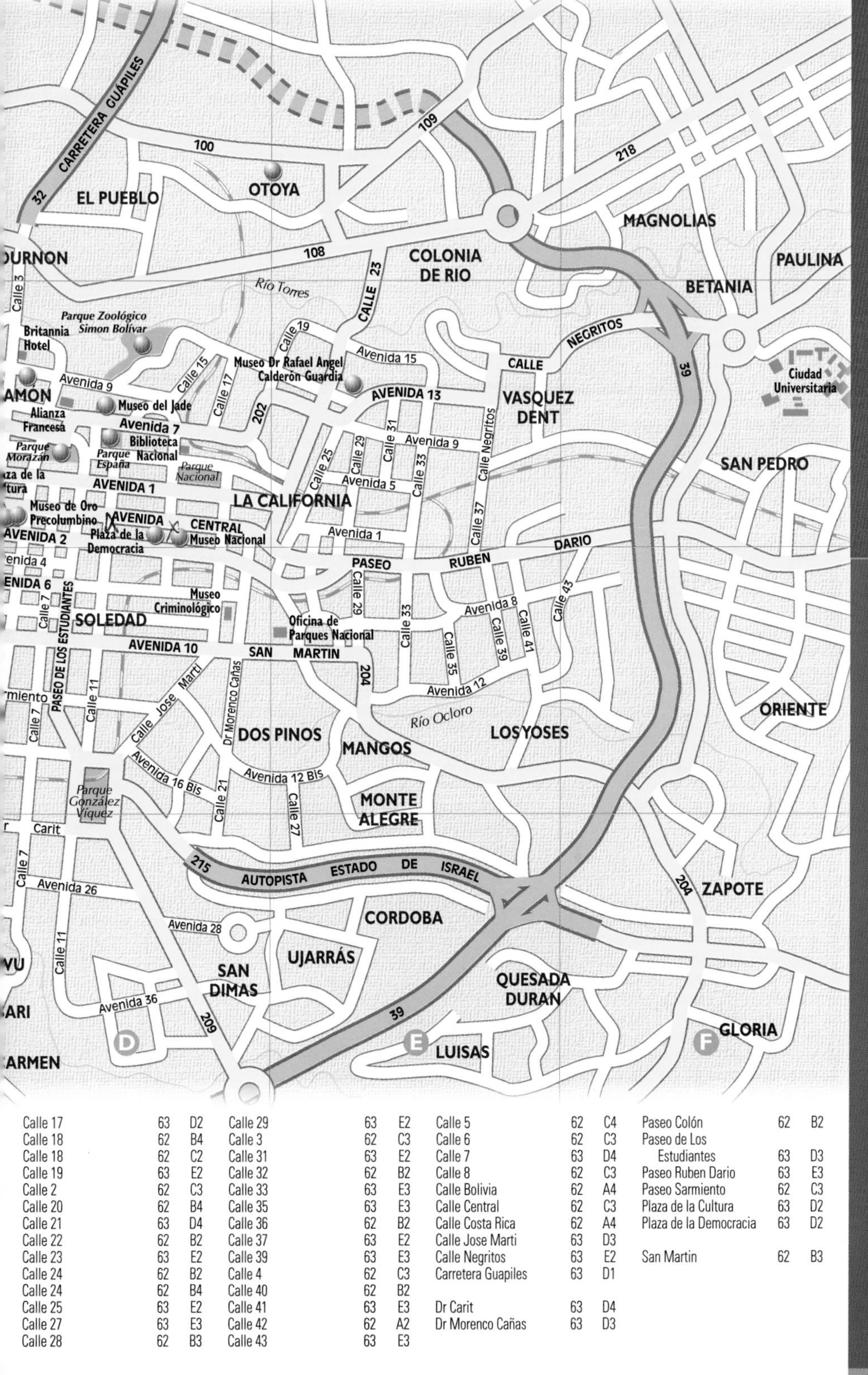

CARRETERA GUÁPILES
32
100
109
218
108
EL PUEBLO
OTOYA
MAGNOLIAS
COLONIA DE RIO
PAULINA
BETANIA
Río Torres
CALLE 23
Calle 3
Parque Zoológico Simon Bolívar
Britannia Hotel
Calle 19
Calle 15
Calle 17
Museo Dr Rafael Angel Calderón Guardia
Avenida 15
CALLE NEGRITOS
39
Ciudad Universitaria
Avenida 9
Museo del Jade
AVENIDA 13
202
VASQUEZ DENT
Alianza Francesa
Avenida 7
Biblioteca Nacional
Parque Morazán
Parque España
Parque Nacional
Calle 25
Calle 29
Calle 31
Calle 33
Avenida 9
Calle Negritos
SAN PEDRO
AVENIDA 1
Avenida 5
LA CALIFORNIA
Museo de Oro Precolumbino
AVENIDA CENTRAL
Calle 37
AVENIDA 2
Plaza de la Democracia
Museo Nacional
Avenida 1
PASEO RUBEN DARIO
Calle 29
Calle 43
PASEO DE LOS ESTUDIANTES
Museo Criminológico
Calle 7
SOLEDAD
Avenida 8
Calle 33
Oficina de Parques Nacional
Calle 39
Calle 41
AVENIDA 10
SAN MARTIN
Calle 35
Calle Jose Marti
Dr Morenco Cañas
204
Avenida 12
Calle 11
Río Ocloro
ORIENTE
DOS PINOS
MANGOS
LOS YOSES
Avenida 16 Bis
Avenida 12 Bis
Calle 21
Calle 27
MONTE ALEGRE
Parque González Víquez
Carit
215
AUTOPISTA ESTADO DE ISRAEL
Calle 7
Avenida 26
204
ZAPOTE
CORDOBA
Avenida 28
Calle 11
SAN DIMAS
UJARRÁS
QUESADA DURAN
Avenida 36
209
39
GLORIA
D
E
F
LUISAS

INTRODUCTION

Northeast from Plaza de la Cultura (▷ 71) lie the two historic districts of Amón and Otoya, neighborhoods built on coffee wealth where colonial buildings now stand as monuments to grand living and architectural extravagance. Amón and Otoya districts testify to San José's bygone wealth and style. Colonial grandeur and contemporary bohemia fuse among leafy streets dotted with hotels, fine restaurants, art galleries and embassies.

The colonial-style architecture of barrios Amón and Otoya memorializes San José's glorious belle epoque. The boom in coffee exports to Europe funded development during the 19th century (▷ 40). With the rise of the coffee elite—*cafetaleros*—infrastructure in the capital improved. Export ships brought back European goods, and fashion, architecture and culture all took their lead from Europe.

Economic growth stimulated expansion in the late 1950s and promoted new prosperity. San José grew at the expense of the surrounding rural communities and its rapid growth quickly destroyed its European charm. A world apart from much of the unprepossessing capital, Amón and Otoya remain the most aesthetically pleasing and fashionable districts for visitors to explore.

From Avenida Central, walk north along Calle 5 and on to Amón, past the leafy retreats of Parque Morazán and Parque España, where traffic noise gives way to bird chatter. On Avenida 9, between Calle 3 and Calle 7, alongside Hotel Don Carlos, the walls lining the street are decorated with ceramic tiles. These districts are good places for a stroll, past colonial houses with low-slung eaves shading broad balconies.

WHAT TO SEE

PARQUE MORAZÁN

The largest of central San José's parks is Parque Morazán. With soaring araucaria trees, serpentine benches and an aging bandstand, more poetically known as the Music Temple, the park is an ideal spot to rest after visiting the shops on its south and west sides. It is named for General Francisco Morazán, who tried to unite Central America in 1842; he was executed shortly afterwards in Parque Central. To the north of the park is the Edificio Metálico, made of cast iron in Belgium and shipped from France in the 1890s; today it is a school.

61 D2

INFORMATION

63 D2 and 63 D1

Opposite and above *Examples of the single-story architecture of the colonial period seen widely in Amón and Otoya, with some more elaborate than others*

TIPS

» The areas around Parque Morazán and Parque España are best avoided at night. They are notorious red-light districts where robbery is not uncommon.

» If you are staying at a hotel in Barrio Amón or Barrio Otoya, a taxi (US$2–US$3) to and from the downtown area, or to El Pueblo in Barrio Tournón, is recommended for safety reasons.

PARQUE ESPAÑA

East of Parque Morazán, bisected by the hazardous Calle 9, is Parque España, a verdant square with Moorish-style, mosaic-tiled fountains and an old pergola. On Sunday it hosts a market. In the middle are the statues of Juan Vázquez de Coronado and Simón Bolívar. Coronado became governor of Veragua in 1562, and he is renowned for his compassionate treatment of the indigenous tribes.
63 D2

COLONIAL ARCHITECTURE

A stroll around Amón and Otoya reveals fine examples of colonial architecture. To the northeast of Parque España, the ornate yet tiny Casa Amarilla (Yellow House) is home to Costa Rica's Ministry of Foreign Affairs and has an exquisite baroque doorway. In the grounds, to the northeast corner, is a large chunk of the Berlin Wall. One block east of the Casa Amarilla, a dazzling white building houses the Mexican embassy. The peppermint-green Alianza Francesa building (tel 506 2222 2283), on the corner of Calle 5 and Avenida 7, was built in 1949. Other treasures in the area are the pastel-pink Hotel Britannia (▷ 81), on Calle 3 and Avenida 11, and the turrets of El Castillo, on Avenida 11 and Calle 3.

ART GALLERIES

In keeping with the area's artistic vigor, a clutch of art galleries can be found along undulating streets, including Galería Namú (▷ 76), an excellent introduction to Costa Rica's arts and crafts.

PARQUE ZOOLÓGICO SIMÓN BOLÍVAR

At the northern reaches of Amón is the Simón Bolívar Zoo, which has a small number of native species. The zoo is popular at weekends but it isn't the best kept place. Conditions have been improving slowly.
Avenida 11, Calle 7 · 506 2256 0012 · Mon–Fri 8–3.30, Sat, Sun 9–4.30 · US$3.50, donations welcome · Go north on Calle 7 until you reach Avenida 11

Below *This building, with its elaborate turrets and religious themes, was the home of a bishop*

CENTRO COSTARRICENSE DE CIENCIAS Y CULTURA

www.museocr.com

The castle-like facade of the Costa Rican Center of Science and Culture, a former penitentiary, just beyond comfortable walking distance from downtown San José, hides a blend of art, history and fun. The Children's Museum occupies a couple of wings. The National Gallery uses the vaulted ceilings and spaces to display art exhibitions. In the Carlos Luiz Saénz Library, prisoner accounts describe life inside the prison. Completing the mix, the National Auditorium is a performance venue. The transformation of what was an unpleasant place is impressive even if the contents don't overwhelm.

62 C2 Calle 4, beyond Avenida 9 506 2238 4929 Tue–Fri 8–4.30, Sat, Sun 9.30–5 Tue–Fri adult US$2, child US$1.30, Sat, Sun adult US$1.75, child US$1.25 Join Calle 4 and head north, or catch a cab See *La Nación* newspaper for exhibition details

MUSEO DE ARTE COSTARRICENSE

www.musarco.go.cr

One of the capital's more memorable museums, the Museum of Costa Rican Art is in the old airport terminal in Parque Sabana. Architect José María Barrantes's conversion, opened in 1940, is the minimalist backdrop to a small but absorbing collection of 19th- and 20th-century art and sculpture by national and international artists. Limited by space, the most representative collection of Costa Rican contemporary art is exhibited chronologically and thematically. Perhaps the most compelling work in the museum, and reason enough for visiting is the Salón Dorado, on the upper level. In 1940, French sculptor Louis Férron created an epic bronze-painted stucco mural relief that depicts Costa Rica's history from the pre-Columbian period to the airport's inauguration. You'll find work by Francisco Zuñiga (1912–98, ▷ 32) in the splendid sculpture garden.

62 A2 Calle 40, Avenida 2 506 2222 7155 Tue–Fri 9–5, Sat, Sun 10–4 US$5, free on Sun To Sabana Cementerio from Avenida 2, 80 colones Taxi from Parque Central US$1.50

MUSEO DEL JADE

▷ 68.

MUSEO DR. RAFAEL ANGEL CALDERÓN GUARDIA

www.mcjdr.co.cr

In Barrio Escalante, a 20-minute walk from central San José, close to Iglesia St. Terente, this museum is recommended for visitors who want to learn more about Costa Rica's political background. There are displays on the life of Rafael Angel Calderón Guardia, the reformist Partido Republican Nacional (PRN) president who laid the foundations for the Costa Rican welfare state in the 1940s. Proposed early reforms were unsuccessful but raised the suspicions of landowners, and stimulated thought in modernizing liberals who suggested that it was the institutions of government that needed to be changed, not just the policies. Set in the beautiful Calderón mansion, the museum also has monthly art exhibitions.

63 E2 Avenida 11, Calle 25 506 222 6392 Mon–Sat 9–5 US$0.50

MUSEO NACIONAL

www.museocostarica.go.cr

Six blocks east of Plaza de la Cultura (▷ 71), the Bellavista Fortress lines the eastern flank of Plaza de la Democracía. Bullet scars of battle from the 1948 civil war (▷ 41) are visible. The converted barracks now house the National Museum. A mixed bag of displays looks at Indian life pre-colonization and the introduction of Catholicism in Costa Rica, with a few rooms given over to colonial-era lifestyle, and art. Highlights are the large collection of pre-Columbian stone spheres and *metates* (mortar stones) and a separate room exhibiting pre-Columbian gold. Downstairs, a small exhibition leads through quarters and prison cells explaining events leading up to the civil war.

One block north, on Calle 17, Avenida Central 2, is the Palacio Nacional (Mon–Fri from 4pm) where the Legislative Assembly sits.

63 D2 Calle 17, Avenida Central 2 506 2257 1433 Tue–Sat 8.30–4.30 Adult US$4

Below *Cannon in the grounds of the Museo Nacional, which is housed in a former military barracks, the Bellavista Fortress*

INFORMATION
www.ins-cr.com
63 D2 11th floor of INS building, Avenida 7, Calle 9–11 506 2287 6034
Mon–Fri 8.30–3.30, Sat 9–1
US$7

MUSEO DEL JADE

North of Parque España is the Instituto Nacional de Seguros (INS), which houses the Fidel Tristan Jade Museum on the ground floor. In addition to the stunning collection of jade carvings with hundreds of beautifully worked pieces, there are displays of pre-Columbian art, pottery and sculpture. All of the museum's jade was recovered from archaeological digs in Costa Rica and sheds light onto the different indigenous cultures. A significant part of the exhibition derives from the private collection of archaeologist Carlos Balser, who came to Costa Rica in 1921.

ANCIENT CRAFT

For the Maya and Aztec cultures, jade was more important than gold and was believed to have medicinal powers. Beyond its beauty and its intrinsic value for those who traded it, the jade collection reveals the increased social stratification in the period between 100BC and AD700. Many of the pieces on display would have been worn by chiefs or shamans as status symbols. Most of the jade in the collection was recovered from sites in the northwest province of Guanacaste. Outcrops of jade are not known in the region, suggesting that either they were exhausted in prehistoric times or that raw jade was imported to the Chorotega area, perhaps from the Montagua Valley in Guatemala (the only site in the hemisphere where jade is now found), to be distributed to craftsmen.

Considered among the finest jade carvings of the ancient Americas, there are many examples of polished axe forms, revealing shamans disguised as zoomorphic deities, including eagles, jaguars, crocodiles, ocelots and even the resplendent quetzal. The pottery and sculptures displayed include *metates* (tripods for grinding corn) and ceramic tables. The final room, often referred to as the Sala Exotica, contains many examples of fertility goddesses, believed to have religious significance.

La Familia, a sculpture outside the entrance by renowned Costa Rican artist Francisco Zúñiga, is an elegant contrast to the institutional INS building.

Above *Detail of a collection of* metates *(300BC–1000AD), which were used for grinding corn*

MUSEO DE ORO PRECOLOMBINO

www.museosdelbancocentral.org

Buried like treasure below the Plaza de la Cultura and accessible through a gated entrance on the eastern side is the Pre-Columbian Gold Museum. Delicate figurines of frogs, spiders and other creatures glisten in the museum. Displays show the development of metallurgical techniques in the Diquis region of southwest Costa Rica, demonstrating fine craftsmanship. Gold work grew steadily in importance from around AD500, marking a move away from the north's Mayan influences, which preferred jade, to the southern influences of Panama and Colombia, with greater importance for gold.

Within the same three-floor underground complex, the small Numismatic Museum displays a selection of notes, coins and bills reflecting Costa Rican history from the 16th century to the present day. An open area is used for temporary exhibitions. The ICT Tourist Office is in the same complex.

63 D2 Plaza de la Cultura 506 2243 4202 Daily 9.30–5 US$9

MUSEO LA SALLE DE CIENCIAS NATURALES

www.lasalle.edu.co/museo

Tucked within La Salle College, opposite the southwest corner of Sabana Park, the La Salle Museum of Natural Sciences is full of stuffed animals and birds, displayed in recreations of their natural habitats. The majority of exhibits, some of which are a tad timeworn, represent Costa Rica's own flora and fauna, from monkeys shown cavorting through the treetops to marine turtles, manatees and even swordfish. There are impressive exhibits of butterflies and geological specimens, and life-size recreations of dinosaurs prowl the foyer. The museum is all at ground-floor level and suitable for visitors in wheelchairs. You can catch the Sabana-Estadio bus from outside the Catedral Metropolitana, downtown, on Avenida 2.

62 A2 Sabana Sur 506 2232 1306 Mon–Sat 8–4, Sun 9–5 US$2

PARQUE CENTRAL

▷ 70.

PARQUE SABANA

West of downtown, Avenida Central becomes six-lane Paseo Colón. At the western end of Paseo Colón, Parque Sabana was the city's airport until the middle of the 20th century. The transformation has created a vast park 30 minutes' walk from central San José. On the western side is the new 35,000-seat National Stadium, built by the Chinese government between 2008 and 2010, a running track, a sports complex and a lake. Inside the park there is the Museum of Costa Rican Art (▷ 67). This partly forested park is a lovely place to walk or jog, or to explore by mountain bike, although it is best avoided at night.

62 A2 Paseo Colón and Highway 1 24 hours Buses marked Sabana Estadio or Sabana Cementerio run from Parque Central along Paseo Colón to the park, 80 colones

PLAZA DE LA CULTURA

▷ 71.

PLAZA DE LA DEMOCRACÍA

Plaza de la Democracía is dominated by the Bellavista Fortress, now the National Museum (▷ 67), which was created in 1989 to celebrate the centenary of Costa Rican democracy. A bronze statue of José Figueres stands in the quiet plaza. Along the western side of the square, which was remodeled in 2009, is a small craft market (daily 8–6). Three blocks west and one block south is the Iglesia Soledad. The church overlooks the charming little Plaza de las Artes, with modern sculptures.

63 D2 Avenida Central, Calle 13–15 24 hours At the middle of town, head east, down Avenida Central. A taxi from Parque Central costs US$1

Left *A gold object displayed in the Museo de Oro Precolombino*
Below *Spectators at a concert in the Plaza de la Domocracía*

INFORMATION

62 C2 Calle 2–Calle Central, Avenida 2–4 24 hours Buses from La Sabana run along Paseo Colón and stop alongside the park, 80 colones

TIPS

» The area immediately west and south of the park is a seedy red-light district and should be avoided.

» Pickpockets are very common in Parque Central. Try to leave all valuables locked up in your hotel and be mindful of camera thieves.

PARQUE CENTRAL

Imbued with a bubbling energy, Central Park may have little in the way of sights, but it reveals the vibrant mosaic of Costa Rican daily life. At the heart of downtown San José, a couple of blocks west of the Plaza de la Cultura, bordered by Avenida 2 and Calle Central, Central Park provides plenty of people-watching opportunities. The park is noted for the grandiose bandstand in the middle; the structure was kindly donated by Nicaraguan dictator Anastacio Samoza. The plaza has been spruced up and now features a bronze statue of a street-sweeper on its north side—a charming curiosity. Although there is no street cafe, you can normally buy an ice cream. At weekends, Sundays in particular, this is a popular spot with locals who saunter through the temporary stalls and stop to admire the lifelike bronze figures.

THE CATHEDRAL AND THEATER

Dominating the eastern side of the square is the slightly cramped Catedrál Metropolitana (tel 506 2221 3826), visited by the late Pope John Paul II in 1983 on his first visit to Central America. A marble statue of the Pope, by Jiménez Deredia, stands outside. The original structure was destroyed by a powerful earthquake, and the 19th-century replacement has been renovated. Inside the cathedral there are eye-catching, stained-glass windows, and the Capilla de Santíssismo Sacramento is adorned with flowers. Gone are the sooty candles, replaced instead with a neat line of electric ones—25 colones will light your bulb for a few minutes, 50 colones and you can brighten two.

Facing the plaza on Avenida 2 is the Teatro Melico Salazar, Costa Rica's most important theater after the Teatro Nacional. Performances and shows at the Melico have a broad appeal, ranging from pop and jazz concerts through to ballet and orchestral works.

Below *The impressive bandstand at the center of the park*

PLAZA DE LA CULTURA

Plaza de la Cultura is the heart of the city, where the sublime Teatro Nacional stands, a graceful reminder of San José's opulent days. On Avenida Central and Calle 3–5, Plaza de la Cultura is a vibrant hub of pedestrian activity, where clusters of locals and visitors, and a few hundred pigeons, gather round to watch the constant flow of people from all walks of life. There are plenty of street cafes, but the Gran Hotel Costa Rica offers the best vantage point for the urban anthropologist. In the drier months, the Plaza de la Cultura is the focus of evening performances of anything from classical orchestras to jazz, blues and cultural events, often with international artists. At the weekend, a small market, selling everything from textiles to herbal remedies, opens up in front of the Gran Hotel. On Tuesday and Saturday, late in the afternoon, a Peruvian panpipe band makes its appearance, in front of Costa Rica's ice cream über-parlor, Pops.

ALL THAT GLISTENS

One of San José's glittering highlights, the Museo de Oro Precolombino (▷ 69), lies beneath the square and is accessed through an entrance on the east side.

DRAMA

On the southern side of the plaza is the neoclassical Teatro Nacional (National Theater), one of the most impressive buildings in the city, and a source of considerable pride. It was funded by a coffee tax in the late 19th century when the country's social elite realized the city was lacking a theater suitable for world-class performances; opera star Adelina Patti evidently omitted the Costa Rica leg of her tour as there was not a venue she deemed sufficiently glorious.

Construction of this national treasure called on the skills of European artisans, including Belgian architects and Italian artists. The colonnades of the exterior are complemented by a lavish interior with a balance of extravagance and detail in the mahogany furniture, crystal chandeliers, gold-leaf murals and paintings. The Carrara marble staircase is adorned with Costa Rica's most renowned painting, *Una Alegoria,* by Italian artist Aleardo Villa, which depicts the coffee harvest. The painting is reproduced on the back of the 5,000 colones banknote. The graceful neoclassical facade is topped by statues of the Muses and inset with alcoves featuring busts of Beethoven and Spanish composer Calderón de la Barca.

The theater opened with a production of *Faust* in 1897. You can check the website for the monthly program.

INFORMATION

63 D2 Calle 3–5, Avenida Central

TEATRO NACIONAL

www.teatronacional.go.cr
Avenida 2, Calle 3 · 506 2221 1329
Mon–Sat 10–5 · US$3

TIPS

» San José has little in the way of geography to help you get your bearings. Running along the northern flank of Plaza de la Cultura, Avenida Central is a useful navigator, forming a neat horizontal line through the city map.

» A coffee stop in the Café del Teatro (▷ 78) grants access to the theater, providing a sneak view of the glorious interior of the Teatro Nacional.

» Many museums and attractions are closed on Sunday or Monday, including the Pre-Columbian Gold Museum and National Theater, so plan accordingly.

Above *A political demonstration attracts a small crowd*

SAN JOSÉ'S SQUARES

A walk through San José reveals a street culture of chaos and clutter where solitary gestures to architectural style stand serene. Colonial-style treasures nestle amid lush patios, kaleidoscopic markets bombard the senses and modern monoliths thrust from squares where Joséfino life ebbs and flows. Leafy parks provide the perfect place to relax.

THE WALK
Distance: 3.5km (2 miles)
Allow: A morning
Start at: Mercado Central
End at: Plaza de la Cultura

★ If you want to see the city wake you'll have to be ready by 6am. For the human dawn chorus, the tour begins at the Central Market, which takes up a whole block bordered by Avenida Central–1 and Calle 6–8.

❶ The Mercado Central (▷ 76) throbs with a cacophony of sounds, sights, smells and tastes. It sells everything from cheese, spices, fruit, vegetables, dried and fresh flowers through to leather sandals, saddles, bridles and simple tourist gifts. The honey is particularly recommended. You can breakfast on tortillas or empanadas and coffee at one of the many stand-up bars, or take a more leisurely sit-down option. The seriously cheap food and drinks are generally cleanly prepared with a turnover so quick the food doesn't have time to go off.

Leave the market on Avenida 1, and continue east for two blocks to the Central Post Office.

❷ The battleship-green Correo Central, understated and often overlooked, seems perfectly balanced in proportion and setting. Behind the elegant, eclectic facade, the echoing halls of post boxes are a bit dour, but upstairs is the interesting Museo Postal Telegráfico Filatélico de Costa Rica. The splendid Café del Correo retains some period pieces and serves coffee and cakes. An ICT tourist office is inside the post office, to the right of the main entrance (daily 8–4). Outside the post office, under the shade of fig trees, Joséfinos have their shoes polished, catch up on the gossip or read *La Nación*.

Leave the post office, turn right and walk one block to the pedestrian thoroughfare of Avenida Central, cross over and then walk one block to Parque Central, bordered by Avenida 2

❸ Parque Central, surrounded by traffic, has a yellow bandstand in the middle. All Joséfino life seems to pass through. Poised to the east is the Catedrál Metropolitana, while to the north, on Avenida 2, is the Teatro Melico Salazar (▷ 77).

Head back north one block onto the pedestrian-only Avenida Central. Perpetually bustling with people rushing around the shops, banks and department stores, this is one of the main arteries of the city. Three blocks east along Avenida Central is Plaza de la Cultura, the heart of the city.

Above *Shady trees in Parque Nacional*

❹ Plaza de la Cultura is dominated by the Gran Hotel Costa Rica (▷ 80–81), one of Costa Rica's oldest hotels. A coffee on the terrace of Café 1930 (▷ 78) is the ideal vantage point to view the smaller Parque Mora Fernández, prettily landscaped and merging into Plaza de la Cultura. Amid the pigeons, Joséfino opportunism rages, from photographers toting cameras to a persuasive medley of shoe shiners and street entertainers. The Teatro Nacional stands in majestic contrast to such urban prose, while on the east side of the square, you can contain your avarice at the underground Museo de Oro Precolombino (▷ 69).

From Plaza de la Cultura head east for six blocks along Avenida Central until you reach the newly relaid Plaza de la Democracía.

❺ Plaza de la Democracía (▷ 69) was created in 1989 to celebrate the centenary of Costa Rican democracy. The main point of interest is the statue of José Figueres. Lining the northern side of the square is the country's Asamblea Legislativa (Legislative Assembly). The eastern flank is dominated by the muscular Bellavista Fortress, which now houses the National Museum (▷ 67).

Behind the National Museum, a pedestrian walkway leads south where some restored early 20th-century houses contain cafes with outdoor seating. The cobbled walkway slopes north, uphill, one block to the Parque Nacional.

❻ The Parque Nacional is packed with palm trees surrounding the Monumento Nacional, a statue representing the five Central American republics ousting the North American filibuster William Walker, and the abolition of slavery in Central America. A statue of national hero Juan Santamaría, donated by the Sandinista Government of Nicaragua, stands in the southwest corner of the park. On the north side, the National Library hides behind a dramatic modernist exterior. At the northwestern corner of the park is the Museum of Contemporary Art and Design. One block east of the square is the old Atlantic Railway station, currently awaiting restoration. Visitors to the museum are welcome to explore the old railway cars on the long-abandoned tracks to the rear.

From Parque Nacional head west down Avenida 3 back toward the middle of town, along the southern side of Parque España.

❼ By day, Parque España (▷ 66) is a refreshingly calm square, graced to its northwest by the Edificio Metálico. Directly north of the square, beside the entrance to the Instituto Nacional de Seguros (INS), is Costa Rica's finest museum, the Museo del Jade (▷ 68). To the west one block and south one block, Parque Morazán is overshadowed by the Aurola Holiday Inn. Take the elevator to the top-floor casino for views of the city.

From Parque España take Calle 11, which runs alongside the INS Building north for one block. Tucked behind the two parks defined by the blocks between Calle 1 and Calle 15 and Avenida 7 and Avenida 11 are the historic districts or barrios of Amón and Otoya (▷ 64–66).

Below *The imposing Correo Central (Central Post Office) also houses a museum and a pleasant cafe*

❽ During the 19th and early 20th centuries, Amón and Otoya barrios were the residential districts of the coffee elites. Along undulating streets, colonial-style mansions, with verdant balconies, recall a French colonial quarter. At pioneer hotels, like the Britannia (▷ 81) on Calle 3 and Avenida 11, flashes of Caribbean-style architecture fuse with sedate Victorian style. On Avenida 9, between calles 3 and 7, the brick walls are decorated with ceramic tiles depicting rural scenes.

From Avenida 7 heading south along Calle 5 for four blocks and then one block west will bring you back to Plaza de la Cultura.

Above *Statues adorn the neoclassical exterior of the Teatro Nacional*

PLACES TO VISIT
BARRIOS AMÓN AND OTOYA
▷ 64–66.

MERCADO CENTRAL
✉ Avenida Central 1 and Calle 6–8
🕑 Mon–Sat 6am–8pm

MUSEO POSTAL TELEGRÁFICO FILATÉLICO DE COSTA RICA
✉ Calle 2, Avenida 1–3 ☎ 506 2223 9766, ext. 205 🕑 Mon–Fri 8–5

MUSEO DEL JADE
▷ 68.

MUSEO DE ORO PRECOLOMBINO
▷ 69.

WHERE TO EAT
CAFÉ DEL TEATRO
✉ Teatro Nacional, Plaza de la Cultura
☎ 506 2221 1329, ext 250

CAFÉ 1930
✉ Terrace, Gran Hotel Costa Rica
✉ Avenida 2, Calle Central ☎ 506 2221 4000

CAFÉ POSADA DEL MUSEO
✉ Avenida 2, Calle 17 ☎ 506 2258 1027

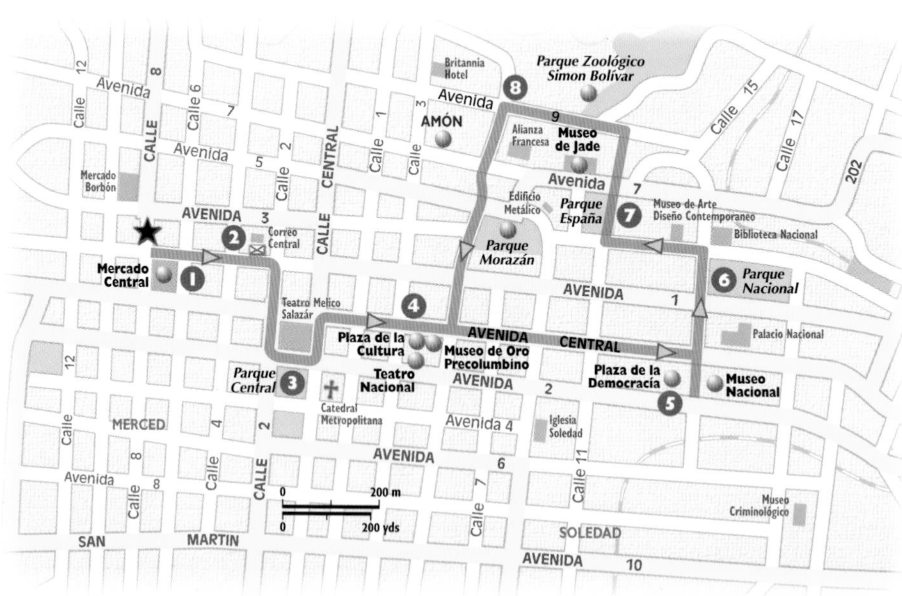

SHOPPING

7TH STREET BOOKS

This friendly bookstore is run by Canadians Marc Roegiers and John McCuen. Just off the Avenida Central, one block east of Plaza de la Cultura, it has a good selection of English-language books, from translations of Latin-American heavyweights like Jorge Luis Borges and Gabriel García Márquez, to contemporary fiction, including Nick Hornby and Anne Tyler. Costa Rica wildlife guides are also sold.

✉ Calle 7, Avenida Central–1 ☎ 506 2256 8251 🕒 Daily 9–6

BOUTIQUE ANNEMARIE

In the main lobby of the Hotel Don Carlos (▷ 81), this souvenir and gift shop has one of the largest selections in Costa Rica, with thousands of handcrafted items and pieces of art on display.

✉ Hotel Don Carlos, Calle 9, Avenida 7–9 ☎ 506 2221 6707 🕒 Daily 9.30–7.30

LA CASONA

This dark, labyrinthine market of *artesanía* shops has lots of interesting stalls to sift through, selling everything from exotic wooden salad bowls, jewelry boxes and sculptures to Café Britt coffee, Guatemalan imported textiles and folkloric paintings. Prices vary greatly from stall to stall, and bargaining is expected. Sunday morning soccer match days are a good time to wander unhassled, with most stallholders glued to fuzzy TV sets.

✉ Avenida Central, Calle Central–1 🕒 Mon–Sat 9.30–6.30, Sun 9.30–5

CENTRO COMMERCIAL EL PUEBLO

The Centro shopping and nightlife complex is a great place for exploring, window shopping, taking a meal and then dipping into a few bars before hitting a disco. Art galleries, shops, travel agencies, fast-food chains, bars and restaurants cater to every taste. The Centro is just beyond comfortable walking distance from downtown San José, but for the fit and energetic, from Plaza de la Cultura, head straight up Calle 3 to Avenida 13 (six long blocks), turn right at El Moro castle, then after 100m (110 yards) the road bends left, crossing the river. From here, it's a 10-minute walk to El Pueblo. In the evening a taxi is strongly recommended—it will cost US$4.

✉ Barrio Tournón ☎ 506 2221 9434 🕒 Daily 11am–2am

ESMERALDAS Y DISEÑOS

www.esmeraldasydisenos.com

This store tucked away in a residential district is one of the best outlets in town for fine jewelry, including exquisite gold pre-Columbian replicas, such as frog pendants and earrings in the form of anthropomorphic jaguars. Ask to see the jewelers at work in their craft studio.

✉ 200m (220 yards) north and 100m (110 yards) west of Torre La Sabana, Sabana Norte ☎ 506 2231 4808 🕒 Mon–Sat 8–6, Sun 8–4

GALERÍA 11–12

www.galeria11-12.com

Anyone who is interested in collecting Costa Rican art should head to the bohemian district of Escazú where the works of Rolando Garitan and Fernando Carballo, two of the country's most renowned contemporary artists, are exhibited at Galería 11–12. The gallery has its roots in the Monday workshop, which was set up in the early 1980s as a meeting place for San José's poets, writers and painters. While the main gallery is geared towards collectors of contemporary art, there are also spaces dedicated to Costa Rica's master painters. Prices range from a few hundred dollars for small pieces to tens of thousands for works by leading artists.

✉ Plaza Itskatzú, Escazú ☎ 506 2288 1975 🕒 Mon–Fri 9am–10pm, Sat 10–10, Sun 1–6

Above *Items at a craft market in San José*

Above *Window displays of swimwear in a shopping mall in the city*

GALERÍA NAMÚ

www.galerianamu.com

Opposite the Alianza Francesa building, Galería Namú is the best one-stop shop for homegrown art. Indigenous art and crafts would be the traditional phrase, but Namú has blended conventional themes of rugs, throws, textiles and mask carvings with many more contemporary developments. The result is some inspired work. Every piece bought comes with an information sheet. If San José is at the start and end of your trip, pop in on the first day, think about what you want to buy while you travel, and then visit again to purchase it just before you leave. If you're just passing, take your credit card and give yourself more than a half hour. Namú also arranges tours to indigenous villages.

Avenida 7, Calle 5–7 506 2256 3412 Mon–Sat 9–6.30, Sun by appointment only Tours from US$10

LIBRERÍA LEHMANN

On the main Avenida Central, this large, well-laid-out bookstore with an academic slant stocks a limited range of Costa Rican wildlife and nature books. For Spanish speakers, there is a good range of contemporary Latin American fiction and just a couple of shelves dedicated to English-language literature: Shakespeare, Emily Dickinson and Oscar Wilde, with the odd John Grisham or Catherine Cookson. Telescopes, globes, CDs, stationery supplies and maps are also sold.

Avenida Central, Calle 3 506 2223 1212 Mon–Fri 8–6.30, Sat 9–5

MERCADO DE ARTESANÍAS

On Plaza Artigas, this market houses several dozen craft vendors selling everything from hammocks to wooden salad bowls and mini oxcarts. Every Saturday in spring it hosts an open-air art exhibition. Bartering is the norm, but expect to pay about 15 to 20 percent less than the original asking price, with additional discounts for cash.

Calle 11, Avenida 4–6 Mon–Sat 9–6

MERCADO CENTRAL

The heart and soul of the city, filled with life, noise and general chaos, the central market is not to be missed. Behind all the daily commerce and greetings you'll find a few typical items for sale, such as leather and wooden goods, many without the price increases found in stores catering to tourists. You may have to look around, but you should find a memorable souvenir. Be aware that pickpockets are known to operate here, so guard your belongings.

Avenida Central–1, Calle 6–8
Mon–Sat 6am–8pm

ENTERTAINMENT AND NIGHTLIFE

BONGOS BAR

This bar has a tropical rain forest theme and is normally the first stop on an El Pueblo bar hop. Happy hour is daily from 6pm to 8pm and is a good time to mix and mingle with yuppie, 30-plus, single Joséfinos. The music runs the gamut of classic rock, sultry Latin dance and 1980s fun and frolics. At the weekend the vibe is more youthful. Saturday is Saturday Safari, and ladies get in free until 10pm.

Entrance to El Pueblo, Barrio Tournón 506 222 5746 Cover charge US$6 (weekends)

EL CARTEL DE LA BOCA DEL MONTE

The unprepossessing exterior of this cavernous bar hides one of San José's best nights out, a 15-minute walk from the National Museum. With scattered beer barrels, sticky tiled floor, alcoves and a gate reminiscent of a subway station, it's pleasingly less polished than the nightspots of El Pueblo and is an institution among San José's bohemian barflies. The cocktail list stretches to more than 100, ranging from traditional margaritas to frozen banana daiquiris and anything else that takes the bartender's mood. A beer will set you back 800 colones (US$1.50). Every Monday, Wednesday and Friday there is live music, and often on the weekend there are improvised performances, from rock to salsa to reggae.

Avenida 1, Calle 21 and 23, close to Cine Magaly 506 2221 0327 Mon–Fri 11.30am–2pm, 6pm–2am, Sat, Sun 4pm–2am US$4 live music cover charge for men (Mon)

CHELLE'S

Head east along Avenida Central to Chelle's where the bright lighting and unwholesome exterior makes it stand out. The other dependable factor is the wonderful selection of drinkers, more concerned with getting a drink than fussing over furnishings. Sticking to a red vinyl seat with a warm beer and a salty *bocas* (snacks) or a smoothie and a cheap lunch was never more fun.

Calle 9, Avenida Central 506 2221 1369 24 hours

JAZZ CAFÉ
www.jazzcafecostarica.com
Out in San Pedro, a US$3 taxi ride from Plaza de la Cultura, this sleek jazz venue offers the best live music in the city with a convivial laid-back feel. Renowned as a launch pad for rising local talent, as well as a top venue for visiting jazz stars, who have included Chucho Valdés, it is a must for jazz devotees. The interior is stylish, the lighting atmospheric and good food and cocktails ensure a relaxed evening's entertainment. There is music almost every night.
✉ Avenida Central, next to Banco Popular San Pedro ☎ 506 2253 8933 🕐 Daily 6pm–12 ✋ Varies according to artist

OLIO
A classy favorite of a mature bohemian crowd, this hip, brick-walled tapas bar with stained-glass lamps oozes warmth. Singles favor the main room and bar, while couples snuggle into romantic nooks. A large wine list includes South American vintages.
✉ Calle 33, avenidas 3 and 5, Barrio California ☎ 506 2281 0541 🕐 Mon–Fri 11.30am–1am, Sat 4pm–12

THE SHAKESPEARE BAR
Inside the Sala Garbo cinema, The Shakespeare Bar is a popular port of call for Joséfinos en route to a movie, dinner or a show at the Laurence Olivier Theater nearby. If you feel like lingering, you can join the aspiring pianists, enjoy a game of darts or chill out to the occasional live music.
✉ Avenida 2, Calle 28 ☎ 506 2258 6787 🕐 Daily 7pm–12

TEATRO EUGENE O'NEILL
www.cccncr.com
This dynamic theatrical wing of the non-profit North American Cultural Center has a varied schedule, ranging from classic productions to contemporary dance to children's plays and pop concerts. With close links to the University, it draws on the talents of San José's rising artistes. In addition to hosting its own productions, performances from the National Dance company and other national organizations can also be appreciated. Prices are dependent on the type of performance; call or check the website for information (in Spanish). Los Yoses is a five-minute taxi ride from the Plaza de la Cultura.
✉ North American Cultural Center, Avenida Central, Calle 37, Los Yoses ☎ 506 2225 9433

TEATRO MELICO SALAZAR
www.teatromelico.go.cr
Performances and shows at the elegant Melico have a broader appeal than those at the National Theater (▷ below). They range from pop and jazz concerts to ballet and orchestral works.
✉ Avenida 2, Calle Central–2 ☎ 506 2233 5424 🕐 Ticket office: Mon–Sat 10–12, 1–5 ✋ From US$2–US$7, up to US$70 for international performances

TEATRO NACIONAL
www.teatronacional.go.cr
A Saturday night visit to the theater is a popular pastime for wealthy Joséfinos. Check the website for the monthly schedule, or stop by for a tour and a coffee in the lovely cafe.
✉ Plaza de la Cultura ☎ 506 2221 9417 🕐 Ticket office: Mon–Sat 10–1, 2–5 ✋ Depending on performance: US$15–US$30; discounts for students and seniors. Visit to theater: US$5

EL TOBOGÁN
A towering wood-and-thatch *palenque* off the Guápiles highway is the city's hottest dance venue on weekends. Though the dance floor is as big as a football field, it packs Latin-music-loving crowds in shoulder to shoulder to dance to live merengue, cumbia and salsa.
✉ 200m (220 yards) north and 100m (110 yards) east of Edificio La República ☎ 506 2223 8920 🕐 Fri–Sat 8pm–2am, Sun 4–9

VERTIGO
www.vertigocr.com
If techno is your thing, don your most stylish duds and hit the dance floor with the city's young sophisticates at this air-conditioned club upstairs in the rather drab "Columbus Building." The huge dance floor allows heaps of space, but Saturdays still can get crowded.
✉ Edificio Colón, Paseo Colón ☎ 506 2257 8424 🕐 Thu–Sat 8pm–4am

FESTIVALS AND EVENTS

MARCH/APRIL

INTERNATIONAL ARTS FESTIVAL
Arts events are held at venues across the city (in even numbered years).

MAY

LABOR DAY
Marches, parades and the president's state of the nation address take place in the capital on Labor Day.
🕐 May 1

OCTOBER

CULTURES DAY
Indigenous peoples march to protest the Spanish conquest.
🕐 October 12

DECEMBER

EL TOPE
As working Joséfinos receive their *aguinaldo* (Christmas bonus), the festive season gets into full swing. The El Tope horse parade begins at noon on December 26 and travels along San José's principal avenues. Many Ticos come from outside the capital to show off their specially trained horses. In the evening, the Festival de la Luz takes place with a flotilla of vibrant floats, and general revelry ensues beneath a firework display. A carnival starts next day at about 5pm, with bull-running (public participation) at El Zapote south of the city.
🕐 December 26

PRICES AND SYMBOLS

The restaurants are listed alphabetically (excluding El, Le, La and Les). The prices given are the average for a two-course lunch (L) and a three-course dinner (D) for one person, without drinks. The wine price is for the least expensive bottle.

For a key to the symbols, ▷ 2.

EL BALCÓN DE EUROPA

Two blocks east of Plaza de la Cultura (▷ 71), this charismatic Italian restaurant dates back to 1909, making it the oldest in Costa Rica. With dark wood-paneled walls covered with photos, the setting and ebullient atmosphere compensate for a hit-and-miss menu. Well-priced pasta dishes are reliable, but some of the meat and fish dishes, the Spanish-style steak excepted, can be on the small side.

✉ Calle 9, Avenida Central–1
☎ 506 2221 4841 ◷ Sun–Fri 11.30–10
L US$15, D US$18, Wine US$15

CAFÉ MUNDO

In a converted mansion in Barrio Amón, north of Parque España, this hip, gay-friendly, Italian restaurant is popular with fast-lunch business workers by day and bohemian Ticos, visitors and expatriates in the evenings. The porch is a lovely setting for the excellent value *plato del día* (US$5). The extensive repertoire of pastas includes fettuccini with vegetables and shrimp sauce, and penne with chicken and vodka. There are pizzas big enough to share, and tomato and herb bread served with olive oil. Hidden behind a wall, the cafe is easy to miss; look for the open gate on the corner.

✉ Calle 15, Avenida 9, Barrio Amón
☎ 506 2222 6190 ◷ Mon–Fri 11–11, Sat, Sun 12–2.30, 5–12 L US$16, D US$21, Wine US$17 200m (220 yards) east and 100m (110 yards) north of the INS building

CAFÉ 1930

On the Parque Mora Fernández, the terrace cafe of the renovated Gran Hotel is a San José institution. The renovation has expanded the cafe, which remains one of the most popular people-watching spots in town. Main course dishes can be bland and overpriced. For light lunches and late-night munchies, however, the club sandwiches, salads and breakfasts are more than satisfying.

✉ Gran Hotel Costa Rica, Avenida 2, Calle Central ☎ 506 2221 4000 ◷ 24 hours
L US$9, D US$22, Wine US$16

CAFÉ POSADA DEL MUSEO

www.hotelposadadelmuseo.com

This bohemian restaurant and art gallery is welcoming, with comfortable terrace seating outside. The menu includes Argentinian dishes like *torta de ricotta, torta de espinacas* and *alfajores*. The excellent three-course set lunches draw the suits, and monthly evening gatherings are popular with artists. A two-minute walk from the National Museum (▷ 67), this restaurant merits a stop for lunch or a coffee.

✉ Avenida 2, Calle 17, diagonal to the National Museum ☎ 506 2258 1027
◷ Mon–Thu 9–7, Fri–Sun 9am–11pm
L/D US$5, Wine US$14

CAFÉ DEL TEATRO

www.teatronacional.go.cr

The National Theater's coffee shop combines neoclassical grandeur and impeccable service to make an unmissable San José experience. Polished marble tiled floors and tabletops, chandeliers and ceiling frescoes have been elegantly restored. Excellent coffee is served and for snacks and lunches there are sandwiches, cakes, fresh juices and salads. It's expensive, but worth it.

✉ Teatro Nacional, Plaza de la Cultura
☎ 506 2221 1329, ext. 250 ◷ Mon–Fri 9–5, Sat 9–4, Sun only during performances
Coffee and cake US$5

LA COCINA DE LEÑA

A five-minute taxi ride from Plaza de la Cultura (▷ 71) takes you to a popular restaurant among gilded Joséfinos. This is Costa Rican *comida típica* (▷ 239) at its finest. The house specials are tenderloin

Opposite *The terrace of the Café 1930*

and Creole chicken broiled with a special sauce. Lighter options include tuna and palm heart salad and tamales. The rustic taverna buzzes at the weekend. Reservations are advised.
✉ El Pueblo Commercial Center ☎ 506 2555 1360 🕒 Sun–Thu 11–10, Fri, Sat 11am–11.30pm 🖑 L US$15, D US$26, Wine US$17

LA ESQUINA DE BUENOS AIRES

Replicating an Argentinian *bodega*, this intimate bar-restaurant is festooned with period prints and infused with the rhythms of tango, drawing a sophisticated local crowd and expatriates in the know. The wide-ranging menu includes onion soup, and shrimp and avocado salad. The filet of sole in blue cheese with boiled potatoes is superb, and the wine list draws heavily from the homeland.
✉ Calle 11, Avenida 4 ☎ 506 2223 1909 🕒 Mon–Thu 11.30–3, 6–10.30, Fri, Sat 12.30–11, Sun 12–10 🖑 L US$15, D US$20, Wine US$18

GRANO DE ORO

www.hotelgranodeoro.com
Just off Paseo Colón, the Grano de Oro hotel's (▷ 81) exciting new restaurant combines elegance with inventive Mediterranean cuisine. The tranquil courtyard patio is perfect for a light lunch, while in the evenings, the intimate candlelit restaurant provides a romantic setting. Appetizers include fried Camembert with hot blackberry sauce and leafy salads. For a main course, try caramelized chicken breast with dried fruits or one of the highly rated, but good-value, seafood dishes, such as poached mahi-mahi with mashed potatoes and leeks.
✉ Calle 30, between avenidas 2 and 4 ☎ 506 2255 3322 🕒 Daily 7am–10pm 🖑 L US$22, D US$30, Wine US$18

JÜRGEN'S

Tucked away in a quiet residential quarter of Los Yoses, this elegant restaurant in Boutique Hotel Jade (▷ 80) represents sophisticated dining at its best. Contemporary art pieces and floral displays complement the menu, which has a French influence. Appetizers include mussels Rockefeller, and entrées range from tilapia with mustard sauce to pork in wine sauce. Service is sharp, and there's a cigar lounge.
✉ Boutique Hotel Jade, Barrio Dent, 200m (220 yards) north of Subaru dealership ☎ 506 2283 2239 🕒 Mon–Fri 12–2, 6–10, Sat 6–10 🖑 L US$18, D US$26, Wine US$20

MACHU PICCHU

This Peruvian restaurant, one block north of Paseo Colón, is an old San José haunt that is popular with tourists. With a spartan dining room and walls hung with a few tokens to the Inca theme, it is the delicious, inexpensive food that is the star here. The seafood menu includes sea bass *a lo macho* (a fillet drenched in Peruvian *aji*—green chili sauce). There are appetizers such as octopus cracklings and ceviche and superb (and strong) pisco sours.
✉ Calle 32, Avenida 1–3 ☎ 506 2222 7384 🕒 Mon–Sat 11–3, 6–10 🖑 L US$8, D US$12, Wine US$6

NEWS CAFÉ

www.hotel-presidente.com
This open-air, contemporary-styled bar-restaurant is a tourist magnet and, while it may have little to do with Costa Rica, it is a reliable downtown option for lunch or a cool beer in the bar. The interior is snug, with TVs in the corner and plenty of newspapers. The burgers are peerless, and there are sandwiches, wraps and salads.
✉ Hotel Presidente, Avenida Central, Calle 7 ☎ 506 2222 3022 🕒 Daily 6am–midnight 🖑 L US$12, D US$16, Wine US$15

PARK CAFÉ

Reservations are de rigueur for this sublime fine-dining option 100m (110 yards) north of Parque Sabana (▷ 69). Serving within the courtyard garden of an antiques store, Michelin-starred chef Richard Neat delivers impeccable tapas and entrées from a world-spanning menu that includes caramelized scallops with ricotta tortellini and pumpkin soup, and lighter fare such as roasted tuna fillet with ginger chutney and artichoke salad.
✉ Calle 44, Sabana Norte ☎ 506 2290 6342 🕒 Daily 12–3, 7–9.30 🖑 L US$18, D US$30

RESTAURANT EL OASIS

The Santo Tomas hotel (▷ 81) restaurant in Barrio Amón, with its poolside dining room, is a soothing antidote to San José's urban jungle. The international menu satisfies most tastes, with grilled pesto tuna, chicken breast with caper sauce, and filet mignon. Save space for desserts such as crêpes, mousse or apple pie. There is also a fine wine list.
✉ Santo Tomas, Avenida 7, Calle 3–5 ☎ 506 2255 0448 🕒 Tue–Sat 4–11pm, Sun 12–7 🖑 L/D US$21, Wine US$18

RESTAURANTE VISHNU

A world-class restaurant for vegetarians and vegans, Vishnu has grown so popular it now has 10 outlets in town. The huge menu spans salads, sandwiches, veggie burgers and fresh-fruit *batidos* (shakes), and for a truly filling meal you can opt for a simple *casado* (set lunch) for US$4.
✉ Avenida 1, Calles 1/3 ☎ 506 2250 6063 🕒 Mon–Sat 7am–9pm, Sun 9–7 🖑 L US$6, D US$10, no wine served

TIN JO

Four blocks south of Plaza de la Cultura, in front of Lucho Barahona Theater, this is one of San José's most popular restaurants. It serves Asian cuisine ranging from steamed Vietnamese chicken to teriyaki salmon, with plenty for vegetarians. At Sunday lunch it is packed with Costa Rican families. Take a taxi in the evenings; the neighborhood can be unsafe after dark.
✉ Calle 11, Avenida 6–8 ☎ 506 2221 7605 🕒 Mon–Thu 11.30–3, 5.30–10, Fri, Sat 11.30–3, 5.30–11, Sun 11.30–10 🖑 L US$18, D US$24, Wine US$17

PRICES AND SYMBOLS

The prices are the lowest and highest for a double room for one night including breakfast, unless otherwise stated. All the hotels listed accept credit cards unless otherwise stated. Note that rates can vary widely throughout the year.

For a key to the symbols, ▷ 2.

BOUTIQUE HOTEL JADE

www.hotelboutiquejade.com

Tucked away in an upscale residential district, this stylish hotel plays up the contemporary theme with avant-garde art, graceful furnishings in creams and autumnal tones, and amenities such as cable TV and WiFi. You can light up a cigar in the lounge bar after dinner in one of the city's finest restaurants, Jürgens (▷ 79).

Calle 41, Barrio California, 300m (327 yards) north of Subaru 506 2224 2445 US$117–US$152 30 Outdoor

CLARION HOTEL AMÓN PLAZA

www.choicehotels.com

Minimalists will retreat from this large, anonymous hotel, designed for the business visitor, in the residential Amón district. The ostentatious lobby sets the tone, lined with marble, crammed with antique furnishings and illuminated by chandeliers. Rooms have internet access, satellite TV, housekeeping, air-conditioning and free local calls. There is a lively 24-hour bar, a cafe-restaurant, a casino, ballroom and a spa with sauna, Jacuzzi and gym.

Avenida 11, Calle 3 506 2523 4600 US$120–US$165 90

COSTA RICA BACKPACKERS

www.costaricabackpackers.com

This splendidly situated and well-run hostel belies the image of cheap and dingy backpacker digs with its landscaped swimming pool, free 24-hour internet, TV lounge and clinically clean him, her and mixed dorms. If you wish, splash out on a private room, one with a king-size bed. The open-air rooftop restaurant doubles as a party space by night.

Avenida 6, Calles 21–23 506 2221 6191 US$12 per person dorms, US$28 private rooms 6 Outdoor

FLEUR DE LYS

www.hotelfleurdelys.com

One block south of Plaza de la Democracía, this restored Victorian mansion is absolutely delightful, with elegant rooms named after native Costa Rican flowers. Each room has a private bathroom, hair-dryer, telephone and cable TV. A French restaurant and a bar will mean the only reason you have to leave the hotel is to visit the Museo Nacional (▷ 67), one block away. There's a tour desk with lots of information. The terrace bar is the perfect place to have a cocktail before relaxing on the porch.

Calle 13, Avenida 2–6 506 2223 1206 US$89 room, US$119–US$139 suites 31

GRAN HOTEL COSTA RICA

www.granhotelcostarica.com

This landmark hotel, in the heart of the city on Plaza de la Cultura, was the first purpose-built hotel in Costa Rica. Despite having been remodeled in 2006, the hotel is steeped in history, and has hosted a roll call of icons from

Opposite *An executive room in the Grano de Oro hotel*

John F. Kennedy in 1963 to the late actor John Wayne. The refurbished rooms are equipped with cable TV, fan and safety deposit box, and there is room service and a laundry. In the lobby, a dining room has replaced the casino, which has been moved to a lower level. The downsized and fenced-in alfresco Café 1930 (▷ 78) remains the best people-watching spot in town.
✉ Avenida 2, Calle Central ☎ 506 2221 4000 💳 US$85, US$139–US$175 suites ⓘ 102, non-smoking available

GRANO DE ORO
www.hotelgranodeoro.com
Two blocks south of Paseo Colón, close to Parque Sabana, this lavish 20th-century mansion—the city's top-rated hotel—offers unadulterated luxury and a warm welcome. The wrought-iron beds set off the rooms, which come with cable TV, Jacuzzi or sundeck spa, mini bar and ceiling fan. The rooms were given a lavish refurbishment in 2009. An exciting new addition, opened in 2007, includes an elegant two-tier restaurant that is now the city's most dramatic place to dine (▷ 79). There is also a spa.
✉ Calle 30, Avenida 2–4 ☎ 506 2255 3322 💳 US$147–US$215 rooms, US$266–US$401 suites ⓘ 37 rooms, 3 suites

HOTEL BRITANNIA
www.hotelbritanniacostarica.com
The landmark Hotel Britannia in colonial Barrio Amón (▷ 64–66) exudes old-fashioned style. The renovated, pastel-pink, plantation-style mansion dates back to the coffee boom and has retained its character while providing first-class service. A wrought-iron gateway leads to a tiled porch lined with pillars and, inside, the courtyard reception continues downstairs to the wine cellar, now a rather expensive restaurant. Conservative rooms, in both the original building and a more contemporary new wing, offer all the expected comforts, with ceiling fans and large tiled bathrooms.
✉ Avenida 11, Calle 3 ☎ 506 2223 6667 💳 US$118–US$32 ⓘ 23

HOTEL CASTILLO
www.hotelcastillo.biz
This 19th-century mansion in Barrio Amón (▷ 64–66) has been restored to offer good-value accommodations. Each room is different, but all appeal with crisp decor, comfortable beds, cable TVs and bathrooms. Rooms 6, 7 and 8 all have fine views across the city and are often reserved in advance. Security is good and discounts are available for longer stays.
✉ Avenida 9, Calle 9, behind INS building ☎ 506 2221 5141 💳 US$57–US$103 ⓘ 12 rooms, 10 villas, 1 suite ❄

HOTEL DON CARLOS
www.doncarloshotel.com
The family-run Hotel Don Carlos in Barrio Amón (▷ 64–66), combines colonial character, great facilities and a sense of style. Spacious, spotless rooms each have a bathroom, cable TV and air-conditioning or fan. The hotel has a collection of artworks; the highlight is a mural of San José in the 1900s by Mario Arroyabe. The staff are friendly and there is information on tours in the area, as well as WiFi and free local calls. The on-site Boutique Annemarie (▷ 75) is one of San José's best souvenir shops.
✉ Calle 9, Avenida 7–9 ☎ 506 2221 6707 💳 US$70–US$80 ⓘ 36 ❄

HOTEL PARQUE DEL LAGO
www.parquedellago.com
This once-staid business hotel close to Parque Sabana (▷ 69) has emerged from a total remake as one of the city's most sophisticated options. The spacious rooms have divinely comfortable mattresses, cable TV, minibar, coffee-maker, and other features. The restaurant and bar is a chic retreat serving consistently satisfying dishes. Other facilities include a spa, internet room, and business rooms.
✉ Paseo Colón, Calles 40–42 ☎ 506 2257 8787 💳 US$130–US$175 ⓘ 30 🅿

HOTEL PRESIDENTE
www.hotel-presidente.com
Hotel Presidente is one block from Plaza de la Cultura. Rooms have parquet floors, cable TV, telephone, air-conditioning and a safe box. Breakfast is served in the popular News Café (▷ 79), which sells international newspapers. There are also a sauna and Jacuzzi, travel agency, casino and airport pick-up.
✉ Avenida Central, Calle 7 ☎ 506 2222 3022 💳 US$101–US$164 ⓘ 110 ❄

ROSA DEL PASEO
http://rosadelpaseo.com
A 10-minute walk from Parque Sabana (▷ 69), this colonial house has a striking bronze and cream facade. A refurbishment of the 104-year-old building extended the hotel to include a small courtyard. Rooms with high ceilings, floorboards, bathrooms and modern comforts are neatly finished, although the Victorian style may be too conservative for some. Rooms without air conditioning have ceiling fans. The master suite has a Jacuzzi and terrace balcony.
✉ Paseo Colón, Calle 28–30, in front of INA building ☎ 506 2257 3212 💳 US$80–US$140 ⓘ 19 ❄ In Junior suites

SANTO TOMAS
www.hotelsantotomas.com
Splendidly situated a stone's throw from the Jade Museum (▷ 68), the Santo Tomas is a gracefully converted mansion. Rooms vary in size, but all retain period features, including glossy colonial tile or hardwood floors. Cable TV and direct-dial phones are standard. A garden has a small swimming pool with Jacuzzi and cascade, and the colonial-themed Restaurant El Oasis (▷ 79) is popular with discerning patrons.
✉ Avenida 7, Calles 3–5 ☎ 506 2255 0448 💳 US$80–US$110 ⓘ 20 🏊 Outdoor

Nature Air™

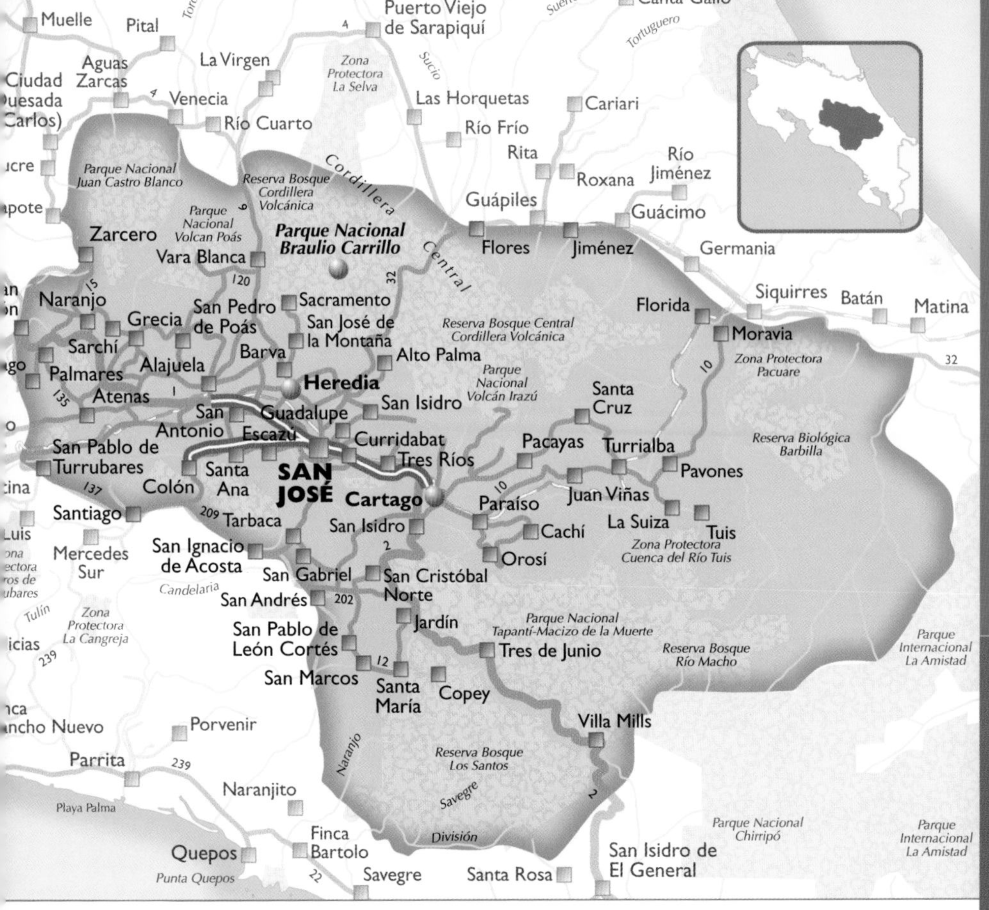

CENTRAL HIGHLANDS

Dramatic vistas around every bend are a hallmark of the diverse Central Highlands, where rugged mountains dominate the scene in every direction. The region rewards travelers with attractions for every taste. Lovely boutique hotels stud the highlands, many in postcard-perfect settings, such as coffee estates on the flanks of a string of volcanoes. Exploring the coffee fields is a key draw to Café Britt and Doka Estates. Combine either with a snaking drive to the summit of the Poás volcano to peer into the bowels of this steaming giant, followed by a visit to La Paz Waterfall Gardens, with its cascades, frog and butterfly gardens, and serpentarium. The route to the top of the Irazú volcano is arguably the nation's most scenic drive, while farther east, Volcán Turrialba is the only place in Costa Rica where you can actually hike into a crater. Turrialba is a base for exhilarating white-water rafting, and for visits to the nation's preeminent pre-Columbian site, at Guayabo.

Many of the nation's most important historic sites are here, too. Alajuela and Heredia, and every other market town, boast a church or cathedral of note, such as in the endearing colonial village of Barva. Cartago's beautiful Basilica de Nuestra Señora de los Angeles is the setting for the nation's most important pilgrimages. Nearby, the ruined church of Ujarrás and the exquisite 17th-century church of Orosi are reason enough to visit the Orosi valley, gateway to rugged hikes in Tapantí-Macizo de la Muerte National Park. In fact, this region boasts dozens of wilderness reserves, including those of the cloud forests of Los Angeles and of Braulio Carrillo National Park. And seeing wildlife is made easy at a score of gardens and zoos, such as Lankester Botanical Gardens, the World of Snakes and Zoo Ave. All this is within a two-hour drive of the capital, while the region's springlike climate adds further appeal.

ALAJUELA

The capital of Alajuela province, this market town, 2km (1.2 miles) from the airport, is a more relaxing base than San José for exploring the Central Valley. Small enough to walk around, the town focuses on the Central Plaza, shaded by huge mango trees. The domed cathedral, damaged by an earthquake in 1990, is one of the 19th-century buildings on the square. A more interesting church is the baroque-style La Agonia, five blocks east of the plaza. National hero Juan Santamaría was born in Alajuela and saved the country in the battle of 1856 (▷ 41). One block north of the plaza, at Avenida 3, Calle 2, is the Museo Histórico Juan Santamaría (Tue–Sun 10–5.30), which describes the war.

254 H6 Frequent, from San José

BAJOS DEL TORO

This remote valley, hidden away on the northern slopes of the Cordillera Central at the base of the Poás volcano, has been overlooked until the past few years due to its relative inaccessibility. The narrow mountain roads that connect the valley to Sarchí and Zarcero are often fog-bound, but emerging below the clouds visitors discover a lush world of trout farms, private rain forest reserves, and simple yet cozy accommodations. A deluxe ecolodge—El Silencio Lodge & Spa—opened in 2008, drawing attention to this tropical Shangri-La that is the main gateway to Parque Nacional Juan Castro Blanco and to the Bosque de Paz Rain/Cloud Forest Biological Reserve (tel 506 2234 6676; www.bosquedepaz.com).

250 H5 Jeep-taxis from Sarchí and Zarcero

CAFÉ BRITT COFFEE PLANTATION TOUR

www.coffeetour.com

As one of the largest coffee processors in the country, Café Britt offers tours of the whole coffee-making process. Professional actors guide you through every stage of the process and the result is informative and enjoyable. Café Britt also combines the tour with other Central Valley activities. For the true caffeine addict there is a Coffee Lover's Tour with visits to the historic coffee mill.

255 J6 506 2277 1600 Adult US$25, child (under 12) US$20; with transportation US$35. Tour: adult US$45, child US$ 40 From pick-up points in San José. Public buses leave from Parque La Merced to Heredia, every 10 min; short taxi ride from Heredia, US$2.50, or 40-min walk Dec 15–Apr 30, 3-hour tours run at 9, 11 and 3; May 1–Dec 14 at 9 and 3 Take the Barva road from Heredia; at first stop sign turn left, right, then left

CARTAGO

▷ 86.

ESCAZÚ

Just outside the city limits to the west of San José, the fashionable suburb of Escazú has little in the way of sights, but bags of charm. Many expatriates living in Costa Rica don't spend a night in the capital, preferring to stay in one of Escazú's characterful hotels. Each of the three smaller towns that make up Escazú—San Rafael, San Miguel and San Antonio farther up the hill—has a church. Up in San Antonio de Escazú, adobe houses around the central plaza create the effect of a village. Facing the square, the modest church of San Antonio de Escazú has a beautiful setting overlooking the valley of San José.

El Día del Boyero (Day of the Oxcart Driver) takes place in March (▷ 104).

255 J6 Buses leave San José from Calle 16, Avenida Central every 10 min From San José, take the main highway west for 10 min, until turnoff signs on the right, then continue driving to the La Cruce intersection

LA GUÁCIMA BUTTERFLY FARM

www.butterflyfarm.co.cr

One of the most popular day trips from San José is a visit to La Guácima Butterfly Farm, the world's second largest exporter of butterflies. Set up in 1984 by Joris Brinckerhoff, a former Peace Corps volunteer, the Butterfly Farm was opened to the public in 1990 and gives a fascinating insight into the life cycle of the butterfly. After a video explains the life cycle, the tour proceeds to the export office to see where the pupae are packed. Then guides lead you to tropical gardens, where they point out some of the 120 native species. The climax of the 90-minute tour is the caterpillar room.

After visiting the laboratories you can wander through the gardens at a more leisurely pace. Visiting in the morning, especially during the green season, is recommended as the insects take shelter when it is raining. Early morning visitors can watch butterflies emerging from chrysalises.

254H6 PO Box 2132-4050, La Guácima, Alajuela 506 2438 0400 Daily 8.45–4.30 Adult US$15, child (5–12) US$7, under 5 free The farm offers direct bus services daily from the main hotels in San José at 7.30, 10 and 2; US$30 including tour Two-hour tours at 8.45, 11, 1 and 3

Above *Visitors on the Café Britt Plantation Tour*

Opposite *The spire of Iglesia de la Agonia in Alajuela*

INFORMATION

255 J6 ☎ 506 2556 0073 Buses leave San José from Calle 5 and avenidas 18–20 every 10 min From Avenida 2 in San José head east and follow the signs. There's a small toll on Highway 2

Above *People relax on the steps of La Parroquia, finally destroyed in 1910*

CARTAGO

Cartago, dominated by Volcán Irazú, is the provincial capital and gateway to the Central Valley's southeast corner. Once the ruling quarter of Costa Rica, Cartago's dominant position was frequently tested and finally faltered in 1823 when San José acquired the capital seat after a series of minor civil scuffles. Since then, nature has challenged the city with many tremors and two devastating earthquakes, first in 1841 and again in 1910, which finally finished off the architectural heritage of the town. Today, the town bustles with the energy of a local market and transportation hub (it is just over 20km/12 miles from San José), and has little to detain the visitor beyond the Basílica de Nuestra Señora de Los Angeles, one of the finest churches in the country, 1km (0.6 miles) to the east of the central park. It holds the diminutive La Negrita, an Indian image of the Virgin Mary less than 15cm (6in) high, which draws pilgrims from all over Central America because she is believed to have great healing powers. After arriving at the Basílica, pilgrims take to their knees, inching their way down the aisle towards La Negrita. It's easy to overlook the finery of the Basílica itself. Destroyed by an earthquake in 1926, it was rebuilt in Byzantine style. The interior is ornately decorated with gold leaf and fine carvings and always has fresh flowers. On the east side, the basement displays religious icons and silver tokens beseeching or giving thanks for a favor. To the east side of the church, pilgrims fill La Negrita-shaped plastic containers and soda bottles with holy water from a spring. La Romera pilgrimage to the Basilica takes place on August 2.

LA PARROQUIA

Cartago's other attraction, La Parroquía, locally known as Las Ruinas, was the city's first parish church, founded in 1575. Frequent tremors meant the church had to be reconstructed several times. Almost completely destroyed in 1841, it was rebuilt only to be destroyed again in 1910. What stands now is what remained then. A small ornamental garden fills the space within, but it is closed for much of the time. In front of the ruins, the central park is a large expanse of pavement, which makes for good people-watching.

HEREDIA

On the lower slopes of Volcán Barva, 11km (7 miles) north of San José, is Heredia, whose history is entwined with that of coffee cultivation in the Central Highlands. Founded in 1706, the town fought for dominance of the country, alongside Cartago, against Alajuela and the eventually victorious San José at the time of independence. Today, though, the quiet town is in danger of losing its position as the fourth city of the republic to more vibrant growth areas such as Liberia or Turrialba. However, Heredians don't seem to be too concerned—traces of colonial heritage and the youthful energy of the Universidad Nacional (National University) give the town a busy grace. This "City of Flowers" has a tranquil charm.

SIGHTSEEING

The sights of Heredia can be seen from one spot through judicious positioning; stand in the northeastern corner of the central plaza and face north. Over your right shoulder is the Basílica de la Inmaculada Concepción, with a short, squat design that has helped the structure survive several earthquakes since completion in 1797. External weathering has taken its toll, but the inside is a complete contrast, starkly crisp and bright white. Looking northwest is El Fortín, a single turret complete with gun slots overlooking a small park. Unfortunately the tower is closed to the public. On the northern side of the plaza is the Casa de la Cultura (tel 506 2261 4485), a beautifully restored colonial house that was once the residence of President Alfredo González Flores (president 1914–17). Today, this fine example of period architecture houses exhibitions and concerts. Keep an eye out for events or just turn up and see what's going on.

BARVA

Barva, 2km (1.5 miles) north of Heredia, is a lovely colonial village with a fine church and many historic red-tile-roofed houses. President González Flores's former home is now the Museo de Cultura Popular (tel 506 2260 1619, Mon–Fri 8–4, Sat, Sun by appointment), furnished with period pieces.

INFORMATION

255 J6 From San José every 10 min from Avenida 2, calles 12–14 (La Merced Church), Avenida 2, calles 10–12

TIPS

›› A taxi to Heredia from San José is about 5,000 colones (US$10); from the airport, expect to pay US$10–US$15.

›› The town offers the best access to Volcán Barva, the main goal of trekkers in Parque Nacional Braulio Carrillo ▷ 90–91.

Above *The Basílica de la Inmaculada Concepción overlooks the adjoining garden*

INBIO PARQUE

www.inbioparque.com

South of Heredia, 15 minutes from San José on the road to Santo Domingo, is INBio Parque, a private educational establishment that explains Costa Rica's biological diversity and its national parks. Excellent tours begin with an audiovisual presentation, before you are taken through four Costa Rican ecosystems. You can experience the Central Highland forest, dry forest, humid forest and wetland. In addition to 51 bird species, there are 538 native plant species, as well as mammals and reptiles. Along the well-marked trails, you can see many species, which may remain elusive during visits to the national parks: white-tailed deer, three-toed sloths, Hoffman's woodpeckers and many others. Interactive exhibits provide insights into poison-dart frogs, tarantulas, ants, orchids and bromeliads. Additions to INBio include a butterfly garden and a lagoon with an underwater viewing gallery, plus a traditional farm.

255 J6 · 506 2507 8107 · Sat, Sun 8–5 · Adult US$23, child (5–12) US$12, under 5 free · North and west of the Shell gas station in Santo Domingo. Pick-up from hotels in San José is possible

JARDÍN BOTÁNICO LANKESTER

Some 5km (3 miles) east of Cartago on the road to Paraíso, Lankester Botanical Garden, an overgrown hobby founded by the British naturalist Charles H. Lankester in the 1950s, has grown to be an internationally renowned collection specializing in epiphytic flora, in particular the orchids of Costa Rica. The 10.7ha (26.5-acre) gardens have around 800 species of national and exotic orchids. These flowers reach their peak blooming from February to May.

The gardens also have ferns and bromeliads, as well as heliconia, palm and bamboo. A cactus garden opened in 2009. More than 100 species of birds visit the gardens. It's a calming place, and respectful noise levels are requested. Short courses cover the care and cultivation of orchids, plant recognition and nature photography. Tour operators in San José offer tours to the gardens, normally as part of a trip to Volcán Irazú (▷ 93), costing from US$55.

255 K6 · 506 2552 3247 · Daily 8.30–4.30 · Adult US$7.50, child US$5.50 · From Cartago take a bus towards Paraíso, ask to get off at the entrance to Jardín Botánico Lankester and from there walk south for 500m (545 yards), turning right at the sign · Taxi from Cartago around US$4

Below *An example of Costa Rica's indigenous orchids at Jardín Botánico Lankester*

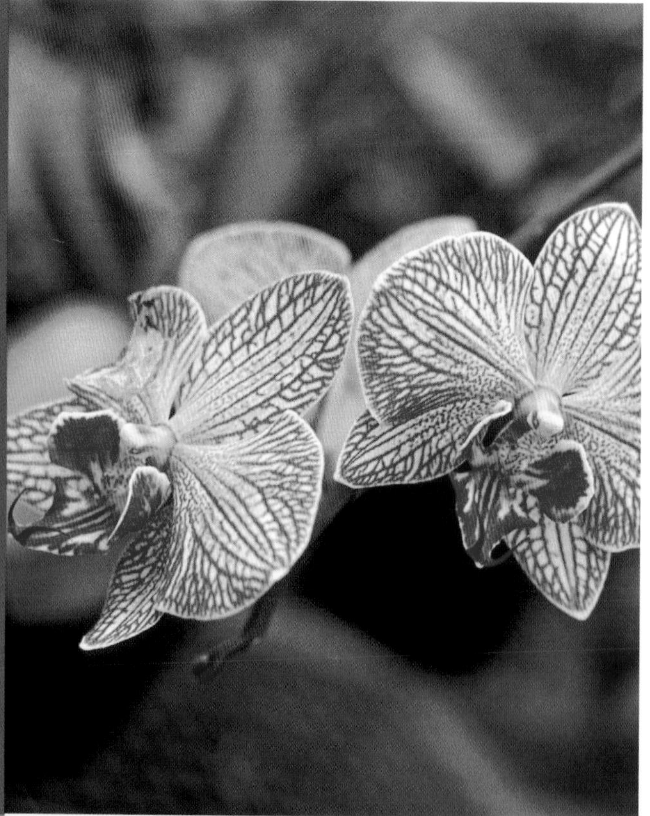

LA PAZ WATERFALL GARDENS

www.waterfallgardens.com

One of the most popular excursion destinations in the Central Highlands, this diverse nature-themed park has enough to keep a family enthralled for an entire day. It reopened in May 2009 after repairs following the January 1, 2009 earthquake that devastated the area immediately surrounding La Paz, which sits on the eastern flank of the Poás volcano.

Flanking a lushly forested valley, it has a steep trail that clings to the canyon-side and lead to a series of spectacular waterfalls. Above, you can explore huge walk-in aviary and butterfly exhibits, a walk-through ranarium (frogs) and serpentarium (snakes), a hummingbird garden, and a recreation of a traditional farmstead. The restaurant here is first-class, and it has deluxe accommodations (▷ 107).

250 H5 · Vara Blanca · 506 2482 2720 · Daily 8–5.30 · Adult US$35, child US$26 · From Heredia, head north via Barva and Birrí, then follow the signs for Vara Blanca · A taxi from San José will cost about US$50. Most tour operators in San José offers excursions

MONUMENTO NACIONAL GUAYABO

Some 18km (11 miles) north from Turrialba lies Costa Rica's top archaeological site, the Indian ceremonial complex of Guayabo National Monument. Excavation at the site only began in 1968, though it was discovered at the end of the 19th century by Anastasio Alfaro. It remains underfunded and rarely visited.

More than 3,000 years old, the site was occupied from 1000BC to 1400, flourishing around AD800, the period when many of the stone structures were constructed. Petroglyphs have been etched on to many of the stones, their meaning undeciphered. Centuries-old aqueducts still carry water to the reservoirs.

Today only a fraction of the protected area has been excavated, although Guayabo does not compare to the great ruins of Guatemala and Mexico.

255 K6 Information office 506 2559 1220 Daily 8–3.30 Adult US$6, child US$4 Buses from Turrialba Taxi from Turrialba about US$20 one-way

OROSI

Tucked within a beautiful vale flanked by steep-sided mountains, the colonial-era village of Orosi boasts Costa Rica's oldest and most exquisite church, Iglesia de San José. Restored in 1735 it has a baroque altar and a small, impressive museum of icons.

The vale is cloaked in coffee fields surrounding Lago Cachí, a man-made lake that provides hydro-electric power at the Cachí dam. On the north side of the lake and overlooking it stands Las Ruinas de Ujarrá, where the ruins of this 17th-century church are the setting for a pilgrimage on Easter Sunday. Stop at Mirador Orosi for spectacular views over the valley.

255 K7 Regular daily buses from Cartago to Orosi. Buses depart Paraíso for Ujarrás Jeep-taxis in Orosi will run you around the valley and to Parque Nacional Tapantí-Macizo de la Muerte

Above *Orosi's beautiful Iglesia de San José is Costa Rica's oldest church*

PARQUE NACIONAL BRAULIO CARRILO

▷ 90.

PARQUE NACIONAL TAPANTÍ-MACIZO DE LA MUERTE

Approached from Orosi and just 30km (18 miles) from Cartago, Tapantí-Macizo de la Muerte National Park is packed with interest. It is one of the country's newest national parks and is also in one of the wettest parts of the country, reportedly receiving as much as 8,000mm (315in) of rain a year. Covering 58,000ha (143,318 acres), Tapantí-Macizo includes the former Tapantí National Park and much of the Río Macho Forest Reserve. The park incorporates a wide range of life zones, from lower montane wet forest to montane rain forest with altitudes rising from 1,220m (4,000ft) to more than 3,000m (9,840ft) at the border with Chirripó.

The diverse altitudes and relative seclusion of the park have created an impressive species list. Tapirs, pacas, racoons and white-faced monkeys are some of more than 45 species of mammal in the area, which include the elusive jaguar and ocelot. The quetzal nests in late spring and can be found near the entrance on the western slopes. In total 260 bird species have been spotted. Frogs love the wet conditions.

Three trails lead off the principal road providing walks ranging from 30 minutes to 2 hours, but don't forget a raincoat. There are several waterfalls that are good for swimming and picnic spots.

Tour operators in San José can arrange guided trips, and horseback riding to the park from Orosi is also an option.

255 K7 506 2551 2970 Daily 8–4 US$10 Buses run as far as Río Paloma, from where it is a 9km (5-mile) walk, or take a jeep-taxi from Orosi Follow signs to Orosi, then take road to park headquarters Small information center with trail maps and slide show

INFORMATION

250 J5 Zurquí entrance station 506 2233 4533 Daily 8–3.30 US$10 Buses heading east from the Gran Terminal de Caribe in San José pass the park entrance (Quebrada González sector) Take Highway 32 San José–Guápiles heading northeast. Toll booth US$0.20. Taxi from San José about US$30

INTRODUCTION

Vast, wild and majestic, Parque Nacional Braulio Carrillo is a world of waterfalls and abundant wildlife. Trail walks and the Rain forest Aerial Tram provide closer encounters. Only 20km (12.5 miles) from San José, the park protects some of the country's most rugged landscapes. Steep-sided gorges, eroded by rivers, lie concealed in forested valleys laced with drifting clouds, which rise to the volcanic peaks of Barva (2,906m/9,534ft) and Cacho Negro (2,150m/7,054ft) where they deposit annual rainfall of around 4,500mm (177in). The result is dramatic waterfalls, most of which are hardly ever seen.

Braulio Carrillo extends from Volcán Barva down to the Caribbean lowlands abutting La Selva. It was created in 1978 to protect the region against damage caused by the construction of a new highway to the Caribbean in 1977. When plans were announced to build a highway to Limón, through prime virgin rain forest, vocal campaigning by conservationists persuaded the government to declare the area a national park. It is divided between the Quebrada González Sector and the Barva Volcano Sector. The main entrance is about 1km (0.6 miles) beyond the Zurquí tunnel, about 20km (12.5 miles) northeast of San José. You can walk the trails on your own, but a guided walk is best as the guides will point out far more than you will see by yourself.

The San José–Guápiles–Limón Highway travels through the park, so you still get an impression of the topography as you travel to the Caribbean. Despite its proximity to San José, groups entering the park do get lost, so go prepared.

WHAT TO SEE

TRAILS

Three trails lead out from the ranger station at Quebrada González. Las Palmas is a 1.6km (1-mile) trail taking about 1.5 hours, and provides excellent birding. El Ceibo is even shorter, taking just an hour and leading to some ceibo trees. The Botarrama Trail, an extension of El Ceibo, leads to the Río Sucio and gets

Above *The clouds that characterize Costa Rica's cloud forests drift across Parque Nacional Braulio Carrillo*

deeper into the rain forest; it stretches for 3km (2 miles) and takes about two hours. The ranger station's list of animals to look for, including monkeys, toucans, peccaries, tarantulas and snakes, makes for an interesting read before and after your trek. Other trails from the Barva ranger station (tel 506 261 269) wind through cloud forest inhabited by quetzals and tapirs.

FLORA AND FAUNA

More than 90 percent of the park is primary forest and contains some 6,000 species of plants. While the higher altitudes struggle to support life, profuse humid rain forest dominates, reaching its greatest diversity at the lower altitudes. More than 500 species of birds have been logged here, including resplendent quetzals in the higher altitudes, toucans, king vultures and the national bird—the sooty robin.

Mammals include three species of monkey, as well as tapirs, pacas, jaguars, pumas and ocelots. To complete the list, reptiles include two of the deadliest snakes in the world, the fer-de-lance and the bushmaster. The best chance of seeing mammals is by hiking one of the short trails that lead through the 450ha (1,112 acres) of the private reserve used for research.

VOLCÁN BARVA

Hiking to the summit of the Barva volcano is one of the best ways to see some of the less explored parts of the national park. The hike to the top passes through the chilly and moist climate of the cloud forest, with moss-covered trees heavily laden with epiphytes and bromeliads.

Birders flock here to catch a glimpse of quetzals, king vultures and three-wattled bellbirds, as well as countless hummingbirds. Monkeys, reptiles and poison-arrow frogs can also be seen. Trails lead to three water-filled craters. From the summit, on a clear day, magnificent views stretch across the Central Valley.

TIPS

- Highway 32 is one of Costa Rica's busiest roads, but driving conditions are dangerous and extreme caution is required.
- The weather can change dramatically. Take maps, a compass, food and water for all trekking in the park.
- Another option for hikers is Monte de la Cruz Reserve (daily 8–4), on the southern slopes of Volcán Barva, with cloud forest that's good for spotting quetzals.
- Access to Barva requires hiking or the use of a rugged four-wheel-drive vehicle. For the serious hiker there is a trail heading north from the top of Barva down to La Selva Biological Station near Puerto Viejo de Sarapiquí. The trip takes about four days, covers 65km (40 miles) and requires planning. Three daily buses travel to Porrosatí from San José de la Montaña and Heredia, from where a poorly marked trail leads to the summit and then out through the park headquarters. The 4km (2.5-mile) trek takes a little over two hours. A more common route leaves from the ranger station, 3km (2 miles) beyond Sacramento.

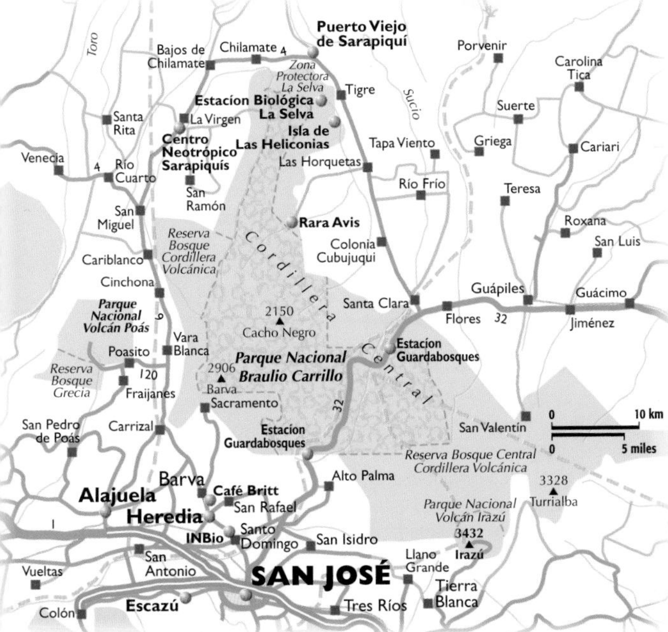

Below *A chestnut-mandibled toucan*

PARQUE NACIONAL VOLCÁN POÁS

Only 37km (23 miles) north of Alajuela, Volcán Poás National Park is the most popular such park in the country. Standing at a lofty 2,708m (8,885ft), the park focuses on the vast crater of Poás Volcano, 1,320m (4,330ft) wide with sloping sides descending for 300m (984ft). Currently filled with a simmering turquoise lake, the crater dries out in more active periods, sprinkling the landscape with sulfur. The most notorious eruption in the 20th century blew an ash cloud skyward some 8km (5 miles). Poás erupted between 1952 and 1954, with more explosions in 1989, 1994 and 2006. Today, vulcanologists believe the magma chamber is just 400–500m (1,300–1,640ft) below the lake. Whenever there is a risk to visitors, the park is closed.

Beyond the drama of the volcano, 79 bird species, including quetzals, reside in the park's dwarf cloud forest, and a trail of just over 1km (0.6 miles) leads to a second crater. Last entry to the trail is at 2.30 and free rambling around the park is not permitted for safety reasons.

Try to arrive early—clouds often hang low over the crater above 1,000m (3,280ft) obstructing the view. But with strong winds throughout the year, gaps in the clouds often offer glimpses. The best time for good views is between December and April. On a clear, windless day, you can wear shorts and T-shirts, but when the clouds arrive, the temperature plummets. Add a dousing of rain and you can get cold, so take a rain jacket.

250 H5 · 506 2482 2165 · May–end Nov daily 8–3.30, Dec–end Apr Fri, Sat 8–4.30 · US$11.80 · A good information center is the final stop for visitors, from where it's a short walk uphill to the lookout · Road access almost to the summit for visitors with disabilities and those unable to walk at this altitude

Below *Sightseers on the Rain Forest Aerial Tram in a section of cloud forest*

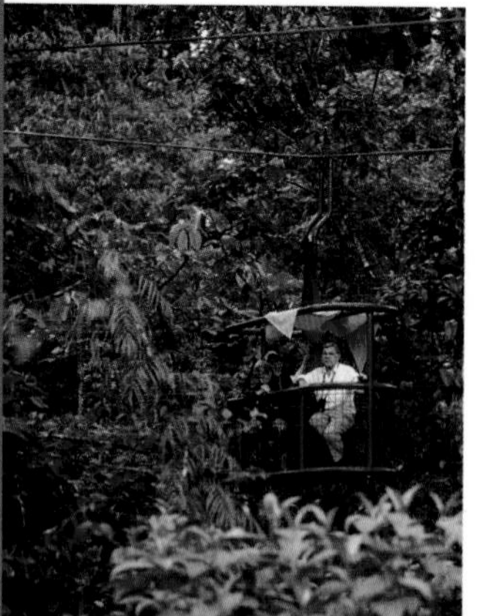

RAIN FOREST AERIAL TRAM

www.rainforesttram.com

Moving silently through the forest at canopy level is the best way of seeing the complexity of the rain forest. Fortunately, the unique attraction of the Rain Forest Aerial Tram, the brainchild of Dr. Donald Perry and John Williams, is that it gives you the chance to do precisely that. Open-air cable cars, with protection from the sun and rain, glide slowly through the forest rising from ground level to the canopy for a close-up view of life above the forest floor. Each car has a bilingual guide who will point out interesting fauna. Their practised eyes will spot birds and animals long before the casual observer does, and you will see the sheer density of plant life and insects found in the upper sections of the rain forest.

At the half-way point, a short walk leads to a vista stretching to the Caribbean lowlands, with views as far as Tortuguero on a clear day. The return journey flies just above the canopy, before coming back to land—an unforgettable experience. In addition to the fascinating ride, the story of the creation of a successful green tourism experience on this scale is equally interesting. The facility includes trails and guided tours, a serpentarium, butterfly and frog garden, and a zipline.

251 K5 · Reservations office on Avenida 7, Calles 5–7 in San José · 506 2257 5961 · Tue–Sun 6.30–4, Mon 9–4 (most tours arrive after 9) · Park entrance and tram ride: adult US$55, child (under 11) US$27.50 · Take any bus heading towards Guápiles from Gran Caribe bus terminal in San José · Package tours from San José, including pick-up from most hotels · Daily 7–6

SAN GERARDO DE DOTA

This small community is tucked into a lovely valley carved by the waters of the Río Savegre, and enjoys a springlike climate year-round. Mists sift through orchards and forests, adding to the surreal beauty, and quetzals are as numerous here as anywhere in Costa Rica. The Quetzal Education Research Center pursues research into the birds' ecology. Hiking trails lead into the cloud forest, which drips with epiphytes and mosses.

255 K8 · Regular daily buses from San José (avenidas 1–3, Calle 16) to San Isidro will drop you at Km80, from where it's a 9km (5.5-mile) downhill hike to San Gerardo. A minibus meets the tour at 7.40am (tel 506 8367 8141) · Follow the Pan-American Highway south from Cartago to Km80, then turn right

SARCHÍ

The small craft village of Sarchí owes its fame to the painted *carretas* (oxcarts) produced locally (▷ 32). Originally distinctive to the area, they are now sold across the country. Sarchí is actually two towns—Sarchí Sur and Sarchí Norte—set among hills offering views across valleys. The heart of the town is to the north, where a tiered plaza leads to a wedding-cake church of lime green which glows at sunset. The oxcarts and other wooden furniture, including rocking chairs, are mass-produced by hand in factories and *mueblarías* (furniture shops). The town has done everything it can to relieve you of your cash: Goods can be flat-packed and shipped home.

254 H5 · Regular daily buses from San José's Coca-Cola Terminal take 1 hour · Taxis in Sarchí make quick journeys between the north and south towns if you want to look around before buying

VOLCÁN IRAZÚ

Easily reached on a day-trip from San José, Irazú is the highest volcano in Costa Rica at 3,432m (11,260ft). A road reaches to the edge of the dramatic lagoon-filled craters, making this one of the busiest parks. Whether buffeted by icy winds, or basking in sunlight, the volcano is worth visiting for the stupendous views. Visit as early in the day as possible for the best chance of a clear view; even if the lower slopes are cloudy, it is possible that the summit is above the clouds.

This "mountain of quakes and thunder" has a lively history. The first documented eruption was recorded by Cartago's governor, Diego de la Haya Fernández, in 1723. There were violent eruptions in 1963, which damaged the crater and showered San José with ash—a dramatic welcome to President John F. Kennedy who was visiting the area at the time. Fumaroles, small lava flows and tremors are proof that the mountain quakes and thunders today.

Once at the top, there are pockets of fragile vegetation on the inhospitable, lunar landscape. The temperature range of -3°C to 17°C (27°F to 63°F) and the poor soil supports a hardy scrub with thick leaves and stunted growth to cope with the winds. Three of the five craters can be visited. The main crater is a cube, 1,050m (3,445ft) wide, 300m (984ft) deep, blown out of the earth. Playa Hermosa crater is a good birding spot, where you may see the ubiquitous volcano junco bird. Otherwise, little survives in this hostile desert.

255 K6 ☎ 506 2200 5025 Daily 8–3.30 US$10 One bus daily at 8am from Avenida 2, calles 1–3, from Gran Hotel Costa Rica Most tour operators in San José have day-trips to Irazú costing US$40 per person Taxi US$40

VOLCÁN TURRIALBA

Volcán Turrialba is the least visited and smallest of the Central Highland volcanoes to merit its own national park, which was established back in 1955. The lack of interest means there is no entrance fee—or at least no one to collect it, officially you get a permit in San José—and no services are provided. At 3,328m (10,916ft), Volcán Turrialba is east of Volcán Irazú on the eastern flank of the Cordillera Central. Three craters show evidence of lava flows, but the last eruptions occurred between 1864 and 1865.

If you want to stay overnight you can camp. Alternatively, a good base is Volcán Turrialba Lodge (tel 505 2273 4335; www.volcanturrialbalodge.com), 2km (1.2 miles) from Finca la Central. Tour options include treks and horseback riding to the crater floor; Turrialba is the only volcano where this is possible.

255 K6 From Cartago to Santa Teresa north of Turrialba, then walk to Volcán Turrialba Lodge in the saddle between Irazú and Turrialba. Also from Turrialba to Santa Cruz and a jeep-taxi to the lodge Day-trips can be organized through tour operators in San José

Above *Its green lake contrasts with the gray crater of Volcán Irazú*

ZARCERO

At the north side of the Central Valley, Zarcero draws crowds to the bizarre Dalíesque topiary that fills the town's square. These creations are the work of Zarcero's most famous son, Evangelista Blanco Breves. Given the job of maintaining the plaza in 1964, he set about the task with a few simple shrubs that have grown, been clipped, grown and clipped again. Breves has created animals, couples dancing, a helicopter and other works.

Zarcero has an exhilarating, mountain climate where dairy cattle fuel the local economy. A local specialty is *palmito*, a white, moist cheese like mozzarella. Fruit jams are another regional product on sale.

250 H5 Regular buses from San José Coca-Cola Terminal

ZOO AVE

www.zooave.org

Owned and operated by the Nature Restoration Foundation, this government-recognized wildlife rescue facility is set in landscaped gardens. Zoo Ave educates visitors about Costa Rican wildlife through interactive exhibits and rehabilitation and release programs. Its breeding efforts are focused on endangered species such as the macaw and the squirrel monkey. Captive breeding programs have successfully introduced dozens of birds as part of the Scarlet Macaw Restoration Program.

While here, you'll see more than 100 species of native and exotic birds including toucans, parrots, black swans, eagles and the quetzal, as well as all four types of monkey that live in Costa Rica, and other mammals and reptiles.

254 H6 ☎ 506 2433 8989 Daily 9–5 Adult US$15, child US$3 Bus from Alajuela to La Garita Follow signs to Zoo Ave from the Pan-American Highway heading west from Juan Santamaría airport Taxi from Alajuela around US$8

OROSI VALLEY

East of Cartago, coffee plantations carpet the Orosi Valley, dotted with peaceful villages where colonial churches, surreal sculptures, pirate legends and the curiosities of Costa Rican daily life provide an engaging circular tour. You will also venture to the border of little-visited Tapantí-Macizo de la Muerte National Park.

THE DRIVE
Distance: 36km (22 miles)
Allow: 1 day
Start/end at: Cartago/Tapantí National Park

★ Cartago, gateway to the southeastern corner of the Central Valley, lies under the looming massif of Volcán Irazú, 20km (12.5 miles) from San José.

Exploring the town (⊳ 86), go first to the Basílica de Nuestra Señora de Los Angeles, one of the finest churches in the country, 1km (0.6 miles) east of the central park. It holds La Negrita, an indigenous image of the Virgin Mary less than 15cm (6in) high, which draws pilgrims from all over the country. Cartago's other attraction, La Parroquía, locally known as Las Ruinas, stands next to the central park. Founded in 1575, it was Cartago's first parish church. Earthquakes toppled successive cathedrals and it was finally abandoned in 1910.

Take Highway 10 southeast of Cartago for 8km (5 miles) to Paraíso, where the road falls away to the hidden secrets of the Orosi Valley, surrounded by steep-sided mountains rising up to cloud level. At Paraíso, the road diverges to go east following the northern shore of the lake to Ujarrás, or south to Orosi. The route described here follows the signs for Ujarrás, about 7km (4 miles).

❶ Ujarrás is famous as the site of Costa Rica's first colonial church, built between 1570 and 1580. Legend has it that in 1666, English pirates were seen off by Ujarrás's citizens, aided by the Virgin. This event is celebrated annually on April 16 or the closest Sunday when the saint is carried in procession from Paraíso to the ruined church.

Continue east from Ujarrás. The valley floor here is flooded by the waters of Lago Cachí, created by the Cachí Dam, which blocks the river before flowing to the white-water rafting spot on the Río Reventazón. Just 2km (1.2 miles) away is Cachí village and its nearby attractions.

❷ The Presa de Cachí (Cachí Dam) is not impressive unless it's releasing water, but it is a natural stopping point before heading along the southern shore to the Casa del Soñador (the Dreamer's House), where Hermes and Miguel Quesada carve figurines using twisted old coffee plant roots and driftwood. A short walk away, on the lake shore, is La Casona del Cafetal, a popular eatery.

Just 3km (2 miles) from Cachí, continuing east around the lake, is the star of the valley, Orosi.

❸ Orosi (▷ 89) is best known for the 18th-century Parroquía de San José, built by Franciscan missionaries. The church has weathered countless tremors and has been restored to near-pristine conditions. Across the cloister, the Museo de Arte Religioso displays religious objects in the former monastery. There are hot springs next to Orosi Lodge, and more in Los Patios, just south of town.

A short way south of Orosi the road splits; the left fork crosses the Río Orosi. The right fork leads towards Tapantí-Macizo de la Muerte National Park, 9km (5.5 miles) from the main road. Go over the Río Macho bridge, take the first right turn and continue along the road for 3km (2 miles) until you reach the private reserve of Monte Sky, requiring a four-wheel-drive vehicle to reach it.

❹ Monte Sky is a mountain retreat bordering the Tapantí National Park. The refuge protects more than 290 species of birds. Monte Sky Space hotel can accommodate up to 20 people. Hiking trails lead through cloud forest to waterfalls.

Tapantí-Macizo de la Muerte National Park is 2km (1.2 miles) east, signposted from Orosi.

❺ Tapantí-Macizo de la Muerte, established in 1994, covers 58,000ha (143,320 acres) of one of the wettest parts of the country. Visitor numbers are still low. The park protects the Río Orosi watershed, which feeds the Cachí Dam hydroelectric power plant. The south boundary of the park joins with the Chirripó National Park (▷ 178–180), extending the protected area that makes up La Amistad International Park (▷ 177).

Right *The lush slopes above Cachí Dam*
Opposite *Church ruins in Ujarras*

PLACES TO VISIT

PARQUE NACIONAL TAPANTÍ-MACIZO DE LA MUERTE

▷ 89.

MUSEO DEL ARTE RELIGIOSA

✉ Orosi Church ☎ 506 2533 3051
🕐 Tue–Fri 1–5, Sun 9–12, 1–5 ✋ US$1

MONTE SKY

☎ 506 2231 3536; www.intnet.co.cr/montesky

WHERE TO EAT

LA CASONA DEL CAFETAL

On the lake's south shore, La Casona del Cafetal draws Sunday crowds to its US$15 buffet.
✉ Lago de Cachí ☎ 506 2533 3280
🕐 Daily 11–6 ✋ L US$32, Wine US$18

WHERE TO STAY

OROSI LODGE

www.orosilodge.com
This lodge, with seven rooms in the Orosi valley has a delightful cafe.
✉ Orosi Valley ☎ 506 2533 3578
✋ US$45–US$58

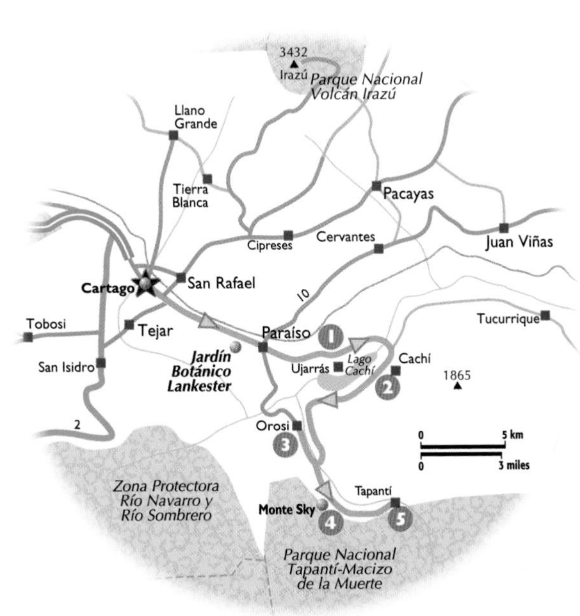

VOLCÁN POÁS AND THE CENTRAL HIGHLANDS

The central part of Costa Rica has a rich, volcanic soil and a benign climate. This drive goes through fertile, farming valleys into hills carpeted with coffee plantations. Crowning it all is the lunar landscape of Volcán Poás.

THE DRIVE
Distance: 73km (45 miles)
Allow: 1–2 days
Start/end at: San José

★ Leaving San José, take the Pan-American Highway west for 5km (3 miles) until the Alajuela exit. A line of villages huddles on the western slopes of Volcán Poás. The area was badly damaged by the January 2009 earthquake, but all the facilities listed here were operating again at the time of printing.

Alajuela (▷ 85), capital of the Alajuela province, once fought to rule the region. Now an energetic market town, the main feature is the central plaza, shaded by mango trees. Five blocks east is the church of La Agonia, restored after the 1910 earthquake. North of the plaza is the Museo Histórico Juan Santamaría, celebrating Alajuela's national hero.

From Alajuela, drive for 1.5 km (1 mile) to the turnoff for Tuetal. Turn left and follow the signs for Xandari Resort & Spa (▷ 107); the steep road to the hotel is badly potholed. It's 5km (3 miles) north of Alajuela.

❶ Enjoying magnificent views from its ridgetop locale, this deluxe spa hotel (▷ 107) set amid its own coffee fields will tempt you to linger overnight, not least for its fabulous contemporary styling. A massage or other treatment at the holistic spa makes a great way to start the day.

Some 2 km (1.25 miles) north of Xandari is the Doka Coffee plantation. When you reach the intersection at Sabanilla, turn left and follow the signs for Doka.

.

❷ On the slopes of the Poás Volcano, the 242ha (600-acre) privately owned Doka Estate (▷ 104) has been in the same family for three generations. Set at 1,372m (4,500ft), it is often lauded as one of Costa Rica's most beautiful coffee plantations. Tours, twice daily, show you the traditional coffee production process from nurturing seedlings, growing bushes and harvesting the beans to the peeling process, fermentation, drying and roasting. The estate's coffee shop, Casa del Café, has great views and, as well as enjoying a cup of their brew, you can buy roasted beans to take home. A butterfly farm was added in 2009, and it even has a bonsai farm open to view.

Leaving the Doka Coffee Estate, continue north along Route 130, passing through coffee country, following the signs for the Poás volcano. Gently undulating hills rise slowly towards the volcanic slopes of Poás. As you climb from Alajuela,

From left to right *Volcán Poás; a Poás ranch; fresh red coffee beans*

the warmth gives way to freshness and then a slight chill.

Passing through Fraijanes, which was badly damaged by the 'quake, you'll reach Poasito. Beyond, the road begins to snake up through cloud forest to the entrance of Parque Nacional Volcán Poás. From Fraijanes, follow route 30 for 8km (5 miles) to a three-way junction (a right turn heads to Poasito); continue north following signs for Volcán Poás, 37km (23 miles) from Alajuela. Try to be there before 10am when clouds engulf the volcano.

❸ Volcán Poás (▷ 92) is the highlight of the 5,601ha (13,835-acre) Volcán Poás National Park. The world's largest geyser-type crater, it has a rim measuring 1.5km (1 mile) in circumference. The park is mostly stunted cloud forest, packed with bromeliads, moss and vines, and is home to a large number of bird species. The restless volcano puffs and belches, giving off pungent fumes, so visitors spend no more than 30 minutes at the crater. The Sendero Boto trail leads off from the crater to a small lagoon, Laguna Boto, in the crater formed by the Poás volcano 8,000 years ago. This is one of the few national parks in Costa Rica that is suitable for visitors with disabilities, with wheelchair access to viewing platforms.

Return south to the junction at Poasito, and turn left. Look for the restaurant Chubascos on the corner, a good place for a fresh fruit *licuado* made with organic strawberries, and follow signs for Vara Blanca, (6km/3.5 miles). Some 200m (220 yards) before the Vara Blanca junction, signs on the left indicate Poás Volcano Lodge (▷ 104, 107), down a 1km (0.6-mile) dirt track.

❹ Poás Volcano Lodge makes an ideal base to explore Poás Valley. In addition to following the lodge's trails, you can take horseback riding tours of the La Legua valley, which begin on Volcán Barva's slopes and continue along the edges of Braulio Carrillo National Park (▷ 90–91). The park contains 600 species of trees, 500 bird species and many native mammals. The most readily

identified plant is the giant-leaved *Gunnera*, also known as "poor man's umbrella."

When you leave the lodge, turn left and continue for 200m (220 yards) to the Vara Blanca gas station, turn left again and continue for 5km (3 miles). The nature park and wildlife refuge of La Paz Waterfall Gardens are on the left.

❺ La Paz Waterfall Gardens (⊳ 88) are a nature park and wildlife refuge with 3.5km (2 miles) of self-guiding trails. They wind through forests to five waterfalls, with viewing platforms, upstream along the Río Paz. One of the major attractions is the butterfly garden, with more than 4,000 species and the world's largest butterfly observatory, plus a superb snake exhibit and walk-through ranarium where you can get up close and personal with dozens of frog species.

From La Paz Waterfall Gardens, return to the Vara Blanca gas station and take Route 120 south, signposted Heredia, via Carrizal, for 21km (13 miles) to the underrated town of Barva, 3km (2 miles) north of Heredia. Lines of coffee bushes run up and down the contours of the slopes.

❻ Barva is usually bypassed en route to Poás. Peaceful and historic, the main attraction is the inspiring, whitewashed church of San Bartolomé, built in the mid-16th century and flanked by single-floor adobe houses. The town's Museo de la Cultura Popular has exhibits of adobe construction techniques, which reveal the settlement's colonial heritage.

From Barva it is 3km (2 miles) south on Route 120 to Heredia (⊳ 87), and then 11km (7 miles) south on Highway 3 to San José.

PLACES TO VISIT

LA PAZ WATERFALL GARDENS

⊳ 88.

DOKA COFFEE PLANTATION TOUR

www.dokaestate.com

☎ 506 2449 5152 🕐 Tours Mon–Sat 9.30, 1.30, Sun by reservation 💰 US$18

MUSEO DE CULTURA

✉ Barva ☎ 506 2260 1619 🕐 Mon–Fri, Sun 8–4 💰 US$1.50

XANDARI RESORT & SPA

www.xandari.com

✉ Alajuela ☎ 506 2443 2020

🕐 Daily 8–5

WHERE TO EAT

RESTAURANTE COLBERT

✉ Vara Blanca ☎ 506 2482 2776

🕐 Daily 7am–9pm

WHERE TO STAY

POÁS VOLCANO LODGE

www.poasvolcanolodge.com

✉ PO Box 1935-3000, Heredia

☎ 506 2482 2194 💰 From US$60, including breakfast

Below *Doka Coffee Plantation*

Opposite *La Paz waterfall*

THE ROUTE OF THE SAINTS

An easy drive from San José enables you to explore the cluster of coffee-producing villages that huddle on the lowlands slopes of the Talamanca Mountains. History failed to record the reasons, but the spirituality of the region lives on with each town named after a saint, and each with a church of differing design.

THE DRIVE
Distance: 41km (25.5 miles) from the Pan-American Highway turnoff
Allow: A day
Start/end at: San José or Cartago taking the Pan-American Highway (Highway 2) south through the Talamanca Mountains

★ From the Pan-American Highway, turn west at Km51, south of Empalme, signposted to Santa María. It's a good road, twisting and turning sharply downhill through pastureland and passing clapboard houses. Eventually it opens up to reveal Santa María de Dota in the Río Pirrís valley (14km/8.5 miles).

❶ In Santa María de Dota stop outside the church. This simple town of just a few thousand residents, it revolves around the main square. Here the focal point is the boxy lime-green church basking on the plaza. The Monumento Liberación Nacional studs the plaza, and the local coffee mill can be toured.

From the plaza in Santa María de Dota, head away from the church and take the road west, signposted San Marcos (it would have been the first right on entering the square). An easy drive winds down the steep slopes of the Río Pirrís. After 6km (3.5 miles) turn left to San Marcos de Tarrazú.

❷ San Marcos de Tarrazú has a more traditional church and even on dull days the cream-painted building looks sunlit. Perched on the hilly slopes, the village appears as if it might be auditioning for a John Ford western. A combination of altitude, soil, sunlight and rain conspires to make conditions ideal for growing superlative coffee. Unpaved roads connect coffee estates with the towns of Santa María, San Pablo and San Marcos. One of the most renowned estates,

Umaña, lies 1km (0.6 mile) from San Marcos, and has been run by the Umaña Jimenez family since the 1890s. While there's little do in San Marcos itself, it is a charming place to stop for refreshment.

Leaving San Marcos's square, continue past the church, going left at the T-junction, and follow the road that bends round behind the church. Cross over a couple of roads, climbing a small section of hill, then turn left, signposted San Pablo de León Cortes, taking the right turn at the next T-junction. It's 4km (2.5 miles) to San Pablo, past coffee fields.

❸ San Pablo's church is different again, polygonal in shape and with some handsome woodwork.

From San Pablo, follow the road to the left; at the T-junction turn right signposted Cartago. The road climbs out of the valley, clinging to the slopes, moving through pine trees. A dip through a small valley, followed by a brief climb and a left turn (about 8km/5 miles) heads to San Antonio.

From left to right *The church in Santa María de Dota; San Marcos de Tarrazu church interior; the Route of the Saints*

❹ San Antonio is another coffee town clamped to the hillside. In town, the largest flat expanse of land is the soccer field.

Return to the main road, which continues to climb through coffee fields giving more great views. After some 9km (5.5 miles), turn right and rejoin the Pan-American Highway (Highway 2) at Km44 to return to Cartago and San José.

WHERE TO EAT

LA CASONA DE SARA

This homey, family-run restaurant is one block north and east of the plaza.

✉ Santa María de Dota ☎ 506 2541 2258 🕐 Daily 7–7

RESTAURANTE BAR VACA FLACA

A rustic log hut amid pines, with cowboy decor and country fare.

✉ Between San Pablo and San Antonio ☎ 506 2274 1868 🕐 Daily 11am–midnight

ALAJUELA

FLOR DE MAYO

www.hatchedtoflyfree.org

For nature lovers, a visit to this macaw breeding facility in the private estate of Richard and the late Margot Frisius is a joyous experience. Visitors can witness hatchlings being raised in incubators and juvenile birds testing their wings in large flyways in preparation for their release.

✉ Río Segundo de Alajuela ☎ 506 2441 2658 🕐 By appointment only 🖐 US$20 donation

LIGA DEPORTIVA ALAJUELENSE

www.lda.org

Alajuela's soccer team, Liga Deportiva Alajuelense, is one of Costa Rica's best. Games are usually held at 11am on Sunday, but check locally, or watch for fans heading to the stadium in Alajuela's northeast. Tickets can be bought at the stadium on match days.

✉ Calle 9, four blocks north and six blocks east of Plaza Central, Alajuela ☎ 506 2443 1617 🖐 US$7–US$15

Above *A great green macaw*

PURAVIDA SPA

www.puravidaspa.com

Surrounded by coffee plantations, the American-owned Good Life Center for Yoga Meditation and Renewal offers five- and seven-day packages that include yoga, meditation, aerobics, spa treatments, hikes and volcano and rafting trips. Accommodations range from tents to luxury villas.

✉ Apto 1112, Alajuela ☎ 506 8392 8079 or 770 783 0238 🖐 US$1,215–US$1,785

SPA VILLAGE AT XANDARI

www.xandari.com

On a coffee *finca* (ranch) north of Alajuela, this luxurious spa provides pampering with a view. Treatments in open-air, palm-roofed pavilions include massage, homeopathic remedies, reflexology, mud wraps and facials.

✉ 5km (3miles) north of Alajuela ☎ 506 2443 2020 🖐 Massages from US$75

ATENAS

MOTORCYCLES COSTA RICA

www.motoscostarica.com

Some 25km (15 miles) from Alajuela, Atenas, the small town famous for its delightful climate, is the base for this friendly operation that organizes motorcycle tours of the Central Highlands, Arenal and the beaches of Guanacaste. For greater freedom, Suzuki sport bikes are available to rent.

✉ Atenas ☎ 506 2446 5015

🖐 From US$2,195 including guides, accommodations, meals, drinks and bike rental. Suzuki motorbike US$50–US$85 per day (3-day minimum) or by the week for less

ESCAZÚ

BARRY BIESANZ

www.biesanz.com

Barry Biesanz is one of the country's top craftspeople (▷ 33). His distinctive carvings use a mix of dark and light woods. The boxes—humidors, jewelry boxes or what Barry calls for "small things"—are exquisite.

✉ Apto 47-1250, Escazú ☎ 506 2289 4337 🕐 Mon–Fri 8–5, Sat 10–4, Sun by appointment only

MULTIPLAZA

www.multiplazamall.com

This, the largest shopping mall in Costa Rica, a 15-minute bus ride from the capital, is where you will find familiar American brands. Librería Internacional has a good selection of English-language fiction and Costa Rican wildlife and cultural guides, and E-Music stocks international music.

✉ North of Escazú on Highway 27 ☎ 506 2201 6025 🕐 Daily 10–9, Sun 10–8

LA GARITA

BOTANICAL ORCHID GARDEN

www.orchidgardencr.com

Opened in 2007, this botanical garden is the product of 30 years labor. About 150 orchid species are raised in greenhouses or grow outdoors, half of them native to Costa Rica. Also here are bamboo groves, heliconias and palms. If you have time, linger for lunch in the gorgeous cafe.

✉ 2km (1.2 miles) west of Pan-American Highway ☎ 506 2487 8095 🕐 Tue–Sun 8.30–4.30 💰 Adult US$12, child US$6

GRECIA

TROPICAL BUNGEE

www.tropicalbungee.com

For adrenaline junkies, exhilarating jumps from a bridge down to the Río Colorado 80m (262ft) below are available on day-trips from San José. With more than 20,000 jumps to their name, this company has a 100 percent safety record. They also offer rappeling, and rock climbing near Cachi.

✉ Grecia ☎ 506 2248 2212 💰 One jump: US$65

WORLD OF SNAKES

www.theworldofsnakes.com

This open-air serpentarium exhibits more than 150 snakes, representing half of the country's serpent species. World of Snakes also has a research and conservation program. Multilingual tours with knowledgeable guides last 45 minutes. The website was under construction at the time of printing.

✉ 1.5km (1 mile) from Grecia, heading towards Alajuela ☎ 506 2494 3700 🕐 Mon–Thu 8–4 💰 Adult US$11, child US$6

LA GUÁCIMA

RANCHO SAN MIGUEL

This stud farm raises Andalusian horses and offers riding lessons. The highlight, however, is the once-weekly dressage show in the tradition of the world-famous Lipizzaner stallions. It's a magnificent spectacle as the horses perform pirouettes, leaps and other maneuvers to Spanish classical music.

✉ 3km (2 miles) north of La Guácima ☎ 506 2439 0909 🕐 Nov–end Jul Sat 8pm 💰 US$26

HEREDIA

BULEVAR BAR

The university ensures buoyant nightlife in quiet Heredia. A block from the university, Bulevar is one of the happening places, with a good mix of students, tourists and young professionals. Food is available and there is live music on Tuesday and Saturday.

✉ Avenida Central, calles 5–7, Heredia ☎ 506 2237 1832 🕐 Daily L1am–1am 💰 Beers US$1.50, cocktails US$3

CENTRAL MARKET

This vibrant market is a compact version of the Mercado Central in San José. Earthy sights, smells and tastes make for an absorbing foray into provincial Heredia. Stalls are crammed with fruit and vegetables, herbal remedies, flowers and inexpensive crafts.

✉ Avenida 6, calles 2–4, Heredia 🕐 Mon–Sat 6–6

LA CHOZA

La Choza is another unpretentious, lively bar that packs a university crowd in every night. The split-level bar has an upstairs balcony and TV screens competing with a mix of Latin pop, rock and salsa. There is karaoke every Thursday at 9pm and marauding mariachis occasionally on Wednesday.

✉ Avenida Central, calles 7–9, 100m (110 yards) west of the main university entrance, Heredia ☎ 506 2237 1553 🕐 Mon–Fri 4–1, Sat, Sun 3–1, Sun football match day 11am–1am

INTERCULTURA COSTA RICA

www.interculturacostarica.com

This school offers language tuition at all levels from beginner upward, with homestays and a range of cultural activities.

✉ Apdo 1952-3000, Heredia ☎ 506 2260 8480 💰 From US$270 a week without home-stay, US$394 with accommodations

OROSI

BALNEARIO DE AGUAS TERMALES

There are two outdoor swimming pools here, a restaurant and basketball court, with plenty of space for sunbathing. Thick, unruly vegetation makes it good for early morning bird- and butterfly-watching.

✉ 300m (330 yards) south and 150m (185 yards) west of Orosi church, next to the Orosi Lodge ☎ 506 2533 2156 🕐 Wed–Mon 7.30–4 💰 US$2

SANTA BARBARA DE HEREDIA

FINCA ROSA BLANCA COFFEE PLANTATION & INN

www.fincarosablanca.com

This small, family-run coffee estate surrounds the world-famous Finca Rosa Blanca boutique hotel (▷ 107). Their coffee is only available for purchase here, but the informative and impassioned tour, escorted by professional barista Leo Vergani, is the best in the country. Linger to ride one of the estate's horses, and stay for lunch or dinner in the superb restaurant. It's one of the few places where you can actually help pick the beans from October to January.

✉ 1km (0.6 miles) east of Santa Barbara de Heredia ☎ 506 2269 9392 🕐 Daily 💰 US$25

SARCHÍ

FÁBRICA DE CHAVERRI

The heart of Sarchí is to the north, but there are workshops in both parts of town. Arriving from the south you come first to Fábrica de Chaverri. The family-run operation was established in 1903 and has seen four generations of Chaverris produce hand-painted oxcarts. A

full-size cart costs US$500 or more, but smaller options are available for less. Worldwide, flat-pack shipping can be arranged.
✉ PO Box 19-4150, Sarchí ☎ 506 2454 4411 ⌚ Daily 8–6

TURRIALBA

RAINFOREST WORLD

www.rforestw.com

One of a couple of small local operators that offers cross-cultural tours with bilingual guides, aimed at low-impact tourism. They combine two-days rafting on the Pacuare River with camping in the Huacas Canyon. There are trips to their private jungle reserve and scenic "float trips" for those who don't enjoy the rapids experience. Not all experience are water-based, so visit their website to see all that's on offer.
✉ Turrialba ☎ 506 2556 0014 💳 1-day trips US$95 per person; custom tours also available

RIO LOCOS TROPICAL TOURS

www.whiteh2o.com

Not the biggest white-water rafting operation in Costa Rica but, they claim, the friendliest. It's Tico-run and has a lot of experience. The company offers runs on the Pacuare, Pejabaye and Reventazón rivers. It has four kinds of kayaks, including inflatables; you can choose to paddle solo or twin
✉ Apdo 285-7150, Turrialba ☎ 506 2556 6035 💳 US$55–US$125 per day

Below *Rafting on the Pacuare River*

SERENDIPITY ADVENTURES

www.serendipityadventures.com

Serendipity provides hot-air balloon tours in the Turrialba area, or to the north around Naranjo or Arenal Volcano, in addition to adventure and nature tours, including a seven-day trip that combines canyoning, rafting, horseback riding and motorcycling. A four-day Cabécar Indian trail tour ventures into the Talamanca foothills.
✉ Turrialba ☎ 506 2558 1000; in USA 877 507 1358 💳 8-day tour from US$2,585; balloon trips from US$345 per person

TICOS RIVER ADVENTURES

www.ticoriver.com

This company specializes in one-day rafting trips along the 31km (19-mile) Pacuare rapids, which combine exhilarating stretches of Class IV rapids with scenic interludes. Three- and four- day trips to Chirripó are offered by the company mid-June to December.
✉ Turrialba ☎ 506 2556 1231
⌚ Leave at 9am and return at 4pm

VARA BLANCA

POÁS VOLCANO LODGE

www.poasvolcanolodge.com

Professional and welcoming, accomplished English horsewoman Emily Cannon runs half-day guided horseback tours. The tour begins on the northern slope of the Barva volcano, passing though scenic backcountry and highland trails fringed with forests on the edge of Braulio Carrillo National Park (▷ 90–91). The forests teem with birdlife and you may spot signs of tapirs, ocelots or jaguars. The horses are well cared for and Emily is knowledgeable about the Poás area and Costa Rica as a whole.
✉ El Cortijo Farm, Vara Blanca ☎ 506 2482 2194 ⌚ Daily 8.30–1.30 💳 US$60, minimum two people

VOLCÁN POÁS

DOKA ESTATE

www.dokaestate.com

The lower slopes of the Poás volcano are cloaked in coffee bushes. At Doka Estate, visitors can learn about production and processing of Costa Rica's main crop at the country's oldest *finca* and mill. Folkloric shows add a dramatic dimension and an open-air restaurant with spectacular views serves traditional fare.
✉ Sabanilla de Alajuela ☎ 506 2449 5152 ⌚ Mon–Sat 9.30–1.30 💳 US$18

FESTIVALS AND EVENTS

MARCH

EL DÍA DEL BOYERO

One of the outstanding features of Escazú is El Día del Boyero (Day of the Oxcart Driver), on the second Sunday of March, which is one of the country's largest festivals. It fills the sleepy streets with oxcart parades accompanied by traditional music and dancers.
✉ Escazú

APRIL

JUAN SANTAMARÍA DAY

Alajuela celebrates the life of the town's most famous son, the young drummer boy Juan Santamaría, who became a national hero when, during the Battle of Rivas in 1856, he torched the headquarters of the reviled American soldier William Walker. To commemorate the event, there is a week of general celebration, bands, concerts and dancing.
⌚ April 11

PRICES AND SYMBOLS

The restaurants are listed alphabetically (excluding El, Le, La and Les). The prices given are the average for a two-course lunch (L) and a three-course dinner (D) for one person, without drinks. The wine price is for the least expensive bottle.

For a key to the symbols, ▷ 2.

ALAJUELA

EL AMBROSIA

Quality restaurants are rare in Alajuela, but this cafe has patio seating and an upbeat ambience. There is a range of coffees and sandwiches, pastries and cookies. At lunch, it is usually busy, drawing the local business crowd for a good-value *plato del día*. Credit cards are not accepted.

✉ Calle 2, Avenida 5, Alajuela ☎ 506 2440 3440 ⏲ Mon–Sat 10–6.30 L US$8, no wine served

ESCAZÚ

CERUTTI

Rated by some as one of the best Italian restaurants in Costa Rica, Cerutti is popular with visiting glitterati, politicos and expatriates. Italian cuisine, including fresh pasta dishes, seafood and fish and meat dishes, is served with panache in a serene 100-year-old house. Understated elegance predominates with crisp white tablecloths and glimmering silverware. Reservations are advised.

✉ San Rafael de Escazú ☎ 506 2228 4511 ⏲ Wed–Mon 12–3.30, 6.30–11 L US$15, D US$24, Wine US$20

LA LUZ

Considered by many to be one of the best restaurants in Costa Rica, this elegant hotel restaurant serves fusion food with Caribbean and Asian tastes. Ironwork chandeliers and heavy wood beams set the tone and the valley view is superb. Appetizers include macadamia-encrusted chicken strips and entrées feature a monumental seafood platter with jumbo shrimps covered with bacon, mussels and squid. For meat-eaters, grilled tenderloin with strawberry sauce is a must. For dessert, the crème brûlée is superb.

✉ Hotel Alta, Alto de las Palomas, Escazú ☎ 506 2282 4160 ⏲ Mon–Sat 6–3, 6–10, Sun 9–4 L US$26, D US$34, Wine US$20 🚗 On the road to Santa Ana

LE MONASTÈRE

www.monastere-restaurant.com

In the hills, this restored monastery is one of the most romantic dining rooms in the Central Valley. French-Belgian cuisine includes salmon with rose petals and caviar, duck foie gras, mahi mahi with Cajun shrimp and wild boar stew with truffles. Dining under the gaze of marble statues and staff dressed in full monks' habits, this is a memorable experience, although the food itself is sometimes a let-down.

✉ Old road to Santa Ana, Escazú ☎ 506 2289 4404 ⏲ Mon–Sat 6.30pm–11 D US$30, Wine US$20 🚗 On the Santa Ana road from Escazú, turn left at the Multicentro Paco and follow the green crosses.

RESTAURANTE CITY LIGHTS TIQUICIA

In the hills south of Escazú, Tiquicia serves traditional food. It's quite an adventure to get here, and the views are unbeatable. With its rustic setting, Tiquicia is an institution and would be more so if the hours weren't so erratic (call ahead and check). Get a taxi or a 4WD vehicle if you are going after rain. Traditional dancers sometimes perform.

✉ Escazú ☎ 506 2289 5839 ⏲ Tue–Fri 5pm–12, Sat 12–12, Sun 12–6 L US$18, D US$25, Wine US$17

Above *Cooking pots in a local restaurant*

LA GARITA

FIESTA DEL MAÍZ SODA/ RESTAURANT

If you're exploring by car, this place merits a visit. The restaurant also produces tasty corn dishes. The decor is unprepossessing, but it is popular as a pit stop for weekenders on their way to and from the Pacific. Credit cards are not accepted.
☒ Jacó road, La Garita ☎ 506 2487 5757 ◷ Tue–Thu 10–8, Fri–Sun 7am–9pm ✋ L US$5, D US$10, Wine US$9 🚘 On the left-hand side of the road, just after leaving La Garita on the way to Jacó

HEREDIA

FRESAS

This open-plan diner beside a noisy traffic nexus serves everything you could want for a quick lunch, including snacks, sandwiches, full meals, fresh fruit juices and, not surprisingly, plenty of strawberries *(fresas)*. They will also deliver. Credit cards are not accepted.
☒ Calle 7, Avenida 1, Heredia ☎ 506 2262 5555 ◷ Daily 8am–midnight ✋ L US$7.50, D US$10, no wine served

LE PETIT PARIS

Three blocks from the Parque Central, this is a little piece of France. Amid Doisneau photographs and 1930s posters of Paris, the ambience changes between the bar, restaurant and leafy patio. The menu is mainly French, but pizza and pasta dishes are also served. It hosts live music on weekends.
☒ Avenida Central–2, Calle 5 ☎ 506 2262 2564 ◷ Mon–Sat 12–10pm ✋ L US$10, D US$15, Wine US$15

VISHNU

Vegetarian dishes at great prices are served in this spotless diner one block from the University. Office workers and students pack in for the value *plato del día* (US$3), which includes a main course dish, salad, soup, fruit juice and dessert. The quasi-legendary vegetarian burger (US$2) is guaranteed to satisfy even the most ardent carnivores. It's difficult to walk past the glass cabinets displaying gooey brownies, *empanadas de piña*, coconut cake and wholemeal and tomato breads.
☒ Avenida Central–1, Calle 7, Heredia ☎ 506 2237 2526 ◷ Mon–Thu 8–1pm, Fri–Sat 8–7, Sun 9–6 ✋ L US$4, no wine

MONTE DE LA CRUZ

BAALBEK BAR AND GRILL

www.baalbekbaryrestaurante.com
This Lebanese restaurant on the slopes of the Barva volcano draws the cognoscenti for the views as well as for the excellent food, such as *mehshe* (chicken and rice in cabbage), and grilled eggplant (aubergine). The menu, complemented by a large wine list, also has international staples such as T-bone steaks and grilled salmon. Choose from the elegant downstairs restaurant or the more intimate booths upstairs.
☒ Los Angeles de San Rafael, 500m (550 yards) below El Castillo Country Club ☎ 506 2267 6083 ◷ Tue–Sun 12–12 ✋ L US$15, D US$25, Wine US$20

OROSI VALLEY

BAR-RESTAURANT COTO

In the middle of Orosi, this rancho-style bar-restaurant and *parillada* (grill) is welcoming and serves simple, tasty Tico dishes. Meat is the specialty; there is a good-value *casados*, fried fish, heart of palm salads and homemade *flan de coco* for dessert. In the evening there is often live music.
☒ Orosi ☎ 506 2533 3032 ◷ Daily 8am–midnight (or until the last person leaves) ✋ L US$8, D US$12, Wine US$16

OROSI LODGE CAFÉ

www.orosilodge.com
The excellent German-run Orosi Lodge has a relaxed and welcoming European-style cafe with mesmerizing views. It is a lovely spot to eat breakfast—birdwatch while you enjoy homemade granola, fruits, croissants and bagels, and scrambled eggs with cheese and bacon served in the frying pan with fresh baked bread. In the late afternoon, banana cakes, apple strudels and carrot cakes to die for pop out of the oven, then the candles are lit, the jukebox plays and lights glitter in the valley.
☒ Orosi ☎ 506 2533 3578 ◷ Daily 7–7 (hotel guests only on Sun) ✋ Breakfast US$5, coffee and cake US$4

SANTA BARBARA DE HEREDIA

EL TIGRE VESTIDO

www.fincarosablanca.com
Well worth a detour, this open-air restaurant has views over coffee fields. It serves gourmet, regionally inspired lunches and dinners that make great use of organic produce grown on-site. Chef Pedro Alas is Michelin-starred.
☒ Finca Rosa Blanca Coffee Plantation & Inn ☎ 506 2269 9392 ◷ Daily 6am–10pm, reservations required ✋ B US$10, L US$10, D US$30, Wine US$20

LA LUNA DE VALENCIA

www.lallunadevalencia.com
For a one-of-a-kind experience, this rustic restaurant run by flamboyant Spanish owner, Vicente Aguilar, simply can't be beat. Vicente whisks up huge paellas in the open kitchen, but gazpacho, ceviche and delicious octopus with wine are also featured. The highlight comes when Vicente tears out of the kitchen to sing an aria, drink wine from a wine-sack or join the flamenco troupe each Thursday night.
☒ San Pedro de Barva ☎ 506 2269 6665 ◷ Thu 7–10pm, Fri–Sat noon–10pm, Sun noon–5 ✋ L US$12, D US$25, Wine US$10

VOLCÁN POÁS

JAULARES

www.jaulares.com
This good lunchtime stop en route to the Poás volcano is steeped in a traditional farmstead ambience. It is known for its *comida típica* (▷ 239) dishes prepared on a wood-burning stove. The black bean soup and jalapeño steak draw the locals, along with excellent daily *casados* (set lunches). Friday nights are best, when local musicians perform.
☒ 1km (0.6 miles) south of Fraijanes, on the San Pedro–Poás road ☎ 506 2482 2600 ◷ Mon–Sat 10–10, Sun 8–6 ✋ L US$5, D US$12, Wine US$14

PRICES AND SYMBOLS
The prices are the lowest and highest for a double room for one night including breakfast, unless otherwise stated. All the hotels listed accept credit cards unless otherwise stated. Note that rates can vary widely throughout the year.

For a key to the symbols, ▷ 2.

ALAJUELA

XANDARI RESORT & SPA

www.xandari.com
With superb views, this former coffee ranch created by US architect Sherrill Broudy, is an impressive hotel (pictured above). The dramatic and stunning design is graced by stained-glass windows, waveform hardwood ceilings, and artworks by Sherrill's wife, Charlene. Each villa has a balcony and bathroom. The restaurant uses local organic produce. Explore trails leading to natural waterfalls, dip in the pool or enjoy a spa treatment.
✉ 5km (3 miles) north of Alajuela ☎ 506 2443 2020; US toll free 866/363 3212 ✋ US$209–US$356 ⓘ 22 villas 🏊 Outdoor

HEREDIA

BOUGAINVILLEA

www.bougainvillea.co.cr
This efficient place 20 minutes' drive outside San José, has consistently ranked in the top tier of highland hotels. Rooms have cable TV, air-conditioning, bathroom and a balcony with Central Valley views. There are gardens and tennis courts and a free shuttle to San José.
✉ Santo Tomás de Santo Domingo, 9km (6 miles) east of Heredia ☎ 506 2244 1414; US toll free 866/880-5441 ✋ US$136–US$160 ⓘ 81, plus 2 for disabled visitors ❄ 🏊 Outdoor

FINCA ROSA BLANCA PLANTATION & INN

www.fincarosablanca.com
This exciting hotel on a bluff over the Central Valley, is capped by the Rosa Blanca suite: a turret with a four-poster bed and floor-to-ceiling windows. Surrounded by coffee fields, the hotel is an architectural delight. Rooms are individually themed; most have murals and mosaic-lined tubs. The garden supplies organic produce for the gourmet restaurant, and the hotel has a spa and stable.
✉ 1.5km (1 mile) from Santa Bárbara, Heredia ☎ 506 2269 9392 ✋ US$328–US$509 ⓘ 15 suites 🏊 Outdoor

LOS ANGELES

VILLABLANCA CLOUD FOREST HOTEL & SPA

www.villablanca-costarica.com
At the edge of its own cloud forest reserve, this former farmhouse is now a stunning state-of-the-art hotel. The cozy cabins have hearths, and bathrooms feature colonial tiles. The restaurant is first-class, and the lounge invites lazing by the fire. Guided birding and hikes, plus horseback rides, are offered.
✉ Los Angeles Cloud Forest Reserve, 12km (7.5 miles) north of San Ramón ☎ 506 2461 0300 ✋ US$155–US$192 ⓘ 35

VARA BLANCA

PEACE LODGE

www.waterfallgardens.com
Overlooking a lush valley, this deluxe hotel is a one-of-a-kind, with its fanciful design. Mammoth-size rooms combine natural stone and timbers, notably in the whimsical bathrooms. Suites have Jacuzzis, and all rooms have fireplaces.
✉ Vara Blanca ☎ 506 2482 2700 ✋ US$295–US$475 ⓘ 25

VOLCÁN POÁS

POÁS VOLCANO LODGE

www.poasvolcanolodge.com
High up in the valley, this lodge has good views of the volcano. Rooms are spacious and there is internet access and outdoor activities.
✉ PO Box 1935–3000, Heredia ☎ 506 2482 2194 ✋ US$85–US$100 ⓘ 9
🚗 From Poasito take right turn toward Vara Blanca. After 6km (3.75 miles), a turnoff to the left is signposted. Sign on gate at El Cortijo farm where the road leads for 1km (0.6 miles) to the house

NORTHERN REGION

Almost every visitor to Costa Rica heads to this region during their stay. The reason? Two of the nation's most world-renowned sites are here. With its picture-perfect cone, Volcán Arenal causes gasps of "oohs!" and "aahs!" as it explodes spectacularly on a virtually daily basis. Dozens of lodges, from simple to sumptuous, near its base let you watch from a safe distance. Thermal spas such as Balneario Tabacón and Arenal Waterfall Gardens take advantage of volcanic springs. And the nearby town of La Fortuna hums as a center for all manner of adrenaline-charged activities: horseback riding, river float trips, kayaking, caving, even heli-touring. No visit to the volcano is complete without driving along the north shore of Lake Arenal, occupying a saddle between the mountains of the Cordillera de Tilarán. This gorgeous wind-whipped lake is Costa Rica's foremost setting for bass fishing and windsurfing.

Set deep in the mountains, the Quaker community of Monteverde is famous for its cloud forest reserve, tempting birders keen to spot the aptly named resplendent quetzal, which nests here. No longer sleepy, Monteverde has blossomed with tourist attractions, including several canopy tours, such as SkyWalk, and wildlife attractions, from the Monteverde Orchid Garden to the Serpentarium and Bat Jungle. You'll need a warm jacket for these cool, mist-nourished heights.

Not so on the steamy, often hot, rain-drenched flatlands below. The rivers that teem from the mountains feed bottle-green rain forests that carpet the northern region. Trails that thread the reserves of La Selva and Selva Verde offer virtually guaranteed sightings of monkeys, sloths, snakes and dozens of other creatures. Birding in Costa Rica is nowhere excelled, a fact underscored by a visit to Caño Negro National Wildlife Refuge, a wetland paradise teeming with migratory waterfowl and a nirvana for anglers who come to hook prize-size tarpon and snook.

INTRODUCTION

The perfect cone of Volcán Arenal is one of the world's most active volcanoes. This breathtaking spectacle crowns a region that abounds with natural wonders and exhilarating activities. Rising from the western plains of the San Carlos valley, three hours by car from San José, Volcán Arenal stands symmetrical, clear and tall against the horizon, puffing fumes and exploding against a fine blue sky (if you are lucky) with the expansive Lake Arenal in the foreground.

Volcán Arenal was a sleeping giant until 1968 when a massive eruption devastated the western flank of the volcano, killing 78 people. That event reignited a pattern characterized by periods of explosive activity and lava flows followed by dormancy for hundreds of years. Since 1968, Arenal has been erupting almost continuously. The most recent major eruption in August 2000 caused the deaths of two people. As the lava flows increase, volcano viewing has been subject to a more cautious approach.

Lake Arenal was formed in 1974 to provide hydroelectric power for the country. The wall damming River Arenal is at the eastern end of the lake near La Fortuna, but the generating plant is at the western end at Tronadora close to Tilarán. East to west trade winds from the Caribbean are channeled through the narrow gap between the Cordillera de Tilarán to the south and Cordillera de Guanacaste to the north. As the winds rise, they dump 4,500mm (175in) of rain each year on Arenal Volcano National Park at the eastern end of the lake, but when they reach the western limits of the lake, rainfall is down to 1,500mm (60in) annually. One final push over the western hills and the drained winds pass over Guanacaste with little moisture left in them, creating conditions ideal for the dry tropical forests of Santa Rosa National Park (▷ 137–139).

A steady supply of people has changed the once-sleepy backwater of La Fortuna, 6km (3.7 miles) away, to an occasionally lively focus of activity, providing a good base for excursions to the volcano and other activities. All trips to the volcano can be done independently or with a tour operator. While there are variations on a theme, most trips to the volcano leave in the late afternoon to get you to the best viewing spot for dusk. Several hotels on the shore of Lake Arenal provide memorable nighttime views of the hot plumes and red lava of Arenal. Friendly La Fortuna provides time to relax and unwind with pools, waterfalls and luxury at the romantically kitsch Tabacón hot springs. Other activities in the area include visits to spectacular waterfalls, and tours of the area by foot, on horseback or by bicycle.

WHAT TO SEE

PARQUE NACIONAL VOLCÁN ARENAL

Dominated by the conical peak of the volcano, Arenal Volcano National Park (tel 506 461 8499) covers 12,106ha (29,914 acres). Upgraded from a reserve to a national park in 1994, it protects the watershed that maintains water levels in Lake Arenal and sustains the volcano's microclimate.

A trip to see the lava flows and eruptions of the Arenal volcano is one of Costa Rica's most popular excursions. As darkness cloaks the region, the dust plumes that skirted down the bare slopes through the day reveal themselves to be glowing lava tumbling, crashing and smashing down the volcano slopes in a spray of natural fireworks. The sight is spectacular and the sound decidedly eerie. Arenal is a classic Stromboli-type stratovolcano, with a symmetrical cone formed by layers of volcanic material. It is the youngest of the stratovolcanoes in Costa Rica, at less than 5,000 years old. Research from the Arenal Observatory Lodge has produced a wealth of data, including the mind-boggling notion that the magma chamber that feeds the eruptions is just 5km (3 miles)

INFORMATION

www.arenal.net

239 F4 · Parque Nacional Volcán Arenal: daily 8–4; Venado Caves: daily 7–4 · Parque Nacional Arenal: US$10; Venado Caves: US$10 · Daily to La Fortuna via Ciudad Quesada from Terminal Atlántico Norte, San José (506 2256 9552), 3.5 hours. Daily from Ciudad Quesada, 1 hour. Daily to Venado, Guatuso from Ciudad Quesada · Trips to Arenal can be reserved through tour operators in La Fortuna and typically cost US$25 if visiting Baldi Thermae, US$60 if going to Tabacón Resort. All-inclusive trips to the Venado Caves cost US$39–US$45 · In La Fortuna, various tour agencies around the main square · From the south leave the Pan-American Highway near San Ramón; a good road leads north for 73km (45 miles). An alternative and longer route passes through Zarcero and Ciudad Quesada. Arriving from Tilarán to the west, a potholed road follows the north shore of Lake Arenal with views across the lake to the volcano. From Arenal to Venado, a dirt road leaves the north shore of the lake. Another route goes north from Tanque, heading west close to Jicarito

Opposite *Brightly colored plants and greenery overlooking Lake Arenal, Central America's largest man-made lake*

TIPS

» If seeing the volcano is the main reason for your visit, the skies are most reliably clear between December and April. Otherwise take into account greater rain between August and November—the waterfall will be more impressive, but walking trails will be muddier.

» Take a flashlight, good shoes and rainproof attire for visiting the volcano, and swimming gear and towel for visiting the thermal springs.

» For the budget conscious, across the road from the Tabacón hot springs is a less expensive option at just US$10 (Mon–Fri 10–9.30, Sat, Sun 8am–9.30pm).

» If you have your own transport, Toad Hall (▷ 127), on the scenic paved road between La Fortuna and Nuevo Arenal, is an excellent cafe for a meal and drink in a prime spot over the lake. It is also one of the best souvenir craft shops in the country.

below the surface. You will be permitted to visit safe areas—the one high ridge used by groups is El Silencio, 2km (1.25 miles) west of Tabacón Resort—but heed warnings. After viewing the volcano, groups head down to one of the thermal baths for a relaxing soak before returning to La Fortuna.

The park has five interesting (and safe) trails starting at the park entrance. The walks take from 25 minutes to a couple of hours and provide the chance to see heliconias, birdlife and mammals such as howler monkeys. Las Coladas trail involves a bit of scrambling over old lava flows, but provides good views of Lake Arenal and Volcán Chato. While trekking solo is permitted, guided hikes and treks can be arranged by tour operators in La Fortuna. Opposite the park entrance is a camping area.

HOT SPRINGS

Hot baths in the area offer the chance for serious rest and relaxation. Some 4.5km (3 miles) north of town, the closest hot springs to La Fortuna are Baldi Thermae (tel 506 2479 9651, daily 10–10, US$25). It has a number of pools starting at a comfortable 37°C (98°F) rising to an egg-poaching 63°C (145°F). Some 12km (7.5 miles) from La Fortuna, and much more fancy, is the Tabacón Resort (tel 506 2519 1999; daily 10–10; adult US$65, child under 9 US$20, under 4 free). The focus of the resort (▷ 129) is a series of mineral pools at a variety of temperatures. While the geothermally heated waters are totally natural, the rest is pure kitsch.

VENADO CAVES

The small community of Venado, about an hour away, is home to the labyrinth of the Venado Caves (tel 506 2478 9081). Formed during the Miocene period, 20 million years ago, the limestone was brought to the earth's surface by tectonic movements. Eight caverns can be visited, each eroded in the limestone by acidic waters. Linked by narrow passages, the caves' stalactites and stalagmites form Gaudí-esque shapes. There are dried-out river beds, waterfalls and bats. Tarantulas, snakes, crickets and frogs are also present. Dress accordingly and be prepared to get wet and dirty. Showers are available, so take a change of clothes. Not recommended for the claustrophobic.

LAKE ARENAL

Ringed by lushly forested hills and under the gaze of Volcán Arenal on its eastern side, Lake Arenal provides a superb setting for watersports. In 1974, it was flooded to form a basin that now supplies the country with 75 percent of its electrical power. In addition to the shoreline hotels, and the hydroelectric power from the Tronadora dam, the wind that blows the length of the lake has created world-class boardsailing conditions, with winds reaching 97kph (60mph). A mostly paved road twists around the northern shore of Lake Arenal, leading to Tilarán via Nuevo Arenal, making for a scenic drive. Boat trips are

Below *The volcano at dawn, as it towers above the national park*

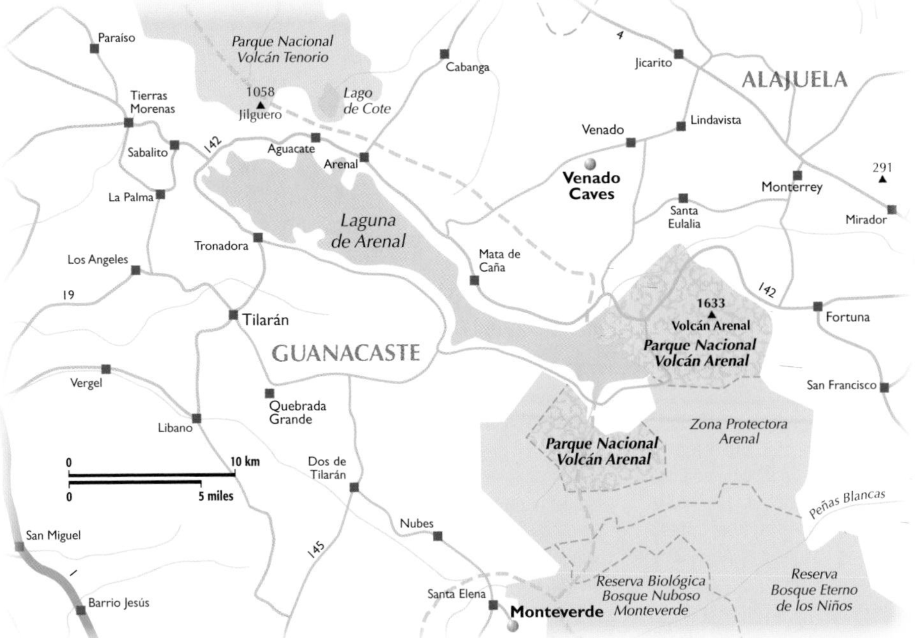

arranged with tour operators or by talking to local boatmen at the northern end of the dam. Fishing for rainbow bass *(guapote)* and *machaca* is possible during the year, with March to July being the best time for bass.

LA FORTUNA

Other than a plaza graced by a church on its west side, sights in La Fortuna are limited. Farther east, Arenal Mundo Aventura (tel 506 2479 9762; www.arenalmundoaventura.com) has waterfall rappelling, zipline tours and other adventures. Heading south, Río Fortuna waterfall (US$7) plunges 70m (230ft) from lush forest to the pool below, creating a hazy mist. Wear good shoes: it is a steep and slippery path. Below the falls there are good swimming spots. You can walk or drive to the falls from town, following the road for 1.6km (1 mile) before taking a 4km (2.5-mile) bumpy road through yucca and papaya plantations. Alternatively, take a half-day horseback-riding tour (US$25).

MORE TO SEE

QUEBRADA CEDEÑA

For a completely natural hot spring experience follow the road for 1.5km (1 mile) to Quebrada Cedeña. It can be difficult to find as there are no signs, but it's completely free; look for local parked cars.

ARENAL BOTANICAL AND BUTTERFLY GARDENS

On the north shore of Lake Arenal is the delightful Arenal Botanical and Butterfly Gardens, with many flowers, birds and butterflies.

☎ 506 694 4273 🕘 Daily 9–4, closed Oct 💳 US$8

RANCHO MARGOT

www.ranchomargot.org

On Lake Arenal's shore, the colonial-era Rancho Margot is an ecologically sustainable organic farm with a stables plus trails into its private rain forest preserve, and you may see native species in its wildlife rehabilitation center.

☎ 506 2479 7259

Below *A windsurfer enjoys the water on Lake Arenal*

CENTRO NEOTRÓPICO SARAPIQUÍS

www.sarapiquis.org

The nonprofit Centro Neotrópico Sarapiquís is more an ecological experience than a hotel, and has become a model for sustainable development. The complex emphasizes the theme of Man and Nature and includes a museum of contemporary indigenous cultures, botanical gardens, an archaeological park and the 350ha (865-acre) Tirimbina Biological Reserve.

In addition to providing a setting for exploring the lowland Caribbean rain forest, the center aims to be a place to learn and be challenged physically and mentally. The museum uses state-of-the-art technology, including audiovisual and animated displays.

The Alma Alta archaeological park, set amid the Centro's orange grove, includes a reconstructed pre-Columbian, 15th-century village and an eco-friendly hotel using solar energy. In 1999, after the construction of the center, pre-Columbian tombs were discovered and excavation work is continuing.

250 J4 US$20, or US$14, museum only From San José to Puerto Viejo de Sarapiquí (▷ 115), pass La Virgen 85km (53 miles), a 90-min drive, from San José. Head west from Puerto Viejo de Sarapiquí toward San Miguel PO Box 86-3069, La Virgen de Sarapiquí, Heredia 506 2761 1004

CIUDAD QUESADA (SAN CARLOS)

Just 24km (15 miles) from Zarcero, Ciudad Quesada, also called San Carlos, is the transportation hub for the northern lowlands. The town is of little interest to the visitor, but it is a useful junction between La Fortuna, Los Chiles and Puerto Viejo de Sarapiquí.

By Costa Rican standards Ciudad Quesada is a large town, but it has a distinctly small-town feel. There is little need to move more than a block or two from the main plaza, which is densely packed with trees and palms. To the east is a cavernous church with an impressive sculpture of Christ hanging above the altar.

East of town, Termales del Bosque (tel 506 2460 4740, US$15) has a botanical garden, forest trails, mineral springs and a zipline canopy tour (US$45).

250 G4 Regular buses to and from Atlántico Norte Terminal, San José. The terminal in San Carlos is 1km (0.6 miles) north of the plaza

ESTACIÓN BIOLÓGICA LA SELVA

www.ots.ac.cr

Some 3km (2 miles) south of Puerto Viejo de Sarapiquí, adjoining Braulio Carrillo National Park (▷ 90–91) at its northernmost boundary, La Selva Biological Station is a renowned research station with astonishing species diversity. Over half of the 875 bird species found in Costa Rica have been sighted on the 1,513ha (3,738 acres) of old growth and tropical wet forests. Toucans, parrots, trogons, monkeys, agoutis, peccaries and coatis are regularly seen. There's even a warning to look out for the seven venomous snakes out of the 56 species found at the station.

Owned by the Organization for Tropical Studies, the facility welcomes guests, usually as part of a day-trip from San José or Puerto Viejo de Sarapiquí. Half-day and three-day birding courses provide a great introduction to the subject.

250 J4 506 2766 6565 Daily 5.45am–4pm US$28, including guided walk; US$85 overnight cabins From San José to Puerto Viejo de Sarapiquí, at 6.45am and 12.15pm, to an intersection; walk the kilometer (half mile) to the entrance 3.5-hour Experience La Selva tour leaves at 8 and 1.30 (US$30) The Station is 3km (2 miles) south of Puerto Viejo de Sarapiquí. Watch carefully for the sign

ISLA DE LAS HELICONIAS

www.heliconiaisland.com

Heliconias Island is a fantastic collection of 80 types of heliconia from across the world, which flower all year round. You can also find other botanical species, including a type of ornamental banana and graceful palm trees. Throughout the gardens, bamboo, ferns, orchids and bromeliads grow with untamed abandon and birdlife is abundant, with long-tailed hermit hummingbirds and orange-chinned parakeets making an appearance. The eye-catching blue morpho butterfly can also be seen. Rarely will you see such variety and diversity in so small an area.

The Dutch owners are knowledgeable, self-taught botanists. Camping on the 2ha (5-acre) island is allowed and the price includes entrance.

251 J4 Apd 48-3069 506 2764 5220 Daily 8–5; call ahead to check US$15 From Puerto Viejo de Sarapiquí (▷ 115) to Montero Montero is 8km (5 miles) south of Puerto Viejo de Sarapiquí. Take the right turn 1km (0.6 miles) south of Río Isla Grande bridge and the Isla Grande petrol station. A right turn, followed by another right turn leads down a grassy track that should be signposted

Below *A lone visitor crosses a bridge at Estación Biológica La Selva*

MONTEVERDE
▷ 116.

PARQUE NACIONAL VOLCÁN TENORIO
Established in 1995, Tenorio Volcano National Park is one of the country's newest such parks, protecting the watershed of the Tenorio volcano (1,916m/ 6,286ft) and 12,871ha (31,804 acres) of mixed forest. The village of Bijagua, which lies in the saddle between Tenorio and Miravalles volcanoes, has facilities, and the park is a popular destination for hiking. A rewarding trip for the hardy, the park has stunning natural features. Soak in hot springs, visit waterfalls or see a park highlight, the Río Celeste, with azure blue waters created by minerals leached from the rock. The most accessible route leads from the Bijagua Heliconias Ecotourist Resort, which lies 3km (2 miles) out of town, along the flanks of the volcano. Other trails, for the more intrepid, lead from the crater lake through cloud forest to the summit, with views of the Arenal volcano and Lake Nicaragua.
249 E3 506 2200 0135 Daily 8–4 US$10 From San José as far as Upala, then a 15km (9-mile) journey to Bijuagua in a four-wheel-drive vehicle to the park From San José go north on the Pan-American Highway to Cañas; 7km (4.3 miles) north of Cañas, Highway 6 heads northeast 34km (21 miles) to Bijagua

PUERTO VIEJO DE SARAPIQUÍ
It is difficult to believe that Puerto Viejo de Sarapiquí, 97km (60 miles) north of San José, was once a flourishing port. Today's laid-back community is a couple of roads linking the riverside dock with the bus station and not much of interest in between. But the road west to La Virgen and the road south to the highway have plenty of lodges, reserves and river-rafting operations.

A few kilometers west toward La Virgen, set in 500ha (1,235 acres) of lowland rain forest, the Selva Verde Lodge (▷ 129) is more accessible than other lodges in the region. It's a good spot for birding and river trips. You can take walks along the multitude of trails—focusing on botany, birding or butterflies—with a resident naturalist. The Río Sarapiquí, which bisects the property, is here a scenic boat journey or, upstream, an adrenaline-pumping challenge. The lodge arranges guided hikes (US$15), boat tours (US$20) and horseback riding (US$25). Next door, the Sarapiquí Conservation Learning Center (tel 506 766 6482) works to ensure that the community benefits from the rain forest's secrets.
250 J4 Almost hourly from San José Gran Terminal del Caribe (506 2222 0610), 3.5 hours Launch to Tortuguero is US$300–US$350 for 1 to 10 people, 5 hours. Daily launch service to Trinidad on the San Juan River, leaving at 1 (US$5), returning the next day at 10am Take the San José–Limón Highway, and after passing through Braulio Carrillo National Park, take Highway 4 north at Rancho Robertos for 33km (20 miles). A longer, scenic route heads north from Heredia via Vara Blanca, but much of it was destroyed in the 2009 earthquake. It is due to reopen in 2010

RARA AVIS
www.rara-avis.com
Reached through Las Horquetas, around 16km (10 miles) north of the San José–Limón road, Rara Avis is a private reserve (an overnight stay is required owing to transportation logistics) perched on the eastern flanks of Braulio Carrillo National Park at an altitude of 700m (2,296ft).

The reserve's faunal diversity is staggering. More than 360 birds have been recorded, including the green macaw. You will probably see monkeys, coatis and anteaters. The really lucky may spot tapirs and jaguars. At the reserve, reached by a bone-shaking 15km (9-mile) journey in a tractor-pulled cart, a network of trails leads through primary forest. Some are rough and muddy, so go prepared. You can hike them with a guide or enjoy the solitude and silence on your own.

Booking accommodations at the reserve in advance is essential especially in the dry season.
250 J4 506 2764 1111 From US$80 inclusive package The 6.30am from San José reaches the hut at Las Horquetas in time to catch the tractor that leaves at 9.30am for the 3-hour journey to Rara Avis. Tractors leave Rara Avis at 2pm to catch the bus back to San José From San José, take the Guápiles–Limón Highway through Braulio Carillo National Park. Follow signs for Puerto Viejo de Sarapiquí. Las Horquetas is 16km (10 miles) farther on

REFUGIO NACIONAL DE VIDA SILVESTRE CAÑO NEGRO
Close to the Nicaraguan border, the Caño Negro National Wildlife Reserve covers 10,171ha (25,132 acres). The reserve draws birds and wildlife to one of Central America's most important wetlands. At its heart is Lake Caño Negro, covering 800ha (1,976 acres) but no more than 3m (10ft) deep, which evaporates at the end of the dry season in May. Swamps, forest and marshes attract a wide range of migratory birds. The reserve is home to Costa Rica's largest colony of Neotropic cormorants and is the country's last refuge for the Nicaraguan grackle. The roseate spoonbill, with its spatulate bill, is a common sight, and you may glimpse the huge jabirú standing 1.5m (5ft) tall—it is Central America's largest bird and critically endangered.

Floating safaris in canoes leave Los Chiles and follow the Río Frío through primary forest. You may see howler, spider and white-faced monkeys, along with sloths and caiman. Most people take the eight-hour tour from La Fortuna, which costs around US$50. Tours organized from Los Chiles cost US$20, and boats can be chartered by groups. Sportfishing for tarpon is available from lodges in the village of Caño Negro.
249 F2 560 2471 1309 Daily 8–5 US$6 Two daily from San José Terminal Atlántico Norte to Los Chiles Take the road north through Santa Rosa toward Los Chiles, then follow the signposted turnoff to Caño Negro, several kilometers (a couple of miles) before Los Chiles. Four-wheel-drive vehicle is required

MONTEVERDE

INTRODUCTION

Majestic and remote, Monteverde encapsulates the essence of Costa Rica—diversity of wildlife, seclusion and at times exhilaration. One of the world's outstanding tropical plant and wildlife sanctuaries, it encompasses eight ecological zones. Monteverde owes its formation to the pursuit of ideals. In 1951, a group of Quakers left the US to avoid the draft. Buying land in Monteverde and clearing the forests for dairy farming, the community soon realized that the forest cover was essential to preserve the soil and created a protected area of 541ha (1,336 acres). In 1972, after a period studying the birds of the cloud forest, George Powell and his wife set out to protect more of the region, joining forces with long-time resident Wilford Guindon to promote the creation of a reserve. Combining the Quaker reserve with a further 328ha (810 acres), the Monteverde Cloud Forest Reserve was created in 1972.

The ideals of its founders have continued as the reserve has grown. Without the backing of large environmental organizations, Monteverde moved from individual passion to global awareness through word-of-mouth recommendations and television nature documentaries. Slowly, the notion of ecotourism began to reap rewards, and the reserve spawned myriad reserves, protected areas and conservation projects across Costa Rica.

Today, there is discussion about the future of Monteverde and other reserves in the area. Some residents want to see the dreadful roads upgraded to improve access. Others want to restrict the potential damage that may be caused, believing that development has already reached unacceptable limits. Decide for yourself whether visiting Monteverde is about quality or quantity.

The secret hideaway that was Monteverde Reserve in the 1970s, when it was founded, is now a well-trodden path. With its head often shrouded in mist, Monteverde Cloud Forest Reserve will keep you alert in anticipation. But before you curse the poor roads from the Pan-American Highway, remember that it has been fundamental in preserving the cloud forest by preventing rampant development of this isolated region. While the reserve is the main reason for visiting the area, there are many other places to explore.

Despite the visitors, the area has a rustic charm. Santa Elena, the main village, trundles along in a state of organized chaos. Nearby is the Santa Elena Cloud Forest Reserve, with a network of trails and The Original Canopy tour (▷ 120). Monteverde's Conservation League also manages the Children's Eternal Rain Forest (▷ 118), with trails that lead to views of the Arenal volcano, lagoons and waterfalls (▷ 110–113).

There are tourist information offices in Monteverde and Santa Elena, but tour operators and hotels in Santa Elena can help with inquiries and by arranging tours. The driest months in the region are from January to May, with the best months for birding being February, March and April. September to November are the wettest months. As this is cloud forest, remember that mist is common and rain can occur throughout the year. Walking is the simplest way of getting around the area, and is certainly feasible around Santa Elena. Buses run from Santa Elena to Monteverde.

WHAT TO SEE

RESERVA BIOLÓGICA BOSQUE NUBOSO MONTEVERDE

Straddling the continental divide, the Monteverde Cloud Forest Reserve covers 10,500ha (25,945 acres) and is privately owned and administered by the Centro Cientifico Tropical, a non-profit research and educational association. The reserve is mainly primary cloud forest shrouded in mist and cloud, giving high humidity. In Monteverde, trade winds from the Atlantic force moist air up the

INFORMATION

www.monteverdeinfo.com
www.acmcr.org
249 F4 Reserve office: 506 2645 5122, for information, tours and reservations Office: daily 7–4.30; Park: daily 7–4 Adult day pass for multiple entry, US$17, cannot be purchased in advance Daily from San José's Terminal Atlántico Norte to Santa Elena; one bus a day from Puntarenas and Tilarán. For Fantasy and Interbus shuttle bus details ▷ 54. From Santa Elena to the reserve five times daily (US$1) Coming south on the Pan-American Highway turnoff at Km149, south of Río Lagarto, for about 40km (25 miles) to Santa Elena (2.5 hours). A four-wheel-drive car is recommended. Going north on the Pan-American Highway, take Sardinal turn off north of Río Aranjuez, then via Guacimal to Monteverde. You can also drive from Tilarán Bureau of Tourism of Monteverde is in Santa Elena (506 2645 6464, daily). Good information on activities in and around the reserve. From the bus station walk back one block to the log cabin west of the church Guided tours lasting 3.5hrs, US$17, guided night tours every evening departing at 7.15pm, US$17. Tours can be reserved. Independent guides can be organized through your hotel Taxi from Santa Elena, around US$7

Opposite *Exploring one of the trails in Monteverde Cloud Forest Reserve*

TIPS

» The total number of visitors allowed in the reserve at any one time is 150, so be there before 7am to make sure of getting in during high season. If you want a guide, hotels will reserve a place for the following day. Alternatively, you can just turn up and see if there are spaces on any tours.

» If you intend to head from Monteverde to La Fortuna, you can avoid the eight-hour bus journey via Tilarán by taking a jeep to Lake Arenal, then a boat, and a jeep for the last stretch. It takes three hours, costs US$25 and is more scenic.

» The best months to visit Monteverde are January to May, especially February, March and April.

» If you are driving a rental car, ensure the agreement allows you to travel to Monteverde.

» To get to Monteverde from Santa Elena, the smart choice is to get transportation up the hill and walk down, enjoying the views as you go.

Tilarán Mountains; the air cools as it rises, and then condenses to make clouds that drop rain. The result is an abundance of plants and epiphyte growth with tree trunks and branches covered in dense blankets of moss and lichens, and linked by twisting vines interspersed with fallen trees and giant tree ferns. A cloud forest is an almost magical place, like the forests of fairy tales. A visit to Monteverde, or any of the many other private reserves in the area, is an opportunity to see nature in grand profusion. Plants grow on every available space, insects breed, birds feed and mammals loiter and stalk. Without a trained eye nearby, you may see only insects and hear a bird take flight, but the experience is no less enjoyable.

Monteverde contains more than 400 species of birds, including the resplendent quetzal, best seen in the dry months between January and May, near the start of the Nuboso trail but also by the reserve's parking area. There are more than 100 species of mammals, including monkeys, Baird's tapir, Costa Rica's six endangered cats (jaguar, jaguarundi, margay, ocelot, oncilla and puma), reptiles and amphibians. The reserve is home to an estimated 2,500 species of plants and more than 6,000 species of insects.

The entrance is at 1,530m (5,020ft), but the reserve's maximum altitude rises to over 1,800m (5,900ft). Mean temperature is between 16°C and 18°C (60°F and 65°F) and average annual rainfall is 3,000mm (118in). The weather changes quickly and wind and humidity often make the air feel cooler, so take a light jacket and rain gear.

The commonly used trails are in good condition and there are easy boardwalks for those who do not want to go far, as well as trails that take about two hours, but you could easily spend all day wandering around. Trails may be restricted from time to time. There is one northwards to the Arenal volcano that is increasingly used, but not easy. Free maps of the reserve are available at the entrance, along with an excellent self-guiding Nature Trail with a guide booklet (US$2). Follow the rules and sign the register, indicating where you are going in case you get lost. Stay on the paths, leave nothing behind and take no fauna or flora out; radios and tape recorders are not allowed.

MONTEVERDE SETTLEMENT

Strung out along the bumpy road between Santa Elena and the Reserve, the settlement at Monteverde has no central focus. It was founded by American Quakers in the 1950s and started life as a group of dairy farms providing milk for a cooperative cheese factory. Quietly churning away, La Lechería (tel 506 2645 5436, Mon–Sat 7.30–5, Sun 7.30–12.30; free) produces excellent cheeses of various types, fresh milk, ice cream and milkshakes to die for. Today, Monteverde maintains an air of pastoral charm, but tourism provides more revenue for the town than dairy produce ever could.

RESERVA BOSQUE ETERNO DE LOS NIÑOS

www.acmcr.org

Adjoining the Monteverde Cloud Forest Reserve is the Children's Eternal Rain Forest, established in 1988 after an initiative by Swedish schoolchildren. Currently covering 22,000ha (54,360 acres), the land was purchased and maintained by the Monteverde Conservation League with children's donations from more than 44 nations around the world. Funds are used for buying additional land and for improving the existing reserve area.

The Bajo del Tigre trail is about 3km (2 miles), taking 90 minutes. Guides can be arranged or you can go on a self-guiding tour. Trips deeper into the forest go to the San Gerardo Field Station, in the western part of the reserve, where there are 7km (4.5 miles) of trails leading through primary and secondary forests and a spectacular view of the Arenal volcano. The Poco Sol Field Station is at the eastern end of the protected areas near Poco Sol Lagoon and reached on the road from San Ramón to La Fortuna, with almost 10km (6 miles) of trails

visiting a waterfall and providing good birding. Accommodations are available at both of the field stations.

✉ Asociación Conservacionista de Monteverde, Apartado Postal 124-5655, Monteverde
☎ 506 2645 5003 🕐 Daily 7.30–5.30 US$5

RESERVA BOSQUE NUBOSO SANTA ELENA

www.reservasantaelena.org

Just 1km (0.6 miles) along the road from Santa Elena to Tilarán, a long, steep 5km (3-mile) track is signposted to this 310ha (766-acre) reserve. It is 83 percent primary cloud forest (the rest is secondary forest) at 1,700m (5,576ft), bordered by the Monteverde Cloud Forest Reserve and the Arenal Forest Reserve. A network of paths spreads for 12km (7.5 miles), with several lookouts where you can see and hear the Arenal volcano on a clear day. The canopy tour is recommended. You climb inside a hollow strangler fig tree, then cross between two platforms along aerial runways 30m (98ft) up, which give good views of orchids and bromeliads, then down a 30m (98ft) hanging rope at the end. There is a small information center where rubber boots can be rented and a cafe is open at weekends. The rangers are very friendly and enthusiastic and there are generally fewer visitors here than at Monteverde. Profits from the scheme go to five local schools.

☎ 506 2645 5390 🕐 Daily 7–4 Adult US$12, child US$ 6 Taxi from Santa Elena US$7; three daily shuttles (US$2)

HUMMINGBIRD GALLERY

Just before the entrance to Monteverde Cloud Forest Reserve is the Hummingbird Gallery, where masses of different hummingbirds can be seen darting around a glade, visiting feeding dispensers filled with sugared water. There is a slide show at Monteverde Lodge (▷ 129)—*Sounds and Scenes of the Cloud Forests* (daily 6.15pm, US$5).

☎ 506 2645 5030 🕐 Daily 8.30–4.30

MONTEVERDE BUTTERFLY GARDEN

A dirt road opposite the Hotel Heliconia leads to the Monteverde butterfly project, a beautiful garden planted for breeding and researching butterflies, which was founded in 1991 by biologist Jim Wolf and his wife, Marta Iris Salazar. The central goal of the project is environmental education. Wandering through the four gardens and three greenhouses you can see hundreds of species, representing nearly half of Costa Rica's butterflies. The netted flyway allows for close encounters with the winged jewels, which fly more on sunny days (if it rains you can visit again at no extra charge). The garden raises more

Above *Sunlight filters through the canopy of trees in the reserve*

TIPS

» Be warned that seeing wildlife requires patience. As with all nature experiences, be realistic in your expectations.

» A guide is a good idea if you want to see wildlife–the untrained eye misses a lot.

» Recommended equipment includes: binoculars (which are available for rent at the entrance, US$10); a good digital camera; insect repellent; sweater and light rainwear. Rubber boots or good walking shoes are a must for the longer walks at all times of year, but especially in the rainy season, and can be rented at the park office for US$1 or at hotels.

than 50 species, and bilingual guides provide insights into the life cycle of these fascinating creatures. The best time for a visit is between 11 and 1.
☎ 506 2645 5512 Daily 9.30–4 Adult US$10, child US$4, including 1-hour tour

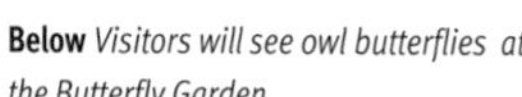
Below *Visitors will see owl butterflies at the Butterfly Garden*

SKY WALK AND SKY TREK

www.skywalk.com

Off the road to Tilarán, 5km (3 miles) north of Santa Elena, the highly professional Sky Walk and Sky Trek operations enable you to experience the wonders of the cloud forest canopy with added adrenaline. Canopy tours are now commonplace in Costa Rica, but Sky Walk is among the best. It includes more than 2.5km (1.5 miles) of trails and uses six suspension bridges straddling deep canyons to take you through the cloud forest at canopy level, the highest bridge being 42m (138ft) above the ground and the longest one being 243m (797ft).

Sky Trek is an even more breathtaking experience, but not for the faint-hearted as you fly through the air on 10 ziplines strung out from giant trees. The longest cable is 427m (467 yards) long and 127m (416ft) high. On clear days the panoramic view from the highest observation tower is incredible. The Sky Tram takes you to the start point.

☎ 506 2645 5238 Sky Walk: daily 7–4; Sky Trek: daily 7–3 Sky Walk: adult US$30, child US$24, under 6 free. Sky Trek: adult US$48, child (8–12) US$38, under 8 free Sky Walk: guided nature hikes at 8 and 10, US$38; Sky Trek tours: 7.30, 9.30, 11.30, 1.30 and 2 Hotel pick-ups can be arranged, US$1

THE ORIGINAL CANOPY TOUR

www.canopytours.com

This canopy tour, the first in the world, is in the grounds of the Monteverde Cloud Forest Lodge, 1km (0.6 miles) from Santa Elena. An intricate series of

11 tree platforms, varying between 8m (26ft) and 28m (92ft), connected by cables, take you zipping and soaring through the various layers of the forest canopy, culminating with 12 rappel descents.

The tour begins with a guided hike through the forest and a talk outlining the biodiversity of the forest, before you climb up to the first platform. One of the unique experiences of the tour is a rope ladder ascent through the core of an immense strangler fig tree. The Monteverde Cloud Forest Lodge connects the Monteverde with the Santa Elena reserve and has private trails, which provide excellent birding.

PO Box 7979-10000 506 2645 5243 Tours at 7.30, 10.30 and 2.30; free hotel pick-ups Adult US$45, child US$35

SELVATURA

www.selvatura.com

About 2km (1.2 miles) beyond Sky Walk, this well-rounded facility also has a zipline canopy tour with 18 platforms and 15 cables, plus 3km (2 miles) of tree-top walkways, with the highest 60m (180ft) above the ground. There is also a hummingbird garden and some 20 species of butterflies flutter around within a domed enclosure (US$10).

The scintillating highlight is the Jewels of the Rain forest Bio-Art Exhibition & Insect Museum, displaying tens of thousands of insects from around the globe. It is part of the private collection of world-famous entomologist Dr. Richard Whitten.

506 2645 5929 Daily 7–5 Canopy tour: adult US$45, child US$30; Walkway: adult US$25, child US$215. Insect Museum: US$10 Canopy tours 8.30, 11, 1 and 2.30 Hotel pick-ups included in package rates

MORE TO SEE

BAT JUNGLE

This fascinating bat exhibit includes a flyway. Documentaries are shown, and visitors don giant ears to gain an appreciation of bats' astounding acoustic abilities.

400m (440 yards) uphill from the gas station in Monteverde 506 2645 6566 Daily 9.30–7.30 Adult US$10, child US$8

ECOLOGICAL SANCTUARY WILDLIFE REFUGE

A private farm with four trails through forest, passing cascading waterfalls, with good chances of spotting wildlife.

506 2645 5869 Daily 7am–7.30pm US$15 Guided tours 7–5.30, US$30

ORCHID FARM

This garden dispays more than 400 species of orchid, including the *guaria morada*, the national flower of Costa Rica, and the world's smallest orchid.

506 2645 5308 Daily 8–5 US$10

RANARIO

The Frog Pond has almost 30 species of frogs and toads. Guided tours last for 45 minutes and you can return as many times as you like throughout the day.

506 2645 6320 Daily 9–8.30 US$10 for day pass 300m (330 yards) west of Monteverde Lodge

SERPENTARIO

www.snaketour.com

More than 25 species of snakes are displayed, along with their prey: chameleons, frogs and so forth.

300m (330 yards) east of Santa Elena 506 2645 6002 Daily 8–8 Adult US$8, child US$5

Above *An orange-kneed tarantula held by a keeper at the Serpentario*

Below *A violet sabrewing in the Hummingbird Gallery*

WALK

MONTEVERDE

You must not miss spending a day at the famous Monteverde Cloud Forest Reserve. A network of well-maintained and mapped trails can be linked together to form a walk of almost any length in this magical forest in the clouds. A guide will know where to go to maximize the fantastic wildlife-viewing opportunities.

THE WALK
Distance: from 2km (1 mile)
Allow: 1 day
Start/end at: Park headquarters

★ The main trail system in Monteverde forms a rough triangle, and that is its name: El Triangulo. From the entrance to the reserve, four trails, including the Bosque Nuboso Trail (▷ 119), the Rio Trail and the Pantanoso Trail, link up to form the boundary of the triangle. Individual trails are occasionally closed for repair, and there is no guarantee that any specific trail mentioned here will be open at the time of your visit, depending on conditions.

The most popular trail is the 1.9km (1-mile) Bosque Nuboso Trail, due to the 27 points along the trail that correspond to information in a self-guiding pamphlet (US$2 in the Reserve's souvenir shop), making it the best trail to explore without a guide. This trail forms the southern edge of the triangle, terminating where it joins the Brilliante Trail, which then takes a northeasterly tack along the line of the Continental Divide as it passes through Monteverde.

At, or near, self-guiding point 4 on Bosque Nuboso, just a few hundred meters from the entrance, many guides pause with their groups, set up their tripods and point their telescopic viewers at aguacate trees just off the trail. Here, frequently, they spot one or more respendent quetzals perched, preening or feeding on the aguacate fruit. This type of avocado has a big seed and little flesh, so quetzals eat great quantities of them.

On the northern side of the triangle, the Rio Trail winds along parallel to a small river, eventually reaching a *mirador*, or lookout, with a splendid view of a waterfall. En route, your guide will point out where the forest turns from secondary growth (an area that has been cleared or logged within the last 75 years) into primary growth, where the trees have never been cut and the largest are up to 150 years old. The guide will identify orchids and other epiphytes, spot and name every bird within sight and talk cloud forest numbers: 150 types of fern, 3,480mm (137in) of rainfall annually, 765 types of tree, 216 mammals, including 110 different bats, among them three vampire species. He will tell you interesting facts: that hummingbird hearts beat 800 times per minute and that there are 80 types of avocado in Monteverde.

When you are ready to return from your walk, times, distances, trails and directions are dictated by many factors, including the location of other guided groups, trail conditions and animal sightings. Your guide might march you off on another trail because a couple of quetzals have been spotted there. But even without a quetzal sighting, the guide's insight and the visual splendor of the forest, make this one of the most memorable places to walk in Costa Rica.

TIPS

» Spend the night in the area and arrive early. Those first in at 7am have the best chance of seeing wildlife and will certainly see larger numbers of birds.

» Use a guide (from US$15 per person). You can share the cost by going with a group. Given the difficulties of spotting wildlife and the crowded conditions, guides are crucial to understanding the reserve's ecosystems. They can't guarantee sightings, but will know, for example, the locations of the aguacate trees where quetzals gather. Guides are uniformly multilingual and knowledgeable about the forest.

» Dress appropriately: it is often cloudy, misty and windy. It can be quite cool so take a light raincoat, a hat or hooded poncho, and shoes with good grips; rubber boots can be rented (US$1). Some trails are finished with textured brick, but there are plenty of slippery patches.

» Take binoculars. If you have a pair, you won't have to wait in line for a look through a guide's telescope. If you are taking a camera, make sure it is semi- or fully waterproof and has a zoom.

PRESERVING MONTEVERDE

As one of the most popular tourist destinations in Costa Rica, Monteverde can get swamped by visitors. Without limits, the foot traffic would be very damaging, so the roads remain unpaved, to deter day-trippers and the reserve's managers have limited visitors to a maximum of 150 per day. Even this is a large number for such a small reserve and it puts a physical strain on the trails, stretches of which may be closed for repair, making some areas inaccessible. The limit has also generated anxiety around the entrance, as guides and tourists scramble to get in first. But despite its popularity, Monteverde remains an inspiring place to visit.

Clockwise from opposite *Vegetation in the Monteverde Reserve; a banded orange heliconian In the Butterfly Garden; a red-eyed tree frog in the Serpentario*

BOCA TAPADA

LA LAGUNA DE LAGARTO LODGE

www.lagarto-lodge-costarica.com

Some 40km (25 miles) from the Río San Carlos, the Laguna de Lagarto, a member of The Ecotourism Association, is frequently recommended for its wildlife watching. The lodge looks directly out to the rain forest and a private reserve of 500ha (1,235 acres) where you can roam along 15km (9 miles) of trails with a guide or head out on your own. Some 365 bird species, including the great green macaw, have been recorded on the property. From the lodge you can take canoeing trips on nearby lagoons, a boat trip to the San Juan River on the border with Nicaragua, or go horseback riding. The hotel is off the beaten path, so these activities are not convenient for non-guests.

✉ Boca Tapada ☎ 506 2289 8163

LA FORTUNA

ARENAL HANGING BRIDGES

www.hangingbridges.com

This attraction in the Fortuna region offers a complex of gentle trails that wander through 250ha (617 acres) of primary forest and across a series of steel suspension bridges, which provide good wildlife spotting and views of the Arenal volcano. Access is via a sharp right turn past the Arenal dam on the Fortuna–Nuevo Arenal road.

☎ 506 2290 0469 🕑 Daily 7.30–4.30 ✋ Adult US$22, child US$12; guided tours US$25

ARENAL RAIN FOREST RESERVE

www.arenalreserve.com

A Sky Tram ride up a mountainside ends at a lookout with views over Lake Arenal and Arenal Volcano. From here enjoy a canopy tour with almost 5km (3 miles) of zipline—the longest single line is 700m (2,310ft) long! More sedentary trails lead through the rain-forest reserve. Snake and butterfly exhibits round out the attractions.

✉ El Castillo ☎ 506 2479 9944 🕑 Daily 7.30–5 ✋ Adult US$55, child US$28

ARENAL WATERFALL GARDENS

www.thespringscostarica.com

New in 2009, this exciting hot springs facility is located at a deluxe new hotel with a grandstand hilltop position a safe 5km (3 miles) from the volcano. Landscaped in Disney fashion, it has 18 thermal mineral-water pools fed by cascades. You can float on inner tubes, there's a spring-fed lake with kayaking, and an impressive wild cat rescue and rehabilitation center will open to the public in 2010, including a "jaguar island."

✉ The Springs Resort & Spa, 6km (3.5 miles) west of La Fortuna ☎ 506 2401 3313 🕑 Daily 8am–midnight ✋ US$40

MONTEVERDE

ARTS AND CRAFTS COOPERATIVE

Just over halfway up the road to the reserve, close to El Bosque restaurant, is CASEM, founded in 1872 by women of the Monteverde area who help provide for their families by working from their homes. The cooperative now sells embroidered shirts, T-shirts, wooden and woven articles and baskets. The shop next door sells Costa Rican coffee and you can also get used coffee sacks as an unusual souvenir, if they have any. More than 140 craftspeople are represented.

Opposite *Observing the surroundings from a hanging bridge near Lake Arenal*

✉ Casemcoop R. L. (CASEM), opposite Stella's Bakery ☎ 506 2645 5190 ⏲ Mon–Sat 8–5, Sun 10–4

BROMELIAS BOOKSTORE AND GALLERY

Some 3km (2 miles) east of Santa Elena is Bromelias, owned by Patricia Maynard. The gallery represents several local artists and craftsmen, with a myriad collection of paintings, batik, stained glass, indigenous musical instruments and jewelry. The arty vibe extends to the alpine-style restaurant festooned with arts and crafts where they serve wonderful home-made chocolate and banana cake, sandwiches and teas. Yoga classes can also be arranged.

✉ 75m (80 yards) east of Stella's Bakery ☎ 506 2645 6272 ⏲ Daily 9–5

LA CASCADA

On the road to Monteverde, La Cascada is the place to head for serious partying until the early hours. Very popular in high season, it may be low key in the early evening, but by 10pm it positively throbs with visitors and locals dancing to live music courtesy of local bands or DJs. Admission price varies accordingly. As well as beer, spirits and cocktails, fast-food bar snacks are served. A Jacuzzi has been added.

✉ Just before the petrol station on the road to Monteverde ☎ 506 2645 5186 ⏲ Thu–Sat 9pm–2am ✋ US$5

DESAFÍO EXPEDITIONS

www.monteverdetours.com

Desafío is a highly recommended tour operator that runs a selection of tailor-made horseback tours in the Monteverde area. Excursions include two-hour secondary forest and farm rides, a good option for novice riders, US$15–US$32; a four-hour ride, which also includes a two-hour hike to the breathtaking 91m (300ft) San Luís Waterfall, US$47; or for the more dedicated, a two-day trip to La Fortuna. Helmets are only provided for children and it is worth noting that English-speaking guides tend to be available only on the larger group tours. Prices are lower the larger the group.

Desafío also runs white-water rafting trips on the rapids of the class III–IV Río Toro. Trips depart at 8.30am and return at 3.30pm and cost US$85 per person, including equipment and hotel transportation in the Arenal area. Half days on the Balsa River (US$65), are much tamer, with interludes that allow for wildlife spotting and for swimming alongside the raft. All guides are bilingual. Remember to call ahead and be aware that river trips are subject to weather conditions being suitable on the day. The company also offers hard-core canyoneering, including waterfall rappelling.

✉ Opposite the supermarket in Santa Elena ☎ 506 2645 5874

ECOLODGE SAN LUÍS

www.ecolodgesanluis.com

Affiliated with the University of Georgia, this facility is part research station and part ecological forest reserve. Guided birding and nature hikes—including to a waterfall—plus horseback rides are among the draws, and visitors seeking a more in-depth knowledge of local ecology can partake of lectures and intensive study courses. A night walk is not to be missed.

✉ San Luís ☎ 506 2645 8049 ⏲ Daily 8–5 ✋ US$20 guided hike, US$10 self-guiding trail hike, US$10 horseback ride

JEWELS OF THE RAIN FOREST

www.selvatura.com/jewels.html

The world's largest private insect collection is displayed in exotic, colorful detail. Entomologist Richard Whitten is usually on-hand to tell fascinating anecdotes as you admire the many thousands of butterflies, moths, beetles and more. from around the world, all exquisitely choreographed by Richard's wife, Margaret. Fascinating videos are screened in an auditorium.

✉ Selvatura ☎ 506 2645 5929 ⏲ Daily 7–5 ✋ US$10

SABINE'S SMILING HORSES

www.horseback-riding-tours.com

A good riding stables, Sabine's places a clear emphasis on fit and healthy horses. Horseback tours from two to five hours and multi-day riding holidays are organized and include the Monteverde to Arenal tour, beach rides, full moon rides and tours to the San Luís waterfall. The most popular excursion, the Campesino Secret Trail, crosses through farmland and cloud forest for three hours.

✉ Pensión Santa Elena ☎ 506 2645 6894 ✋ 3-hour ride US$40

LA TABERNA

The Taberna, close to the Serpentarium, is a good place to enjoy an early drink on the outdoor terrace, or more ebullient socializing and dancing after 9pm. Infectious beats stir locals and visitors to some serious hip gyrating, with a Latin musical repertoire including salsa, son and merengue, although 1980s rock usually competes for the airwaves by the early hours. There is a restaurant serving snacks, sandwiches and burgers, and some below-average fish and meat dishes.

✉ 1km (0.6 miles) from Santa Elena ☎ 506 2645 5883 ⏲ Wed–Sun 11am–2am

LA VIRGEN

RANCHO LEONA

www.rancholeona.com

Some 9km (5.5 miles) north of San Miguel is La Virgen, and one good reason to stop there is Rancho Leona. The main attraction is excellent kayaking on the Río Sarapiquí, and excursions are available from beginner to advanced level with two nights' accommodations included in the all-inclusive price of US$75. There is a quiet patio for reading in the lush gardens, an Indian-style sweat lodge and in-depth local knowledge of all the nearby attractions, all fueled by a healthy but filling menu of dishes served in the open-air restaurant.

✉ La Virgen, 9km (5.5 miles) north of San Miguel ☎ 506 2761 1019

PRICES AND SYMBOLS

The restaurants are listed alphabetically (excluding El, Le, La and Les). The prices given are the average for a two-course lunch (L) and a three-course dinner (D) for one person, without drinks. The wine price is for the least expensive bottle.

For a key to the symbols, ▷ 2.

ARENAL

LA CHOZA DE LAUREL

www.lachozadelaurel.com

Recreating the mood of a typical Tico farmstead with cloves of garlic and antique pots and pans dangling from the beamed ceiling, this charming open-air restaurant serves hearty country fare prepared *a la leña*—on a wood-fired stove. Its cheap lunchtime *casado* specials combine meat, veg and starch.

✉ 100 m (110 yards) west of the plaza in La Fortuna ☎ 506 2479 7063 🕑 Daily 6am–10pm ✋ L US$6, D US$12, Wine US$14

GINGERBREAD

www.gingerbreadarenal.com

Israeli professional chef Eyal Ben-Menachem has condensed the influence of his world travels into an eclectic and creative menu typified by jumbo shrimp with couscous and lentils. You can always count on a succulent filet mignon, but the menu leans heavily toward fresh gourmet seafood that fuses French, Mediterranean and Californian inspirations. Even the breads and jams are homemade. The stone patio with wrought-iron tables is a lovely venue come rain or shine. Lunch is available by telephone reservation for groups of four or more only. Note that credit cards are not accepted.

✉ 4km (2.5 miles) east of Nuevo Arenal ☎ 506 2694 0039 🕑 Tue–Sat 5pm–9pm ✋ L US$14, D US$22, Wine US$20

RESTAURANTE HELICONIAS

www.hotelarenalkioro.com

With unrivaled grandstand views of the volcano, this smart hotel-restaurant with vast picture windows is the place to enjoy superlative international cuisine, which majors on meat and shellfish. An octopus cocktail appetizer and sea bass in caper sauce are among the treats. Service is exemplary.

✉ Hotel Arenal Kioro, 10km (6 miles) west of La Fortuna ☎ 506 2461 1700 🕑 Daily 6.30am–10pm ✋ L US$16, D US$26, Wine US$15

RESTAURANTE LUIGI

As its name suggests, Luigi is an Italian restaurant. Open to La Fortuna's main street, it has a great location, and the modestly elegant setting is romantic at night. Wood-fired pizzas and homemade pastas are the highlights, but it also serves continental dishes, such as beef Stroganoff, and local seafood. It excels at flambées.

✉ 200m (218 yards) west of the plaza in La Fortuna ☎ 506 2479 9636 🕑 Daily 6am–11pm ✋ B US$8, L US$14, D US$24, Wine US$15

TOAD HALL

www.toadhall-gallery.com

Toad Hall cafe, a 45-minute drive from Fortuna, serves a mix of fresh food with home-grown salads, fruit juices and divine chocolate brownies. The views of the lake

Above *A sizzling display of the prepared ingredients for many local dishes*

and volcano are great and its art gallery gift shop is one of Costa Rica's best.
✉ La Unión de Arenal ☎ 506 2692 8001 ⓢ Daily 8–4 ✋ L US$10, no wine

TOM'S PAN

This small, rustic, German-run bakery-restaurant often fills up with German tour groups who come to devour Teutonic staples, such as sauerkraut, and dumplings with bacon. It also serves American breakfasts, and the homemade pastas and homebaked breads and pastries are worth the journey.
✉ Nuevo Arenal ☎ 506 2694 4547 ⓢ Daily 7:30am–4pm ✋ B US$8, L US$12, Wine US$15

LAS VENTANAS

www.thespringscostarica.com

If the views from Restaurante Las Heliconias seem unnervingly close to the action, this superb restaurant—the most elegant in the region—offers a grandstand view from a safer distance. You can look through a wraparound wall-of glass, angled to permit plunging views to the river. From elegant place settings to tuxedo-clad wait-staff, the effect of the place will leave quite an imprint. The fusion menu marries French influences to Costa Rican ingredients. The result is delicious. Be sure to sample a dessert.
✉ 8km (5 miles) west of La Fortuna ✉ 506 2401 3313 ⓢ Daily 12–3, 6–10 ✋ L US$15, D US$32, Wine US$20

CHACHAGUA

COCO LOCO ART GALLERY & CAFÉ

www.arenalbyowner.com

An adjunct to one of the finest art and crafts galleries in Costa Rica, this small cafe is a delightful place to break a journey to and from La Fortuna and the Central Highlands, with herbal teas a selection of coffee drinks, and divinely refreshing fresh-fruit smoothies.
✉ 8km (5 miles) southeast of La Fortuna ☎ 506 2468 0990 ⓢ Daily 8am–5pm ✋ L US$10,

HORQUETAS DE SARAPIQUÍ

HACIENDA LA ISLA

www.haciendalaisla.com

This lovely hacienda-style boutique hotel has a gourmet, open-air restaurant under thatch. The Belgian owner's wife, Chef Anna, uses ingredients from the hacienda's own extensive orchards and gardens to create Latino fusion cuisine, such as tenderloin in dark beer sauce with fine asparagus and duchesse potatoes. The restaurant overlooks a fish-filled lagoon at the forest edge—a superb setting, often enlivened by monkeys.
✉ Horquetas ☎ 506 2764 2576 ⓢ Daily 7am–10pm ✋ B US$10, L US$15, D US$25, Wine US$25

MONTEVERDE/ SANTA ELENA

MORPHOS CAFÉ

Morphos, one of the most consistently recommended restaurants in Santa Elena, serves a selection of daily specials featuring hearty fish and meat staples as well as standards such as pasta. The dining room is a social hub by day with hikers devouring sandwiches, while candlelit tables add romantic appeal by night.
✉ Opposite the supermarket, Santa Elena ☎ 506 2645 5607 ⓢ Daily 11–9.15 ✋ L US$10, D US$18, Wine US$15

PIZZERIA DE JOHNNY

www.pizzeriadejohnny.com

En route to the national park, 1km (0.6 miles) from Santa Elena, restrained elegance prevails at the long-established Johnny's, often lauded as the region's best restaurant. Good wood-ovened pizzas are liberally topped with fresh ingredients, and appetizers include garlic mussels and bruschetta. There is a good wine list, and for lighter fare or a lunchtime snack, choose from a selection of sandwiches. The balcony has several outdoor tables.
✉ On the Santa Elena–Monteverde road, Monteverde ☎ 506 2645 5066 ⓢ Daily 11.30–9.30 ✋ L US$10, D US$16, Wine US$16

RESTAURANT DE LUCÍA

Across the street from the Hotel de Lucía Inn, Lucía's is a piece of Italy that has received countless recommendations. Tasty vegetarian cuisine, including lasagne and tortillas, are served alongside meat and fish dishes in a relaxed and informal setting. The daily specials of meat and fish are brought to your table and cooked to taste. This is a popular place, so reservations are advised.
✉ On the road to the Monteverde Butterfly Garden ☎ 506 2645 5337 ⓢ Daily 7am–9pm ✋ L US$13, D US$20, Wine US$18

EL SAPO DORADO

www.sapodorado.com

Costa Rican and Quaker traditions fuse with aplomb at the widely recommended restaurant of the El Sapo Dorado Hotel, on the Monteverde road. Global and national dishes merge vegetarian and vegan options with Tico dishes, and organic produce is used in each inventive meal. The serene views over Nicoya from the terrace extend the sense of well being. If you have specific dietary needs, be sure to call ahead and the staff will be happy to oblige.
✉ Entrance to El Sapo Dorado hotel, Monteverde ☎ 506 2645 5010 ⓢ Daily 6.30–9.30, 12–3, 6–9.30 ✋ B US$7.50, L US$14, D US$20, Wine US$18

SOFIA

Without a doubt the best fine-dining option in the Monteverde area, this elegant yet unpretentious restaurant is overseen by chef-owner Karen Nielsen, who conjures magical fusion dishes with a *nuevo Latino* twist. The menu inlcudes dishes such as goat cheese *quesadilla* with roasted eggplant and tomato or seafood *chimichanga*. Time your visit for live music nights, ranging from choral to jazz. It is probably a good idea to reserve a table, too.
✉ Beside the bullring ☎ 506 2645 7017 ⓢ Daily 11.30am–9.30pm ✋ L US$12, D US$25, Wine US$20

PRICES AND SYMBOLS

The prices are for a double room for one night including breakfast, unless otherwise stated. All the hotels listed accept credit cards unless otherwise stated. Note that rates can vary widely throughout the year.

For a key to the symbols, ▷ 2.

ARENAL

ARENAL COUNTRY INN

www.arenalcountryinn.com

With views of Arenal Volcano, this is converted former working hacienda, set among tropical gardens, about 1km (0.6 miles) out of town. The large, fully equipped *cabiñas* have private bathrooms, safety deposit box, flat screen TV, air-conditioning, minibar and private terrace. Breakfast is served in the breezy open-air dining room—once a cattle-holding pen—and you can rest by the large pool before heading out to explore. Facilities for disabled guests are good. The service is excellent and it's probably Fortuna's best in-town inn.

✉ Apt 678 2010, Arenal ☎ 506 2479 0101 US$71–US$109 20 bungalows Outdoor On the road to San Ramón, 1km (0.6 miles) before La Fortuna church

ARENAL KIORO

www.hotelarenalkioro.com

Less than 1km (0.6 miles) east of Tabacón, this all-suite hotel is the premier resort in the region; it has unrivaled proximity to the volcano and it is known for its all-round luxury. Occupying a ridgeline at the base of the unnervingly close volcano, the lavishly appointed Kioro is designed to maximize guests' viewing experience in every regard. The spacious junior suites have walls of glass, rattan furnishings, satellite TV, direct-dial telephones, safes, as well as Jacuzzis for indulgent grandstand vistas. The deluxe marble-clad bathrooms have his-and-hers showers and sinks. The airy and elegant restaurant, serving excellent fusion fare, also has a wall of glass, as do the adjoining bar and the games room and gym. Thermal waters heat the twin swimming pools. A good list of activities includes horseback riding, mountain biking, fishing and boat tours, but the sumptuous spa is reason enough never to leave the property.

✉ Between Fortuna and Lake Arenal ☎ 506 461 1700 US$310–US$345 53 rooms Outdoor

ARENAL OBSERVATORY LODGE

www.arenalobservatorylodge.com

The only hotel on the south side of the volcano, this is also the highest and offers superb grandstand views. Dating back to 1973, the observatory was once a research station for the Smithsonian Institute, but now has 40 rooms, most with views of the volcano. Lodgings vary from basic rooms, with shared bath, in La Casona farmhouse, to the luxurious Smithsonian rooms with glass walls, tiled floors, separate dining areas and queen-size beds. The hotel also provides stunning views across the Río Agua Caliente valley and Lake Arenal.

✉ Between Fortuna and Lake Arenal ☎ 506 2479 1070 US$110–US$168, includes an early morning guided hike to Arenal Volcano (US$6) 40 Outdoor Four-wheel-drive vehicle recommended, but not essential along the stretch of 9km (5.5 miles) leading to the lodge (taxi-jeep from Fortuna US$12)

HOTEL LOS HÉROES (PEQUEÑA HELVECÍA)

www.hotellosheroes.com

Some 30km (18 miles) from Fortuna, this Alpine-style chateau is a wonderful blend of Tico hospitality

Opposite *The thermal baths at Tabacón Grand Spa Thermal Resort*

and Swiss patriotism. All the rooms have a private bathroom and views of the lake; some have a terrace. The main restaurant serves fondues and other Swiss classics, and a restaurant revolves through 360 degrees. Devotion to all things Swiss includes a 60cm (23.6in) gauge railway with a couple of diesel engines going up the hillside crossing two bridges and passing through a couple of tunnels for 2km/1.25 miles (three times a day, US$3), and a small yet beautiful private family chapel. Credit cards are not accepted.

Lake Arenal, Nuevo Arenal 506 2692 8012 US$65–US$115, including breakfast 12 rooms, 2 suites Outdoor

LA MANSION INN

www.lamansionarenal.com

The romantic La Mansion overlooks Lake Arenal, providing split-level bungalows with different levels of luxury. All rooms have lake-view terraces with sweeping panoramas and come with a CD player (you can borrow discs from the hotel). The price includes luxury breakfast with champagne, served in your room or in the terrace restaurant which specializes in European cuisine. Horses and canoes are available for guests to rent for a small charge. The impressive Royal Cottage has its own private infinity pool, Jacuzzi and gardens.

9km (5.5 miles) from Nuevo Arenal 506 2692 8018 US$225–US$495 16 bungalows, 4 suites, 1 cottage Outdoor It is a 45-minute drive from La Fortuna to the Mansion Inn, passing El Tabacón hot springs, then the dam. A dirt road leads straight to the inn, about 9km (5.5 miles) before Nuevo Arenal

TABACÓN GRAND SPA THERMAL RESORT

www.tabacon.com

Some 12km (7.5 miles) from La Fortuna, Tabacón Resort's hotel is on most Arenal tourist agendas for its thermal mineral pools (▷ 112). Rooms are spacious, with air-conditioning, cable TV, hair-dryer and bathrobes to slink around in while gazing at the views of the volcano. After visiting the mineral pools (free entry for hotel guests) you can have dinner at the reasonably priced restaurant. The Iskandria Spa provides all manner of beauty and relaxation treatments. Please note that some tour operators won't book guests into this hotel because it lies in the potential path of a lava flow should the Arenal volcano experience a sudden major eruption.

Tabacón 506 2479 2000, toll free in US 1-877 277 8291 US$322–US$513 including free access to the mineral pools 95 rooms, 11 junior suites

BIJAGUA

CELESTE MOUNTAIN LODGE

Opened in 2008 by Frenchman Joel Mitchell, this one-of-a-kind eco-sustainable property sits at the base of the Tenorio volcano with sensational views toward the Miravalles volcano, too. Made of sturdy steel beams, with a vast open-walled atrium lounge and restaurant, the hotel's cantilevered 21st-century architecture includes louvered wall-to-ceiling windows in stylish bedrooms. Gourmet "tico fusion" meals are served family style. Wheelchair-bound visitors are hauled along mountain trails in a special one-wheel rickshaw.

3km (2 miles) northeast of Bijagua 506 2278 6628 US$129 18 rooms

MONTEVERDE

MONTEVERDE LODGE

www.monteverdelodge.com

Climbing the hill from Santa Elena to Monteverde, a dirt road to the right leads to the Monteverde Lodge, owned by Costa Rica Expeditions. The spacious suites are rustically chic, and all have two double rooms and a private bathroom with solar-heated water. It's a graceful hotel, which impresses from the outside and has a vast lobby complete with open fire and a dining room with excellent views. The environmental considerations extend to the solar-heated Jacuzzi, set in a glass atrium. Package deals are available; children under 10 sharing a room go free.

Monteverde 506 2257 0766 US$110–US$190 27

EL SAPO DORADO

www.sapodorado.com

Coming along the gravel road from Santa Elena up to Monteverde, a steep road to the left arrives at the Golden Toad where the Tico/US owners reflect the synthesis of Costa Rican and Quaker traditions. Secluded suites each have a private bath with hot water showers: choose from Sunset Suites, overlooking the Nicoya Peninsula, the newest and largest Fountain Suites, with fridge, or Classic Suites, which have an open fire for the cooler months. In the restaurant (▷ 127), vegetarian options merge with traditional dishes. The lodge has its own trail that skirts the Monteverde reserve.

Monteverde 506 2645 5010 US$107–US$122 30 suites

PUERTO VIEJO DE SARAPIQUÍ

SELVA VERDE LODGE

www.selvaverde.com

One of the country's first wilderness lodges, Selve Verde still sets a standard to beat. Birding groups flock here for the excellent guided programs, and it also offers canoeing, plus a small butterfly garden. The forested riverside setting provides just the right jungle feel, and the simple yet spacious accommodations in stilt cabins put you in touch with the rain forest through glassless screened windows. Rooms in the Creek Lodge share bathrooms; those in River Lodge are most sumptuous and have private bathrooms.

Chilamate, 8km (5 miles) west of Puerto Viejo de Sarapiquí 506 2766 6800 US$110–US$135 45 rooms Outdoor

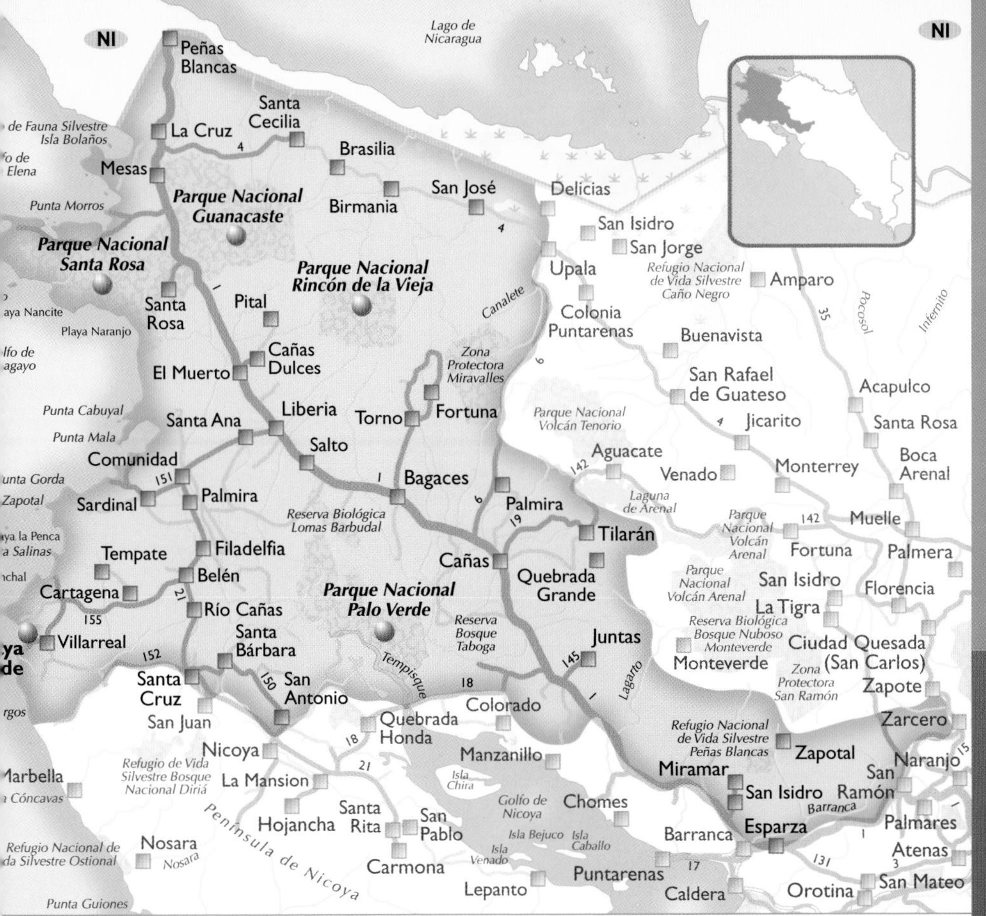

GUANACASTE

Whereas the rest of the country is clad in various lush shades of green, Costa Rica's uniquely dry northwest quarter is parched for six months a year, when dry forest species blossom in an explosion of gorgeous pastels. Cattle ranching is the main activity, and many haciendas around the historic town of Liberia double as ecological activity centers where guests can saddle up and/or ride ziplines and ATVs (quad bikes). In pre-Columbian times, this region was a thriving cultural center. Descendants of the Chorotega tribe keep a ceramic tradition alive in Guaitíl village.

The flatlands are framed to the east by volcanoes. Rincón de la Vieja National Park tempts hikers with trails to bubbling mud pools and hot springs, and an adventurous trek to the summit. At Las Hornillas Volcanic Activity Center, on Miravalles, you can even splash around in warm oozy mud. The relatively open forests guarantee fabulous wildlife viewing at Rincón de la Vieja, Palo Verde and Santa Rosa national parks—the latter centered on La Casona, an historic hacienda considered a National Treasure. Santa Rosa is also an important nesting site for marine turtles, which come ashore at dozens of beaches along Guanacaste's Pacific shore, notably at Playa Grande.

Guanacaste's gorgeous beaches boast accommodations from backpacker hostels to ultra-deluxe resorts, several of which have championship golf courses. Tamarindo, the largest resort, is the main base for surfing, a popular activity up and down the coast. Offshore, the warm waters teem with cetaceans, marlin and other game fish. No surprise, then, that the once sleepy fishing villages of Playas del Coco, Playa Flamingo and Tamarindo double as centers for scuba diving and sportfishing.

The Pan-American Highway slices north–south through the heart of Guanacaste, granting easy access to all the sites. Visitors can even fly direct from North America to Liberia's Daniel Oduber Quirós International Airport.

CENTRO DE RESCATE LAS PUMAS

http://laspumas.org

About 5km (3 miles) north of Cañas, this rescue center for wild cats displays all six species found in Costa Rica, including jaguars. Most animals were confiscated by the National Parks Service as illegal pets, or were injured or orphaned in the wild. Other mammals here include deer, foxes, monkeys and peccaries, and hundreds of parrots and other birds.

249 E4 Around 5km (3 miles) north of Cañas 506 2669 6044 Daily 8–5 Adult US$10, child US$5 Regular Liberia–Cañas buses will drop you off outside the entrance

GUAITÍL

Guaitíl is an easy excursion from Santa Cruz. The roads that meander throughout the Nicoya Peninsula are lined with rows of pots and plates, most of which are produced in Guaitíl. The people of this small town have retained the traditional skills for making the hand-built and oven-fired red and black pottery. More than 30 years ago, Coopearte, a women's cooperative, was formed by Hortensia Briceño, and Guaitíl and its pottery gained international recognition.

The tiny linear town has studios along the road and around the soccer field. If you're interested in the manufacturing process, you may be shown the techniques and the plants used.

249 C5 Seven buses daily from Tamarindo at 6.45am to Santa Cruz, then to Guaitíl every few hours. Hourly from Liberia, Nicoya to Santa Cruz and from San José Guaitíl is 12km (7.5 miles) southeast of Santa Cruz on the Santa Barbara road

JUNTAS DE ABANGARES

www.minatours.com

Fame flickered for this little town in the late 19th century when gold finds attracted prospectors.

A century later, a few prospectors still mine for gold, but the main attraction is a mining museum at La Sierra de Abangares (tel 506 2662 0033, Tue–Fri 8–5) with mining artifacts from the boom times, including the ruins of an old stamping mill *(mazos)* used to crush the ore. Around the mill, trails provide good opportunities for seeing some of the area's 90 species of birds.

In the middle of Juntas, details of the history of mining in Costa Rica are available at the office of Mina Tours (tel 506 2662 0753), whose owner's mother, Ofelia Gamboa Solorzano, is the daughter of one of the pioneers.

The road through Juntas is an alternative route—four-wheel drive advised—to Santa Elena and Monteverde for those traveling south from Guanacaste or using the Tempisque ferry.

249 E5 From Cañas to Juntas at 9am and 2pm Juntas lies east of the Pan-American Highway

LIBERIA

Guanacaste's provincial capital, Liberia, stands at the intersection of the Pan-American Highway and Highway 21 to the Nicoya Peninsula. Since 2002, when the international airport opened, the status of Liberia has soared, along with the number of visitors arriving directly from the US for instant Guanacaste gratification. Commercial interests have thrived, altering the town's colonial feel. Its traditional, white buildings, which evolved to survive the blazing heat that bakes the town in the dry season, now sit alongside glitzy shopping plazas, and are at their best on Calle Real.

At the end of the day, promenaders gather in the central plaza. On the main boulevard, between calles 10 and 12, is an equestrian statue dedicated to the horsemen of the plains.

248 C3 10 a day from San José's Tracopa terminal (▷ 55)

MIRAVELLES: LAS HORNILAS

www.lashornillas.com

Miravalles is the only volcano in Guanacaste not enshrined in a national park, and there are few trails. The western slopes are tapped for geothermal electricity, thanks to steaming underground waters that spout to the surface. Privately owned Las Hornillas Volcanic Activity Center has a trail around bubbling mud pools and fumaroles. You can even wallow in warm mud pools—a soothing tonic. It also has thermal swimming pools and a waterslide.

249 D3 506 8839 9769 Daily 8–5 US$20 Regular buses from Bagaces to Guayabo then jeep-taxi to Las Hornillas

Opposite *A walkway gives a view down to floor of the rain forest*
Below *Churning local clay in a large pestle at the pottery in Guaitíl*

INFORMATION

www.sinac.go.cr

248 C2 · 506 2666 5051 · Daily 8–4, by reservation only · US$6

You will need a four-wheel-drive vehicle to get to the park. From Liberia, the Pan-American Highway heads north towards the Nicaraguan border. After 42km (26 miles) a right turn, opposite the turnoff for Cuajiniquíl, leads onto a dirt track, from where it is 17km (10.5 miles) to the Maritza Field Station

TIPS

» You have to book basic dormitory accommodations at the three stations, Cacao, Maritza and Pitalla in advance with the Santa Rosa National Park administration (▷ 137).

» It is essential to call the national park office before setting out for the park as the biological stations may be closed.

» This is one of the least developed parks in Costa Rica, so be prepared for very basic conditions. You will need to take your own food unless you can make arrangements with park authorities.

» You can see Lake Nicaragua from the top of Volcán Orosi.

Above *Orosi volcano is in the park*

PARQUE NACIONAL GUANACASTE

The lynchpin of the Guanacaste Conservation Area, this remote national park has abundant birdlife and trails. Close to the Nicaraguan border, at Costa Rica's northwestern fringes, Guanacaste National Park, created in 1991 and linking two older parks, protects 34,651ha (85,622 acres), in an area covering the Orosi and Cacao volcanoes. The park includes rain forest, tropical wet forest, cloud forest and tropical dry forest. There is a network of hiking trails and a wildlife inventory of more than 140 mammal species, 300 bird species, 100 amphibians, 5,000 butterflies and 10,000 insects. With fewer visitors than other national parks, the rewards are great for those with the time and endurance to navigate this remote region.

TRAILS AND BIOLOGICAL STATIONS

Maritza Station is the most comfortable of the stations, and the closest to the Pan-American Highway. Leave the highway 10km (6 miles) north of the turning for Santa Rosa, opposite the turn for Cuajiniquíl. Trails from the station lead through gallery, dry and transitional dry-humid forest. Short trails of around two hours lead to the petroglyph site close to Cerro El Hacha, where you can see some 800 petroglyphs. You can walk to the summit of Cacao, a long day's walk. Higher up the slopes at 1,100m (3,609ft) above sea level is Cacao Station. Temperatures here are lower, rainfall higher and this part of the park has areas of transitional dry-humid forest and cloud forest. Access is from the Pan-American Highway, 23km (14 miles) north of Liberia at Potrerillos. If you want to trek between the park's stations, decide whether you want to start or end in relative comfort: Cacao Station is far more basic than Maritza and doesn't have electricity. A four-hour hike goes through cloud forest to the top of the volcano; check at the station for permission before setting out. Pitilla Station may be physically close to Cacao, but access is 28km (17 miles) east along Highway 4 from the junction with the Pan-American Highway, then south at Santa Cecilia along 9km (5.5 miles) of dirt road. It is one of the best spots for birding, but be prepared for basic conditions at the lodge.

PARQUE NACIONAL PALO VERDE

See thousands of birds wading through this watery wonderland and deciduous forest at the Lomas Barbudal Reserve. At the northernmost limits of the Gulf of Nicoya, the floodplains of the Tempisque River are protected by Palo Verde National Park, covering 18,651ha (46,068 acres). Lodges and haciendas scattered along the Pan-American Highway provide good bases for exploring the park. A journey this far is rewarded by excellent birding. The road leaves the Pan-American Highway at Bagaces, from where a four-wheel-drive vehicle covers the 28km (17.5 miles) to the Palo Verde Station. At the northern limits of Palo Verde National Park, Lomas Barbudal Biological Reserve protects precious tree species. The four-wheel-drive track for Lomas Barbudal is 10km (6 miles) north of Bagaces, along the Pan-American Highway, close to Pijije. The reserve's office is 6km (3.75 miles) down this road, which eventually joins the road to Palo Verde National Park. The park headquarters is within Palo Verde, 8km (5 miles) from the entrance. An off-road vehicle is required.

FLORA AND FAUNA

The park's 12 habitats, including marshes, lagoons, mangroves and forests, are home to the largest concentration of waterfowl and wading birds in Central America—275 resident and migrating species—and it is the country's only nesting site of the jabirú stork. Many of the bird species are found on the Isla de los Pájaros. Mammals are also abundant and 150 species of tree have been recorded. The annual raptor migration in October and November is a spectacular phenomenon.

Several trails in the park lead from the Palo Verde Biological Station, where accommodations are available. Some 6km (3.7 miles) along the Pan-American Highway, near San Joaquín, Hacienda Solimar (tel 506 669 0281) is a ranch recommended for birders.

RESERVA BIOLÓGICA LOMAS BARBUDAL

An important reserve for the protection of rare tree species, Lomas Barbudal includes mahogany, rosewood and the cortez tree, which blooms riotously a few days after a rain shower in the dry season. With seven habitats, Lomas Barbudal is home to 130 bird species, including the scarlet macaw. The reserve's savannas and dry forest support cacti and bromeliads, and the insect life is unusually rich.

INFORMATION

www.ots.ac.cr

248 D4 · 506 2200 0125

Reserve office: daily 8–4 · Palo Verde: US$10; Reserva Biológica Lomas Barbudal: donation requested

Accommodations are available at Palo Verde Biological Research Station · 506 661 4717

TIPS

» The area receives the largest concentration of waterfowl and wading birds between September and March, with a distinct dry season between December and March.

» The Lomas Barbudal reserve is at its most breathtaking in March when the cortez trees are ablaze with yellow flowers.

» In the dry season, wildlife concentrate near the depleted water supplies. One of the best ways to spot mammals is to wait quietly near a water hole.

» Instead of driving to the park from Bagaces, rent a boat from the town of Puerto Humo and journey upriver passing Isla de los Pájaros. Upstream from the park, crocodiles gather among the encroaching vegetation.

Below *White ibis fly over marshland in Parque Nacional Palo Verde*

PARQUE NACIONAL RINCÓN DE LA VIEJA

Steaming geysers, blue lagoons and bubbling mud emphasize the volcanic nature of this park, where wildlife thrives. More than 600,000 years old, Rincón de la Vieja volcano was formed by the eruption of several volcanic cones that eventually merged to become one, straddling the continental divide. The name means Old Lady's Corner; according to Guatuso legend, an old witch living on Rincón de la Vieja sends smoke skyward whenever she is annoyed. It is also believed that the park once served as a natural lighthouse for sailors off the Pacific coast. The last major eruptions occurred from 1966 to 1970, although there were minor eruptions in 1999, when it belched out ash clouds as far west as Santa Rosa National Park.

HIGHLIGHTS

Located in Guanacaste's cordillera, 27km (17 miles) northwest of Liberia, Rincón de la Vieja National Park protects 14,161ha (34,992 acres) of territory, ideal for hiking and horseback riding. The park lies astride the cordillera creating the conditions for a wide variety of species. Steaming mud pools, hot springs, steam vents and fumaroles have earned the park the nickname "Little Yellowstone." The main attractions lie between the Santa María and Las Pailas ranger stations, but exploring the park fully takes three days. There are hikes to the summit with fine views (on clear days) across the lowlands.

Most places of interest are reached from either the Las Pailas or Santa María Hacienda rangers' stations, which are linked by a path. The massif, rising to a height of 1,916m (6,286ft) at the Santa María volcano, is visible from Liberia, and the lower summit of Volcán Rincón de la Vieja has a lagoon at the southern end, which can be reached on a two-day trek. There are four ecosystems and 250 species of birds. Howler monkeys, armadillos and coatis are among the mammals. Ticks and other biting insects also abound. A number of trails lead from Las Pailas and Santa María Hacienda rangers' stations: the Enchanted Forest and Hidden Falls trails head to thermal pools, 3km (2 miles) from Santa María entrance. A 30-minute hike from the park office, there is a beautiful Prussian-blue lagoon: The intense hue is a result of the mineral properties of the stones lying beneath the water.

INFORMATION

248 D2 ☎ 506 2200 0296
US$10, an extra US$3 toll for the access roads to the parks entrances
There are two routes into the park: the southern route, which has less traffic, goes from Puente La Victoria on the western side of Liberia and leads, in about 25km (15.5 miles), to the Santa María sector, closest to the hot springs. The northern route turns east off the Pan-American Highway 5km (3 miles) northwest of Liberia to Curubandé. Beyond Curubandé, you reach Posada El Encuentro, cross the private property of Hacienda Lodge Guachipelín (US$3 for road maintenance), and beyond Rincón de la Vieja Mountain Lodge Taxi from Liberia US$30–US$40. Hotels in Liberia will book a taxi for US$15 per person, minimum 6 people; depart at 7am, 1 hour to entrance, return at 5pm

TIPS

» At the summit, the Laguna Jilgueros is a good site for spotting wildlife, including tapirs.
» Take insect repellent; the water provides a breeding ground for mosquitoes.
» Do not drink water from the streams; volcanic springs contain high levels of chemicals.

PARQUE NACIONAL SANTA ROSA

INTRODUCTION

Home to La Casona, a symbol of Costa Rica's national pride, this park has open dry tropical forest where wildlife is relatively easy to see. At Playa Nancite you can watch sea turtles come ashore to nest.

Tucked in the northwestern corner of Costa Rica, 48km (30 miles) south of the Nicaraguan border, Santa Rosa National Park holds a special place in the hearts of local and international visitors for its historical and natural importance. The National Park has grown to encompass the 38,673ha (95,560 acres) of the entire Santa Elena Peninsula, and now protects the largest remaining area of dry tropical forest in Central America. South along the coastline, Playa Naranjo is one of Costa Rica's most beautiful beaches, and one of the hardest to reach. The historical significance of the region is an essential part of the national identity. Some 7km (4.5 miles) from the entrance of the park is the Casona de Santa Rosa, which resonates with every Costa Rican as the site of the country's struggle in 1856 against William Walker's attempts to take over and unite Central America. Tragically, La Casona was almost completely destroyed by fire in May 2001, but has since been rebuilt as an exact replica. While it is possible to reach Santa Rosa National Park by bus, the reforestation zone of Murciélago is more difficult to access, and a four-wheel-drive vehicle is essential for navigating the region. Visitors can camp at the administrative entrance to the park from where a number of short trails lead out and a detailed trail map is available. Within the more remote Murciélago sector is Playa Blanca, a white sand beach that you can visit in the dry season in a four-wheel-drive vehicle. At other times of the year you will need permission from park authorities. Access to the beautiful and deserted turtle-nesting beach of Playa Nancite is restricted to biologists only owing to the importance of the seasonal *arribadas* (arrivals).

As early as 1663, the land that now forms the Santa Rosa National Park was treasured for cattle raising with the founding of a ranch in the area. The inauguration of the National Park in 1971 saw a shift away from ranching to conservation for the coastal region, which was complemented by the creation of the Guanacaste and Rincón de la Vieja national parks. The creation of the Rincón Cacao Biological Corridor added the final piece of a migratory corridor that incorporates nine of the twelve ecosystems found in Costa Rica, leading

INFORMATION

248 B2 Park administration: 506 2666 5051 Open 24 hours, but the entrance may be barred to traffic before 8am US$10, surfers US$15 Any bus between Liberia and La Cruz will pass the entrance. For the Murciélago sector, buses leave Liberia for Cuajiniquíl at 5.30am and 3.30pm, returning at 7am and 4.30pm Follow the Pan-American Highway north of Liberia for 32km (20 miles), then turn west at the signpost. Access to the Murciélago sector is 10km (6 miles) north of the main entrance, via the road west towards Cuajiniquíl The park entrance sells maps, bird lists, a small brochure and museum guide

Above *Playa Naranjo is a popular surfing destination*
Opposite *A trail heads across a river in the Parque Nacional Rincón de la Vieja*

TIPS

» Isla Desnuda provides the best opportunities for wildlife spotting very early in the morning or late afternoon. Despite the low-level light, it should also provide the best opportunities for photography.

» Entrance to Playa Nancite is restricted to permit holders. Apply to the park authorities for a permit at least 20 days before your intended visit, but most permits are taken by researchers during the mass turtle nestings.

» The park has several *miradores* (lookout points) that provide wonderful panoramas revealing the region's vast frontier landscape and sheer diversity. The best views are from Mirador Tierras Emergidas and Mirador Yalle Naranjo, located en route from the administration center to Playa Naranjo and the coast.

» Behind La Casona, there are good views across the surrounding area.

» The small beach of Playa Blanca, with its pristine white sand, is one of the most isolated and beautiful beaches in Costa Rica and is also one of the safest bathing areas in the region.

Below *A capuchin monkey rests in a tree*

from the Pacific to the volcanic peak at Rincón de la Vieja, which rises to 1,916m (6,286ft).

In the world of conservation, the Area de Conservación Guanacaste (ACG—Guanacaste Conservation Area) is a beacon of hope, and in 1999 the Santa Rosa National Park was declared a UNESCO Natural World Heritage Site. Official estimates say the region protects some 235,000 species—more than exist in the entire US. Proving that conservation is an ongoing process, work continues to protect more of the area and add to the migratory corridor.

WHAT TO SEE

FLORA AND FAUNA

The immediate appeal of Santa Rosa National Park is the abundant and relatively easy-to-see wildlife. During the dry season, from November to May, the mainly deciduous trees shed their leaves and the animals depend on shrinking water holes until they dry up completely. The open dry tropical forest makes it easier to spot the white-tailed deer descending from the park's upper reaches and the dozing howler monkeys found within the park. Many unique species of tree can be seen, including the *pochote*—called the naked Indian—and the region's namesake, the *guanacaste*. There are estimated to be some 115 species of mammal in the park, including white-tailed deer, coatis, and spider and white-faced monkeys. In coastal regions, mangrove swamp is the predominant vegetation. Between August and December on Playa Nancite, the phenomenon of the *arribada* involves thousands of olive ridley turtles arriving on the beach. To the north, the Murciélago sector, reached through Cuajiniquíl, protects over 70 species of bat found in this part of the park.

LA CASONA

The Santa Rosa Hacienda—La Casona—has become an essential visit for every Tico. Records show the property was created in 1663, but the strategic significance of the region was bought to the fore by the prying eyes of American filibuster William Walker (▷ 41). In the 1850s, Walker saw the hacienda as an essential foothold for his imperialist ideals. An advocate of slavery, he believed the independent aspirations of Central America had strayed too far from the interests of its northern neighbor. Having walked into Nicaragua and gained the presidency, Walker's attention turned to Costa Rica, next step to the south. His attempts to conquer Costa Rica were started at, and floundered at, La Casona. The Costa Ricans, under the leadership of José María Cañas, defeated Walker's band of filibusters on the afternoon of March 20, 1856. The strategic significance of the area was reinforced again in 1919, when troops marched from Nicaragua to overthrow President Federico Tinoco, and again in 1955 during the presidency of José Figueres Ferrer "Don Pepe." On both occasions the invading troops were defeated.

History made this unassuming hacienda building important, but that importance led to its destruction. The arson attack of May 2001, by a couple of vengeful hunters angry that hunting was banned in the park, completely destroyed the collection of military paraphernalia and exhibits recording the lifestyle and events that took place at La Casona. The building was reconstructed using money raised through private donations from Ticos outraged at such a sacrilegious act. Restoring La Casona to its former glory was an impossible dream, but the addition of original features, including late 19th-century roof tiles salvaged from the flames, have added a historical aura to an otherwise sterile replica.

TREKS, TRAILS AND BEACHES

Behind La Casona, the short (1km/0.6-mile) Indio Desnudo (Naked Indian) nature trail, with annotated signposts, takes a loop through fine stands of dry tropical forest past the red peeling bark of the gumbo limbo tree. Sendero Los

Patos, which begins 5km (3 miles) beyond the National Park administration center, provides good opportunities for wildlife spotting. The Tierras Emergidas trail runs parallel to the entrance road. The longest feasible one-day trek is to Mirador Valle Naranjo, some 6km (4 miles) from the administration buildings. Longer treks to Playa Naranjo and Playa Nancite (access to Playa Nancite is restricted, see below) require an overnight stay and should be booked with the administration offices. (There is a four-wheel-drive track leading to both beaches, but do not rely on being able to use it. Many vehicles get stuck!) The trek descends gently over 12km (7.5 miles), moving through dry tropical forest and a multitude of butterflies. By the time you reach the lower altitudes, your eye will be well trained in spotting the iguanas, crabs and monkeys that are much in evidence. With luck, you may even see green macaws, white-lipped peccaries, tapirs and possibly pumas, which are reported to be increasing in number in the park. A left fork leads to Playa Naranjo, which has more trails than Playa Nancite. Toward the southern end, Sendero Carbonal leads to the brackish Limbo Lagoon, where you may find the American crocodile.

Playa Naranjo itself is awesome. Stretching around the bay, it is a popular surfing spot. In the bay is the surfing high spot of Witches' Rock—one of the oldest geological formations in Costa Rica, dated at 680 million years old.

Above *A gnarled tree in the dry tropical forest of Parque Nacional Santa Rosa*

PLAYA NANCITE

Playa Nancite is treasured as the nesting site of three species of sea turtle, the largest at almost 2m (6.5ft) in length being the leatherback and the second largest the green turtle. The olive ridley may be smaller, but makes up for it in sheer numbers, arriving in thousands in an incredible natural phenomenon. At night from August to December, thousands of olive ridleys gather in the offshore waters, enduring a mating cycle that lasts up to nine hours. After mating, the female turtles arrive in thousands over a three- to seven-night period and each deposits between 90 and 120 eggs in deep nests where they incubate in the sand for 50 days. After hatching, the young turtles struggle to the surface, then cross the beach to the treacherous coastal surf. All manner of terrestrial and marine predators feast on the young during this dangerous trek. The vast number of eggs produced in one small space gives each individual a greater chance of survival. Estimates suggest that at the peak of the *arribadas* (arrivals) as many as 75,000 turtles may nest on the beach, before migrating as far north as Mexico and south to Peru. They return every two or three years. Researchers at the Santa Rosa Investigation Center have been studying the phenomenon since it was first discovered in 1972.

In recent years, figures suggest the numbers of olive ridleys arriving at Nancite have been increasing after a sharp decline, the causes of which remain unknown.

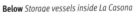

Below *Storage vessels inside La Casona*

MORE TO SEE

BAHÍA JUNQUILLAL WILDLIFE REFUGE

This refuge is also part of the Santa Rosa National Park. It's a popular spot with local families. There is a peaceful, pleasant beach with facilities for camping.

BAHÍA DE SALINAS

From the Murciélago sector of the park, a dirt road continues north, eventually reaching one of the quietest corners in the country, Salinas Bay (a four-wheel-drive vehicle is essential, even in the dry season). Locals claim that the beaches of Jobo and Rajada are the best in the country.

AIRSTRIP

Close to Cuajiniquíl is the airstrip built by Oliver North during the 1980s to supply the Nicaraguan Contras. It was built on a property formerly owned by the Nicaraguan leader, Somosa, before it was purchased for the National Park.

PLAYA GRANDE

Playa Grande and Parque Nacional Marino las Baulas de Guanacaste are important nesting sites for turtles. Beautiful Playa Grande's appeal is clear. Stretching like a golden carpet into the distance, the beach is as popular with surfers as it is with leatherback turtles. It is considered to be one of the best surf spots in the country; the beach forms the most western point of the Nicoya Peninsula and receives swells from the north, south and west. Along the coast of a peninsula created by Tamarindo's estuary, 485ha (1,198 acres) of beach and mangrove swamps are protected in the Parque Nacional Marino las Baulas de Guanacaste, with an additional 22,000ha (54,360 acres) covering the marine reserve.

PARQUE NACIONAL MARINO LAS BAULAS DE GUANACASTE

Away from the beach, the estuarine waters of the national park protect mangrove swamps, where all six Costa Rican mangrove species are found. From a drifting boat you can see a great deal of wildlife, including caiman, crocodiles and roseate spoonbills. Created to protect the nesting habitat of the leatherback turtle, Marino las Baulas de Guanacaste National Park has successfully reduced the poaching of turtle eggs from the beaches of Playa Grande. But while the local solution may be working, the broader global picture does not bode well. There has been a dramatic drop in the numbers of leatherbacks in the park (▷ 28). In 1988, the annual *arribadas* saw 1,365 females coming on shore to lay their eggs; by 2003, this figure had fallen to 155 before rebounding in 2005, when more than 400 arrived, but numbers have fallen to below 100 in the past few years. Growing to a massive 2m (6.5ft) in length and weighing as much as half a ton, mature females arrive at the beach between October and March, where they haul themselves up the beach to deposit between 80 and 100 eggs the size of table-tennis balls before returning to the ocean, exhausted. Turtle-watching tours are usually arranged from, and begin in, Tamarindo, a short boat trip across the mouth of the estuary. The national park office, at the town's entrance, runs trips to the beach in the nesting season. The beach is closed 6pm–6am, except for guided turtle-viewing tours (US$10, by reservation only), and fines are issued for anyone found on the beach without permission.

INFORMATION

248 A4 Park office: 506 2296 7074 US$10 (6am–6pm) Buses from Tamarindo to San José stop at Huacas, from where it is 9km (5.5 miles) to Playa Grande Playa Grande is 1 hour by car from Liberia. From the junction at Huacas the main road leads straight ahead to Matapalo and after 9km (5.5 miles) to Playa Grande Taxi from Huacas costs around US$10

TIPS

» At low tide, it is a beautiful walk (30 minutes approximately) along Tamarindo beach to Playa Grande. At high tide, river taxis will take you across the estuary (US$1) or, like the surfers, you can swim across. There are beach clubs and bars at the southern end of the beach.

» Take care when swimming as the current can be strong.

» Break-ins of parked cars is common. Do not leave any items in your car.

Above *The beach is a leatherback turtle nesting site and is popular with surfers*

PLAYA TAMARINDO

www.crparadise.com

Some five hours' drive from San José, and just 90 minutes from the Daniel Oduber Quirós airport in Liberia, Tamarindo has grown from a small village to an extremely popular sun and surf destination. Sunsets draw out all sections of Tamarindo society at dusk to watch the sinking sun. Either side of the magic moment, Tamarindo is a flurry of activity. While the town is driven by surfing, an increasingly upscale blend of hotels, bars and restaurants makes it a good beach stop.

The beach is attractive, with a craggy coastline fringed with tamarind trees. Beach hikes lead south from Tamarindo to Playa Langosta, then south to Playa Avellanas and Playa Negra. If you are lucky, you may see monkeys. To the north, a 3km (2-mile) walk takes you to Playa Grande (▷ 140), a leatherback nesting site. Aquatic activities are many and varied, but watch out for strong tides in places. Tamarindo's three surf breaks make it a good place for beginners. Snorkeling, kayaking, sailing and fishing can also be arranged. You can easily walk around Tamarindo, but mountain bikes and scooters are available for rent from the main street, running parallel to the beach.

248 A4 On the main road in Playa Conchal ☎ 506 2653 2251, daily 8–6 Shuttle bus services (▷ 54, 55) with Fantasy Bus Grayline and Interbus between Tamarindo and San José (US$35), Jacó and Sámara

PLAYAS DEL COCO

One of Guanacaste's northernmost beaches, Playas del Coco is a lively beach community, with a rash of hotels to suit all budgets. Restaurants range from humble spots to temples of gastronomy. Unlike Tamarindo to the south, a more sedate vibe prevails, as Playas del Coco is a popular destination for Costa Ricans on the weekends. Coco is one of the country's most popular dive spots, with operators providing courses and trips to more than 30 dive sites within a 20-minute boat ride from town (▷ 145). The town is also a departure point for trips to Witches' Rock (▷ 139, 234), and is a good base for sportfishing. For more peace and solitude, head 3km (2 miles) southwest of Coco to Playa Ocotal, where rocky headlands shelter tiny coves that have been developed as dive sites and provide excellent snorkeling. Often considered the poor relation of Tamarindo, Playas del Coco's profile will change if investors get permission to build a marina here.

248 B3 Daily buses from San José Tracopa terminal via Liberia Leave the Pan-American Highway at Liberia, where a left turn on Highway 21, passing Daniel Oduber Quirós airport, leads west for 35km (22 miles) to Playas del Coco

REFUGIO DE FAUNA SILVESTRE ISLA BOLAÑOS

www.sinac.go.cr

Close to Nicaragua's border, in Salinas Bay, Isla Bolaños Wildlife Refuge is a small island reserve protecting 25ha (62 acres) of stunted forest. Protected status is afforded to this barren land because it is one of Costa Rica's few nesting sites of the brown pelican, and the only known nesting site of the American oystercatcher. You may also see graceful frigatebirds. Access is limited during the nesting season, but you can walk around the island at low tide. Boat trips can be organized from Puerto Soley.

248 B1 ☎ Area de Conservación Guanacaste: 506 2666 5051 During the nesting season (Jan–Mar) no visits are permitted. Contact Area de Conservación Guanacaste or the National Park service in San José (☎ 506 2248 2451) for access during the rest of the year US$6

REFUGIO NACIONAL SILVESTRE PEÑAS BLANCAS

www.fpncostarica.org

Peñas Blancas National Wildlife Refuge is one of the least-visited protected areas of Costa Rica. The reserve extends to 2,400ha (5,930 acres) and is distinctive for its rugged volcanic terrain and white rock deposits of diatomite, composed of skeletal remains of planktonic algae. Covering altitudes from 600m (1,968ft) to 1,200m (3,937ft), the refuge includes tropical dry, semi-deciduous and premontane forest. The region was once logged, but visitors can still enjoy the birds and butterflies, and may see peccaries or deer. There are no services in the park, but wilderness camping is allowed. Getting to the refuge is difficult without private transportation.

253 F5 ☎ Fundación de Parques Nacionales: 506 2257 2239. Area de Conservación Pacífico Central (ACOPAC): 506 2416 7068 Daily 8–4 US$6 Leave the Pan-American Highway east of Esparza, at Macacona, and head north to Peñas Blancas. There is a trail to the refuge from Peñas Blancas, but take a topographical map

Below *A small tour boat is just putting out to sea from Playa Tamarindo where several pleasure craft are moored offshore*

GUANACASTE'S NORTHWESTERN BEACHES

Guanacaste's remote beaches have become more popular since the opening of the international airport at Liberia. This tour takes in some of the best. You can choose which to see and where to stop. Take your time and spend a couple of days in the area.

THE DRIVE
Distance: 96km (60 miles)
Allow: 1 day
Start/end at: Playas del Coco/Tamarindo

★ Head west from Liberia for 20km (12.5 miles) to a main junction at Comunidad. Take the right fork and follow signs for Playas del Coco, Playa Panama and Playa Hermosa. Continue past Sardinal for another 14km (8.5 miles) until you come to another junction; follow signs to the right. The first turnoff leads to Playas del Coco (▷ 141).

❶ Playas del Coco is the original beach escape for Joséfinos. Laid-back during the day, the pace picks up by night. The narrow, gray sand beach, while pleasant, is nothing special. The village has a lively nightlife, plus many operators offering diving and sportfishing trips.

At the entrance to Playas del Coco a street to the left heads south, with a sign for Ocotal; look for Rich Coast Diving on the corner (▷ 145). Take this road to a T-junction, then turn right. Follow the signs to Ocotal, and take the left-hand turn when you get to the junction bisected by a large tree. It is 3km (2 miles) from Coco to Ocotal.

❷ Playa Ocotal is a more secluded bay than its northern neighbor, without the easy access. The rocky headlands have made it a rewarding dive site. Snorkeling at the southern stretch is excellent when the water is clear, and it is good for swimming.

From here you have two options. You can return to the main road leading from Highway 21 to Playas del Coco and continue for 10km (6 miles). A right spur heads north to Playa Hermosa, which can be reached from two side roads from the main road.

❸ Playa Hermosa, on the southern tip of Bahía Culebra, is a golden beach good for swimming and general watersports. With a west-facing beach, the sunsets are impressive, and cruises are popular at twilight. The resort is evolving rapidly.

Some 5km (3 miles) past Playa Hermosa, you come to the most northern of the Guanacaste beaches, Playa Panama.

❹ The development of Playa Panama and the Bahía Culebra is driven by the state-sponsored Papagayo Project. It has seen the beginnings of a transformation of this scenic bay into a collection of mega-resorts and high-rise apartments. With investment by Mexican and European companies, the place is intended to become the largest leisure city in Central America. The effect that such development will have on the area, and the demand for water in the country's driest region, has led to much criticism from environmentalists.

Or, after visiting Playa Ocotal, return to the main junction at Comunidad

Opposite *Enjoying the beautiful white sands of a Costa Rican beach*

then head south for 11km (7 miles) to Belén. From Belén, it is a 24km (15-mile) drive to the village of Huacas, and several popular beaches to the north, west and south. At Huacas, take the northern fork. The road follows the coast past Playa Conchal, Playa Brasilito, Playa Flamingo, Playa Potrero and distant Playa Pan de Azúcar.

❺ The white bay of Playa Conchal, or Shell Beach, made up of tiny shells, is good for swimming and snorkeling in its clear waters.

The vast Paradisus Playa Conchal Beach & Golf Resort occupies the land behind the beach. It is easier to approach Playa Conchal from Playa Brasilito to the north.

❻ The beach at Playa Brasilito is not overly attractive, but good transportation and a range of services make it a useful base if you want to explore this part of the coast on a tight budget.

If you've had enough driving for one day, head straight for Playa Grande (see ❾) at this point. Otherwise, continue through Brasilito and take the paved road as it turns right and continue on for 3km (2 miles), following the signs for Playa Flamingo. Turn left along the beach, heading toward the group of hotels on the mountainside to the left.

❼ Playa Flamingo has traditionally been the sportfishing capital of the peninsula; however, its large marina was closed down by health authorities in 2006. A beautiful white sand beach (originally known as Playa Blanca) is the main draw, but the town has a good collection of services, comfortable hotels and fine-dining restaurants. Nestling in the hills are the homes of the Hollywood glitterati. Despite the name, there are no flamingos here.

Just before Flamingo beach there will be a turnoff to the right with signs to Playa Potrero. Continue along the 3km (2-mile) dirt road, which is in relatively good condition.

❽ The dark sand beach of Playa Potrero, beyond the rocky headland, stretches north from Playa Flamingo. A pleasant 3km (2-mile) walk north of Potrero is Playa Penca and, beyond it, the forest-fringed sandy bay of Pan de Azúcar, reached with an offroad vehicle

Return to the main Highway 21, back at the Huacas junction, which leads straight ahead to Matapalo and after 9km (5 miles) to Playa Grande The last 5km (3 miles) are on an unpaved road.

❾ Playa Grande (▷ 140) is a quiet, extensive beach area, popular with surfers and leatherback turtles. Along the coast of a small peninsula created by the Tamarindo Estuary, 485ha (1,198 acres) of beach and mangroves are protected in the Parque Nacional Marino las Baulas de Guanacaste.

From Playa Grande it is a delightful 30-minute walk south to Tamarindo. At high tide you will need to take a short water taxi ride across the estuary (US$3). However, by car you will need to return to Huacas and turn south for Villareal, then turn west to reach Tamarindo.

❿ The hectic surf town of Playa Tamarindo is very popular and is the largest beach resort in the region. The expatriate community is serviced by restaurants, bars and shops lining the main street. Heading south, beyond the headland is the idyllic Playa Langosta. To avoid crowds, stay in Playa Grande.

WHERE TO EAT

PAPAGAYO STEAKHOUSE & SEAFOOD
✉ 200m (220 yards) before the beach Playas del Coco, ▷ 141
☎ 506 2670 0298

MARIE'S
▷ 148.

GREAT WALTINI'S
▷ 148.

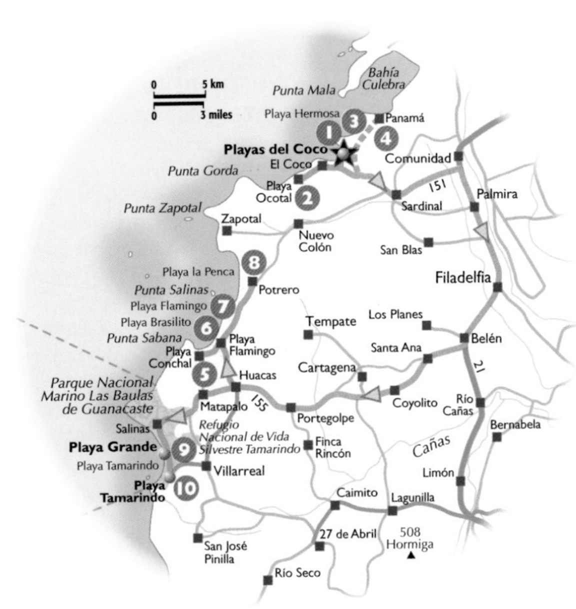

CAÑAS

SAFARIS COROBICÍ

www.nicoya.com

This company specializes in scenic rafting trips, which focus less on the thrills and spills and more on contemplation of the natural setting, improving the chances to see wildlife. This is a good option for all the family.

✉ Cañas ☎ 506 2669 6091 🕐 Hourly trips 7–3 ✋ US$37 for 2 hours, US$60 for 4

GOLFO DE NICOYA

ISLA CHIRA

Not many visitors make the boat trip from Puntarenas or Puerto Moreno to visit this large and barely populated island in the middle of the Gulf of Nicoya. Yet it's a fascinating study, not least for its salt ponds, picked upon by herons, roseate spoonbills and other waders; and for its frigate bird and pelican rookeries in the mangroves.

LIBERIA

AFRICA MÍA

www.africamia.net

Making the most of Guanacaste's African-like savanna, this theme park opened in 2006 as a recreation of the East African plains, with zebras, ostriches and antelope. Tours are offered in a safari-style bus.

✉ 7km (4.5 miles) south of Liberia ☎ 506 2666 1111 🕐 Daiy 8–6 ✋ Adult US$18, child US$12

PARQUE NACIONAL RINCÓN DE LA VIEJA

HOTEL HACIENDA GUACHIPELÍN

www.guachipelin.com

This cattle ranch, bordering Rincón de la Vieja National Park, focuses on sustainable tourism. It offers a range of activities in a stunning natural setting. A one-day Guachipelín adventure pass covers all the activities and attractions, from snorkeling to horseback riding and a canopy zipline.

✉ Parque Nacional Rincón de la Vieja ☎ 506 2666 8075 ✋ Guachipelín adventure pass US$75

PLAYA AZUL

LA VIDA SPA

www.thesanctuaryresort.com

Aimed at burned-out executives, La Vida Spa offers treats such as Swedish massages, facials, manicures, pedicures and holistic therapies, including reiki. Seven themed pools feature various treatments: the Polynesian pool is filled with green tea and ginger; the Costa Rican pool has warm, mineral-rich Costa Rican mud. Rooms cost from US$110 per night.

✉ The Sanctuary Resort, Playa Azul, Nosara ☎ 506 2682 8111

PLAYA CONCHAL

GARRA DE LEÓN

www.solmelia.com

Garra de León is, in the resort's own words, an "eco-golf experience course," with broad fairways and Pacific views. The par-72 course offers four sets of tees. The cart is included in the price, and private instruction is offered.

✉ Playa Conchal Beach and Golf Resort, Playa Conchal ☎ 506 2654 4123

✋ 18 holes in high season from US$150 for guests, non-guests US$195. Guests age 17 and under play free

PLAYAS DEL COCO

FLOR DE ITABO

www.flordeitabo.com

While Playa Flamingo to the south

Opposite *Sailing in Papagayo Bay*

gets the main sportfishing business, the Flor de Itabo hotel in Coco (▷ 150) has a good reputation, with professional captains and all the gear if you want to charter a boat. A variety of multi-day big game fishing trips can be arranged.
✉ PO Box 32, Playas del Coco ☎ 506 2670 0292 ✋ Boat charter from US$650 per day; six days big game fishing from US$775 per person for group of four

OCOTAL DIVING SAFARIS
www.ocotalresort.com
One of the oldest and most respected dive companies in the region, Ocotal offers trips to the Bat Islands—great for spotting big pelagics such as whale sharks and, for truly lucky divers, swordfish. Guests at the Ocotal resort get a free dive daily, and it also has snorkeling, sailing and fishing.
✉ El Ocotal Beach Resort & Marina ☎ 506 2670 0321 ✋ Dive packages begin at US$682 for five nights, with two days' diving

RICH COAST DIVING
www.richcoastdiving.com
Rich Coast is run by experienced divemasters Martin and Brenda van Gestel. As well as PADI courses, they offer packages, direct or booked through hotels in Coco, starting from two-tank dives at US$80. Dives at Las Islas Catalinas cost US$110. There are also fishing, sailing and snorkeling trips.
☎ 506 2670 0176. In the US and Canada 1-800-4-DIVING

PLAYA FLAMINGO

ECOTRANS
www.ecotranscostarica.com
This company specializes in eco-adventures throughout the region, from ziplining and kayak trips to nature tours of Palo Verde National Park and float trips on the Corobicí River. It's a handy one-shop provider and can also provide minibus transfers.
✉ 200m (220 yards) south of the marina, Playa Flamingo ☎ 506 2654 5151

FLAMINGO EQUESTRIAN CENTER
http://equestriancostarica.com
Bilingual instructor Amanda Gardner offers a wide range of classes in basic horsemanship, dressage and jumping for all ages and levels. Workshops are held throughout the year.
✉ Calle Antigua, Playa Flamingo ☎ 506 8846 7878 ✋ Horseback ride US$35 per person

SHANNON SAILING
www.flamingobeachcr.com
the cruising yacht *Shannon* has hosted nautical adventures off Guanacaste since 1991, allowing close encounters with the region's abundant marine life, including dolphins, rays and whales. The half-day snorkeling and sunset cruise includes a sail to Playa de Amor and guided snorkels. There are surfing trips to Ollie's Point, "extreme sailing," and live-aboard diving expeditions to Isla del Coco.
✉ Las Brisas Center 1, Playa Flamingo ☎ 506 2653 8437 ✋ Sunset cruise US$75

PLAYA GRANDE

LAS BAULAS NATIONAL MARINE PARK
Turtle-watching tours depart from Tamarindo and other northwestern beaches from November to March to Playa Grande. Trips leave at night and must be organized through hotels. Reservations can also be made at Las Baulas National Marine Park. During the nesting season, you must be accompanied by licensed guides on the beach at night.
✉ Playa Grande ☎ 506 2653 0470 ✋ US$16, plus park entrance and guide

PLAYA HERMOSA

DIVING SAFARIS OF COSTA RICA
www.costaricadiving.net
One of the longest-running dive operations in the country, the company offers all the standard dive options and some good packages mixing aquatic activities with land-based options. Most dives are within a 30-minute radius, with abundant marine species, including the promise of whale sharks.
✉ Playa Hermosa ☎ 506 2672 1259 ✋ From US$65 for a two-tank dive

PLAYA JUNQUILLAL

PARADISE RIDING
www.paradiseriding.com
Guanacaste is *sabanero* (savanna) heartland; many ranches offer horseback-riding tours. Criollo horses are available for all levels and most rides require no previous experience. Tours are from two hours to longer four-hour beach gallops. Guides are professional and bilingual.
✉ Playa Junquillal ☎ 506 2658 8162 ✋ US$25 for 2 hours, US$55 for 4 hours

PLAYA PANAMA

RESORT DIVERS OF COSTA RICA
www.resortdivers-cr.com
Resort Divers offers daily, half-day, two-tank dive trips which leave at 8.45am. Each dive is guided (bilingual) and limited to a group of no more than six divers. There are local dive sites and trips farther afield to the Catalina Islands and Isla de Murciélagos where bull sharks, cow-nosed rays and eagle rays proliferate. Puffer fish, parrot fish and sleeping turtles can also be glimpsed on a night dive. Scuba-diving courses are also offered, ranging from PADI open-water courses, to advanced and rescuer courses. Resort Divers also offers ATV (quad bike) tours and deep-sea fishing.
✉ Playa Panama ☎ 506 2672 0103 or 506 672 0106 ✋ Half-day from US$65

PLAYA TAMARINDO

AGUA RICA DIVING CENTER
www.tamarindo.com/agua
This professional and relaxed dive center runs PADI-certification courses. Pacific coast diving trips in the Tamarindo area are offered, but the zenith of Costa Rican diving is without doubt a live-aboard diving excursion to Isla del Coco, which is also available from Agua Rica. The multilingual guides provide excellent information.
✉ Centro Commercial Diriá ☎ 506 653 0094 🕒 Mon–Sat 9.30–6.30,

Sun 3.30–6.30 5-hour trip to Catalina Islands US$95

BAR 1

www.bar1tamarindo.com

This chic, open-air bar would fit right at home in New York or LA, with its sexy, sophisticated decor. Theme nights include movies on Tuesday, and a DJ spins techno, world beat and Latin tunes on weekends. Night nibbles include sushi.

Plaza Tamarindo, 200m (220 yards) south of La Rotunda 506 2653 2586 Daily 6pm–2am

CAPITÁN SUIZO STABLES

www.hotelcapitansuizo.com

Swiss owner Ursula Schmid is an avid rider and she maintains a superb stable opposite the hotel. Hourly rental costs a mere US$10 per hour, or opt for a guided ride if you prefer.

Hotel Capitán Suizo, Playa Langosta 506 2653 0075

CASAGUA HORSES

www.paintedponyguestranch.com

On the main road between Belén and Tamarindo, Casagua Horses is expertly run by American/Tico couple Kay Dodge de Peraza and Esteban Peraza. All ages and levels are welcome, and you can chose between Western- and English-style saddles. Tours range from countryside trails where you can see howler monkeys to the adults-only Cantina tour, which gives you the chance to play cowboy, riding along the old oxcart trails and visiting wild west towns. If you are staying in Costa Rica for a while, you can improve your horsemanship with private lessons and even learn the high-stepping Tope, Spanish-style.

Finca Casagua,in front of Rancho Cartagena, between Portegolpe and Lorena 506 653 8041 1–2 hour tour from US$30

COSTA RICA ART AND PAINTINGS

www.natalyn.com

The work of Tamarindo artist Natalie Lynn is divided into several themes, including nature, wildlife and Mayan symbolism, inspired by her trips to the Guatemalan jungle and Bali. Sea creatures and jungle critters abound in her vibrant, naive murals. Check out her work online and then contact her for a private appointment.

Playa Tamarindo 506 2653 0241 US$1,500–US$10,000

Below *Horseback riding along Playa Montezuma in Guancaste*

MANDINGO SAILING

www.tamarindosailing.com

Mandingo Sailing is run by German couple André and Maria Hammerschmidt, who offer cruises and snorkeling trips on board their schooner yacht, the *Lemuria*. Romantics are welcomed for the sunset cruise. On board you can look for cavorting dolphins, enjoy a glass of wine and wait for the heavenly Tamarindo sunset. From December to March you may see breaching humpback whales and sperm whales. Or spot pufferfish, rays and reef fish on a sail and snorkel trip.

Tamarindo Diriá Hotel, 200m (220 yards) from La Rotunda, Playa Tamarindo 506 8831 8875 Sunset cruise US$80 per person; half-day snorkel trip US$55 per person

MONKEY BAR

www.tamarindovistavillas.com

At the entrance to town, on the main road, this lively bar is a popular hangout among the local surfing community, with frequent live music of Latin, rock, jazz or blues, and amazing sunset vistas from its elevated vantage point. Meals come in large portions and the sociable and unpretentious vibe makes it a good place to meet people and talk beach breaks and swells.

Tamarindo Vista Villas, Playa Tamarindo 506 2653 0114 Daily 10–10

NIBBANA

www.nibbana-tamarindo.com

This beachside bar-restaurant, just behind Century 21 on the main road, has a Caribbean vibe by day with reggae playing. In the early evening, it plays host to surfers and livens up with searing cocktails and an ebullient party spirit. Pizzas, salads, sandwiches and fruit cocktails provide light refreshment until 6pm, and in the evening meat and seafood dishes are served. There is live music at sunset every Sunday, and an internet cafe.

200m (220 yards) from La Rotunda, Playa Tamarindo 506 2653 0447 Daily 7am–12am

OFF-ROAD ADVENTURES
www.offroadcostarica.com
Costa Rica's rugged terrain screams out to be explored in true "Indiana Jones" fashion. Take your pick of an open-top Toyota LandCruiser—yes, you get to drive—or a former U.S. Army truck for these four-wheel-drive adventures along mud tracks, with river fordings and pools to splash through (in wet season). Dry season trips can be dusty! After your rain forest safari, head to the beach for R&R, including volleyball, banana-boat rides and sea kayaking.
✉ Playa Tamarindo ☎ 506 2653 1969 ✋ US$75 by truck; US$150 by Toyota Land Cruiser. US$20 extra for a canopy zipline ride

PASATIEMPO
www.hotelpasatiempo.com
Set back from the main road, a 10-minute walk from the heart of town, this buzzing bar-restaurant in a rancho setting has large TV screens showing sports, a pool table and wide-ranging music. One of Tamarindo's best nights is Pasatiempo's Tuesday night open-mike jamming session.
✉ Take the left fork 100m (110 yards) before La Rotunda, Playa Tamarindo ☎ 506 2653 0096 🕒 Daily 8am–midnight

TAMARINDO BEACH CIGAR LOUNGE
The aroma of fresh tobacco leafs draws you into this handsome cigar lounge, with an adjunct room where skilled rollers turn raw leaves into fine cigars for export. The walk-in humidor displays several unique homegrown brands, such as La Flor de Palmares, boxed in a charming miniature *carreta*, or Costa Rica oxcart; and the Espresso, a flavorful *robusto* made of leaves aged with roasted espresso beans.
✉ On the Playa Langosta road, Playa Tamarindo ☎ 506 2653 0862 🕒 Daily, rollers: 8–5, bar: 4pm–midnight

TAMARINDO SPORT FISHING
www.tamarindosportfishing.com
Tamarindo is famed for its world-class sportfishing, and veteran skipper Randy Wilson offers crews and facilities. Catches, using his special catch and release technique for the conservation-minded angler, include marlin.
✉ 300m (330 yards) west of the entrance to Tamarindo airstip, Playa Tamarindo ☎ 506 2653 0090 ✋ Half-day trip from US$850, day trip from US$1,500

FESTIVALS AND EVENTS

MARCH

LIBERIA FIESTAS
A series of events taking place in Liberia featuring Guanacaste folklore, rides and concerts.
🕒 First week of March

JULY

ANNEXATION OF GUANACASTE
Guanacaste's decision in 1824 to be part of Costa Rica rather than Nicaragua is celebrated with fiestas in Liberia, folk dances, parades, bullfights, cattle shows and concerts.
✉ Liberia 🕒 July 25

PUNTA ISLITA

CASA SPA PUNTA ISLITA
www.hotelpuntaislita.com
Near to Corozalito, this spa resort offers more than 30 treatments that combine traditional therapies with the ancient beauty skills of the Chorotega indigenous groups. Modern Cleopatras can try the milk and honey massage, while the Piña Colada pedicure is a must for hike-ravaged feet. For all-out indulgence, finish with lunch at the 1492 restaurant. This spa does not cater to non-guests.
✉ Punta Islita ☎ 506 2661 4044 ✋ 4-night spa package from US$2,488

QUEBRADA GRANDE

CURUBANDA LODGE
www.curubanda.com
Snuggled in the saddle between Volcán Cacao and Volcán Rincón de la Vieja, this lodge occupies a 450ha (1,112-acre) *finca*, with its own forest reserve extending up the mountain slopes. Horseback rides are a specialty, and guided hikes lead up the slopes of Rincón de la Vieja. Its forte is agrotourism: you can even milk cows or help birth goats at the *finca's* 200ha (494-acre) cattle farm. Its elevation at about 700m (2,300 feet) is a breath of fresh air after the heat of the lowlands.
✉ Dos Ríos de Upala, 22km (13.5 miles) east of Portrillos, 23km (14 miles) north of Liberia ☎ 506 2691 8177

ROSARIO

TEMPISQUE SAFARI
www.tempisquesafari.com
This 90ha (222-acre) cattle *finca* and forest reserve on the banks of the Río Tempisque doubles as a wildlife rescue and breeding center. Crocodiles splash in a lagoon, scarlet macaws roost in the trees, and a zoo includes white-tailed deer, peccaries, wild cats, capybaras and monkeys. There's even an ostrich! Tours are by cart pulled by water buffalo, and include a boat trip along the banks of Palo Verde National Park.
✉ Rosario ☎ 506 2689 1069 🕒 Daily 9–4 ✋ US$20 per person

SANTA CRUZ

HACIENDA PINILLA
www.haciendapinilla.com
Less than one hour by car from Liberia's airport, this par-72 links golf course on the Pinilla hacienda has "the best greens in Central America," claims the course's PGA head golf professional David R. Vallejos. Four sets of tees cater to players of different abilities. Clubs and shoes are available for rental and the club provides lessons. The clubhouse has a bar and grill.
✉ Playa Langosta ☎ 506 2680 3000 ✋ 18 holes: US$85 for hotel guests; US$185 for non-guests, cart included

PRICES AND SYMBOLS

The restaurants are listed alphabetically (excluding El, Le, La and Les). The prices given are the average for a two-course lunch (L) and a three-course dinner (D) for one person, without drinks. The wine price is for the least expensive bottle.

For a key to the symbols, ▷ 2.

LIBERIA

PANADERÍA ALEMANIA

This open-air, German-run restaurant is far more than the bakery its name suggests. Shaded by a guanacaste tree, it offers an airy space for enjoying a cheap set-lunch *casado*, fresh seafood dish, or nightly special, followed by dessert, including apple strudel. It has a complete bakery selling fresh breads, pastries, cheesecakes, etc.

✉ Avenida Central, Calle 10 ☎ 506 2665 2061 ◷ Mon–Sat 7am–11pm, Sun 11–11 ✋ L US$9, D US$22, Wine US$18

RESTAURANTE PASO REAL

Facing the plaza in the heart of the city, this friendly seafood restaurant is a great place to select from a wide-ranging menu that spans King Neptune's larder. The ceviche is excellent, as are the Mexican-style shrimp jalapeños and the fish with brandy sauce. The fish of the day can be anything from mahi mahi to red snapper. The indoor restaurant has a large-screen TV and can get noisy when packed with locals; the place to be is the patio terrace overlooking the square.

✉ Avenida Central ☎ 506 2666 3455 ◷ Daily 11–10 ✋ L US$12, D US$20, Wine US$12

PLAYAS DEL COCO

SUELY'S

Two French sisters operate this tree-shaded, open-air restaurant, with wooden decks and a lively color scheme. The eclectic fusion menu is ever-changing, but might include such treats as tuna tartare, pan-seared brie, and a seafood medley featuring jumbo shrimp, mussels and scallops on saffron rice with a leek fondue drizzle. Desserts include the fabulous chocolate volcano.

✉ 1km (0.6 miles) west of Playas del Coco, on the road to Ocotal ☎ 506 2670 1696 ◷ Daily 11.30–11 ✋ L US$12, D US$28, Wine US$20

PLAYA FLAMINGO

MARIE'S

Marie's, on the beach, is one of Flamingo's most highly regarded restaurants. The evening chalkboard of specials lists the catch of the day. Appetizers include ceviche, and avocados stuffed with succulent shrimp. For breakfast, try the papaya pancakes with a bright orange flush, and for a quick, satisfying lunch there are good-value *casados*, fajitas and burritos. With a relaxed setting, excellent service and good prices, this is resort dining at its best.

✉ Playa Flamingo ☎ 506 2654 4136 ◷ Daily 6.30am–9.30pm ✋ B US$5, L US$12, D US$20, Wine US$13

PLAYA GRANDE

GREAT WALTINI'S

www.hotelbulabula.com

Run by American owners Wally and Todd, Great Waltini's is the liveliest dining spot in Playa Grande, drawing local expatriates for killer cocktails at the bar: the Jumbo-sized "Waltini Martini" and "Bert's Jumbo rum punch" will put you on your back! Fusing influences from throughout the Americas, the menu has everything from quesadillas and crabcakes to such entrees as filet of ahi tuna sautéed with white wine and garlic butter. Leave room for the "Siberia" chocolate drink dessert.

✉ Hotel Bula Bula (▷ 150) ☎ 506 2653 0975 ◷ Tue–Thu 5.30–8.30, Fri–Sat 5.30–9 ✋ D US$22, Wine US$18

PLAYA HERMOSA

THE BISTRO

www.lafinisterra.com

Overlooking Playa Hermosa, with lovely views framed by tamarind trees, this balcony restaurant is a great place to escape the heat. The nouvelle Costa Rican cuisine includes daily specials such as filet mignon with peppercorn sauce, and international staples like Caesar salad and pasta dishes.

✉ La Finisterra Hotel, 100m (110 yards) uphill from the Hotel Playa Hermosa ☎ 506 670 0227 🕒 Daily 10–10 ✋ L US$15, D US$25, Wine US$18

GINGER

Dramatically contemporary, this open-air tapas restaurant beneath a cantilevered glass canopy looks almost too hip to be true. The chic dining space wraps around a trapezoidal bar where all-too-diminutive cocktails are served. Canadian chef Anne Hegney Frey, however, delivers mouthwatering tapas with a light touch: fried calamari, exquisite ginger rolls and a ginger ahi tuna as soft as a sigh. Occasional wine tastings are hosted.

✉ 200m (220 yards) inland of the beach on the Playa Panama road ☎ 506 2672 0041 🕒 Tue–Sun 5–10 ✋ D US$32, Wine US$25

TAMARINDO

CAPITÁN SUIZO

Another chic hotel-restaurant (▷ 151) serving nouvelle dishes. The curving, open-air bar serves cocktails and is spacious enough for dining. The adjoining wall-less restaurant is airy, thanks to a soaring palenque roof. Service is relaxed yet professional, delivering fusion dishes that merge European and Pacific influences and ingredients. A favorite is tilapia in caper sauce.

✉ Capitán Suizo hotel, Tamarindo ☎ 506 2653 0975 🕒 Daily 7am–9.15pm ✋ L US$13, D US$26, Wine US$18

DRAGONFLY BAR AND GRILL

www.dragonflybarandgrill.com

Among the latest in a breed of nouvelle restaurants recently opened in Tamarindo by professional chefs, this one stands out, not least for its canvas canopy "roof" supported by glazed tree trunks and lit by romantic paper lanterns. Owner Tish Tomlinson and chef Kevin Mulry have combined talents to produce an exciting menu, ranging from beef satay with ginger soy sauce appetizer to main dishes such as pistachio-crusted mahi mahi and chili-rubbed pork chops with chipotle mashed potatoes. Divine!

✉ 100m (110 yards) north of Hotel Pasatiempo, Tamarindo ☎ 506 2653 1506 🕒 Mon–Sat 5–11pm ✋ D US$30, Wine $20

EL JARDÍN DEL EDÉN

The classiest restaurant in town, this delightful and chic thatched mezzanine restaurant overlooks a floodlit multi-tier pool and cascade. The marble-topped bar is a great place for cocktails before settling at a romantic booth or candlelit table to taste Peruvian chef Omar Grados's Pacific fusion delights: mussel soup with saffron and tenderloin flambé with martini are typical dishes.

✉ Hotel Jardín del Edén ☎ 506 2653 0137 🕒 Daily 12–10 ✋ L US$16, D US$35, Wine US$26

KAHIKI RESTAURANT

A 10-minute stroll from the middle of town, this American-owned restaurant draped with fairy lights delivers chalkboard specials of Asian-fusion fare. Oven-roasted, herb-rubbed pork tenderloin, seared tuna with wasabi cream and shrimp and calamari ceviche salads are some of the specials that might appear. The open-air dining area is informally stylish. No reservations. Credit cards are not accepted.

✉ 200m (220 yards) along the road to Playa Langosta, Tamarindo ☎ 506 2653 3816 🕒 Wed–Mon 11–2, 5–10 ✋ L US$10, D US$25, Wine US$15

NOGUI'S SUNSET CAFE

Right on the beach, this popular Tico-run cafe serves the best breakfasts in Tamarindo: three-egg omelets, stuffed tortillas, banana bread with cinnamon cream cheese and fruit and pancakes. For lunch there are tacos, pizzas, salads and sandwiches, including the best BLT in town. The real draw, however, is the beachside setting. Service can be slow, but always gracious.

✉ Beachfront, off La Rotunda, Tamarindo ☎ 506 2653 0029 🕒 Thu–Tue 6am–9.30pm ✋ B US$5, L/D US$10, no wine

OLGA'S COFFEE SHOP

There are many snack and coffee outlets in Tamarindo, but this is a tremendous newcomer. Named for its charming owner, it gets plenty of light through walls of glass. Free WiFi is an added reason to linger. Enjoy great granola and yoghurt breakfasts, organic salads, sandwiches and desserts.

✉ 100m (110 yards) west of Plaza Tamarindo ☎ 506 8395 5338 🕒 Mon–Sat 7–7, Sun 8–2 ✋ B US$5, L US$10

PANADERÍA DE PARIS

www.lalagunadelcocodrilo.com

At the northern end of town, the Panadaría de Paris is the mother of all bakeries in this part of the world. French owners Josette and Claude have imported their Parisienne pastry savoir faire. The aroma of freshly baked bread, croissants, pain au chocolat, tarts, cookies and banana bread drifts from the streetside bakery. For lunch there are baguettes and pizza or quiche slices. Credit cards are not accepted.

✉ Hotel La Laguna del Cocodrilo (▷ 151) ☎ 506 2653 0255 🕒 Daily 6am–7pm ✋ B US$5, coffee and cake US$5

RESTAURANTE SEASONS

www.hotelarcoiris.com

Gourmet Israeli chef Shlomy Koren is in charge at this chic restaurant. His menu is heavy on Mediterranean dishes, including some Levantine favorites, infused with a nouvelle twist. It's hard to resist such dishes as stuffed rigatoni with shrimp in creamy tomato sauce. Choose from a poolside patio or indoor dining.

✉ Arco Iris hotel ☎ 506 8368 6983 🕒 Daily 12–2, 6–10 ✋ L/D US$27, Wine US$20

PRICES AND SYMBOLS

The prices are for a double room for one night including breakfast, unless otherwise stated. All the hotels listed accept credit cards unless otherwise stated. Note that rates can vary widely throughout the year.

For a key to the symbols, ▷ 2.

PARQUE NACIONAL GUANACASTE

HACIENDA GUACHIPELÍN

www.guachipelin.com

This working cattle ranch at the base of the Rincón de Vieja volcano has become one of Costa Rica's leading activity centers, providing a back-to-nature experience. Former stables are now comfortable albeit simply appointed rooms with ceiling fans and views. The open-air restaurant serves regional dishes, and a second restaurant draws people for its folkloric music and dance. A pool and activities that include horseback riding, canyoneering, white-water rafting, tubing on rapids and a zipline tour provide an all-round vacation.

✉ Curubandé, 18km (12 miles) east of the Pan-American Highway and 8km (5 miles) west of the park ranger station ☎ 506 2666 8075 US$89 standard, US$100 superior 34 Outdoor

PLAYAS DEL COCO

FLOR DE ITABO

www.flordeitabo.com

On the road leading to the town, just 1km (0.6 miles) from Playas del Coco, this Italian-run hotel has accommodations ranging from standard and luxury rooms, to apartments, bungalows and suites. All have private bathrooms, air-conditioning and cable TV; deluxe rooms also have kitchenettes and master suites have Jacuzzis. Seafood and steaks are served in the restaurant, and the ceramic-tiled pool has a swim-up bar. The hotel specializes in sportfishing, and there's a casino (7pm–2am). The hotel offers free transfers from Daniel Oduber Quirós airport in Liberia.

✉ PO Box 32, Playas del Coco ☎ 506 2670 0292 Standard double US$85, deluxe suite US$135, apartments (sleeping six) US$145 Outdoor

LA PUERTA DEL SOL

www.lapuertadelsolcostarica.com

Hidden down a side road, there's a family feel to this Italian-run place. The suites all have a living room, bathroom, air-conditioning and fan, telephone and safe box. The pool can be used for free scuba try-outs. Enjoy good homemade pasta in the Italian restaurant.

✉ 100m (110 yards) from the beach at the northern end of town, Playas del Coco ☎ 506 2670 0195 US$88–US$110 10 Outdoor

PLAYA GRANDE

HOTEL BULA BULA

www.hotelbulabula.com

Near the southern end of the beach, beside the tiny dock for Tamarindo, this lively hotel is set in exquisite gardens with a small pool. Owners Walt and Todd run it with loving care that extends to the decor and unusual touches, such as fresh-cut flower arrangements in rooms, and batik sarongs provided for around the pool. The restaurant, Great Waltini's is the finest around (▷ 148). Guests get use of the hotel's beach club and free water-taxi rides to Tamarindo.

✉ Playa Grande ☎ 506 653 0975 US$120 10 Outdoor

HOTEL LAS TORTUGAS

PLAYA GRANDE

www.lastortugashotel.com

Close to the turtle sanctuary of Playa Grande, this ecologically conscious

Above *The pool at the Hacienda Guachipelín*

hotel has been constructed by owner Louis Wilson to prevent light reaching the beach and affecting nesting turtles. Rooms either have air-conditioning or have been designed to benefit from cross ventilation. Backpackers now have a dorm option. The open-air restaurant serves international and local dishes.
✉ Playa Grande ☎ 506 653 0423
US$50–US$120 ⓘ 8 dorms, 12 rooms
Outdoor

PLAYA HERMOSA

HOTEL PLAYA HERMOSA

www.hotelplayahermosa.com

New owners have metamorphosed this place. The remake includes Bali-style, two-story villas with junior suites around a landscaped pool, and gracious standard rooms facing the beach. All rooms are fitted with flat-screen TVs and WiFi. A new restaurant and lounge bar are also in the works—a welcome addition to Playa Hermosa, where most eateries and bars are off the beach.
✉ The first beach turnoff, on the main road to Playa Hermosa ☎ 506 2672 0046 US$175–US$275 ⓘ 38 rooms
Outdoor

PLAYA LANGOSTA

CALA LUNA

www.calaluna.com

The Cala Luna, in a peaceful spot 10 minutes' drive south of the airport, offers unabashed luxury. Each of the villas has a pool, cable TV, telephone, CD player and kitchen. Yoga classes are available by appointment. The Cala Moresca restaurant serves regional and Italian dishes and American breakfasts.
✉ Playa Langosta ☎ 506 2653 0214
Rooms US$205, villas from US$410 excluding breakfast ⓘ 20 rooms, 21 villas
Outdoor

SUEÑO DEL MAR BED & BREAKFAST

www.sueno-del-mar

Among tropical vegetation, right on Playa Langosta, this is one of the most charming hotels in Costa Rica. With a rugged, Robinson Crusoe setting, the adobe design combines colonialism with contemporary comforts. Each room is decorated with frescoes. Balinese-style bathrooms and four-poster beds.
✉ Playa Langosta ☎ 506 2653 0284
US$221–US$272 ⓘ 4 rooms, 1 *casita*
Outdoor

TAMARINDO

ARCO DE IRIS

www.hotelarcoiris.com

A hip, youthful hotel with sepia-toned rooms. Bungalows have stunning contemporary bathrooms and are a stone's throw from a gorgeous pool and stone deck. Restaurante Seasons (▷ 149) is new, serving gourmet fusion dishes with a Levantine touch. The all-female staff perform diligently with a smile.
✉ On the hillside, 300m (330 yards) south of Plaza Tamarindo ☎ 506 2653 0330
US$89–US$99 ⓘ 9 rooms Outdoor

BEST WESTERN TAMARINDO VISTA VILLAS

www.tamarindovistavillas.com

A hillside hotel overlooking the ocean with excellent facilities, including a pool with swim-up bar, a Jacuzzi and the Monkey bar-restaurant, a surfer hang-out. The feel is youthful, and with bicycles, surf boards and golf clubs for rent, it is a sociable base. The 17 villas all have living rooms and kitchens. Rooms and villas have air-conditioning and TV.
✉ At the northern entrance to town
☎ 506 2653 0114 Double US$114–US$138, suite US$178–US$279 ⓘ 12 rooms, 17 villas Outdoor

CAPITÁN SUIZO

www.hotelcapitansuizo.com

This Swiss-run, beachfront hotel has stylish rooms in thatched bungalows. Each has a mezzanine sleeping area and is neutrally decorated, with a fridge, patio, or a balcony. The restaurant overlooks gardens visited by howler monkeys; paths lead to the pool. The service is faultless.
✉ South end of Tamarindo town toward Playa Langosta ☎ 506 2653 0075
Rooms US$190–US$290, bungalows US$250–US$290 ⓘ 22 rooms, 8 bungalows Outdoor

LA COLINA APARTHOTEL

www.la-colina.com

With fine sea views, La Colina is self-catering accommodations on a grand scale. Everything is big: the bed, the walk-in fridge, the pool. All suites have air-conditioning, fans, telephone, TV and kitchen. Hammocks swing below pergolas.
✉ 200m (220 yards) east of the main road, Tamarindo ☎ 506 2653 0303
Apartment suite for 2 US$125, penthouse sleeping up to 4 US$280 ⓘ 15 suites, 3 penthouses Outdoor

EL JARDÍN DEL EDÉN

www.jardindeleden.com

Standing on a hill outside the main part of town, this stylish hotel set in gardens is run by French owner Nicolas Segonne. Each room is designed with west-facing windows for sunset views. Sophisticated contemporary furnishings play on country themes—Tunisia, Japan, Mexico or Bali—while the African-themed rooms have de rigueur zebra skins and leopard-print fabrics, and even huge elephant heads over the beds. The expensive restaurant is one of the best in town (▷ 149). A private path leads directly to the beach.
✉ 400m (440 yards) uphill from the main road, Tamarindo ☎ 506 2653 0137
US$170–US$215 ⓘ 2 apartments, 34 rooms Outdoor

LA LAGUNA DEL COCODRILO

www.lalagunadelcocodrilo.com

Run by French couple Josette and Claude, this beachside hotel is at the north end of town. Each bright room has a blue-tiled bathroom. Ground-level rooms have air-conditioning and terraces with sea views. At 5pm, you can watch as Claude feeds the crocodiles that swim in the estuary alongside the hotel's garden.
✉ Opposite Tamarindo Villas, Tamarindo
☎ 506 2653 0255 US$60–US$115
ⓘ 10

CENTRAL PACIFIC AND NICOYA

The Central Pacific and southern Nicoya form a transition zone between the dry northwest and the humid southwest of Costa Rica, and the forests thicken from north to south. Coastal national parks such as Carara and Manuel Antonio offer sufficient rationales to visit, thanks to their ease of access, well-maintained trails and fabulous wildlife viewing. Sightings of sloths, toucans and troupes of monkeys are virtually guaranteed here, as they are at less popular but equally rewarding venues such as the wildlife refuges at Curú and Cabo Blanco. Those hoping for a close-up look at crocodiles won't be disappointed on a boat safari on the Tárcoles River. And eyeball-to-eyeball encounters with forest canopy critters are made possible at such ventures as the Rain forest Pacific Aerial Tram, near Jacó.

Jacó is Costa Rica's largest beach resort town, and a magnet for surfers. Nearby, Playa Herradura is the setting for the nation's annual surfing championship. A water-taxi links Jacó to Malpaís, at the southwest tip of the Nicoya Peninsula. Malpaís, and equally laid-back Montezuma, close by, offer the ultimate in offbeat experiences. They appeal to both backpackers and moneyed travelers with surf camps and deluxe hotels along dramatically beautiful shores hemmed by forested mountains. Passenger and car ferries from the regional capital and port town of Puntarenas offer connections between southern Nicoya and the Central Pacific. The town is also the departure point for exciting day-long excursions to Isla Tortuga—a palm-shaded tropical paradise ringed by white sands and turquoise waters.

Sportfishing is a forte of this region. The marinas at Playa Herradura and Quepos are the main centers, as well as for sailing craft that will whisk you out to sea to spot dolphins or for relaxed sunset cruises that show off this coast at its best.

DOMINICAL

www.dominical.biz

A 44km (27-mile) drive south from Quepos along the Costanera Sur (coast road) leads to Dominical, a small town at the mouth of the Río Barú. Dominical owes its success to the surf that pounds the coastline. If you want to surf, or learn how, it's a great spot. Locals can offer advice on places to go. Most hotels and restaurants lie along the road from Quepos or line the beach. Apart from surfing, there are tours and trips to Hacienda Barú, plus hiking and horseback riding in the forested hills of Escaleras. A turnoff 10km (6 miles) along the road to San Isidro leads to a couple of waterfalls, the largest being Nauyaca Waterfalls, 50m (164ft) high (tel 506 2787 8013, tours 8 and 2, US$45).

255 K9 Hourly buses from San José to San Isidro de El General from avenidas 1–3, Calle 16. From San Isidro several daily buses go to Dominical It is a 3.5-hour drive from San José. Go south on the Pan-American Highway as far as San Isidro de El General, where a right turn leads to Dominical

HACIENDA BARÚ

www.haciendabaru.com

Hacienda Barú is an eco-friendly adventure park set in a privately owned National Wildlife Refuge. The owner, Jack Ewing, and his wife arrived in 1972 at a time when Costa Rican conservation was in its infancy. By the end of the 1980s, the cattleman-turned-conservationist had bought and protected the diverse property of 19.2ha (47.4 acres), where 310 bird species have been recorded.

Interpretive pamphlets allow you to wander the trails alone as slowly as you like, and guides are available if you prefer. Trails lead through forest, to an observation tower where you may see sloths, monkeys and peccaries.

Activities include tree climbing, and a night spent in the jungle. The beach is used by nesting olive ridley turtles and the rare hawksbill turtles that arrive from July through October. Basic accommodations are available.

255 K9 506 2787 0003 The Quepos–Dominical bus passes the hacienda Daily Guided walks start at US$20 per person, rising to US$60 for a night in the jungle Open-air restaurant Hacienda Barú is 2km (1.25 miles) north of Dominical on the Manuel Antonio road

ISLA TORTUGA

www.calypsocruises.com

Isla Tortuga, 3km (2 miles) southeast of Curú (▷ 159), is a rugged, forested island fringed by a gorgeous white sand beach melting into jade waters good for snorkeling. The owners welcome day visitors arriving on boats. Kayaks and aqua-bikes are available, sand volleyball is popular, and a loop trail that leads into the forested hills offers lovely views over the Gulf of Nicoya. Many visitors are content to laze in a hammock beneath palms. The journey to the island is a treat in itself, passing between the Islas Negritos wildlife refuge—twin islands that protect an important nesting site for frigate birds, brown boobies and other seabirds. Calypso Cruises (tel 506 2256 2727, from US$109, including transfers from San José) has trips aboard the sleek *Manta Ray* catamaran.

253 E7 Boat excursions from Montezuma; Calypso Cruises offers tours daily from Puntarenas

JACÓ

The popular, bustling resort of Jacó is the closest beach to San José, a three-hour drive away. Costa Rica's original surf capital has no shortage of activities. While Jacó is hardly paradise, the beach is 3km (2 miles) in length, with the busy main street, lined with bars, shops and businesses, running parallel.

The climate for beach lovers is ideal from December to April when breezes keep temperatures in the mid 20s°C (around 77°F). The surf is best from May to November. Swimmers take care—dangerous currents cause deaths each year.

Bahía Herradura, used in the 1992 movie *1492: Conquest of Paradise*, is north of Jacó. Playa Hermosa, a low-key surfing community, is a peaceful enclave, 5km (3 miles) to the south of Jacó.

Local activities include zipline, horseback rides and kayak trips, plus the Pacific Rain forest Aerial Tram (tel 506 2257 5961; www.rainforesttram.com). In recent years, Jacó's image has been tarnished by a visible sex industry and crime.

254 G7 Several daily from San José Coca-Cola Terminal Shuttle transfers with Interlink (506 2283 5573; www.interbusonline.com) and Grayline (506 2220 2126; www.graylinecostarica.com), US$35 Jacó is west of the Pacific *costanera* parallel to the beach, 117km (73 miles) from San José

Left to right *A surfer on Dominical beach; horses on Jacó beach*

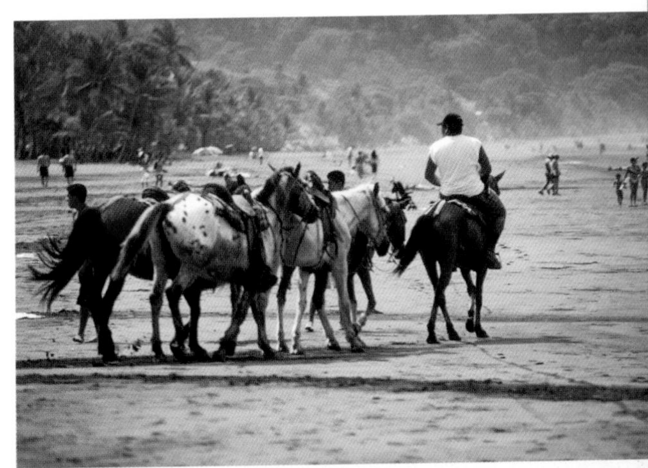

MALPAÍS

www.nicoyapeninsula.com

At the southern tip of the Nicoya Peninsula, Malpaís is a small village strung across a 3km (2-mile) road which abuts Cabo Blanco Nature Reserve (▷ 159). As wild and remote as its name suggests, Malpaís (meaning "bad land") is famed as a superb surfing destination. The area's appeal extends beyond its powerful surf breaks. Long white sands, creeks and natural pools stretch along the rugged coast. Fringed with forest, the beach abounds with howler monkeys and birdlife. To the north, Malpaís joins with Santa Teresa, a tiny former fishing village that has seen rapid development. Stylish lodges offer yoga, while rustic cabins satisfy surfers. Activities range from sportfishing to horseback riding, and even ultralight flying.

253 D7 Daily bus service from Cóbano to Malpaís From Paquera follow road to Cóbano, from where a road leads west for 11km (6.8 miles) to Carmen, then south for Malpaís

MONTEZUMA

A testing journey to the southern tip of the Nicoya Peninsula, four hours from Puntarenas, takes you to Montezuma. This once sleepy hamlet made its way onto the tourist circuit thanks to its laid-back alternative lifestyle and setting. At busy periods, the mainly budget hotels are full, so check in early. Although it gets crowded, there are lovely walks along beaches, rounded off by rocky points.

Some 20 minutes on foot up the Montezuma River is a waterfall with a swimming hole. Intrepid walkers can continue up to more waterfalls, but accidents and deaths have been reported. Operators offer a range of tours, including snorkeling at Isla Tortuga (US$45), horseback-riding tours (US$25), and mountain bike rental (US$5 per day). A popular trip is the boat taxi to Jacó (US$35), which goes to the Pacific coast in one hour. Cabo Blanco Nature Reserve is an enjoyable day-trip.

253 E7 Regular buses from San José to Puntarenas. Then from Paquera to Montezuma (1 hour 15minutes) Launches from Puntarenas to Paquera (1 hour 15 minutes) Road paved from Paquera to Montezuma, passing through Cóbano. During the rainy season a four-wheel-drive vehicle is recommended

NICOYA

Nicoya may be the provincial capital, but it is really just a pleasant market town distinguished by the country's second oldest church, the adobe Iglesia de San Blas. Although the pulpit dates back to the 16th century, the building was consecrated in 1644; it contains a museum of pre-Columbian objects. Before the Spanish conquest, Nicoya was the heart of the Chorotega community and takes its name from the local Indian chief. It is an important transportation hub, with links to the beach communities of Sámara and Nosara to the south, the Tempisque ferry to the east, and Playa Naranjo on the tip of the peninsula. Fiesta de la Yegüita, takes place on December 12 (▷ 166).

252 C5 Regular daily buses from San José. Hourly between Liberia and Santa Cruz Area de Conservación Tempisque (ACT) office on the square can help with visits to nearby Barra Honda National Park

NOSARA

www.nosara.com

Nosara, 26km (16 miles) north of Sámara, is a small village with little to see, which makes it ideal if you like lazing on beaches. Most people come for the three unspoiled beaches nearby or to see the mass nestings of the olive ridley turtles at Ostional (▷ 159). Playa Nosara is north across the Nosara River. Playa Pelada, the prettiest beach, south of the river, is popular for surfers and has a bat cave. Playa Guiones is an expanse of white sand backed by dunes and forest. Nosara village is a hot walk 5km (3 miles) north of Playa Guiones. Much of the property backing Pelada and Guiones beaches is owned by expatriates; the hills above Nosara are dotted with homes of the rich and famous. Activities include hiking in the privately owned Reserve Biológica Nosara (tel 506 2682 0035). Horseback riding, fishing and boat trips into the mangrove swamps of the Nosara River can be arranged.

252 B6 Daily direct bus from San José at 6am A good paved road leads from Sámara to Nicoya

PARQUE NACIONAL BARRA HONDA

www.sinac.go.cr

To the west of Nicoya, a limestone outcrop contains Costa Rica's largest cave system and forms the heart of Barra Honda National Park. In the network of 42 caves only 19 have been explored. Because access is difficult, the caves are in excellent condition. A guide is compulsory to visit the caves, accessed by a fixed ladder. Caving is dangerous in the rainy season (May to November), and the dry season is hot; ensure that you have enough water.

252 D5 506 2659 1551 Daily 8–4 Entrance: US$10; cave descents: US$36, including guide and equipment Daily from Nicoya to Quebrada Honda (first bus at 10.30am, last bus returns at 4.30pm, giving you only 2 hours in park); then an hour's walk to Santa Ana and the park offices from bus drop-off point

PARQUE NACIONAL CARARA

Just 90km (56 miles) from San José, Carara National Park has the most accessible forest in the country and is a popular protected area. There are self-guiding trails for you to see some of its 750 plant species, plus perhaps scarlet macaws, monkeys and poison-arrow frogs. Uphill from the park is La Catarata Manantial (tel 506 2645 1215, Dec–end Apr daily 8–3, US$20), a private reserve with a waterfall and natural pools. It's a hike but worth the effort.

254 G7 506 200 5023 Daily 7–4 US$8 Regular buses from San José or Puntarenas to Jacó go over the Río Tárcoles bridge and past the park entrance Fom San José, head west on the Orotina Highway to Río Tárcoles bridge; 3km (1.8 miles) past the bridge is the ranger's station

PARQUE NACIONAL ISLA DEL COCO

One of the largest uninhabited islands in the world, this remote UNESCO World Heritage Site is a diving paradise. More than 550km (340 miles) southwest of Costa Rica, the volcanic Isla del Coco rises from the sea floor at the western tip of the Coco Tectonic Plate. With an area of just 23sq km (9sq miles), the island rises steeply to the highest point of 634m (2,080ft) at Cerro Yglesias. The coast is lined with steep cliffs and the rugged terrain creates numerous rivers; some of the resulting waterfalls plunge into the ocean. Only the bays of Wafer and Chatham make the island accessible. Temperatures of 30°C (86°F) and an annual rainfall of 7,000mm (276in) guarantee cloud cover and verdant rain forest. The island's isolation means that several endemic species exist. Of the 87 bird species, 3—the Coco Island flycatcher, cuckoo and finch—are only found here. Green, hawksbill and olive ridley turtles visit the bays. Offshore, the protected waters are rich with coastal reefs. Over 300 species of fish are in the waters, but the real interest lies in the hammerhead sharks that school in their hundreds, and the abundance of white-tipped sharks, whale sharks and manta rays.

BURIED TREASURE

The island showed no signs of habitation prior to the arrival of the Spanish. Poorly marked on navigational maps, only experienced sailors could find it. Legend claims that the pirates Benito Bonito, William Davies and Captain Thompson buried treasure here between the late 1600s and 1821, including the Lima Booty, which is supposed to include a life-size statue of the Virgin Mary and Child in solid gold. Since then, more than 300 expeditions have searched for the sunken treasure. The island was a prison between 1872 and 1874. An exploratory trip in 1898 to reopen the penitentiary became a scientific expedition that realized the area's natural importance. Marine life is the main draw, and most visitors are serious divers, arriving on live-aboard boats.

INFORMATION

252 inset 506 2283 0022
Coco is an uninhabited island. Most people stay offshore on board the dive vessel, *Okeanos Aggressor* (www.aggressor.com) as part of an all-inclusive package. Passengers are shuttled to the island to enjoy spectacular birding (▷ 164)

TIPS

» A permit is required to visit the island.
» Diving is only recommended for very advanced divers due to strong currents.

Above *A scalloped hammerhead shark swimming over a coastal reef near the Isla del Coco*

PARQUE NACIONAL MANUEL ANTONIO
▷ 160.

PARQUE NACIONAL MARINO BALLENA
www.marinoballena.org
On the Pacific coast, between Punta Uvita and Punta Piñuela, the Ballena (Whale) Marine National Park is one of the least-developed national parks. The main attractions are underwater: coral reefs and the abundant marine life that includes dolphins and, occasionally, humpback whales. Offshore, Las Tres Hermanas and Isla Ballena mark the southern boundary of the park, providing nesting sites for frigate birds, white ibis and brown pelicans.

Although there are three ranger's stations (they are rarely staffed), and signposts line Highway 34, the Costanera, facilities in the park are nonexistent. However, a turtle nesting project at Bahía is administered by the local community and visitors are welcome. Boat trips to the islands can be arranged from Bahía, and diving is starting up.

Next to the Marino Ballena National Park, south of Uvita, is Rancho La Merced (tel 506 2771 4582), a wildlife refuge with more than 500ha (1,235 acres) of rain forest and mangroves. The area can be explored, ideally on horseback, with trips to waterfalls, the beach, the mangroves or around the ranch.

258 K9 ☎ 506 2786 5392 Park office in Playa Ballena: daily 8–4 (erratic) US$6, but this is rarely collected Buses to Uvita from San José Coca-Cola terminal Take the Costanera southeast from Dominical for 17km (10.5 miles) to Uvita, the main access point for the park

PUNTARENAS
West of San José, the gritty provincial capital of Puntarenas is the main transportation link on the Pacific coast. The northern side of this thin coastal sand spit is a bustling array of scruffy fishing and ferry docks. The southern side, six blocks away, is made up of the Paseo de los Turístas, a promenade and beach dotted with bars, cafes, restaurants and hotels. Neither aspect is particularly successful; both fishing and beaches are distinctly average.

The Parque Marino del Pacífico (Avenida 4, Calle 2, tel 506 2661 5272, Tue–Sun 9–5; $7), in the old railway station, has an aquarium.

253 F6 Casa de la Cultura, Avenida 1, Calle 3, ☎ 506 2661 5036, 8–6 Regular buses from San José Terminal to Puntarenas Vehicle and passenger ferries to Paquera on the south side of the peninsula

Above *A tuna fishing boat just outside the fishing port at Puntarenas*

QUEPOS
On the Pacific coast, some 145km (90 miles) from San José, Quepos bears a legacy, in name at least, from the Quepo Indians who inhabited the region at the time of the Spanish conquest in 1519. As the main access point for Manuel Antonio National Park, which lies 7km (4 miles) over the rocky Punta Quepos peninsula, this lively town pulsates with crowds that converge in search of the palm-fringed beaches and wildlife encounters of the National Park (▷ 160–161).

Quepos has successfully moved beyond a dependency on banana exports. The United Fruit Company began large-scale production in the 1930s, but plantations in the region were overwhelmed by disease in the 1950s and, economically, Quepos was crippled. The oil-producing African palm has replaced banana agriculture in the region (palm oil is used in the production of margarine and soap).

The lively bars and restaurants buzz and hum, but hanging silently in the background, the atmosphere of an old port town remains. A marina completed in 2010 has enhanced Quepos's reputation as a sportfishing hub, and the town now has many restaurants.

254 H8 Six times daily from the Coca Cola terminal in San José Highway 34, the Costanera, passes Quepos 2km (a mile or so) to the east; look for the signs

REFUGIO NACIONAL DE VIDA SILVESTRE CURÚ

www.curu.org

Between Bahía Ballena and Paquera, Curú National Wildlife Refuge vies for the title of smallest protected area in the country with a mere 70ha (173 acres). Rising from three beaches, good for swimming and snorkeling, there are five ecosystems, including mangroves. Mammals are equally diverse, with deer, pacas, racoons and monkeys. The privately owned refuge is a good place to spot marine turtles nesting, in season. The Montezuma–Paquera bus can drop you at the locked gate. Make advance reservations for basic accommodations.

253 E7 506 2641 0100 Daily 7–3 US$8 Buses from Montezuma (leaving from Hotel Montezuma at 8am) to Paquera pass the park entrance

REFUGIO NACIONAL DE VIDA SILVESTRE OSTIONAL

A short drive north of Nosara is Playa Ostional, a wide beach protected for the natural spectacle of the *arribada*, when tens of thousands of *lora* (olive ridley turtles) arrive to nest. Along with Playa Nancite to the north, Ostional is one of the world's most important nesting sites for the turtles. The *arribadas* occur between July and November with the largest numbers arriving between August and October, at the end of the lunar cycle. But you can normally see some turtle activity at any time of the season. The beach is occasionally used by leatherback and green turtles. Locals are permitted to harvest turtle eggs under a program that incorporates conservation goals with the community's needs.

The beach is part of Ostional National Wildlife Refuge, protecting 352ha (870 acres) of land, including Nosara beach and a marine zone. The reserve's forest supports groups of howler and capuchin monkeys. On the north bank of the Río Nosara, mangroves, good to explore by kayak, are home to 100 bird species.

252 B6 Daily 8–4 US$10 (night); a guide (US$10) is compulsory during nesting season Daily from San José at 5am to Santa Cruz, then 13.20pm bus to Ostional Trips to the nesting grounds are arranged through hotels in Nosara and Sámara Ostional is a 30-min drive north of Nosara. Visit the ranger station for details. Four-wheel-drive vehicle needed in the rainy season

RESERVA NATURAL ABSOLUTA CABO BLANCO

Neatly covering the southwestern tip of the Nicoya Peninsula, Cabo Blanco is a precious reserve, both ideologically and biologically. Created in 1963, it is the oldest protected area in the country apart from the frontier corridor to the north with Nicaragua. The reserve is the legacy of Nicolás Wessberg and his wife, Karen Mogensen, who set out to preserve the stands of moist forest as development gradually denuded the surrounding area. The 1,800ha (4,448 acres) of the reserve were finally donated to the National Parks program in 1994, when Doña Karen bequeathed the land to the state.

Today, the reserve is easily visited on short trips from Montezuma. It is composed of tracts of evergreen and deciduous species in a beautiful moist forest that fringes the beaches and rocky headlands. With roughly 2,300mm (90in) of rain a year, this is one of the wettest spots on the peninsula. A couple of trails lead through the park, which for its size has a good variety of wildlife, including porcupines, armadillos and three species of monkey. The reserve is also an important site for seabirds, including brown pelicans, frigate birds and the largest nesting colony of brown boobies. Just beyond Cabo Blanco is beautiful Playa Balsitas, with lots of pelicans and howler monkeys; however, this area of the reserve is closed, although there are plans to open a trail from Malpaís.

253 D7 506 2642 0093 Wed–Sun 8–4 US$10 Buses depart Montezuma at 8.15, 10.15, 2.15 and 6.15. A private shuttle service (506 2642 0802) leaves Montezuma at 8am and 9am and picks you up outside the park at 3pm or 4pm, US$3 Local boatmen can arrange transportation farther up the peninsula or to the mainland. It's best to try and get a group to spread the cost A taxi will cost around US$10 per person

SÁMARA

www.samarabeach.com

Around five hours's drive from San José, Sámara—a popular surfers' and backpackers' destination—is a smallish village with a rugged quality, set in a horseshoe bay, lined with thick jungly vegetation. Although relatively small, the beach is peaceful and excellent for bathing. With several good international restaurants, internet facilities, a language school and a surf school, the village has a relaxed pace, where the gentle trickle of residents from around the world blends well with the ticking over of everyday life.

The place offers a good excuse to get away for a few days and relax by the sea. For the more energetic, there are activities and excursions that can be arranged, with a clutch of tour operators offering watersports and horseback-riding tours in the area.

252 C6 Direct bus from San José Tracopa terminal. Daily from Nosara

Below *An olive ridley turtle*

INFORMATION
255 J8 506 2777 5185 Tue–Sun 7–4 US$10 For San José to Quepos, ▷ 158. From Quepos main terminal to the road at Manuel Antonio, every 30 mins Arrive early to get a parking space. You can have your car watched for US$3 per day (car theft is not unusual; lock valuables in the trunk) Accredited wildlife guides (tel 506 8894 1358) can be arranged at the entrance to the park, or you can make arrangements at your hotel, US$20 per person Taxi from Quepos costs US$6

Above *An aerial view of the national park, showing Cathedral Point*

INTRODUCTION

Manuel Antonio is a crowd-pulling area of outstanding natural beauty, with short hiking trails, magnificent vistas, monkeys and rich birdlife. And the golden beaches are just as special. Around 150km (90 miles) southwest of the capital (four hours by car) Manuel Antonio National Park is a genuine tropical wilderness and acclaimed as one of the most scenic landscapes of Costa Rica. Whether you are a lover of golden beaches and crystalline waters, or like to wander through tropical forests teeming with wildlife, there is something in this park for you.

The threat to Manuel Antonio's natural wealth began with the arrival of the Spanish. After the indigenous peoples had been sold or wiped out by illness, land was cleared for farming. Much of the region was used for banana plantations, but the stunning vistas of the peninsula attracted foreign buyers. With locals denied access, state authorities became aware of plans to clear the land for agriculture. In haste, Manuel Antonio was declared a national park in 1972. Since then, development has been limited to the access road to the west of the park. There is no denying that a booming tourism industry—150,000 people visit each year—and a national park do not sit easily together, but the extent of the damage depends on your perspective. The environmental impact is clear to see. Monkeys rather depressingly scavenge for food. Litter, pollution, sewage and petty crime are serious issues, and with up to 600 visitors each day, wildlife flees to quieter areas. For the time being, at least, development is limited but the future could be very different.

From the southeastern corner of Quepos (▷ 158), a road winds up and over the peninsula of Punta Quepos, passing the smart hotels, restaurants, bars and boutiques that flourish along this rocky outcrop, and have earned the area the title of Costa Riviera. The park's entrance is by the bridge over the Quebrada Camaronera tidal estuary; parking charges apply. As you enter the park, pick up a map and information on the trails, beaches and flora and fauna. Guides can be hired. Activities range from kayaking and surfing to dolphin watching and scuba diving.

WHAT TO SEE

FLORA AND FAUNA

Manuel Antonio National Park is one of the smallest in the country, but its flora and fauna is impressive, with an inventory of 109 species of mammals and 184 species of birds. High annual rainfall makes this a humid forest. The diversity is complemented by mangroves. Offshore, a dozen islands provide nesting sites for seabirds; the waters are rich with marine life, and biologists have identified 78 fish species. Punta Catedral, once an island, is now connected to the mainland by a sandbar. A trail, with viewing points, climbs over the headland. The former island is home to primary and secondary forest, and an early morning walk will find you face to face with surprisingly timid wildlife, including pacas, agoutis and iguanas. With a guide you'll see a lot more. Longer trails head east along the coastline passing the tree-fringed beaches of Manuel Antonio, heading out to Playa Escondido and on to Punta Serrucho and Playa Playitas. The trails are the best place to see monkeys, including white-faced capuchins and the rare squirrel monkey. But it is equally enjoyable to stroll just beyond the park entrance to one of the five sandy beaches, with gentle gradients, good for swimming.

MORE TO SEE

RAINMAKER CONSERVATION PROJECT

www.rainmakercostarica.com

A short trip northeast of the park, a network of cable bridges between trees link platforms that afford a unique bird's-eye view of the forest canopy. The project aims to protect the Fila Chonta mountain range on Costa Rica's Pacific side. Almost entirely virgin rain forest, the privately owned reserve contains more than 70 percent of all the species of flora and fauna found in Costa Rica. The Rainmaker Canopy Walk consists of six sections totalling 250m (270 yards), linking platforms attached to trees, providing close encounters with this pristine wildlife haven. Rainmaker operates sustainable tourism, and the canopy design precludes harmful impact on the forest.

✉ 17km (10.5 miles) from Parrita in the village of San Rafael Norte ☎ 506 2777 3565
🕒 Tours: Mon–Sat 8.45, 10.45, 12.45, plus birding at 5.30am 💲 US$70, including meals

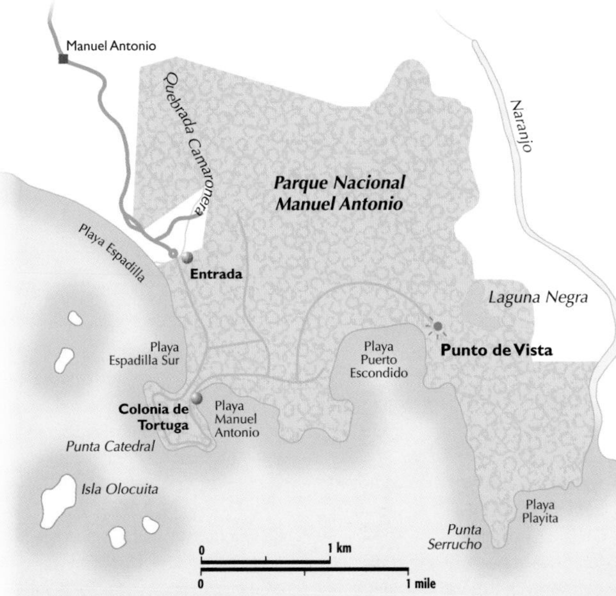

TIPS

» The best time to visit the park is early; aim to be at the entrance by 7am to increase your chances of viewing wildlife.

» When hiking the trails, be aware of snakes that can easily be mistaken for jungle vines.

» Some of Manuel Antonio's beaches are lined by the poisonous manzanillo tree.

» Walking to the park from Quepos is not advised. Searing heat, steep inclines, serpentine twists and hazardous traffic make for a challenging and potentially dangerous hike.

» When returning from the park, the standard bus fare to Quepos is 200 colones per person.

Below *The forested floor of the national park*

THE PACIFIC COAST ROAD

This is a fascinating journey down the Pacific coast from the resorts of Jacó, Quepos and Manuel Antonio to plantations in the far south. Getting lost is difficult: You follow one road down the coast. The road runs parallel to the coastline, but only occasionally touches it.

THE DRIVE
Distance: 230km (143 miles)
Allow: 2–3 days
Start at: Orotina
End at: Palmar Norte

★ Starting in Orotina, Highway 34, the Costanera (coastal road) begins smoothly; the section from here to Jacó (40km/25 miles) is some of the best road in Costa Rica. On this stretch the road winds through the coastal hills. It's easy to go fast, and there are often police waiting to write out tickets, so watch your speed.

❶ From the Río Tárcoles bridge you can see some of the country's best free entertainment. Park your car on the south side of the bridge close to the police kiosk (avoid leaving valuables in it) and look over the side to watch the crocodiles in the water below.

Carry on down the road to Parque Nacional Carara at Km22.

❷ Carara National Park (▷ 156) is one of the country's most popular and accessible. Its primary forest contains more than 750 plant species. The park also protects pre-Columbian archaeological sites, some of which date back to 300BC. At the southern end of the park, close to the rangers' station, are a couple of self-guiding trails of just over 1km (0.6 miles), where you may see scarlet macaws, spider monkeys and poison-arrow frogs.

At Km40, take the turn that heads west to Jacó.

❸ Jacó is a busy, if mediocre, surf spot (▷ 155). A little way beyond Jacó, a road leads to the huge, ferocious waves of Playa Hermosa, popular with experienced surfers.

A short distance farther down the road, a turning goes to Playa Hermosa. Continue south on the highway, with sea views. Down the coastline at Punta Guapinol, there's a scenic stopping point. The road continues past the secluded Esterillos beaches and to Parrita, from where a rusty, one-lane bridge marks the beginning of the palm oil plantations that stretch south to Río Savegre. The oil from the palms is used in ice cream, mayonnaise, baked goods and detergents. At Km89 an old bridge marks a turnoff west to Quepos and Manuel Antonio National Park. This is a good place to spend a night or two. En route, you'll pass the signed turnoff for the Rainmaker Conservation Project (▷ 161).

❹ Quepos (▷ 158) has successfully moved beyond a dependency on banana exports to provide for

Opposite *Nauyaca Waterfall, Perez Zeledon*

visitors. The restaurants and bars along the seafront jostle with the sportfishing outfits.

South from Quepos, a 7km (4-mile) road snakes over the rocky Punta Quepos peninsula past luxury hotels and smart restaurants to Parque Nacional Manuel Antonio. Mid-price hotels are a short walk back from the beach.

❺ Manuel Antonio National Park (▷ 160–161) is, justifiably, one of the most visited parks in the country. Visitors come for glorious white sand beaches backed by jungle, and close encounters with monkeys and other wildlife.

The road from Quepos ends at the park, so return to Quepos to rejoin the main road, which south of Quepos, was finally paved in 2009. Progress is slow. You will pass more palm oil plantations, and a processing factory at Finca Llorana. After the Río Savegre crossing (Km18) there's a shift to bananas. The western slopes of the Central Mountains encroach on the coast, pushing the road up to the shoreline at Matapalo. The scenery builds for another 26km (16 miles) past Hacienda Barú (▷ 155) to Dominical.

❻ Dominical (▷ 155), like Jacó to the north, has a reputation as a surf destination, albeit a more laid-back option. Activities range from surfing to hiking, horseback riding and fishing. A diversion from Dominical goes to the 50m-high (164ft) Nauyaca Waterfalls, 10km (6 miles) along the road to San Isidro de El General.

Follow Highway 10 south again. Wide and fast, it speeds you south. At Km6 from Dominical a road turns shoreward to Rancho La Merced.

❼ Rancho La Merced (▷ 158) is a working cattle ranch and wildlife refuge south of Uvita, with more than 500ha (1,235 acres) of tropical rain forest, as well as mangrove estuary. The area can be explored, ideally on horseback, with trips going to the beach, the mangroves or around the ranch. Walking tours go to nearby waterfalls.

Farther on, the road heads to Playa Bahía, which leads to Parque Nacional Marino Ballena.

❽ Marino Ballena National Park (▷ 158) is a starting point for boat trips to see dolphins and whales, at the right time of year (December to April and August to October).

From Playa Bahía it's a short distance south through the coastal communities of Ojochal, with several stylish accommodation options. Spend the night at one, then rejoin the Pan-American Highway at Palmar Norte.

PLACES TO STAY

SI COMO NO

www.sicomono.com

✉ 2.5km (1.5 miles) from Manuel Antonio National Park entrance, ▷ 160–161

☎ 506 2777 0777

MONO AZUL

www.monoazul.com

✉ Apdo 297, Manuel Antonio, ▷ 170

☎ 506 2777 2572

WHERE TO EAT

PACIFIC BISTRO

✉ 75m (82 yards) north from Jacó's downtown bridge (▷ 167) ☎ 506 2643 3771 🕐 Wed–Sun 6pm–10pm

EL GRAN ESCAPE

www.elgranescape.com

✉ Quepos Centro (▷ 168) ☎ 506 2777 0395 🕐 Wed–Mon 6am–11pm

SAN CLEMENTE BAR & GRILL

✉ On the main road in Dominical (▷ 167)

☎ 506 2787 0055 🕐 Daily 7am–10pm

PLACES TO VISIT

RAINMAKER CONSERVATION PROJECT

✉ North of Manuel Antonio, ▷ 161

☎ 506 2777 3565 🕐 Mon–Sat 8–3

HACIENDA BARÚ

www.haciendabaru.com

✉ 2km (1.25 miles) north of Dominical (▷ 155) ☎ 506 2787 0003

CABUYA

LOS ALMENDROS

www.studioalmendros.com

Some 3.5km (2.2 miles) from Cabo Blanco National Park, this beachside studio and lodge offers classes for individuals interested in health, spirituality and movement arts professions with tai chi, yoga, singing, theater and Latin American dance classes.

✉ Between Montezuma and Cabuya ☎ 506 2642 0378 Two-week workshops US$100

DOMINICAL

ASOCIACIÓN DE AMIGOS DE LA NATURALEZA DEL PACÍFICO CENTRAL Y SUR (ASANA)

www.asana.co.cr

The Association of the Friends of Nature for the Central Pacific and Southern region is a conservation group that offers a volunteer program developing a wildlife corridor project—the Tapir Biological Corridor—from Manuel Antonio to the Osa Peninsula. You'll work on trail maintenance, tree planting and other tasks. Turtle protection projects are also available.

☎ 506 2787 0254 (Franklin Sequeira)
☎ 506 2787 0001 (Jack Ewing)
US$75 per week, including food and accommodations

CINEMA ESCALERAS

Started by movie-lovers Harley and Kimberley Toberman in 2003, this bijoux cinema, on a mountainside with great sunset views, shows classic movies on Friday. Saturday night is Spanish movie night.

✉ Dominical Fri, Sat 5pm dinner, 6pm movie No charge, but 2,500 colones donation appreciated

CONFUSIONE

www.domilocos.net

In the Hotel Domilocos, this Italian-run venue offers superb cuisine that is some of the best outside San José. A treat, but the local cognoscenti come here early to snag a seat for the four-nights-a-week live music that includes a classical violinist on Thursday and Saturday and an acoustic guitarist on Friday and Sunday.

✉ 500m (545 yards) south and 100m (110 yards) east of the soccer field ☎ 506 2787 0244 Daily 6–11.30pm

ISLA DEL COCO

OKEANOS AGGRESSOR

www.aggressor.com

Coco Island (▷ 157) is heralded as the apogee of diving in Costa Rica, and is one of the most exciting dive spots in the world, primarily due to the huge numbers of hammerhead sharks in the area. Owing to the strong currents and sharks, the island is not suitable for beginners. *Okeanos Aggressor* is a 33m (110ft) vessel with comfortable berths for 22 guests. Departing from Puntarenas on the 30- to 36-hour trip, the *Aggressor* offers 8-day and 10-day charters all year.

☎ 506 2228 6613. Toll free in the US on 800-348-2628 From US$2,495 for 8 days, US$2,895 for 10 days, per person

ISLA TORTUGA

CALYPSO TOURS

www.calypsocruises.com

Off the southeastern tip of the Nicoya Peninsula, a handful of sand-fringed islands are easily visited from the peninsula, Puntarenas or San José. The most popular is a luxury cruise to Isla Tortuga, a pair of small uninhabited islands to the south of Curú, with beautiful white sand beaches, and crystal-clear water ideal for swimming, snorkeling and other aquatic activities. It's one of the most popular trips in Costa Rica.

✉ Apt 1053 1007, San José ☎ For reservations 506 2256 2727 Day trips US$109–US$119 with lunch

Above *Calypso Tours organizes visits to Isla Tortuga, with its wonderful beaches*

JACÓ

OZ SPORTS BAR

One of Jacó's more stylish nightspots, this is a popular hang-out among weekending Joséfinos and expatriates. The minimalist design is light and airy, and the large circular bar is flanked by two widescreen TVs showing round-the-clock sports entertainment. There are also pool tables, pinball machines and videos. Live music is on Friday nights with a good range of *bocas* (snacks) to keep you going until dinner.

✉ Calle La Central, Playa Jacó ☎ 506 2643 2162 🕒 Daily 11am–3am

WATERFALLS CANOPY TOUR

www.waterfallscanopy.com

On the road to Herradura, 4km (2.5 miles) from Jacó, the Waterfalls Canopy Tour is owned and run by biologist Luis Fonseca. After the adrenaline rush of the canopy tour, there is a 27m (90ft) rappel, Tarzan swing and tree houses. Guided or self-guiding trails can be followed. Night canopy tours are for a minimum of 10 people. Full-day tours are available from San José, which include a butterfly tour, frog tour and crocodile-watching at Río Tarcoles.

✉ Playa Jacó ☎ 506 2643 3322

✋ 2-hour canopy tour US$60

MANUEL ANTONIO

AMIGOS DEL RIO

www.amigosdelrio.net

Amigos del Rio offers rafting trips along the challenging Upper Savegre River for all levels of experience. White-water kayaking and ocean kayaking around Manuel Antonio can be arranged, as can jungle tours in humvee vehicles. Amigos del Rio's guides are knowledgeable and professional.

✉ Manuel Antonio ☎ 506 2777 0082

✋ Full day US$99

SANTA JUANA MOUNTAIN TOUR

www.sicomono.com

This ambitious ecotourism project, deep in the Fila Chonta mountains, east of Quepos, attempts to integrate rural community members in tourism. Adventure trips give participants a look at *campesino* (rural) lifestyle and include a typical meal, plus a chance to see butterfly breeding, reforestation and other sustainable practices. Afterwards, you can splash around in natural swimming pools.

✉ EcoQuest Tours, Manuel Antonio ☎ 506 2777 0850 ✋ Adult US$75, child US$30

MONTEZUMA

LIBRERÍA TOPSY

This bookstore has a good collection of multilanguage fiction, predominantly English, and other reading matter to buy, rent or exchange, along with international newspapers and magazines. A collection of Latin American literature includes works by Gabriel García Márquez and Pablo Neruda. You can buy stationery, including maps and travel journals.

✉ Opposite the Bakery Café, Montezuma ☎ 506 2642 0576 🕒 Mon–Fri 8–1, Sat–Sun 8–noon

LOS MANGOS HOTEL

www.montezumayoga.com

Nicoya's New Age explosion has hit the Los Mangos Hotel, on the road out of town toward Cobaya. Hatha Vinyasa yoga classes are held in an open-air pavilion amid dense jungle. All levels are catered to in 90-minute classes. One-on-one classes can be arranged on request.

✉ Montezuma ☎ 506 2642 0076 🕒 Sun–Fri 9.30am ✋ Single class US$12, 10 classes US$100

OROTINA

THE ORIGINAL CANOPY TOUR

www.canopytour.com

Mahogany Park near Orotina is home to this Original Canopy Tour franchise, with a 3.5-hour tour going through three different ecosystems. The third platform rests on a strangler fig over 30m (98ft) in height, which links to a fourth on a 44m-high (144ft) kapok tree.

✉ Orotina ☎ 506 2291 4465 🕒 Daily tours at 8, 10, 12, 2.30 ✋ US$45; all-inclusive trip from San José US$60

PANACA

www.panacacostarica.com

Kids in tow? Then they may love this Colombia-run, farm-focused zoo, agricultural fair and exhibition center. Take a tour by horse-drawn cart to view the park, which has equine, porcine and similar themed areas. More than 2,000 animals from around the world are displayed, including more than 150 purebred species of dogs, which put on a dog show. Equestrian shows are featured, along with a parade of *carretas* (oxcarts).

✉ San Mateo de Orotina, 5km (3 miles) northeast of Orotina 🕒 Daily 8.30–6

✋ Guided tour US$15

PLAYA HERMOSA

DEL MAR SURF CAMP

www.costaricasurfingchicas.com

The only all-female surf camp in Costa Rica, the Del Mar offers all-inclusive packages with accommodations at Hotel Pacífico, surfing lessons from female instructors, all equipment, massage and yoga. Beginners should be aware that Hermosa's waves can be large and powerful.

✉ Hotel Terraza del Pacífico, Playa Hermosa ☎ 506 2643 3197 ✋ US$250 full day, including yoga class, breakfast and dinner

HOTEL TERRAZA DEL PACÍFICO

www.terrazadelpacifico.com

At the surfing mecca of Playa Hermosa, just south of Jacó, the specialized surf hotel, Hotel del Pacífico, attracts surfers from all over the world over to its events, including the spectacular night surf contest, where stretches of Hermosa beach are illuminated.

✉ Playa Hermosa ☎ 506 2643 6852

PLAYA HERRADURA

VILLA CALETAS

www.villacaletas.com

Far more than a hotel, this lavish resort boasts an astonishing position atop a mountain, with no less astonishing views up and down the coast and across the Gulf of Nicoya. A visit to lunch or

dine at either of its two cliff-top restaurants is a must for anyone passing by. A full-service Serenity Spa provides holistic treatments. Villa Caletas is renowned for its live concerts, including jazz, in its small amphitheater built into the cliff.
3km (2 miles) north of Playa Herradura 506 2637 0505 Overnight rates begin at US$180

QUEPOS

BLUE FIN SPORTFISHING CHARTERS

www.bluefinsportfishing.com
This operator offers full- and half-day sportfishing charters. The conditions are excellent, with waters teeming with dorado, marlin and tuna. A range of boats is available and all charters include IGFA tackle, safety kit and a bilingual captain.
Apdo 223-6350, Quepos 506 2777 2222 Leave at 7am and return 6pm From US$525 half-day, US$725 full day

CANOPY SAFARI

www.canopysafari.com
Canopy Safari was the first such operator in the southern region. With an ecologically sensitive ethos, canopies are constructed to ensure that the environmental impact is minimal. As well as the white-knuckle rush of zipping through the canopy, the well-organized excursion includes hiking, swimming, breakfast or lunch and refreshments. Friendly guides inform about the flora and fauna.
PO Box 351, Quepos 506 2777 0100 Half-day trips (5 hours) from US$65

IGUANA TOURS

www.iguanatours.com
Iguana Tours was the first professional tour operator in Quepos and offers white-water rafting, horseback riding and excellent and challenging kayaking tours along the stunning Manuel Antonio coastline. For a quieter trip, you can meander through the inland waterways for five hours, with mangrove areas and prolific wildlife.
Quepos 506 2777 2052 Tours depart 8–1 or 1–2 US$65

FESTIVALS AND EVENTS

JULY

FESTIVAL OF THE VIRGIN OF THE SEA

Ends with a parade of brightly decorated boats sailing out into the gulf.
Puntarenas Second week of July

DECEMBER

FIESTA DE LA YEGÜITA

The festival is spectacularly celebrated with parades, dancing, fireworks, bullfights and music.
Nicoya December 12

RANCHO SAVEGRE

www.costaricahorsevacation.com
Rancho Savegre, a cattle range covering 810ha (2,000 acres) some 15km (9 miles) from Quepos, offers a wide variety of guided riding tours, from beach gallops to rain-forest treks and rides to coffee plantation towns. Well-cared-for horses are equally suitable for beginners and accomplished riders. Wear long trousers and sneakers or boots—no sandals.
Quepos 506 8834 8687 Daily 7.30am–1.30pm 3-hour ride from US$58

SANTA TERESA

LUZ DE VIDA RESORT

www.luzdevida-resort.com
This holiday village embodies the relaxed escapism and healthy mindiset for which Santa Teresa has become known. Activities on land and sea can be arranged, from surfing classes to yoga, deep-sea fishing, waterskiing and horseback riding on the beach.
Santa Teresa 506 2640 0568 Doubles US$85–US$105

TÁRCOLES

JUNGLE CROCODILE SAFARI

www.junglecrocodilesafari.com
Prepare for a thrilling ride up the Río Tárcoles with the prospect of witnessing your guide hand-feed a giant crocodile! Early morning is best, when the crocs sun themselves on the banks. Roseate spoonbills, whistling ducks, egrets and scarlet macaws are among the many bird species typically seen close up.
Tárcoles 506 2637 0338 Daily 8.30, 10.30, 1.30 and 3.30 US$25

Below *Crocodiles below Río Tárcoles Bridge, between Orotino and Jacó*

PRICES AND SYMBOLS

The restaurants are listed alphabetically (excluding El, Le, La and Les). The prices given are the average for a two-course lunch (L) and a three-course dinner (D) for one person, without drinks. The wine price is for the least expensive bottle.

For a key to the symbols, ▷ 2.

DOMINICAL

SAN CLEMENTE BAR & GRILL

The San Clemente Bar & Grill is a Dominical landmark, the epicenter of expatriate life and a lifeline for brigades of surfers. Walls are festooned with broken surf boards and covered with sporting memorabilia. With a satellite TV showing sports events, a pool table and lively banter, it positively throbs. Huge platters of spicy Tex-Mex food are served, including burritos, fajitas and nachos, and on all-you-can-eat Taco Tuesday you can satisfy the hungriest appetite for less than a dollar.

✉ On the main town road, Dominical ☎ 506 2787 0055 🕑 Daily 7am–10pm 💰 L US$10, D US$15, Wine US$15

JACÓ

PACIFIC BISTRO

Pacific Bistro is, arguably, one of the finest gastronomic experiences on the Pacific coast. Chef Kent Green produces an Eastern-inspired menu of chalkboard specials, ranging from seared yellowfin tuna steaks to mahi mahi with sake. Each dish is a riot of tastes and textures, while the backdrop is lanterns and cobbled white stonework. The serene location, tucked away from the Jacó crowds, is appealing.

✉ 75m (82 yards) north from Jacó's downtown bridge, Jacó ☎ 506 2643 3771 🕑 Wed–Sun 6pm–10pm 💰 D US$20, Wine US$16

MANUEL ANTONIO

BARBA ROJA

www.barbaroja.co.cr

With glorious panoramas of Manuel Antonio, this is one of the area's most popular eateries, as much for the setting as for the daily menu, which specializes in seafood dishes. At 6pm, crowds flock here to pay tribute to the setting sun, the uninterrupted views and to enjoy the punchy fruit daíquiris and piña coladas. There are daily happy hours and homemade breakfasts and lunches.

✉ Midway between Quepos and Manuel Antonio ☎ 506 2777 5159 🕑 Tue–Sun 10–10 (often open only for dinner in the low season) 💰 B US$8, L US$15, D US$25, Wine US$16

CLARO QUE SI

With its chic, contemporary decor and romantic, open-air, wooden deck with overhead sail-canopy, this restaurant is striking. The fusion menu wows, too, with such dishes as stuffed ravioli with seafood and spinach, and divine chocolate ice cream pie dessert.

✉ Hotel Si Como No (▷ 170) ☎ 506 2777 0777 🕑 Daily 6.30pm–10.30pm 💰 D US$25, Wine US$15

SUNSPOT POOLSIDE BAR AND GRILL

www.makanda.com

This intimate, open-air restaurant is the ultimate romantic venue: a poolside terrace enveloped by jungle and lit at night by candlelight. The lunch menu offers salads, sandwiches and quesadillas, while evening brings more creative fare, supported by a good wine list. Fresh foccaccia with homemade herb butter starts off dinners that can include scallops with blackberry and balsamic reduction. Pizzas from a wood-fired oven are a specialty.

✉ Makanda-by-the-Sea, on the road to Hotel El Parador ☎ 506 2777 0442 🕑 Daily 11–10. Closed Oct 💰 L US$20, D US$45, Wine US$24

Above *Sunspot Poolside Bar and Grill*

MONTEZUMA

BAKERY CAFÉ

This friendly bakery-cafe in the heart of the village, run by Costa Rican/ Swiss couple Luis and Priska Rojas, is a perfect spot for a wake-up call. With a cluster of tables in a natural jungle garden, visited by cheeky monkeys, it combines tranquility with mostly vegetarian food. The cafe serves breakfast fare, ranging from omelets to *gallo pinto* (▷ 239). Lunches include vegetarian burgers and sandwiches. Credit cards are not accepted.

✉ Opposite Librería Topsy, Montezuma ☎ 506 2642 0458 ⊙ Daily 6–6 ✋ B US$5, L US$8

NECTAR BAR & RESTAURANT

www.florblanca.com

At the far north end of Playa Santa Teresa, this beachfront hotel-restaurant could well be the finest on the Pacific coast of Costa Rica. Chef Spencer Groves delivers skillfully prepared Pacific-Latin fusion fare, eaten beneath the stars to the sounds of the ocean and hip ambient music to set the tone for a romantic evening. Sushi is served at the laid-back bar during the afternoon. The frequently changing menu is heavy on seafood, but also includes such temptations as Chinese five-spice marinated duck breast with caramelized red onion and butter-wilted spinach.

✉ Florblanca Resort, Playa Santa Teresa ☎ 506 2640 0230 ⊙ Daily 7am–3pm cafe only, 6pm–9pm main restaurant ✋ L US$26, D US$40, Wine US$25

EL SANO BANANO

www.elbanano.com

At the heart of Montezuma, breakfast and nighttime action pivots around the Healthy Banana restaurant, which serves satisfying meals with a vegetarian slant. Alongside heart of palm salads, lasagne and enchiladas, a daily chalkboard of specials has fish and meat dishes. A 7.30pm dinner accompanies the nightly DVD (free with dinner order) on a drop-down screen. It will even prepare boxed take-out lunches, and its fresh-fruit *batidos* (iced shakes) are just the thing on hot days.

✉ On the main town road, Montezuma ☎ 506 2642 0638 ⊙ Daily 7am–10pm ✋ B US$5, L US$12, D US$20, Wine US$24

OJOCHAL

CITRUS

When it opened in October 2008, this restaurant brought a whole new level of sophistication to the Parque Nacional Marino Ballena district. Chef-owner Marcella Marciano knows how to work wonders in the kitchen, delivering mouthwatering treats in a stylish 21st-century setting. The chic decor is infused with Balinese inspirations, and the stylish bar invites lingering until closing. Flamenco and even belly dancing enliven the evenings.

✉ At the entrance to Ojochal, just off Highway 34 ☎ 506 2786 5175 ⊙ Tue–Sat 11–10 ✋ L US$15, D US$25, Wine US$18

PLAYA HERRADURA

ANFITEATRO SUNSET RESTAURANT

The sublime mountaintop setting with staggering views over the Gulf of Nicoya are reason enough to dine at the Anfiteatro restaurant, adorned with gracious antiques and fine art pieces. New Age music lends to the serene mood. Fortunately, this supremely elegant restaurant with an outdoor terrace also delivers the goods. Only the freshest ingredients go into the creative dishes, which might include a beef tenderloin carpaccio appetizer, and a main course of marlin with coconut milk and rum sauce. A month-long gastronomic festival is held in mid-summer.

✉ Hotel Villa Caletas, 3km (2 miles) north of Playa Herradura ☎ 506 2637 0505 ⊙ Daily 7am–10pm ✋ B US$10, L US$18, D US$36, Wine US$28

QUEPOS

CAFÉ MILAGRO

www.cafemilagro.com

This smart cafe serves great coffee, breakfasts, light meals, pastries and cakes, with books and newspapers also for sale. Snacks include delicious bagels, banana bread, brownies and sandwiches. Don't leave without trying the Skippy shake: chocolate ice cream blended with peanut butter. There's a tranquil garden patio at the rear. It also has a branch midway between Quepos and Manuel Antonio.

✉ On the seafront at north end of town, Quepos ☎ 506 2777 1707 ⊙ Daily 6am–10pm ✋ B US$6, L/D US$12

EL GRAN ESCAPE

www.elgranescape.com

On the main seafront road, El Gran Escape is one of Quepos's long-standing restaurants. A sportfishing theme prevails, with the breezy open-plan dining area decorated with marlin sculptures and inflatable sharks. The menu features, not surprisingly, freshly caught fish and seafood with a Caribbean influence: succulent coconut shrimp, seared tuna, tamarind and red pepper snapper. For carnivores, there are juicy 12oz steaks, and a Mexican selection that runs the gamut of burritos, fajitas and chimichangas. There is also a sushi bar, with all-you-can-eat specials, and a candlelit Italian restaurant next door.

✉ Quepos Centro ☎ 506 2777 0395 ⊙ Wed–Mon 6am–11pm ✋ L US$14, D US$20, Wine US$18

SÁMARA

LAS BRASAS

This confident Spanish restaurant, next to the soccer pitch, on the main street running up from the beach, is one of Sámara's most popular, smart eateries. Airy and spacious, with chunky wooden tables and chairs and, often, strolling musicians, it has a lively atmosphere. The house specials include gazpacho, paella, tortilla and, for eight people minimum, with advance notice, a whole roasted suckling pig.

✉ Costado de la Plaza del Deporte, Sámara Centro ☎ 506 2656 0546 ⊙ Mon–Sat 12–10 ✋ L US$12, D US$18, Wine US$17

PRICES AND SYMBOLS

The prices are for a double room for one night including breakfast, unless otherwise stated. All the hotels listed accept credit cards unless otherwise stated. Note that rates can vary widely throughout the year.

For a key to the symbols, ▷ 2.

ESTERILLOS

XANDARI BY THE PACIFIC

www.xandari.com

A sibling to the spectacular Xandari Resort and Spa (▷ 107), this superlative beach hotel utilizes the same winning designs and artsy touches. Villas exude romance and good taste in their use of hardwoods, mosaics and bright cushions. Generous bathrooms have a wall of glass opening to courtyard gardens, while the wall of glass in the lounges offer ocean views. The lap pool in the garden is inviting, and the restaurant is the best for miles.

Playa Esterillos Este 506 2778 7070 US$235–US$370 12 villas Outdoor

ISLITA

HOTEL HACIENDA PUNTA ISLITA

www.hotelpuntaislita.com

Perched upon a headland with dramatic ocean views, Punta Islita is among Costa Rica's top tier of hotels and is justifiably a member of the Small Luxury Hotels of the World. The wall-less lobby lounge beneath a soaring *palenque* is breathtaking and overlooks a sunken bar serving an infinity pool. Rooms are appointed with rough-hewn furniture, including draped beds, satellite TV, coffee-maker and minibar.

Punta Islita 506 2290 42592 US$360 rooms, US$395 suites, US$450 *casitas*. Check the internet for seasonal specials 20 rooms, 8 suites, 5 *casitas* Outdoor

JACÓ

COPACABANA HOTEL & SUITES

www.copacabanahotel.com

On the beach, at the northern end of town, this complex is one of Jacó's most popular choices. Each airy studio has a shower, air-conditioning and/or fans and a fridge. New suites offer a modicum of luxury. The pool area has a swim-up bar, and the open-air restaurant serves good food and has plenty of birdlife. By night, the pace is livelier.

Jacó 506 2643 1005. Toll free in the US 1-866-436 9399 US$99–US$149 32 Outdoor

LOS SUEÑOS MARRIOTT OCEAN & GOLF RESORT

www.lossuenosresort.com

A 15-minute drive from Jacó, on unappealing Playa Herradura, Los Sueños Resort is one of the most expensive hotels in Costa Rica. Shameless luxury combines with a huge range of amenities, all set in a forest of 445ha (1,100 acres). The four-floor complex, with casino and gym, is a pastiche of Spanish colonial style. There is an 18-hole golf course and a marina.

800m (875 yards) west from the entrance to Playa Herradura, Jacó 506 2630 9000. Toll free in the US: 1-888/223-2427 US$295–US$441 201 Outdoor

VILLA CALETAS

www.villacaletas.com

Looming high above Jacó, with 360-degree vistas, this lavish hotel is a dizzying cocktail of mock Victorian, Greek, French and Latin styles. Each room and villa is replete with every possible convenience. The Caletas amphitheater hosts concerts and weddings. There are gardens, a pool, a sumptuous spa and gym with sublime views, and two restaurants that serve acclaimed cuisine. In 2008 the owner opened Zephyr Palace, adjacent, as the most sumptuous hotel in the country.

9km (5.5 miles) north of Jacó 506 2637 0505 US$207–US$547, plus tax 35 Outdoor

Above *Hotel Hacienda Punta Islita*

MALPAIS

MALPAIS SURF CAMP

www.malpaissurfcamp.com

A five-minute walk from rugged Malpais Beach, this offers excellent accommodations for all budgets. Thatched-roof cabins allow for an at-one-with-nature experience, to a soundtrack of howler monkeys and birdlife. Bungalows, grouped around the pool, have patios and tiled bathrooms to satisfy those seeking more comfort and fewer creatures. The lodge serves erratic, but often excellent meals and is a real social hub in the evenings.

Malpais 506 2642 0031 US$15–US$95 16 Outdoor

MANUEL ANTONIO

ARENAS DEL MAR

www.arenasdelmar.com

New in 2008, this hotel boasts a unique draw for the area: it's the only deluxe hotel with beach access, although most rooms have a hilltop setting with sensational views along the beach to Manuel Antonio National Park. The lavish bedrooms are dolled up in contemporary fashion and have WiFi, plasma TVs and decks with their own whirlpool tubs. The Bali-inspired lobby merges with an open-air bar and restaurant that hovers above the beach.

Above Playa Espadilla, off the road to Hotel El Parador 506 2777 2777 US$260–US$430 38 one- and two-bedroom suites Outdoor

COSTA VERDE

www.hotelcostaverde.com

The World War II aeroplane—decked out as Ollie's Folly Bar—perched at the brow of the hill, marks the downhill run to the beach and the imminent arrival of Costa Verde hotel. Checking in at the train carriage reception, you're led to one of five multi-floor apartment blocks with comfortable to luxurious suites, all with ocean or jungle views, including the Boeing 727 suite, inside an actual jet-liner. Trails lead into the forest. You're bound to be woken by howler monkeys as they crash through the trees.

Manuel Antonio 506 7277 0584 Toll free in the US 1-866/854-7958 US$98–US$130 room, US$143–US$166 studio, US$190–339 penthouse 46 rooms, 2 bungalows 2 outdoor

MAKANDA BY THE SEA

www.makanda.com

One of the best hotels in Manuel Antonio, the studios and villas here are equipped for pure indulgence and designed with subtle Japanese minimalism. In the split-level studios guests have a stunning view as the day unfolds, seen from the perfectly positioned sofa, hammock or bed. You can wander to the infinity pool, Jacuzzi, or the nearby almost-private beach.

Manuel Antonio 506 2777 0442. Toll free in the US 1-888 MAKANDA US$265 studio, US$350–US$400 villa 11 Outdoor

MONO AZUL

www.hotelmonoazul.com

Mono Azul is some 5km (3 miles) from Manuel Antonio beach. This characterful hotel has clean, functional rooms with fan, bath and hot water. Luxury rooms have the added comfort of a TV and air-conditioning. The Blue Monkey's appeal lies in the hotel's ecological focus and wide range of services including pools, games room, library, internet cafe and bar-restaurant. Co-owner Jennifer Rice, a minister, presides over weddings.

Apdo 297, Manuel Antonio 506 2777 2572 US$51–US$74 room, US$74–US$119 villa 28 Outdoor

SI COMO NO

www.sicomono.com

This is one of Costa Rica's most acclaimed hotels. Refurbished rooms have ocean or forest views, and comforts include a solar-heated Jacuzzi, two pools and wet-bar, and you can dine at the Claro Que Si seafood restaurant or the Rico Tico grill. The spa has a solarium and whirlpool and a 40-seat cinema. The hotel has its own wildlife refuge, with a butterfly garden.

2.5km (1.5 miles) from park entrance, Manuel Antonio 506 2777 0777 US$238–US$384 58 2 outdoor

MONTEZUMA

AMOR DE MAR

www.amordemar.com

A short walk south of town is this relaxing hotel. It occupies a craggy cove at the tip of the bay, with manicured gardens that lead from the cafe-restaurant to the crashing waves of the beach. The lodge-style hotel is immaculate, with a variety of rooms, with or without a bath. For groups or families, there is also a *casita*, formerly the owner's home, which is available by the week.

100m (110 yards) from the estuary bridge on the road to Cabuya, Montezuma 506 2642 0262 US$57–US$125, *casita* (small house) US$226 per day 11 rooms, 1 *casita*

NATURE LODGE FINCA LOS CABALLOS

www.naturelodge.net

This blissful eco-lodge crowns the hilltop a five-minute drive from Montezuma. Rooms at the Spanish-style ranch have a private bath and a terrace with ocean views. There is an infinity pool, horse tours and a patio restaurant. Birdlife passes through the migratory corridor in the jungle below.

3km (2 miles) north of Montezuma on the road to Cóbano, Montezuma 506 2642 0124 US$97–US$156 12 rooms Outdoor

YLANG YLANG BEACH RESORT

www.ylangylangresort.com

This one-of-a-kind boutique hotel blends the laissez-faire Montezuma ethos with creature comforts. The location is the main draw, overlooking a rugged section of beach, encroached by forest and home to birds and monkeys, reached by hiking along the sands. Accommodations range from safari tents and bungalows to double rooms, all with bathrooms, air-conditioning and fans. A free-form swimming pool is fed by a water cascade and there is a lush garden. ✉ 800m (870 yards) to the north of town, Montezuma ☎ 506 642 0068 US$160 tents, US$195 rooms, US$215 suites, US$265–US$295 bungalows 6 tents, 3 beach rooms, 3 beach suites, 7 bungalows Outdoor

NOSARA

L'AQUA VIVA HOTEL & SPA

www.lacquaviva.com

Each year sees Nosara go more upscale, and 2009 was no exception with the opening of this lavish, Balinese-theme resort with stunning architecture combining soaring thatched ceilings with Modernist treatments. Centerpoint is a multi-tiered, trapezoid pool, although the hip bar competes as a jaw-dropping statement. The huge bedrooms are furnished with oriental antiques, but also have modern amenities.

✉ On the main road 1km (0.6 miles) north of the bank, in Beaches of Nosara ☎ 506 2682 1087 Rooms US$190, suites US$325 35 rooms and suites Outdoor

HARMONY HOTEL

www.harmonynosara.com

Less than a two-minute stroll from the beach, this gracious, contemporary-themed resort enfolds a landscaped pool complex shaded by palms. A remake has blessed the rooms and one- and two-bedroom bungalows with trendy furnishings and WiFi, although not all units are air-conditioned; all have fans. A tennis court, yoga studio, and a lovely restaurant round out the facilities.

✉ 400m (436 yards) west of the bank in Beaches of Nosara ☎ 506 2682 4114 Rooms US$190, bungalows US$270–US$330 24 rooms, 11 bungalows Outdoor

SAMARÁ

BELVEDERE

www.samara-costarica.com

This friendly and efficient hotel, in a quiet area a short stroll from the beach, has a family atmosphere. Rooms are placed around leafy patios, all with a bath and solar-heated water. Facilities include a Jacuzzi and there are apartments for long stays. Aerial tours by ultra-light can be arranged.

✉ 100m (110 yards) from the entrance to town, on the left, Sámara ☎ 506 2656 0213 US$45–US$95 12 Outdoor

FLYING CROCODILE LODGE

www.flying-crocodile.com

A contender for one of the most original hotels in Costa Rica, the Flying Crocodile takes its inspiration from Catalan architect Antoni Gaudí. Each lodge is a confection of undulating, shimmering and encrusted forms. The hotel doubles as an ultra-light flying center, offering tours for US$70–US$100. If you prefer to keep your feet on the ground, bicycles, horses and motorbicycles can also be rented.

✉ Playa Buena Vista, 10km (6 miles) north of Sámara ☎ 506 2656 8048 US$49–US$59 shared rooms, US$80–US$100, air-conditioned rooms 9 bungalows Outdoor

MIRADOR DE SÁMARA

www.miradordesamara.com

On a hilltop above Sámara, this dazzlingly white aparthotel has fully equipped apartments and is an ideal choice for families and long-stay visitors. Cool and comfortable, each apartment has a bathroom and kitchen, and a private balcony. The hotel also has four spacious rooms and there is a freshwater pool.

✉ Sámara ☎ 506 2656 0044 US$90 rooms, US$105 apartments, including breakfast 4 rooms, 10 apartments Outdoor

SANTA TERESA

FLORBLANCA RESORT

www.florblanca.com

You can't get closer to the ocean than staying at what may well be Costa Rica's most fashionable beach hotel. Hidden among lushly foliated grounds, this chic, unpretentious retreat defines casual calm and serenity. Imbued with a combination of Balinese and New Mexican architecture, the vast villas have outdoor bathrooms, while lounges with terra-cotta floors open directly to the jungle. The fusion restaurant is one of the finest outside the capital. A twin-tier swimming pool, plus gift shop, TV lounge and yoga studio round out the facilities.

✉ Playa Santa Teresa ☎ 506 2640 0232 US$475–US$850 10 villas Outdoor

SAVEGRE

RAFIKI SAFARI LODGE

www.rafikisafari.com

This is as wild as things get in Costa Rica. Deep in the valley of the Río Savegre, at the base of forested mountains, this thatched lodge is run by a South African family in traditional safari fashion. Guests sleep in deluxe tents atop decks with balconies; they even have full bathrooms with flush toilets. White-water rafting and kayaking are specialties of the lodge, which has a spring-fed pool adjoining a lagoon that draws birds and mammals.

✉ Near El Silencio, 19km (12 miles) east of Highway 34 ☎ 506 2777 2250 US$300, including meals 10 four-person tents Outdoor

Below *The superb restaurant at the Florblanca Resort*

SOUTHERN REGION

Known above all for Parque Nacional Corcovado—considered Costa Rica's crown jewel of rain forest venues—this region is actually the most diverse in the nation. The coast and the interior are worlds apart. The Talamanca Mountains, which rise south of San José, reach 3,820m (12,533 feet) atop Cerro Chirripó, at the heart of Parque Nacional Chirripó. The popular hike to the summit ends in Costa Rica's ultimate high. Southward the bulk of the Talamancas is protected within La Amistad International Peace Park—a virtually unexplored world protecting numerous indigenous reserves.

The rivers that spill from the mountains empty into the Térraba-Sierpe Wetland Reserve, a mangrove habitat that can be explored from Sierpe. Boats also depart this riverside hamlet for Bahía Drake, popular with scuba divers keen to explore the reefs around Isla del Caño. Whales frequent these waters and can often be seen from the shores of Bahía Drake, Ballena National Park and Golfo Dulce (Sweet Gulf). You're never far from nature in this region, be it the relatively manicured trails of Wilson Botanical Gardens or the challenging and wet, wet, wet wilds of Corcovado National Park.

Waves crash ashore all along this rugged coastline, drawing surfers to hang 10 at prime spots such as Dominical and Pavones, known for a ride that on good days can exceed 1km (0.6 miles). Set deep in a bay within Golfo Dulce, the banana-loading port of Golfito is also a base for sportfishing, as is Zancudo, a sleepy, breeze-caressed hamlet that unspools along miles of black sand. Equestrians will find no end of options. Rancho Merced Wildlife Refuge lets visitors saddle up to play cowboy; you can explore both shore and mountain at Hacienda Barú; or even ride to hidden waterfalls deep in the Escaleras Mountains from Dominical. Despite its distance from San José, the region is well served by scheduled flights and buses.

BAHÍA DRAKE

A crescent-shaped bay on the north end of the Osa Peninsula, Drake (pronounced Dra-kay) Bay is named after Sir Francis Drake, the English buccaneer who, in March 1579, beached his ship on Playa Colorada in the bay in order to repair it. Drake is good for swimming, but the beach is pebbly and attracts lots of hotel boats. The main appeal is diving off Isla del Caño (▷ 185), and nearby Parque Nacional Corcovado (▷ 181–184). If you want to learn to dive, PADI dive centers offer courses to beginners. Diving in the area is mainly to view fish rather than coral but divers may spot white-tipped sharks and rays. Several hotels also arrange sportfishing.

Researchers have recorded 25 species of dolphins and whales in Drake Bay, including humpback whales and bottlenose dolphins, as well as sea turtles. Corcovado Expeditions runs dolphin- and whale-watching tours; the best time is mid-November to end April. Day-trips to Isla del Caño, Corcovado and the mangroves of the Sierpe-Térraba estuary are offered by Corcovado Expeditions.

258 L11 · Daily buses from San José Tracopa terminal to Palmar Norte. Overland connections to Sierpe, then boat to Drake · Corcovado Expeditions office in Aguijitas · 506 8833 2384 · Leave Pan-American Highway at Chacarita and follow road to Rincón. A right fork leads to Aguijitas. The road, only passable in dry season, demands a four-wheel-drive vehicle

BORUCA

Nestling in the Río Térraba valley, two hours south of San Isidro de El General, the small community of Boruca is the focal point of the Boruca Indians, a tribe numbering less than 3,000 people. For much of the year the village of 200 people is almost lifeless. The rather unprepossessing homes scattered around an unkempt church belie a rich cultural heritage that has been eroding steadily since the arrival of the Jesuits in 1649. Today a cultural museum, sitting in the shadow of the church, is a sad reflection of the value placed on indigenous people in the country. But each year on the last day of December and the first two days of January the hardships of agricultural life are discarded in the celebrations of *La Danza de los Diabolitos*, the Dance of the Devils. If you can time your visit to coincide with the festival, visitors are welcomed.

258 M10 · From San José to Buenos Aires seven times daily. From Buenos Aires buses daily to Boruca at 11.30 and 3.30 · Galería Namú (▷ 76) runs ecotours to the area, US$65 per person per day · Take Pan-American Highway as far as the signs for Buenos Aires. Turn left and continue to Brujo, crossing bridge over the Térraba River, then turn right onto an uphill road which is signposted Boruca, from where it is a 40-min drive · Taxi from Buenos Aires US$45

GOLFITO

The regional hub of Golfito is important as much for its tax-free trade status as for its positioning as the stepping off point for Playa Zancudo and Pavones to the south. It flourished when the United Fruit Company set up in the port in the 1930s. Bust followed boom when the company pulled out in 1985. Arriving from the south, you'll gasp at its lovely, albeit steamy, setting within a bay. To the north is the administrative heart of Golfito and the *depósito libre*—the tax-free zone for Costa Rican merchants. It is the source of the town's relative affluence. Across the bay, or around the north shore, is Playa de Cacao, Golfito's closest beach. Today Golfito is a sportfishing hub, and a new marina promises future fortune.

259 N11 · Calle 5, avenidas 18–20 · Daily bus service from the Tracopa terminal in San José; regular service from Ciudad Neily · From Puerto Jiménez · Highway 14 leaves Pan-American Highway at Río Claro, 15km (9 miles) north of Ciudad Neily

JARDÍN BOTÁNICO WILSON

www.ots.ac.cr

The Wilson Botanical Gardens, 6km (3.5 miles) south from San Vito, are one of the world's premier collections of tropical plants, open for day visits and overnight stays. The Wilson Gardens are part of the Las Cruces Biological Station, owned and operated by the Organization for Tropical Studies. As with La Selva and Palo Verde, the station is a focus for biologists, students, birders and naturalists, keen to take advantage of the phenomenal diversity of the region.

The gardens have a network of trails and paths through the 10ha (25 acres) that take from 20 minutes to two and a half hours to walk, and self-guiding leaflets provide information allowing you to wander through the gardens at your own pace. Alternatively, go with a guide who will point out some of the 700 species of palms in the garden; there are a total of 1,000 in the neotropics. Resident bird species number 331. For the complete experience, accommodations in airy cabins are available.

259 N11 · 506 2773 4004 · Daily 8–5 · US$8 · A full-day guided tour costs US$24, half-day US$18 · From Golfito, take Pan-American Highway south toward the Panamanian border; on reaching Ciudad Neily, head north

Opposite *Stilt-houses in the bay outside Golfito*

Below *The delightful Jardín Botánico Wilson*

PALMAR NORTE AND PALMAR SUR

At a major intersection on the Pan-American Highway, 120km (74 miles) south of San Isidro de El General, Palmar Norte is of particular interest to people fascinated by big trucks. The town, an important transport hub, is one big truck stop. Roads lead southeast to Golfito and the Panama border, south to Sierpe, northwest to follow the Pacific coast and inland to San José.

The most interesting features of the area are the mysterious, spherical stone carvings, *esferas piedras*, left by the Diquis culture. The region is littered with these curious objects, which are most easily seen outside the Instituto Agropecuario in Palmar Norte or in Palmar Sur's main square, which lies on the opposite bank of the Térraba River, a couple of kilometers (a mile) to the south.

As with much of Costa Rican archaeology, the construction and purpose of the stones, believed to be around 2,000 years old, is still open to debate. The largest stone carving in the region, at 1.7m (5.6ft) across, is thought to weigh 9 tons (▷ 37).

258 L10 Several daily express buses go to and from San José. Regular buses go to San Isidro de El General. Several daily buses to Sierpe, the first at 7am for the boat from Sierpe to Drake

PARQUE INTERNACIONAL LA AMISTAD

▷ 177.

PARQUE NACIONAL CHIRRIPÓ

▷ 178.

PARQUE NACIONAL CORCOVADO

▷ 181.

PARQUE NACIONAL PIEDRAS BLANCAS

Primordial and challenging, this relatively unexplored park pulses with wildlife, ranging from sloths, coatis, peccaries, caimans and turtles to red-eyed leaf frogs, iguanas and ocelots.

The park's real attraction is the opportunity to experience the jungle without sharing it with hundreds of other visitors. Smart lodges organize guided hikes on the network of trails, and the park also runs the Esquinas Rain forest Lodge (▷ 193).

The land was initially purchased by the Austrian government to preserve the rain forest from loggers.

258 M11 506 2775 8001 Daily 8–4 US$6 2 buses daily from San Jose Terminal Alfaro to Golfito. Get off at Villa Briceño, 45km (28 miles) before Golfito. If staying at Esquinas Rain forest Lodge, arrange for them to pick you up From Briceño on the Pan-American Highway a rough road leads to Esquinas Rain forest Lodge and Piedras Blancas

PAVONES

Formerly a sleepy village, Pavones, a three-hour journey south of Golfito, has become a world-class surfing destination, with surfers arriving in droves to ride the country's longest left-hander which, if the swell is right, can allow for an awesome three- to four-minute ride.

April to September is the best time for surfing. Regardless of the time of year, surf culture prevails, testified by the mellow vibe, basic accommodations, and the suntanned and sculpted torsos on show. While surfing is the main activity in the area, fishing, horseback riding, kayaking trips, hiking to waterfalls, snorkeling and sunset tours can easily be arranged.

Pavones's two rocky, black-sand beaches, Río Claro and Pavones, stretch south at the mouth of the Golfo Dulce to Punta Banco, with the remote tropical retreat of Tiskita Jungle Lodge (▷ 193). If you want a quiet beach, Playa Zancudo, is a better choice than Pavones.

259 N12 Buses daily from Golfito to Pavones at 10.30 and 3. For transportation from San José to Golfito ▷ 175 A water taxi from Golfito (US$5 per person) is the best way to reach Pavones; contact the ABOCAP (Asociación de Boteros 506 2775 0712) Just outside Golfito, take the turnoff at El Rodeo and then the car ferry to Pavones

Above *Coconuts cluster below palm fronds*

PLAYA ZANCUDO

Leaving the bay of Golfito and heading south you cross the mangrove estuary of the Río Coto Colorado and eventually arrive in Zancudo, with not only a fine long beach but excellent sportfishing facilities too. Arriving at dusk, you are greeted by the beams of the setting sun shining through the coconut palms. For beach lovers, Zancudo has a captivating charm that has attracted American and European expatriates who have created a balance of laid-back comforts while avoiding any complicated trappings. In contrast to Pavones, the beach provides good bathing conditions, and at dusk the town gathers to enjoy the mesmerizing sunset. Fishing fans will find a top-notch fishing lodge, which organizes trips to deep waters that offer world-record-size fish.

259 N12 1 bus a day from Golfito at 2pm The best way to town is by water taxi. Contact Zancudo Boat Tours 506 2776 0012, US$20 per person, minimum US$50. Or visit Land Sea Tours' office in Golfito (506 2775 1614), which will arrange transportation from town Drive to Zancudo from Paso Canoas, or by cutting through on the Golfito–Río Claro road 10km (6 miles) from the Pan-American Highway, turning right at Bar El Rodeo and catching the ferry across the Río Coto Colorado. Either way, be prepared to get lost as signposts are poorly marked

PARQUE INTERNACIONAL LA AMISTAD

The largest park in the country and with incredible natural diversity, La Amistad reaches beyond national boundaries. As the largest protected area in Costa Rica, La Amistad protects the Talamanca mountain range of south-central Costa Rica, covering an expanse of 199,147ha (492,092 acres), and extending south into Panama. La Amistad demonstrates how Costa Rica lies at the convergence of North and South American flora and fauna. Its inventory of species is unparalleled. Secluded, difficult to reach and lacking in services, the park is the preserve of the intrepid and time-rich. There are three rangers' stations at Tres Colinas, Estación Pittier and Altamira. On the Pacific side, your best access point is at the Monte Amou Lodge.

INTERNATIONAL AMISTAD BIOSPHERE RESERVE

La Amistad National Park is the cornerstone of the International Amistad Biosphere Reserve, created by the United Nations in 1982. The reserve includes Tapantí-Macizo de la Muerte National Park (just south of Cartago), Chirripó National Park, four Indian reserves and several other protected areas. When Panama created the adjoining La Amistad National Park in 1990, the entire Talamanca mountain range became a World Heritage Site.

TALAMANCAS

The Talamancas are the highest non-volcanic mountain range in Central America, created by uplift of the earth surface which was subsequently eroded by glacial activity and heavy rainfall. That rainfall—up to 6,000mm (236in) a year in places—has created steep-sided slopes that have kept humans out of some areas of the park. Temperatures range from 25°C (77° F) down to -9°C (16°F). Eight of the twelve ecosystems found in Costa Rica are present, including lowland tropical rain forest, cloud forest and *páramo* (neotropical ecosystem) Altitude peaks at 3,820m (12,530ft) at Cerro Chirripó. Over 9,000 species of flowering plants are found here, as well as Costa Rica's six species of cat, the quetzal and the harpy eagle.

INFORMATION

256 M8 506 2730 0846 at Altamira Daily 8–4 (call ahead to check station is manned) US$6 4 buses daily from San José Tracopa terminal to San Vito. Get off at Las Tablas, then jeep-taxi to Carmen or Altamira. From Carmen it is a 4km (2.5-mile) hike to Altamira, then a 1.5km (1-mile) walk to the entrance

TIP

» Serious trekkers can contact the Asociación Talamanqueña de Ecoturismo y Conservación (ATEC, ▷ 207) about a 10-day trans-Talamanca hike.

Above *The nonvolcanic Talamanca mountain range*

INFORMATION
www.chirripo.com
256 L8 506 2742 5083
US$15, 2 days, then US$10 for each additional day. Each night at the refuge costs a further US$10 Local buses from San Isidro de El General, ▷ 185, to San Gerardo de Rivas and Parque Nacional Chirripó at 5am and 2pm, returning at 7am and 9.30pm. They leave from the bus terminal, south of the main plaza. Regular buses ply all routes with terminals on or close to the highway Around US$500 for a 3-day organized round trip. Contact the regional specialists, Costa Rica Trekking Adventures, who will organize your trip 506 771 4582

Above *Las Morenas Lake seen from the summit of Parque Nacional Chirripó*

INTRODUCTION

Costa Rica's second largest national park (50,150ha/123,920 acres) embodies the adventure and biodiversity of the country. The park's main attraction lies in the challenge of conquering Cerro Chirripó, the country's highest peak, at 3,820m (12,533ft).

On August 19, 1975, Chirripó National Park was officially established. It was expanded in 1982 and designated a UNESCO Biosphere Reserve before being granted World Heritage Site status in 1983. Chirripó, meaning "land of eternal waters," evolved through volcanic and tectonic activity. A series of glacial lakes, rock bed striations and curved moraines provide evidence of Chirripó's history. Geologists believe that 25,000 years ago, during the last ice age, the area was covered with glacial ice. The last glaciers disappeared 10,000 years ago. Before the arrival of the Spanish, the *páramo* highlands were considered to be sacred by the area's indigenous population, a reverence that precluded exploration. In 1904, Agustín Blessing, a Talamancan priest and missionary, became the first man to conquer Cerro Chirripó.

With neighboring La Amistad International Park, Chirripó protects the Talamanca Mountains from south of Cartago down to the border with Panama. The ecological wealth of the park is due to the diversity of landscape that ranges from pastures at 1,000m (3,280ft) around San Gerardo de Rivas to the barren scenery at the peak of Cerro Chirripó. The park's main access point is San Gerardo de Rivas, which has good transportation links to San Isidro (20km/12.5 miles northeast), and where there is a rangers' station (daily 6.30am–4.30pm). Inside the park there are *refugios* (huts) at Llano Bonito (open sided, insect ridden), halfway to the summit, and another basic refuge about 3km (2 miles) farther uphill. The Centro Ambientalista lodge, 5km (3 miles) from the summit, has bunk beds and cooked meals (by pre-arrangement); reservations are strongly advised via the ranger station.

Temperatures vary immensely; the driest period is between mid-December and mid-April, when most people visit the park. During Semana Santa, the park gets very crowded, and on weekends the *refugios* often fill up quickly. At night, temperatures drop, at their lowest, to -9°C (16°F), and with thick fogs and windspeeds in excess of 80kph (50mph), conditions can be bitter. Warm clothing is essential, as is rain gear from May to the end of December. It is possible to walk a circuit of the park, but you will need a guide or good topographical maps. You can rent porters to carry your equipment to the hut (tel 506 742 5073, US$30 per day).

Most of the local lodges are able to assist with arrangements. If all you want to do is climb the peak and let someone else do the organization, most tour operators in San José will arrange it.

WHAT TO SEE

FLORA AND FAUNA

The ecological richness of Chirripó is difficult to imagine. In a world of subtle tropical variations, the presence of classic glacial formations like U-shaped valleys, moraine deposits and glacial lakes appear out of place. From around 3,000m (9,840ft), the barren *páramo* landscape is of stunted forest, mosses, alpine grasses and savanna covering a broad open plateau. The oak landscape just below the summit area is recovering from a fire in 1992.

Around the summit, trails lead to the rocky outcrop of Cerro Crestones, the Valles de los Conejos (Valley of the Rabbits) and the Sabana de los Leones (Lions' Savanna).

At lower altitudes, and warmer temperatures, meadows give way to cloud forest (more than half of the park's total area), with an incredible diversity of flora and fauna, in particular the birds, of which there are over 400 species including the resplendent quetzal. The park contains some 263 species of amphibians and reptiles and is home to the largest tapir population in the country, as well as significant numbers of pumas, jaguars, coatis, monkeys and other species of mammals.

CLIMBING CERRO CHIRRIPÓ GRANDE

For those in search of a good long trek, a two-day trip in Chirripó National Park is the answer. As far as walks go, it's a pretty tough number, but the trail is well marked and there's little chance of getting lost. While technically and navigationally the ascent of Cerro Chirripó Grande is straightforward, with a reasonable level of fitness required, conditions can be brutal, with cold temperatures and muddy terrain.

The trail skirts through evergreen forest, floats among cloud forest cloaked in swirling mists and eventually leads onto the barren *páramo* savannas. Along its length, the fauna changes constantly and the views from the top to the Atlantic, the Pacific and down the spine of the Talamanca range are spectacular, especially at sunrise.

Climbing steadily from a starting altitude of 1,400m (4,600ft), the 18km (11-mile) ascent takes eight to ten hours (conservative estimate) to the Centro Ambientalista el Paramoa *refugio* at 3,400m (11,155ft) above sea level, where there is basic accommodation, equipped with running water, toilets and a cold shower. Leaving by 6am will get you past the steep open plains under the shade of the tree canopy, therefore avoiding the merciless sun. From the refuge, it's a couple of hours, mostly on the flat, to ascend the last 400m (1,300ft) of the hike. Organizing the two- or three-day trip is straightforward. The refuge has 15 dormitory rooms, with 4 beds in each, and a kitchen for preparing food. Basic accommodation at the refuge is reserved

TIPS

» Supplies in San Gerardo de Rivas are limited. If you are hiking, buy them in San Isidro before arriving in the area.

» With often freezing conditions, a stove for cooking and making hot drinks is essential.

» Don't underestimate the severity of the climate, and remember that sunscreen is essential this close to the equator.

» The refuge can get very full, particularly in the dry season from January to April, and on weekends, so book in advance if possible. Sleeping bags and small gas stoves are available for rent for a small fee.

» Topographical maps, necessary for long-distance hikes in the park, are available from the Instituto Geográfico Nacional or Lehmann's bookstore in San José (▷ 76).

» Basic maps of the park can be bought from the MINAE office (in San Gerardo) for US$0.80.

Below *One of the peaks in the park, shrouded in cloud*

Above *Trees drip with moisture in the humid rain forest*

through MINAE (the Ministerio del Ambiente y Energia), which has offices in San Isidro (tel 506 2270 8040) and San Gerardo de Rivas (tel 506 2742 5083).

DAY ONE

Start the trek early, around 6am or earlier if possible, and aim to get to the lodge in one day. It is a long, sometimes slippery, uphill trek with barely any level ground, let alone downhill sections, to break the monotony. While the scenery compensates, you don't want to be struggling toward the top with nightfall approaching. Water is available at the very basic, open-air Llano Bonito refuge at 2,500m (8,200ft), reached after about three hours. It is possible to stay at Llano Bonito but the conditions vary and are not reliably clean.

DAY TWO

Another early start, leaving the lodge around 3.30am, the trek goes along a mainly level trail to the final summit push, a rock scramble of approximately 200m (650ft or so), to the peak for sunrise. Desolate and harsh, this lunar landscape is only 10 degrees from the equator.

If short of time, you can head downhill and catch the 4pm bus to San Isidro. Other trails in the area are easily navigated, although you may feel more comfortable with maps or a guide.

MORE TO SEE

THERMAL SPRINGS

Close to San Gerardo de Rivas, these hot springs are rather handy for weary legs after the stiff climb. From the rangers' station turn left toward Herradura and follow the signposts. Admission for the day is US$2.

CERRO CRESTONES

If you have time, rather than taking the straightforward descent from Chirripó (the most popular route), you could take things more slowly and enjoy the simple trek to the outcrops of Cerro Crestones.

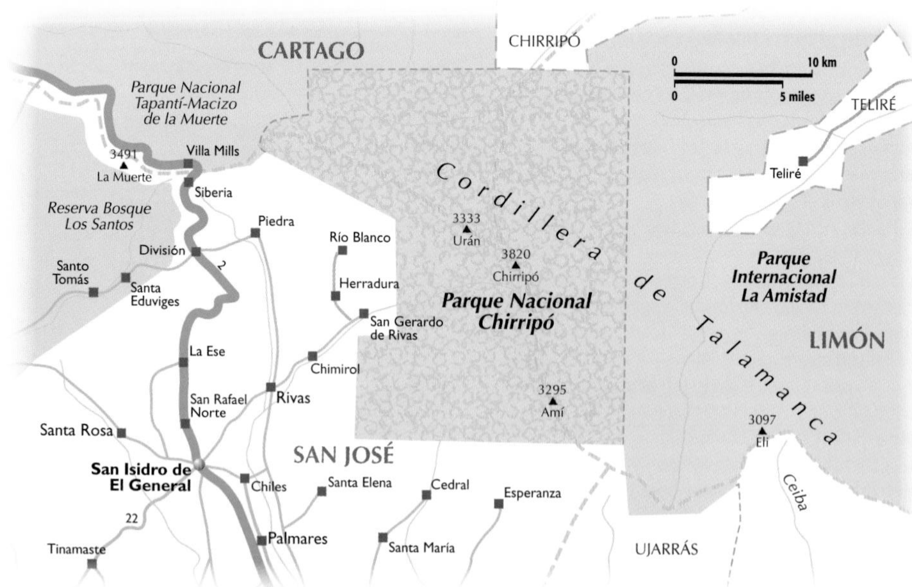

INTRODUCTION

The most magnificent jewel in Costa Rica's green crown, this paradise for wildlife watchers gives visitors the rare chance to take long-distance treks through lowland rain forest and across flawless beaches. Corcovado was granted National Park status in 1975 and protects the largest area of tropical rain forest in the country. Some 30sq km (11.5sq miles) were deforested before it became a national park; the area's timber was more valuable than its gold.

Gold mining in the park was started by the indigenous populations in the eighth century. The Costa Rican gold rush of the 1930s ushered in a renewed period of mining, and the 1970s saw the introduction of damaging techniques, causing the contamination of the southern third of Corcovado. In 1979, an economic slump caused banana prices to plummet, but the price of gold rocketed and many men relocated to Corcovado. By the mid 1980s there were 3,000 illegal miners in the park. A technique known as placer mining has since proved responsible for 80 percent of the park's landslides. Soil sediment and the leaching of mercury, compounded the problem. And the human presence in the forest led to hunting and poaching. Following reports by the World Wildlife Fund, the park was cleared of gold prospectors in 1985.

In the southwest corner of Costa Rica, the park protects one third of the Osa Peninsula (42,469ha/104,940 acres). Three rangers' stations provide access to the park. San Pedrillo, to the north, is reached through Drake, from where you need to charter a boat or walk round the headland. Los Patos in the middle of the peninsula is reached from La Palma, served by buses coming from the Pan-American Highway to Puerto Jiménez. The final option is through La Leona to the south, reached from Carate, which has road access from Puerto Jiménez, 43km (27 miles) away. You can visit the park using any combination of entrances and exits.

INFORMATION

258 L12 506 2735 5580. To reserve accommodations (essential), contact MINAE, Puerto Jiménez on this number US$10 per day, or US$20 for a 5-day pass, reservations required for overnights in ranger's stations 1 daily bus from San José Terminal Atlántico Norte to Puerto Jiménez Costa Rica Expeditions (▷ 238) organizes the Corcovado Rain forest Odyssey, a 3-day, 2-night trip, which includes air transportation and accommodations at the Corcovado Lodge, all meals, a bilingual naturalist guide and canopy tour, US$718. Check the website for last-minute discounted special offers, www.costaricaexpeditions.com Leave the Pan-American Highway at Chacarita and take a potholed road that follows the southern shore of the peninsula to Rincón; 14km (8.5 miles) beyond Rincón is La Palma, from where the road heads west to the Los Patos station

Above *Trusting a hanging bridge to cross muddy water in the Osa Peninsula*

TIPS

›› If short of time or money, the simplest way to the park is to take the pick-up truck from outside Carolina's (▷ 191) in Puerto Jiménez to Carate, from where you can go on short treks in the south of the park.

›› Entering the park through Carate and exiting through La Palma, or vice versa, is the simplest and cheapest option.

›› Always sign the rangers' book before you set off on a hike, regardless of length or difficulty. If you do not return, they will come to look for you.

›› Many of the river trails along the beach will be impassable at high tide, and visitors have often been stranded. Consult the rangers before you set off and be sure to obtain a tide chart from the park information office.

›› A rugged road from Puerto Jiménez requires fording three rivers and is often impassable to jeeps.

›› Setting off early on hikes is recommended, but leave after dawn to minimize chance encounters with snakes.

›› Accommodations must be booked through the MINAE office in Puerto Jiménez.

›› If making an independent trek, bring topographical maps from the Instituto Geográfico Nacional in San José.

Above *San Pedrillo beach is in the national park*

The closest point approaching the park from the south is Carate, an excellent base for short trips to the park. It has good links with Puerto Jiménez to the east. From the capital, most people using public transportation choose to access the park from Puerto Jiménez, by *colectivo* trucks or jeep-taxi. You can get off the bus at La Palma, 24km (15 miles) north of Puerto Jiménez, from where a 12km (7.5-mile) road leads to the park entrance. If you choose the route from Carate to La Leona, be prepared for a hot, exposed beach hike. A station at El Tigre, at the eastern entrance to the park, offers a series of short trails. Budget permitting, you can get an air taxi from Puerto Jiménez to Carate, San Pedrillo and even Sirena for as little as US$100 per person with five people. Trails range from short tracks that take just a couple of hours to marathon challenges involving two-day hikes along beaches and through dense humid tropical forests where you have to negotiate swamps and rivers and camp overnight in the jungle. Basic accommodation is available at the rangers' stations in San Pedrillo, Los Patos, La Leona and, the most commonly used, Sirena. Bring a sleeping bag and mosquito net. You can camp for US$2 a night, and meals are available.

WHAT TO SEE

FLORA AND FAUNA

After Monteverde and Arenal, Corcovado National Park is probably the most recorded part of Costa Rica. National Geographic, Discovery Channel, the BBC and countless naturalists have described its delights, and with good reason. Often heralded as Costa Rica's Amazon, it contains the greatest expanses of primary forest on the Pacific and is true to the popular image of a rain forest: diverse species, soaring trees, magnificent buttresses and creeping vines. As ever, it's the combination of temperatures in the high 20s°C (around 82°F) and rainfall as high as 5,500mm (215in) that has endowed the park with eight different ecosystems. Cloud forest on some of the higher summits gives way to montane forest, which covers over half the park. There is swamp forest around Corcovado lagoon, mangrove forests along the river estuaries, herbaceous swamps and pristine coastline, as well as more than 13 vegetation types, with over 500 species of tree.

Wildlife is equally diverse. Corcovado is home to the largest population of scarlet macaws in Central America. All six big cats in Costa Rica are found in the park, and the beach at Llorona to the north is used as a nesting site by four species of turtles. The staggering inventory extends to 140 species of mammals, more than 10 percent of the mammal species in the entire Americas, 367 species of birds, including the endangered harpy eagle, reptiles, 40 types of freshwater fish and 177 species of amphibians, such as the red-eyed tree frog and the poison-arrow frog. Monkeys abound: Corcovado and Manuel Antonio (▷ 160–161) national parks are the only two areas in Costa Rica where you will find the squirrel monkey. When it comes to wildlife spotting, your expectations should be realistic; you'll need a guide, patience and a good deal of luck to tick significant numbers off your list.

SIRENA

The area around the Sirena rangers' station is the best place for viewing wildlife, where treks through wild, virgin landscapes last from 30 minutes to a few hours. You can explore inland paths and the Corcovado lagoon. It's definitely worth staying overnight at Sirena.

It's about 18km (11 miles), and a full-day hike, from Carate to Sirena, a coastal trail, which you can make in one day as long as the tides don't work against you; check with the wardens to ensure that you can get through. About 40 minutes beyond Carate is La Leona station. From La Leona to the end of Playa Madrigal is another two and a half hours of walking, over a partly sandy beach with some rock pools and shipwrecks. At points the trail rises steeply into the forest and you are surrounded by mangroves, almonds and coconut palms. Look for scarlet macaws feeding on the almond trees that skirt the beach. A couple of rivers break the beachline. The first, Río Madrigal, is about 15 minutes' walk beyond La Leona. Clear, cool and deep enough for swimming, it's a refreshing stop and a good place to spot wildlife.

From Sirena there are opportunities for shorter hikes. The one-hour Guanacaste trail, named after the nGuanacaste trees found along it, begins 0.5km (0.3 miles) from Sirena rangers' station. It starts through dense primary forest that gives way to sparser secondary forest. The trail can be muddy and hazardous in places and several rivers need to be crossed. The Esuvellas trail is slightly longer and can be accessed from behind the rangers' station. Shaded by canopy, the trails are level and relatively easy, with just a couple of rivers to negotiate. From Sirena you can walk north along the coast to Llorona, continuing north on a forest trail and then along the beach to the station at San Pedrillo. You can stay here and eat with the rangers if you've made a reservation.

Left *Forest-floor tree formations*
Below *A strawberry poison arrow frog*

Left *Massive ceibo trees are common in Corcovado National Park*

LOS PATOS

From Sirena you can hike inland on a trail to Los Patos (20km/12.5 miles), that will take between six and nine hours, passing several rivers full of reptiles. This is only recommended for very experienced hikers, with searing heat, high humidity and no breeze. However, the rewards are great, providing some of the best opportunities to see elusive mammals. The rangers' station at Los Patos has a balcony, which is a great observation point for birds.

From Los Patos you can carry on to the park border, before criss-crossing the Río Rincón to La Palma, a settlement on the opposite side of the peninsula (13km/8 miles), a further six-hour hike. From La Palma there is transportation to Puerto Jiménez.

SAN PEDRILLO TO LA LEONA

Close to Drake Bay, San Pedrillo is the most northern of the three rangers' stations. From the east side of the rangers' station, a 90-minute trail ascends to the northern parameters of the National Park. Before the plateau, there is a lookout point from which you may see dolphin and whales.

From the boundaries of the park, you can hike to Playa San Josecito or return towards the rangers' station and hike to the San Pedrillo River (one hour). This is a steep descent and can be dangerous in the rainy season. Crossing the San Pedrillo River takes you to a magnificent waterfall (swimming is not advised). Crossing the river from the left side will bring you back to San Pedrillo.

Walking the coastal path from San Pedrillo to La Leona takes three days, without allowing for time spent exploring trails around Sirena. The Sirena River is the park's deepest river, but not for the nervous. Crocodiles can be seen resting on the banks and sharks feed at the river mouth at high tide (only cross at low tide). There is myriad birdlife along the riverbanks and beautiful waterfalls at Playa Llorona.

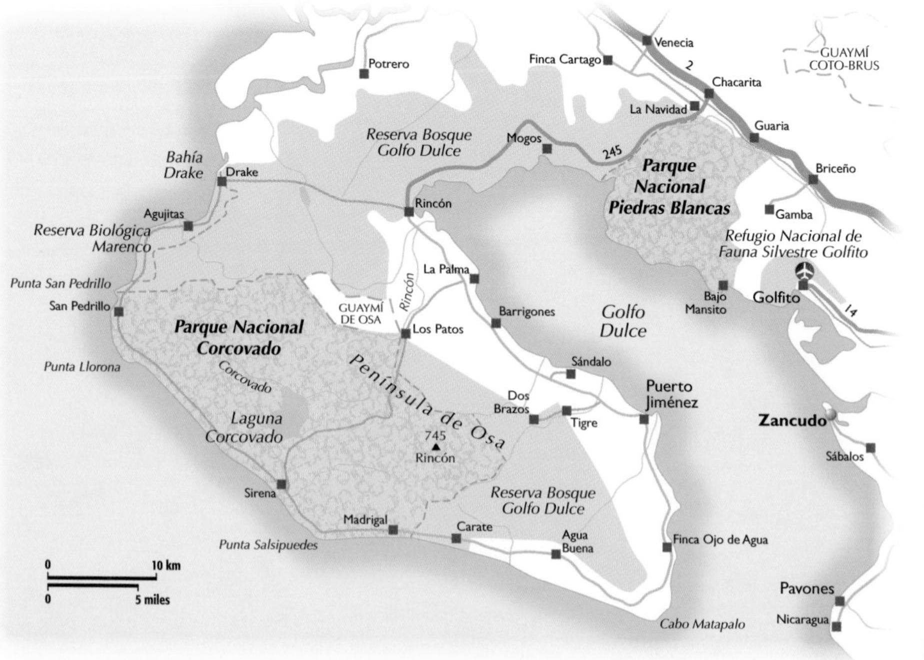

Above *Beached boats at Puerto Jiménez*

PUERTO JIMÉNEZ

The main point of entry for Corcovado National Park, Puerto Jiménez is the most significant town on the Osa Peninsula. Once the gold-mining hub of the area, with a single, dusty main street, Puerto Jiménez retains the feel of a lawless frontier town. Today it is a popular destination with a laid-back lifestyle, reasonable beaches and the beautiful national park not far away. One attraction of the town, five blocks square, is its relative freedom from road traffic. There are budget accommodations, a smart sportfishing lodge, good walks to the jungle and beaches only a couple of blocks from the main street. You don't even have to go that far to see wildlife: Scarlet macaws roost in trees around the football pitch.

If your accommodations are out of town, make arrangements to be picked up from the airstrip, dock or bus station. Regular pick-ups make the trip to Carate from Puerto Jiménez, from where you can go to Corcovado.

258 M12 Ferries cross Gulfo Dulce to Golfito three times daily Ask at Carolina's Restaurant (▷ 191) on the main street, and visit Escondido Trex (506 2735 5210, www.escondidotrex.com). They offer tours on the Osa Peninsula and around the Dulce Gulf The 79km (49-mile) road from the Pan-American Highway to Rincón is badly eroded; from Rincón a potholed dirt road heads south for 35km (22 miles) to Puerto Jiménez

RESERVA BIOLÓGICA DURIKA

www.durika.org

Lying 17km (10.5 miles) east of Buenos Aires, this private reserve spreads over 800ha (1,976 acres) in the Talamanca Mountains. The community aims to encourage reforestation and conservation of the region, and ecotourism plays a part in that process. Good trails through the area and to nearby Cerro Durika (3,280m/10,760ft) g ive an insight into this rarely visited part of Costa Rica. Accommodations are available in five rustic cabins. All sorts of healthy pursuits for mind and body are on offer, including yoga, kung-fu and short hikes to *campesino* (peasant farmer) and Indian communities, and longer hikes to the mountain peaks. The steep, winding access road is one of the most daunting drives in the country. A jeep-taxi from Buenos Aires is recommended.

259 M9 Apdo Postal 9-8100 506 2730 0657 US$35 per person Several daily buses from San José to Ciudad Neily and Paso Canoas pass through Buenos Aires Reserve is 17km (10.5 miles) east of Buenos Aires, off the Pan-American Highway, reached by four-wheel-drive vehicle via a challenging mountain drive

RESERVA BIOLÓGICA ISLA DEL CAÑO

Some 20km (12.5 miles) west of the Osa Peninsula, Caño Island Biological Reserve has a striking coastline formed by jagged cliffs, white sandy beaches and coral reefs. It is a popular day trip from Sierpe and Drake Bay. The island's main interest on land is archaeological. Remains indicate that the island was used as a pre-Columbian cemetery. The stone spheres found in the mainland's Diquis Valley are present here, adding to the mystery of how and why they were made.

The island attracts divers and snorkelers. The 2,700ha (6,672-acre) marine reserve protects coral reefs, parrotfish, olive ridley turtles and the giant conch. Excellent dive sites include "The Depth of the Devil," with reef sharks, barracuda and rock pinnacles thrusting from the deep.

258 K11 506 2735 5580 US$6 The only way to visit the island is as part of a tour. Most people take an all-inclusive tour from Corcovado, around US$80 per person The office for the Osa Peninsula Conservation Area is in Puerto Jíménez (daily 8–1, 2–5)

SAN ISIDRO DE EL GENERAL

www.ecotourism.co.cr

The largest town south of San José is known as San Isidro and rests at the base of a broad fertile valley created by several rivers. Completion of the Pan-American Highway in the 1950s has seen the town grow as a transportation hub for journeys north, south and east. Its principal areas of interest are in a seven-block square. The town is the main departure point for ascents of Cerro Chirripó, and descents of the Río General white-water rapids.

San Isidro is best known to Ticos for one significant event: José Figueres Ferrer (▷ 41) used it as a foothold from which to launch the civil war of 1948. The conflict gave birth to the modern political era in Costa Rica and led to the abolition of the nation's army.

In the mid-1950s, the cathedral of San Isidro Labrador, patron saint of the town, was consecrated. For some, the contemporary concrete church is a bold statement, with magnificent stained glass. Inside, it is bright and breezy with a fresh approach to religious iconography. The old marketplace, now the Complejo Cultural, at Calle 2, avenidas 1–0, contains the Museo Regional del Sur (Mon–Fri 8–12, 1.30–4.30).

255 K8 Hourly from San José, Calle Central, avenidas 22–24 CIPROTUR, the Centro de Información y Promoción Turística del Pacífico Sur, Calle 4, avenidas 1–3 506 2771 6096; a regional tourist board

ALONG THE TALAMANCA FOOTHILLS

The rugged Talamanca massif is your constant companion on this challenging but scenic journey through the Valles de El General and Valle de Coto Brus. It's a two-day drive, with time for a detour into the coffee-clad hills of the Valle del Río Chirripó.

THE DRIVE
Distance: 170km (106 miles)
Allow: 2–3 days
Start at: San Isidro
End at: Ciudad Neilly

★ Beginning in San Isidro (▷ 185), Highway 2 (the Pan-American Highway) is a well-paved slingshot south from town. After barely 1km (0.6 miles), however, keep your eyes peeled for a turnoff to the left—a sharp uphill chicane—for San Gerardo de Rivas and Chirripó. After 7km (4.5 miles) you pass through Rivas, a charming village at the foot of the mountains.

Before Rivas, stop to admire the "Piedra de los Indios," a huge rock carved with pre-Columbian petroglyphs; it's signed roadside on your right immediately north of Rancho la Botija (▷ 191), a farmstead-restaurant where you can stop for a hearty traditional lunch.

At Rivas you leave the paved road and begin to climb into the mountains on a rock and gravel road, with the river below to your right. The road narrows, with switchback bends and heart-stopping drop-offs. The air grows cooler and coffee bushes appear, welcoming you to the mountain hamlets of Canaan and, beyond, San Gerardo de Rivas.

San Gerardo (▷ 179, 180) is a great base for hiking and for relaxing in thermal springs. Spend the night at Talamanca Reserve, set in its own forest reserve, with good hiking and ATV trails (tel 506 2742 5080; www.talamancareserve.com). Next morning retrace your route back down the valley to Highway 2, and turn south. Watch for potholes as you follow the paved road past pineapple plantations, centered on the town of Buenos Aires, hidden north of the highway. Further south you'll cross the Río General and follow its looping course to its junction with the Río Coto Brus; they twine to become the Río Terraba. The purplish heights of Cerro Kamuk form a dramatic backdrop.

The Térraba cuts west through a deep gorge through the Fila Costeña mountains en route to the Pacific. The Reserva Indígena Boruca (▷ 175), deep in the mountains, offers an immersion in indigenous culture. You can buy fabulous carved balsa masks at the source. The muddy mountain road to Boruca is challenging during or after rains.

From the river confluence, follow the Río Térraba barely 1km (0.6 miles) and turn left to cross the bridge over the river. Use caution: Entire slabs of paving are often missing! From here, Highway 137 hugs the northern flank of the Fila Costeña as you follow the Río Coto Brus. The highway now runs in a winding roller-coaster atop a ridge-crest of the Fila Cruces mountains, with gorgeous views to both sides. Drive very carefully. As with all these roads, landslides are frequent, especially after heavy rains. A final climb delivers you in San Vito.

San Vito was founded by Italian coffee farmers in the 1850s. A life-size statue in the triangular hilltop plaza is dedicated to "La Fraternidad Italo-Costarricense." Recent years have witnessed a demise of the local coffee industry. Accommodations include Las Cruces (tel 506 2773 4004; www.ots.ac.cr).

Climbing south out of town, expect fog to shroud the highway, so be vigilant. At Km6 from San Vito you pass Las Cruces Biological Station (▷ 175). Plan to make a stop here, timing your arrival no later than mid-afternoon.

Las Cruces Biological Station is a 290ha (717-acre) forest reserve and Organization of Tropical Studies research center. Agoutis, monkeys and up to 400 species of birds are easily seen while walking the trails of the Jardín Botánico Wilson (▷ 175). It has accommodations, but reservations are essential.

La Cruces sits atop the mountains. From here you'll descend gradually to the ridge-crest of the Fila Cruces. A roadside *mirador* (lookout) offers refreshment and a stupendous view over the vale of the Río Coto-Colorado. The town of Ciudad Neily is laid out below, reached via a precipitous, snaking descend down the mountainside.

PLACES TO VISIT
JARDÍN BOTÁNICO WILSON
✉ 6km (4 miles) south of San Vito, ▷ 175
☎ 506 2773 4004; www.ots.ac.cr

WHERE TO EAT
RANCHO LA BOTIJA
✉ Rivas ☎ 506 2770 2146; www.rancholabotija.com

Right *Sunrise in Parque Nacional Chirripó*

WHAT TO DO

BAHÍA DRAKE

CAÑO DIVERS

www.piratecovecostarica.com

You may see sharks and rays when diving in Drake Bay with Caño Divers. You can arrange your dive through your hotel.

✉ Pirate Cove Hotel, north end of Bahía Drake ☎ 506 2234 6154 ✋ Two-tank diving day US$110

NIGHT INSECT TOUR

www.thenighttour.com

Entomologist Tracie Stice—aka "The Bug Lady"—leads enthralling nocturnal tours into the rain forest in search of bugs by the score, or thousands. You'll be amazed by the fascinating lore she imparts, leaving you with a new appreciation for creepy crawlies. The website is very informative.

✉ Drake Bay ☎ 506 8867 6143 🕐 Nightly 7.30pm ✋ US$35

BORUCA

FIESTA DE LOS DIABLOS

At year's end, head to the Reserva Indígena Boruca, where villagers dressed as devils celebrate a fictional defeat of colonial Spanish forces, represented by a community member dressed as a much-abused bull. Festivities are helped along by copious quantities of corn liquor and by traditional music with pipes, gourds and drums.

✉ Boruca, 30km (18 miles) east of Palmar Norte

CIUDAD NEILY

PARADISE GARDEN

Robert Beatham has spent more than a decade planting and tending his tropical fruit and nut farm and botanical garden. He gives fascinating tours, which begin with a sampling of unusual edible species and include eye-opening education on the medicinal uses of plants such as "wandering jew" (good for treating diabetes).

✉ 1.5 km (1 mile) west of Ciudad Neily ☎ 506 2789 8746 🕐 Daily 6am–5pm ✋ By donation

PAVONES

ARTE NATIVO

Opposite Esquinas, Arte Nativo sells locally made art and jewelry. Owner Candyce Speck's painting are sold here. She offers the only internet service in town (daily 8–8).

✉ 400m (440 yards) south of Supermares ☎ 506 8821 6563

SHOOTING STAR STUDIO

www.shootingstarstudio.org

This studio gives the study of yoga a new twist: it caters to surfers, on a yoga deck just 9m (30ft) from the beach. The owners, Alexander Outerbridge and Amy Khoo also have the only surf shop in town

✉ By the soccer field, Pavones ☎ 506 8393 6982

PLAYA SAN JOSECITO

CASA ORQUÍDEAS

Some 30 minutes by water taxi from Golfito, you can visit Casa Orquídeas, a family-owned botanical garden with a collection of herbs, orchids and local plants and an entertaining, hands-on tour explaining their medicinal properties.

✉ Land Sea Tours, Playa San Josecito ☎ 506 8829 1247 🕐 Sat–Thu 8–5, 8.30 tours ✋ US$8 per person guided tour, min 4 people

Above *Dolphins leaping from the waters—a sight to cheer dolphin spotters*

PLAYA ZANCUDO

ZANCUDO LODGE

www.zancudolodge.com

On the narrow peninsula of Zancudo, there are plenty of angling opportunities. Zancudo Lodge offers offshore fishing on their fleet of 12 well-equipped boats for marlin, dorado, wahoo and tuna and inshore fishing for roosterfish, snapper and grouper.

✉ Playa Zancudo ☎ 506 2776 0008 🕐 Peak season Dec–end Jun 🖐 3-day all-inclusive trip US$3,195

SAN GERARDO DE RIVAS

AGUAS TERMALES

www.sangerardocostarica.com

After an energizing trek up Cerro Chirripó, soothe your weary muscles in these natural springs, which feed landscaped pools popular with local families on weekends. There are changing facilities. It's on private property, and the small entrance fee includes secure parking.

✉ Herradura, 500m (550 yards) northwest of San Gerardo de Rivas ☎ 506 2742 5210 🕐 Daily 7am–6pm 🖐 US$2

CHIRRIPÓ CLOUDBRIDGE RESERVE

www.cloudbridge.org

If the trek up Cerro Chirripó seems too challenging, take to the trails at this private reserve close to the Cerro Chirripó trailhead. Some 12km (7.5 miles) of *senderos* (trails) lead to waterfalls, and you can relax in a meditation garden.

✉ 2.5km (1.5 miles) northeast of San Gerardo de Rivas 🕐 Daily 8am–5pm 🖐 By donation

SAN ISIDRO DE EL GENERAL

CENTRO BIOLÓLOGICO LAS QUEBRADAS

www.ecotourism.co.cr/fudebiol

The community-protected reserve of Centro Biológico las Quebradas is a 2.5km (1.5-mile) walk from Quebradas. The Centro protects the birds, bromeliads and butterflies of the Quebradas River basin.

✉ San Isidro de El General ☎ 506 2771 4131 🕐 Tue–Fri 8–2, Sat, Sun 8–3 🖐 US$6

LOS CUSINGOS

www.cct.or.cr

Some 30 minutes southeast of San Isidro by car is this small bird reserve, home to Costa Rica's eminent ornithologist, Dr. Alexander Skutch, co-author of *A Guide to the Birds of Costa Rica*. Visits to the 76ha (188-acre) reserve are by appointment only and limited to students, researchers, naturalists and birders.

✉ Quizarrá de Pérez Zeledón, San Isidro de El General ☎ 506 2200 5472 🕐 Mon–Sat 7–4, Sun 7–1, by appointment 🖐 US$10 per person

SELVA MAR

www.exploringcostarica.com

In the San Isidro de El General area, white-water rafting is a popular activity. The El General river is the largest white-water river in Costa Rica, with more than 166km (103 miles) of suitable streams. While the valley is scenic, the novice rafter tends to head for the forested sections of the Pacuare and Reventazón rivers, leaving the General's class III–V rapids to the specialists. A variety of rafting trips can be organized locally through Selva Mar.

✉ Calle 1, avenidas 2–4, San Isidro de El General ☎ 506 2771 4582 🖐 1-day trip US$95 per person

SAN VITO

FINCA CÁNTAROS

www.fincacantaros.com

Finca Cántaros specializes in local arts and crafts, including Chorotega pottery, woven textiles and hand-crafted wooden products from the Guaymí and Boruca, and coffee fresh from the harvest in the Coto Brus valley. Cántaros is one of the best craft shops in Costa Rica. The website was still under construction at the time of printing.

✉ On the road south to Ciudad Neily, San Vito ☎ 506 2773 3760 🕐 Sat–Sun 8.30–4 🖐 US$2

VALLE DE LOS SANTOS

FINCA EDDIE SERRANO MIRADOR DE QUETZALES

This is the place to see the resplendent quetzal; a sighting is almost guaranteed. A short trail leads 3km (2 miles) through forests of giant oak to waterfalls and a look-out point.

✉ Pan-American Highway km70 ☎ 506 2390 7894 🕐 Daily 8–5 🖐 2-hour tours US$6

Below *Experience exhilarating rafting on the Pacuare River*

PRICES AND SYMBOLS

The restaurants are listed alphabetically (excluding El, Le, La and Les). The prices given are the average for a two-course lunch (L) and a three-course dinner (D) for one person, without drinks. The wine price is for the least expensive bottle.

For a key to the symbols, ▷ 2.

GOLFITO

BILGE BAR

www.bananabaymarina.com

Catering principally to sailors who tie up at the marina, of which this is a part, this restaurant gets its light through walls of glass. U.S.-style breakfasts satisfy, as do burgers (try the fish burger), salads and sandwich lunches. Fresh seafood dishes are always available, from a spicy Louisiana gumbo to specials of the day.

✉ Banana Bay Marina, 1km (0.6 miles) southeast of Golfito town center ☎ 506 2775 0838 ◷ Daily 6am–10pm ✋ B US$8, L US$12, D US$18, Wine US$15

CASA ROLAND

Bringing a touch of much-needed elegance to the Golfito dining scene when it opened in 2008, this upscale, albeit gloomy, restaurant in the middle of the hotel—inexplicably it has no windows—has a creative globe-spanning nouvelle menu. Seafood is the strong suit. Try the jumbo shrimp with whisky and mustard sauce. Carnivores will salivate at the beef tenderloin with portobello mushroom.

✉ Casa Roland Marina Resort, Zona Americana ☎ 506 2775 0180 ◷ Daily 7–10, 12–10 ✋ B US$10, L US$16, D US$30, Wine US$20

LE COQUILLAGE

www.samoadelsur.com

Popular with sailors, this spacious open-air restaurant, at Centro Turístico Samoa, revolves around a ship-shaped bar. Fast foods include burgers and pizzas, but it dishes out hearty *gallo pinto* breakfasts (▷ 239) and tasty seafood dinners such as *corvina al ajillo* (garlic sea bass).

✉ Avenida Principal, 1km (0.6 mile) northwest of Golfito town center ☎ 506 2775 0233 ◷ Daily 6am–11.30pm ✋ B and L US$10, D US$12, Wine US$12

MATAPALO

BRISA AZUL

www.laparios.com

One of the finest ecolodges in Costa Rica serves fine cuisine beneath a soaring thatched *palenque*. The menu changes daily and includes fish, meat and vegetarian dishes. Starters include *ayote* soup (beans with pork loin chunks) and red peppers stuffed with Turrialba cheese. For main courses try the house special, *Osa Bouillabaisse*. On the dessert menu are a traditional *tres leches* (▷ 240) and the Drunken Watermelon. There is an excellent wine list featuring Chilean and Uruguayan wines.

✉ Ecolodge Lapa Rios, Matapalo ☎ 506 2735 5130 ◷ Daily 7am–8.30pm ✋ L US$31, D US$44, Wine US$21

PARQUE NACIONAL PIEDRAS BLANCAS

ESQUINAS RAIN FOREST LODGE

www.esquinaslodge.com

The wildly beautiful Esquinas Lodge, surrounded by Piedras Blancas National Park, is one of the Osa Peninsula's most magical jungle retreats. The restaurant has a stunning setting with views of the jungle and tropical gardens. The menu includes seafood caught daily in the Golfo Dulce, and organic fruit and vegetables.

✉ Parque Nacional Piedras Blancas ☎ 506 2741 8001 ◷ Daily 7am–9pm ✋ L US$29, D US$38, Wine US$19

Above *Shops in Jiménez town center*

PAVONES

CAFE DE LA SUERTE

www.cafedelasuerte.com

A surf-crowd favorite, this colorful open-air, cafe-style restaurant beside the soccer field specializes in health-focused fare and vegetarian dishes. Start out the day with a bowl of granola, yoghurt and fruit. Lunch might mean a falafel sandwich. The English-speaking, world-traveled owner serves delicious fresh-fruit shakes, plus espressos and cappuccinos. It has WiFi.

On the north side of the soccer field, Pavones 506 2776 2388 Mon–Sat 7.30–5.30, plus dinner in high season B and L US$8, D US$12, no wine served

PUERTO JIMÉNEZ

CAROLINA'S

Right in the middle of town, Carolina's serves decent breakfasts and is recommended for its simple fish and seafood and as a place to find out about tours with Escondido Trex at the rear of the restaurant. For a no-frills lunch, the fish and chicken *casados* are hard to beat, and with plenty of visitors it also makes for a lively hang-out.

Main street, Puerto Jiménez 506 2735 5185 Daily 7am–10pm B US$4, L US$4, D US$12, Wine US$15

JUANITA'S MEXICAN BAR & GRILL

No frills at this lively local dive, where the music gets cranked-up, but the eclectic please-all-comers menu offers burgers and even fish 'n' chips, in addition to Mexican and Tico staples.

Just off main street, Puerto Jiménez 506 2735 5056 Daily 6am–midnight L US$8, D US$10, Wine US$10

PEARL OF THE OSA

With a lovely beachfront setting, a casual ambience and unpretentious menu, this is the place to be for a relaxed meal of fresh ceviche, a set-meal *(casado)* or delicious tuna melt or burger. It also has fresh seafood dishes. The place packs in locals on Friday nights for live music and pastas.

Playa Platanares, 3km (2 miles) east of town 506 8848 0752 Daily 11–9 L US$10, D US$15, Wine US$14

SAN ISIDRO DE EL GENERAL

RANCHO LA BOTIJA

www.rancholabotija.com

The road to San Gerardo de Rivas, 6km (4 miles) east of San Isidro, passes Rancho La Botija, a cattle and coffee estate. Its restaurant is set around a central *trapiche* or sugar mill, with a menu that includes tasty dishes at good prices. Service is friendly.

San Isidro de El General 506 2770 2146 Tue–Sun 9–5 for non-guests, unless a reservation has been made for dinner L US$12, D US$24, Wine US$16

SAN VITO

PIZZERIA LILIANA

Right in the middle of town, Pizzeria Liliana is true to the Italian heritage of San Vito, and comes highly recommended for its upbeat vibe and comprehensive menu, which extends to 20 classic Italian dishes. Plentiful portions of homemade pasta, pizza, fish and meat dishes are all served with Italian wines.

100m (110 yards) from the plaza, San Vito 506 2773 3080 Daily 10–10 L US$8, D US$18, Wine US$18

ZANCUDO

CABINAS SOL Y MAR

www.zancudo.com

This is the preferred hang-out for expats. Breakfasts—omelets, pancakes, etc.—include homemade breads and pastries. Burgers here are always popular. And the chef conjures up Thai dishes, plus such tempting nightly specials as tuna with capers, squash and green beans with roasted pepper sauce.

Zancudo 506 2776 0014 Daily 7am–9pm B US$8, L US$12, D US$18, Wine US$15

OCEANO

Sit on logs for stools and dine at tabletops made of diced tree-trunks at this charming restaurant open to the elements. Canadian owners Mark and Stephanie Homer fuss over guests and also deliver the goods, such as waffles, *huevos rancheros*, fresh seafood dishes, and a killer brownie sundae.

400m (437 yards) south of Zancudo village 506 2776 0921 Daily 11–11, closed Mon in low season L US$8, D US$16, Wine US$15

Below *The elements of a traditional Costa Rican* casado *(set meal)*

PRICES AND SYMBOLS
The prices are for a double room for one night including breakfast, unless otherwise stated. All the hotels listed accept credit cards unless otherwise stated. Note that rates can vary widely throughout the year.

For a key to the symbols, ▷ 2.

BAHÍA DRAKE

AGUILA DE OSA INN

www.aguiladeosa.com

The "Eagle of Osa Inn" is tucked on the cliffside at the mouth of the Río Agujitas. Steep staircases lead up to the stone-lined rooms and suites, so this is not suitable for disabled travelers. The wood-paneled guest rooms are appointed with Guatemalan spreads, and breezes ease in through huge screened, glassless windows. A circular, open-air restaurant-bar looks over the rivermouth, where the inn's own dive shop and sportfishing boats are located, and most guests signing up here do so on dive and fishing packages, although other activities are available.

✉ 600m (656 yards) south of Agujitas ☎ 506 8850 2929 ✋ US$900 two-night package ⓘ 11 rooms, 2 suites

DRAKE BAY RESORT

www.drakebay.com

In a magnificent location opposite Aguila de Osa, this resort combines a rejuvenating back-to-nature experience with a range of activities and services. Spacious tropical cabins, sleeping up to five people, all have queen-size beds, private bathrooms with hot water, porches and splendid ocean views. The ocean-view pool and wild tropical setting complete the sense of well-being. There is email access and the resort has its own private dock. A range of packages is available, from the standard three-nights accommodation, including all meals, transportation from San José and two guided tours, to more tailored birding, scuba diving, kayaking, mountain biking and fishing tours.

✉ Drake Bay ☎ 506 2770 8012. In the US 561 2762 1763 ✋ Standard 3-night package US$660 per person ⓘ 20 cabins 🏊 Outdoor

MATAPALO

BOSQUE DEL CABO

www.bosquedelcabo.co

Just a short distance beyond Lapa Ríos, this low-key yet luxurious cliff-top resort competes with less fanfare. The resort is surrounded by rain forest yet has dramatic ocean vistas from the villas that hang suspended over cliffs looking over the Pacific Ocean at the tip of the Osa Peninsula. Scarlet macaws frequent the grounds while monkeys often troop across the rooftops of the 10 thatched villas, which have solar-powered electricity, screened-windows, outdoor garden-showers, and spacious verandas for soaking up the views. Six luxury bungalows have king-size beds. Delicious health-conscious meals are served beneath soaring thatch. Trails include a suspension bridge to a botanical garden, plus Bosque del Cabo has its own zipline canopy tour.

✉ Bosque del Cabo ☎ 506 2735 5206 ✋ US$185 standard, US$200 deluxe, US$380–475 *casas* ⓘ 10 villas, 2 *casas* 🏊 Outdoor

LAPA RÍOS LODGE

www.laparios.com

Around 17km (10.5 miles) from Puerto Jiménez the road rises steeply to pass over Cabo Matapalo where you will find the Lapa Ríos Lodge, set in a private rain forest

Opposite A thatched safari lodge — **Opposite** *A thatched safari lodge*

reserve covering 400ha (988 acres). Luxurious thatched bungalows are equipped with bamboo furniture. Each bungalow has a private deck with views to the ocean or rain forest, and a bathroom with an indoor and an outdoor shower. The open-air restaurant serves international cuisine, complete with a full bar and observation deck. There are yoga classes, massages, and a pool to contemplate the paradise. This eco-conscious hotel employs only locals, and the heart-of-the-forest location ensures the daily presence of monkeys.

☎ 506 2735 5130 US$276 per person, including three meals per day 16 bungalows Outdoor

PARQUE NACIONAL CORCOVADO

CASA CORCOVADO JUNGLE LODGE

www.casacorcovado.com

Almost at the San Pedrillo park entrance to Corcovado National Park, in a lush jungle setting, these comfortable thatched bungalows and suites are dotted about a private reserve of 69ha (170 acres). Rustic but impeccably finished, each bungalow has wooden furniture, tiled floors, ceiling fans and beds draped with mosquito nets. This good luxury choice offers a variety of tailor-made packages with transfers to and from San José, a choice of tours including hiking in Corcovado, trips to Caño Island, birding, scuba diving and horseback riding.

✉ Corcovado ☎ 506 2256 3181 Closed Sep 1–Nov 30 Two- to seven-night packages, including meals, tours, taxes, transportation and park fees from US$1,750 14 bungalows No entry by road; access is by a 90-min boat ride from Sierpe

LUNA LODGE

www.lunalodge.com

Wrapped in dense jungle on a valley side in the mountains a short distance from Corcovado, Luna Lodge is a perfect base for exploring the rain forest. Yoga is a popular activity here, and owner Lana Wedmore leads yoga workshops on a dojo suspended over the hillside. The lodge caters to various budgets with safari-tents on wooden decks and hacienda-style rooms, plus circular bungalows with outdoor courtyard showers, Guatemala spreads, and leather rockers on private verandas. Guests gather for health-conscious meals served family-style under thatch. Harpy eagles have been sighted flying overhead, and many animals pass by at almost fingertip distance.

✉ 600m (656 yards) north of Carate, 1km (0.6 miles) east of the park entrance ☎ 506 8380 5036. Toll free in US 888/409 8448 Tent US$105, rooms US$135, bungalows US$175 5 tents, 3 rooms, 8 bungalows Driving involves fording several rivers, a sometimes dangerous and impossible task in wet season. Fly into Carate and have the lodge pick you up

PARQUE NACIONAL PIEDRAS BLANCAS

ESQUINAS RAIN FOREST LODGE

www.esquinaslodge.com

Surrounded by the virgin wilderness of the National Park (▷ 176), this lodge, financed by the Austrian government, is a model for sustainable tourism and one of Costa Rica's few not-for-profit ecotourism projects. The 14 snug rooms, with tiled floors, ceiling fans, private baths and mosquito screens, all have verandas overlooking the tropical gardens and forest. The large thatched bar and restaurant serves local and Austrian dishes and there's a pool for cooling off after a day's hiking. The lodge employs local people and uses all profits to support projects in the small community of La Gamba. Multiple tours and activities are offered. Credit cards are not accepted.

✉ La Gamba, Golfito ☎ 506 2771 8001 US$230 per person, with meals 14 Outdoor It's 4km (2.5 miles) to Esquinas from the Pan-American Highway, or arrive from the south via Golfito along a difficult and occasionally impassable road—especially in the wet season

PUERTO JIMÉNEZ

IGUANA LODGE

www.iguanalodge.com

Returning visitors who haven't seen this beachfront lodge in a few years will be delighted by the upgrades to its Iguana Club Rooms, now appointed in deluxe fashion, with lush linens and lavish travertine-clad bathrooms. Guests can still opt for four more rustic stilt-cabins or two new deluxe cabins, the latter with private bathrooms; guests taking the former units may need to descend at night to the shared garden bathrooms. Owners Toby and Loren Cleaver from Colorado lavish attention on theirguests. The restaurant-bar here is one of the best around, especially for live-music Fridays. Guests often get to see exotic creatures roaming the beach—it's a nesting site for marine turtles and a roosting site for scarlet macaws..

✉ Playa Platanares, 3km (2 miles) east of Puerto Jiménez ☎ 506 8848 0752 Room US$120, US$155 cabins, including dinner 8 rooms, six cabins

PUNTA BANCO

TISKITA JUNGLE LODGE

www.tiskita-lodge.co.cr

South of Pavones, at the mouth of the Golfo Dulce, is Punta Banco and the incredibly remote tropical retreat of the Tiskita Jungle Lodge. A collection of cabins and rooms set in a private biological reserve spreading over 223ha (550 acres), this is surely the ultimate "escape from it all" lodge in Costa Rica. Cabins are comfortable, with broad balconies and quite spectacular outdoor bathrooms. Hearty national dishes using the freshest fruit and produce are served in the rustic open-air restaurant. Activities include a swimming pool, natural tide pools and trails leading through the primary and secondary rain forest. Arriving at Tiskita is normally by chartered plane to the Lodge's private airstrip.

✉ Punta Banco ☎ 506 2664 4443 US$272 including meals, guided walk and taxes 16 cabins

THE CARIBBEAN LOWLANDS

Laid-back almost to a fault, the Caribbean lowlands move at a more lackadaisical pace than the rest of the nation. Culturally distinct, much of the population carries the bloodlines of black Jamaicans who arrived more than a century ago to build the Atlantic railroad and work the banana plantations that still smother the lowland plains. The zesty cuisine of the region is distinct, too, infused with coconut milk and spices.

The access point by road is the bustling commercial town of Limón, a popular cruise ship port-of-call midway between Nicaragua and Panama. North of Limón, the coast comprises a watery world of sand spits, lagoons and swampy forest, culminating in the varied ecosystems of Tortuguero National Park and Barra del Colorado Wildlife Refuge. Tortuguero is an unbeatable destination for viewing wildlife by canoe or boat; trips are easily arranged at the many ecolodges that line Tortuguero Lagoon. Sportfishing for tarpon and snook lures anglers to Barra del Colorado and the rivermouth hamlet Parismina, each blessed with a choice of dedicated lodges.

South of Limón, the Talamanca Mountains provide a rugged backdrop for palm-fringed beaches and the offbeat villages of Cahuita, Puerto Viejo de Talamancas and Manzanillo. These capitals of cool are favored by backpackers and surfers from around the world. Many have settled and established eclectic hotels and casual open-air restaurants serving globe-spanning cuisine and fresh-caught local seafood. Cahuita and Manzanillo, respectively, abut Cahuita National Park and Gandoca-Manzanillo Wildlife Refuge, which harbor a wealth of wildlife, from monkeys to marine turtles and freshwater dolphins. Turtles nest all along the Caribbean coast, a region whose major appeal might simply be the option to adopt the local laissez-faire by lazing the days away in a hammock.

The Beach House
unsound
unsound
unsound

PARQUE NACIONAL CAHUITA

Cahuita National Park has some of Costa Rica's best coral reefs. Its beaches capture the Caribbean's essence. The Afro-Caribbean village of Cahuita, 43km (27 miles) south of Puerto Limón, epitomizes the south Caribbean: laid-back but with enough energy to keep things ticking along. The beaches stretching from the southern limits of the town are perfect, shaded by coconut palms reaching out to the ocean. These golden sands mark the northernmost point of Parque Nacional Cahuita. The park was created in 1970 to protect the coral reef that lies off Punta Cahuita. The best example of coral in the country, the reef can be reached on a tour, or snorkelers can swim out to see the brain coral and leafy sea fans in the glassy water. The reef has suffered from the earthquake of 1991 and from the chemical run-off from plantations and increased sediment caused by deforestation. Two rangers' stations give access to the park. At the southern end of Cahuita town, Kelly's Creek station works on a voluntary donation system. The Puerto Vargas station at the southern end of the park charges a US$10 entrance fee.

WILDLIFE

A path follows the coastline around Punta Cahuita, moving through the coconut palms and entering the mixed forest, where you have a good chance of seeing howler monkeys, coatis, racoons, snakes, butterflies and perhaps even scarlet macaws. Areas of swamp are good places to see green ibis, yellow-crowned night herons and northern boat-billed herons.

A DAY'S HIKING

You can most easily stroll the entire park by entering from Cahuita. Walking through, a comfortable day's hike of 7km (4 miles), you eventually arrive at Puerto Vargas and the junction with Highway 36, from where you can catch a bus back to Cahuita. Alternatively, take an early morning bus south to Puerto Vargas and walk back, heading north, to Cahuita.

INFORMATION

257 P7 506 2755 0302 Puerto Vargas daily 8–4; Kelly Creek 6–5 Puerto Vargas US$10; Kelly Creek by donation Several daily from San José Terminal Gran Caribe Cahuita is down an unassuming road off Highway 36, 10km (6 miles) south of Penshurst. From San José head east along the Guápiles road to Puerto Limón and turn south

TIPS

» Valuables go missing if left unattended on beaches.

» The best time for snorkeling is mid-February to April.

Above *A swimmer heads into the water off Playa Negra*

Opposite *The Beach House, Cahuita*

PARQUE NACIONAL TORTUGUERO

INFORMATION

251 L4 ☎ 506 2709 8086

US$10, which is paid to the headquarters at the southern end of the town before beginning any trip through the waterways. Guides cost US$5 per member of the group Transport by boat to Tortuguero is easily arranged. The simplest option is from Moín, a few kilometers (a couple of miles) north of Limón from where you hire a private boat heading up the coastal canal (US$220 for two people). It is also possible to catch a public *lancha* (motor boat) from La Pavona from GEEST Casa Verde, a short bus ride from Cariari. Or you can charter a vessel from Puerto Viejo de Sarapiquí, the most expensive option. Most all-inclusive packages leave from Caño Blanco Marina, close to Matina. If you need to charter a vessel there are several options. Willie Rankin (☎ 506 795 2556) travels from Moín to Tortuguero Nighttime trips along the beach are coordinated through the lodges or the information kiosk in town

Above *A small craft in the park*

INTRODUCTION

It's a waterborne adventure to reach this wildlife-filled rain forest paradise, but Tortuguero is one of Costa Rica's treasures. The sea turtles grab the headlines, but look for frogs, jaguars and Jesus Christ lizards too. Tortuguero National Park, 84km (52 miles) north of Puerto Limón, is the most important nesting site for green turtles in the western hemisphere. The park's 29,068ha (71,827 acres) is made up of a network of waterways that meander through the vast alluvial plain created by rivers flowing off the Central Highlands' eastern slopes. By the time the rivers reach the coast they have slowed almost to a standstill, and with high rainfall, the dense forest is often flooded. The flat landscape is bursting with plant life crowding up to the edge of waterways, only occasional gaps providing a glimpse of the world within.

The land between Limón and the Río San Juan on the border of Nicaragua is tantamount to an offshore island. It can only be reached by air or river travel through the inland waterways and canals surrounding Tortuguero or Barra del Colorado. It is the largest area of tropical wet forest in Costa Rica. During the 1940s, logging companies exploited the area for timber and the coastal canals of the northern Caribbean were built in the mid-1960s to connect the river-dwelling indigenous communities and to provide a more efficient means of transporting lumber to Limón. However, this is still one of the least accessible parts of the country.

Tortuguero village was first populated in the time of pirates, when turtles provided a supply of meat for the mariners. The turtle harvest continued until research by Archie Carr, a prominent figure in the Costa Rican conservation movement in the 1950s, suggested that the green turtle was probably heading for extinction; virtually every nesting female turtle in Tortuguero was caught and exported for turtle soup. And indeed, Tortuguero, which means "turtle seller," still makes a living from its turtles.

The research continued with the creation of the Caribbean Conservation Corps (tel 506 2224 9215). Archie Carr's work and energy were crucial in the creation of Tortuguero National Park. Today, the corporation has an exhibition to the north of town (tel 506 2709 8091, daily 10–12, 2–5.30) and continues tagging work with the turtles monitored by satellite. Nonetheless, the conservation ethic remains weak among the local populaton and visitors are requested to report anyone digging up turtle nests.

While listening for nesting turtles on beaches after dark is the major attraction, trips inland along the natural rivers and man-made channels are a year-round pleasure. The usual way to see the forest is from a small launch passing along narrow creeks. Turtle tours can be arranged through your lodge or the tour operators in Tortuguero. Most people visit Tortuguero as part of a package tour from San José. Flights from San José with Sansa and Nature Air land at the airstrip, 4km (2.5 miles) north of town.

Tortuguero village is the hub of the area. Flowing north from the landlocked village is the Laguna de Tortuguero, which leads for 5km (3 miles) to the Caribbean. Lodges have spread along either side of the waterway, and on the canal running parallel inland to the west. You can also find rustic accommodations in the village and organize a guide independently and several local tour operators have set up shop here. The ranger station at the south end of the village has information about the turtles and the area. You need to register here for turtle tours if you are not part of a lodge package.

WHAT TO SEE

TURTLE WATCHING

The main reason for visiting Tortuguero is to see nesting turtles. The Caribbean beaches of the National Park protect the nesting sites of the green turtle and, in smaller numbers, the huge leatherback, hawksbill and loggerhead turtles. To see one of these magnificent creatures emerge from the ocean surf, haul itself up the beach and dig a nest is an unforgettable experience. And to witness the tiny hatchlings emerge from their sandy burrow before heading frantically for the ocean, like wind-up mechanical toys, is similarly memorable.

Tours to see nesting turtles take place at night. Strict rules govern the tours, which are led by authorized guides. You must be accompanied and flashlights, cameras, video cameras and smoking are prohibited. Tours last for two hours; some may find trudging blindly along the beach and struggling through undergrowth difficult. You are advised to wear dark clothes and closed shoes. These restrictions are designed to limit disturbance to turtles; being quiet is also requested.

As with many activities in Costa Rica, getting the timing right to see this natural phenomenon is essential. The green turtles lay their eggs at night between June and October, with the hatchlings emerging from the depths of their sandy nests until November at the latest. Leatherbacks can be seen between March and June.

WILDLIFE

Tortuguero is one of the country's most diverse national parks and home to over half the bird and reptile species in the country. There are more than 300 bird species in Tortuguero. The looping flight of the keel-billed toucan crossing the open waterways is a common sight, and you may be lucky and see an endangered green macaw. Wildlife viewing in the area is spectacular and best seen from a boat. Mammals are numerous, with howler monkeys and sloths commonly spotted, while hidden within the undergrowth the tracks of jaguar, ocelot and tapir go unseen by most, as do endangered manatees that graze in the watery channels. The fishing bulldog bat, a large bat with a 60cm (23in) wingspan hunts on the waters of the canals. Reptiles and amphibians are on the scene in large numbers: you may see crocodiles and tiny poison-dart frogs.

TIPS

» With an average temperature of 26°C (79°F) and rainfall between 4,500mm and 6,000mm (176in and 236in) a year, Tortuguero is one of the wettest spots in the country. While rainfall is slightly less in February and March there is a high chance of rainfall throughout the year.

» According to the information center, July to October is the best time to see green turtles nesting. The leatherback or baula nests between March and June.

» Keep an eye on the tagged turtles at www.ccturtle.org

Above *A kayaking expedition along the Tortuguero River*

TOURING THE WATERWAYS

From Tortuguero Lagoon a network of smaller channels is accessible by launch. If you travel in silence and with a good guide, you are certain to see much wildlife. Most tours leave early in the morning when birdlife is most in evidence and the chance of seeing mammals is also higher. Tours with lodges are normally included in the price. If you organize your own tour you have a slightly greater variety to choose from. On a self-organized tour you can take a guide, who uses paddle power. Most boats use motor engines. On entering the park they are legally required to switch to electric engines to reduce noise. Keen to maximize the time clients spend wildlife viewing, many guides stay in the channels as long as they can. In order to make up time when they return to the main river, they may increase speeds so that waves crash against the banks. Never encourage your guide to go fast and report any guides speeding in signed go-slow manatee habitat zones.

MORE TO SEE

CERRO TORTUGUERO

At the mouth of Tortuguero Lagoon, Cerro Tortuguero rises to 119m (390ft). While the height is nothing in an area that is overwhelmingly flat, the views from the top are spectacular. Walks up the overgrown trail can be arranged through local guides.

LOMAS DE SIERPE

Rarely visited, these hills rise to 335m (1,100ft) to the west of Tortuguero. They make a good day-trip for those wanting a more challenging trek.

PARISMINA

Perched at the mouth of the Río Parismina, the small riverside hamlet of Parismina is one of the best places in the world to fish for tarpon and snook. Several dedicated fishing lodges cater to anglers.

Below *Branches reflected in the waters at Caño Palma biological station*

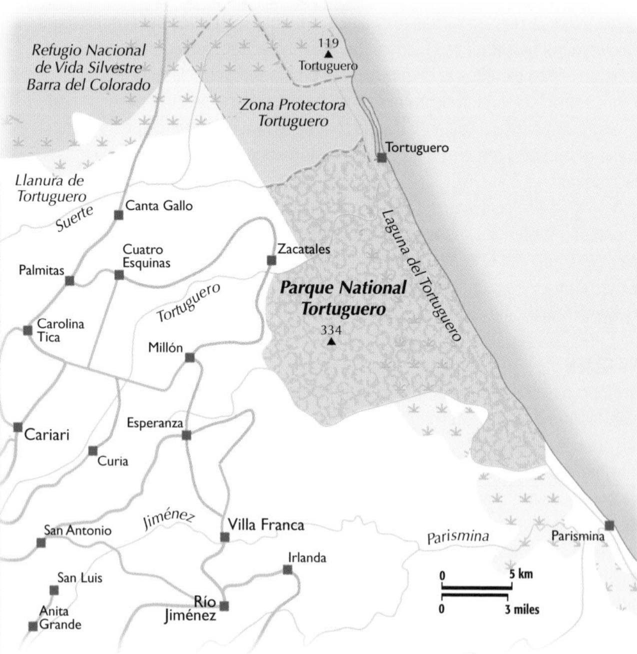

PUERTO LIMÓN

Arriving in Puerto Limón, you can feel the difference in atmosphere and it isn't the high humidity. Columbus dropped anchor on Isla Uvita off the coast, and waves of workers arrived from China and the Caribbean, creating a unique cultural diversity.

Usually visited only in passing, the best time to be in Limón is forCarnaval (▷ 208). A cruise terminal draws cruise ships, but in-town attractions are few and most passengers sign up for excursions farther afield. There is a 24-hour police booth on the main square.

257 N6 Frequent buses from the Gran Terminal del Caribe in San José From San José head east on Highway 32 to Limón

PUERTO VIEJO DE TALAMANCA

Puerto Viejo,17km (10.5 miles) south of Cahuita, with its good beaches, excellent surfing and vibrancy, has become the main party town of the Caribbean coast. Surfers seek out the glorious Salsa Brava wave.

To the east, the enjoyable golden beaches of Playa Cocles, Playa Chiquita, Punta Uva and Manzanillo offer a quiet retreat along a road lined with hotels and restaurants. Away from the beach, you can explore botanical gardens or visit the Keköldi indigenous reserve.

With the arrival of expatriates, setting up homes in backwaters, the Afro-Caribbean make-up of the town is being slowly diluted.

257 P7 Daily from San José Terminal Gran Caribe Asociación Talamanqueña de Ecoturismo y Conservación (ATEC), on the main street, 200m (220 yards) from the beach, Old Harbor 506 2750 0191, Mon–Sat 8am–9pm, Sun 10–6 From Puerto Limón, take Highway 36 south and follow the signs for Cahuita and Puerto Viejo

REFUGIO NACIONAL DE VIDA SILVESTRE BARRA DEL COLORADO

Tucked up in the northeastern corner of the country, Barra del Colorado is reached by daily flights or a boat journey of several hours. One of the most cut-off parts of the country, the sleepy backwater is divided into Barra del Sur, which has the airstrip and lodges, and Barra del Norte, on Isla Calero, the largest Costa Rican island. The major attraction is good sportfishing for snook and tarpon (best from September to April) and the Wildlife Reserve.

The Silvestre Barra del Colorado National Wildlife Refuge is one of the country's largest protected areas, covering the border with Nicaragua along the Río San Juan. A torrential 6,000mm (236in) of rain a year and temperatures averaging 26°C (79°F) create conditions similar to those in Tortuguero. Established in the mid-1980s, its potential for ecotourism remains untapped. Accommodations are available at sportfishing lodges.

251 K3 506 2709 8086 Daily 8–4 US$6 for 1 day, payable at Cuatro Esquinas ranger station in Tortuguero Boats can be arranged from Tortuguero, taking 1.5 hours. Costs vary from US$30, if arranged by your lodge, to US$100. Ask around. It is possible to sail from Puerto Viejo de Sarapiquí

Below *Surfing off Puerto Viejo is as popular with locals as visitors*
Right *Relaxing by Puerto Viejo beach*

REFUGIO NACIONAL DE VIDA SILVESTRE GANDOCA-MANZANILLO

At the southeastern corner of Costa Rica, Gandoca-Manzanillo National Wildlife Refuge protects some of the country's most pristine wetlands.

The land portion of the refuge protects creeks, lagoons and the only natural population of mangrove oysters on the Central American Caribbean. The inland waterways are home to manatees, crocodiles and caiman, while the forests provide a refuge for tapir, jaguars and monkeys. Over 300 bird species have been recorded.

White sandy beaches to the south of Punta Mona are used by leatherback, loggerhead, green and hawksbill turtles. Below the surface, the 4,436ha (10,961 acres) of marine reserve protects large areas of coral.

Fish species in the reserve number over 500, and mammals are topped off with three species of dolphins—the bottlenose, Atlantic spotted and the little-known tucuxi. Local organizations work to ensure that tourism and nature interact with minimum impact (for volunteer opportunities, ▷ 208). Exploring the coast is straightforward, but a guide is recommended if you go inland.

257 Q7 ☎ 506 754 1103 or 506 759 0600 Daily 8–4 US$6 Bus from San José to Puerto Viejo (▷ 55), then local bus to Manzanillo Trips to the land sections of Gandoca-Manzanillo can be organized through ATEC (see Puerto Viejo de Talamanca ▷ 207) Drive east from Puerto Viejo for 12km (7.5 miles) along the road to Manzanillo. You can also walk all the way, along the beach

RESERVA BIOLÓGICA HITOY CERERE

Biologists speculate that Hitoy Cerere Biological Reserve may provide some of the greatest diversity in Costa Rica. Some 60km (37 miles) south of Puerto Limón, the reserve extends to 9,950ha (24,586 acres) and offers some tough day-hikes.

Rainfall in the park is a steady 3,500mm (138in) a year, with temperatures in the high 20s°C (low 80s°F). Three trails lead from the rangers' station through the lush forest rich with epiphytes and many streams, rivers and waterfalls. Wildlife is profuse, with sloths, howler monkeys and white-faced monkeys to be seen, while on the ground you may see otters, peccaries and even jaguars and tapir. More than 100 species of bird have been spotted in the park.

257 N7 ☎ 506 2758 3170 Daily 8–4 US$10 Buses from Puerto Limón for the Estrella Valley pass 15km (9 miles) short of the rangers' station The easiest way to visit the reserve is on a tour from Cahuita or Puerto Viejo with ATEC (▷ 207) From Penshurst, a road heads inland climbing the Estrella Valley to Hitoy Cerere Biological Reserve. It's a tough drive and needs a four-wheel-drive vehicle

SIQUIRRES

Siquirres, 25km (15 miles) after Guácimo, is another banana town and the largest settlement along this section of Highway 32. Few people stop here, but you can tour La Esperanza banana plantation (tel 506 768 8683). Also nearby is Parque Nacional Barbilla, with 11,944ha (29,513 acres) of tropical forest. Created in 1982, the park still has no facilities.

256 L5 On Highway 32, 58km (36 miles) west of Puerto Limón

VERAGUA RAIN FOREST RESEARCH AND ADVENTURE PARK

www.veraguarain forest.com

Opened in November 2008, this ambitious projects occupies 1,300ha (3,212 acres) of premontane rain forest. INBio has a research facility here, and visitors can watch scientists at work in a glass-wall laboratory. A riverside trail good for spotting poison-dart frogs is accessed by an open-air tram—a chance to spot monkeys, sloths, and colorful birds in the treetops as you descend and ascend the canyon at bird's-eye level. Veragua has informative exhibits, plus a serpentarium and walk-through frog-garden.

257 N6 Veragua ☎ 506 2296 5056 Daily 8–5 US$65 adults, US$45 children Veragua and local tour companies offer tours inclusive of transport from San José Turn south from the Guápiles highway at Liverpool; an off-road vehicle is recommended for the 10km (6-mile) dirt road to Veragua

Below *A soda (food stand) in Manzanillo*

Opposite *The remains of the San José to Limón railway, Siquirres*

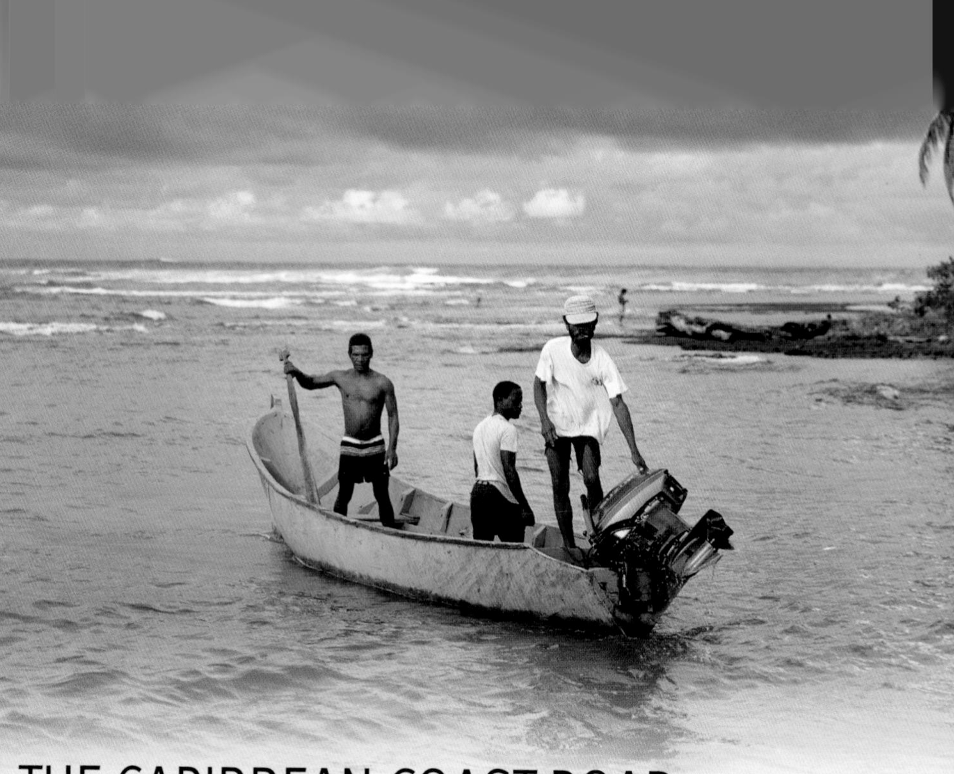

THE CARIBBEAN COAST ROAD

From Puerto Limón, the road south runs close to the sea for over 80km (50 miles) past palm-fringed beaches. This drive follows it south to the Refugio Nacional de Vida Silvestre Gandoca-Manzanillo, and has interesting diversions into the Talamanca Mountains.

THE DRIVE
Distance: 89km (55 miles)
Allow: 1–2 days
Start at: Puerto Limón
End at: Manzanillo

★ This drive follows the coast road south, past tempting beaches, toward the border with Panama.

Raw, unpolished and challenging, Puerto Limón (▷ 201) juts out from a monotonous coastline, and throbs with the dubious energy endemic to many port towns. Limón's fortunes have ebbed and flowed since it first became the melting pot for the influx of workers who arrived to build the railroads.

An optional short diversion is to travel north of Limón to Playa Bonita, 5km (3 miles), following the coastline, and less than 2km (1.25 miles) farther north to the town of Portete. Farther on over the hill, 7km (4 miles) west is Moín.

❶ Playa Bonita has the best beaches near Limón. A handful of houses form Portete where fishing boats are moored in the bay. Moín has the international docks where modern-day banana boats are loaded with the 2.1 million tons of bananas Costa Rica exports each year.

West of Limón, a 30-minute drive along a paved road takes you to Highway 32 and starts the 43km (27-mile) coastal journey south to Cahuita. A thin line of palms breaks the view of the beautiful beaches, but they are marred by the dangerous currents found along the coastline north of Cahuita. Some 20km (12.5 miles) south of Puerto Limón, head inland at Bananito and take the rough road (four-wheel-drive essential) leading to secluded Selva Bananito Lodge. Reaching it involves crossing four rivers. In 2008, storms severely damaged many roads in the Caribbean Lowlands; before setting out call ahead to verify that roads and bridges are passable.

❷ Selva Bananito (▷ 206) is a relaxing, family-run rain forest lodge with cabins made from earthquake-salvaged hardwoods. Balconies, complete with hammocks, have spectacular views to the mountains. Without electricity, evenings are lit by candles and days start with the sun and the dawn chorus of the rain

Opposite *Boat owners bring their craft to the beach to pick up visitors for sportfishing or snorkeling trips, Puerto Viejo*

forest. Only make this detour if you plan to spend the night and take two days rather than one for this drive.

Back on the main road, a short way north of Penshurst ❸, a road heads inland climbing the Estrella Valley eventually arriving at Hitoy Cerere Biological Reserve (▷ 202)—a tough drive that requires a full day. Blink and you'll miss Cahuita, hidden down a road off Highway 36, 10km (6 miles) south of the petrol station at Penshurst.

❹ Cahuita (▷ 197), perched on a craggy peninsula, has a population of 4,200, imbued with the laissez-faire Caribbean lifestyle. Heading north out of town, a dirt road shadows Playa Negra. South of town, a small creek leads to the golden sands that mark the northernmost point of Cahuita National Park, home to some of the best coral reefs in the country.

From Cahuita it may be possible to walk along the beach at low tide to Puerto Viejo (best not tried alone) or take the coast road 17km (11 miles) south to Puerto Viejo de Talamanca.

❺ Puerto Viejo de Talamanca is an intriguing blend of indigenous and Afro-Caribbean cultures. A former fishing village, it is a mêlée of bright shacks, cosmopolitan restaurants and rustic lodges, all woven through the forest that lines the rugged beach. This is Costa Rica's top destination for young, party-loving visitors.

At Hotel Creek, north of Puerto Viejo, the paved road heads into the hills to the village of Bribrí.

❻ Bribrí is only of interest to visitors because it has a bank. The town is at the foot of the Talamanca Mountains and the Talamanca Indian Reserve. Access to the park is limited, and the most viable option is to plan a trip with ATEC in Puerto Viejo (▷ 207).

From Puerto Viejo, the road south to Manzanillo provides a wide range of accommodations. The strip is developing quickly, and surf-camps, upscale hotels and even fine-dining restaurants now line the route. Several sandy beaches provide a quieter retreat. Some 4km (2.5 miles) away from Puerto Viejo, past Playa Cocles, is Punta Cocles. Playa Chiquita, a further 2km (1.25 miles) away, has several hotels. Next is Punta Uva (Grape Point). The road south ends in Manzanillo, 12km (7 miles) from Puerto Viejo.

❼ Manzanillo is the end of the road, but is growing and evolving as a hip backpackers destination. Aquamor (▷ 207) runs diving and kayaking trips out of Manzanillo and has established more than 100 dive sites, including diving trips to the Gandoca lagoon.

Manzanillo is followed by the white sand beaches and rocky headlands of Punta Mona, and then the Gandoca-Manzanillo Wildlife Refuge at the southeastern corner of Costa Rica.

❽ The wonderland of Refugio Nacional de Vida Silvestre Gandoca-Manzanillo (▷ 202) contains some of Costa Rica's most significant wetlands. Waterways and forests teem with birdlife and mammals, while the coastal waters protect significant endemic species of coral.

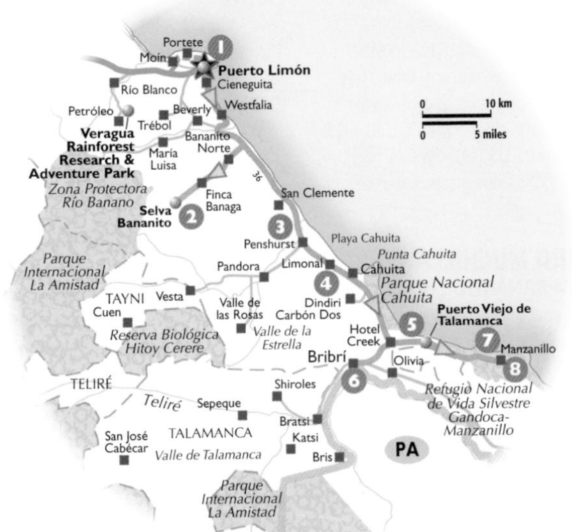

WHERE TO EAT

MISS EDITH'S

✉ 75m (82 yards) east of the police station in Cahuita, ▷ 209 ☎ 506 2755 0248 ⏲ Mon–Sat 11.30–10, Sun 12–10

LA PECORA NERA

✉ 2km (1.2 miles) south of Puerto Viejo, Playa Cocles (▷ 209–210) ☎ 506 2750 0490 ⏲ Tue–Sun 5.30pm–midnight

RESTAURANTE MAXI

A local institution serving fresh fish to hip, people-watching diners. The sea views are great.

✉ On Manzanillo's beach (▷ 209) ☎ 506 2759 9086 ⏲ Daily 11.30–10

BARRA DEL COLORADO

CASA MAR

www.casamarlodge.com

With an idyllic setting on the river, the rustic Casa Mar lodge sleeps 24 people and offers excellent conditions for catching monumental tarpon and snook; lodge owner and local legend Bill Barnes is the current world record holder for catching an 11.8kg (26 lb) snook on a fly rod. Each night you can dine on the fresh catch of the day. Contact the California office to arange a visit.

✉ 2634 West Orangethorpe Avenue, Suite 6, Fullerton, California (mailing address) ☎ 506 2381 1380. Toll free in the US 800 543-0282 💳 5-night package US$2,495

RIO COLORADO LODGE

www.riocoloradolodge.com

Fishing packages, expertly run by Dan Wise, can be organized from this lodge. Where the Colorado River flows into the Caribbean sea, you can fish for snook and the prize of all game fish—tarpon. Trips take place with experienced guides in jungle rivers and lagoons. Night-time turtle-watching tours are available July through September.

✉ PO Box 5094, 1000 San José (mailing address) ☎ 506 2232 4063 🕐 All year; peak season Jan–Mar 💳 Day fishing US$635; 5-night package from US$1,908; 7 nights US$2,838

SILVER KING LODGE

www.silverkinglodge.net

Regarded as the most luxurious lodge on the north Caribbean coastline, the Silver King Lodge offers impressive fishing using 10 v-hull boats in open water and unsinkable Carolina skiffs in inland waters. They also accommodate nature tourism and non-fishing guests. It's a great place to stay, with a good restaurant, a bar, free laundry, a pool and use of kayaks.

✉ Barra del Colorado ☎ 506 8381 1403. Toll free in the US 1-800 947-3747 💳 Day fishing US$550 including accommodation, meals and drinks

CERRO MUCHILLA

SELVA BANANITO LODGE

www.selvabananito.com

Some 20km (12.5 miles) south of Puerto Limón, heading inland at Bananito, a challenging road leads to extreme seclusion. Selva Bananito is a remote, family-run, rain forest lodge, close to Cerro Muchilla on the border of La Amistad Biosphere Reserve. You can enjoy activities such as tree climbing and rappelling, mountain biking, hiking, waterfall swimming, horseback riding or birding. They'll pick you up or provide a map if you want to drive. Tours are included on package deals, or you can visit for the day.

✉ Apt 2333-2050, San Pedro ☎ 506 2253 8118 💳 Activities range from US$30–US$50; 3-day all-inclusive rates from US$431

GUÁCIMO

EARTH

www.earth.ac.cr

The School of Humid Tropical Agriculture is home to a 400-ha (988-acre) rain forest reserve plus gardens, including a banana plantation, used in scientific research. The facility is open to public visits and has trails and fascinating guided tours that provide insights into tropical ecology and sustainable practices. A full-day tour is offered by Costa Rica Expeditions (www.costaricaexpeditions.com).

✉ Escuela de Agricultura de la Región Tropical Húmedal, 1km (0.6 miles) east of Guácimo ☎ 506 2713 0000 🕐 Mon–Fri 9–5

GUÁPILES

GALLERY AT HOME

Patricia Erickson has gained national

Opposite *Puerto Viejo beach*

recognition for her paintings. Bamboo furniture and sculptures are made by Patricia's husband. Call ahead for an appointment.
Guápiles 506 2711 0823 By appointment US$200–US$2,000

RÍO DANTA RESTAURANT AND RESERVE

www.grupomawamba.com
Río Danta Restaurant and Reserve is on Highway 32, 6km (3.5 miles) after the junction at Santa Clara that heads north to Puerto Viejo de Sarapiquí. In addition to being a good stopover for tours to Tortuguero, the reserve's nature trails meander through primary forest where you can see poison-arrow frogs and birds. The gardens are bright with heliconias and bromeliads among soaring palm trees.
Grupo Mawamba, PO Box 10980-1000, Guápiles 506 2710 2626 Daily 1am–1pm Nature trails US$4

MANZANILLO

AQUAMOR

www.greencoast.com/aquamor
The Talamanca Dolphin Foundation (tel 406 586 5084, www.dolphinlink.org) and Aquamor have trained local captains and guides in dolphin etiquette to keep the impact of dolphin-watching in the area to a minimum. Volunteer programs require a commitment of at least one week, and charge from US$6 per night camping in the community of Gandoca. Lodging with local families is also available. As well as dolphin-watching, Aquamor also runs a PADI diving school and offers kayaking and snorkeling trips.
Manzanillo 506 2759 9012
Dolphin-watching US$40, diving from US$35, snorkeling from US$18

TARPONVILLE

www.tarponville.com
The only fishing lodge along the southern Caribbean coast of Costa Rica taps the virtually untouched waters of Gandoca Lagoon, where anglers are guaranteed exciting fights with feisty tarpon. March to May and September to October are the best months. The lodge has simple yet adequate accommodations and sits in the midst of Gandoca-Manzanillo Wildlife Refuge (▷ 202).
Manzanillo 506 2759 9118
5-day fishing package from US$1,675

MATINA

PACUARE NATURE RESERVE

www.parisminaturtles.org
Between the Caribbean lowlands and the Talamanca mountains, a few kilometers (a couple of miles) east of Matina, the 800ha (1,976 acres) of the Pacuare Nature Reserve contain amazing biodiversity, produced by high rainfall and altitudes between 100m and 700m (330ft and 2,300ft). The privately owned reserve has 6km (3.5 miles) of virgin beach that protects the nesting sites of marine turtles. Leatherbacks nest from March to June, with green turtles arriving between June and August. A volunteer program run by Rain forest Concern (www.rain forestconcern.org) has a minimum stay of one week in a lodge overlooking the beach. The reserve is also a secluded spot for birding.
Matina 506 2719 7702. Toll free in the US 800-344 6118); outside US: 506 541 2677 Volunteering US$100 per week

PARISMINA

RÍO PARISMINA LODGE

www.riop.com
This fishing lodge has 12 cabins, a restaurant, bar and pool at the mouth of the Parismina River. The fishing tours led by experienced English-speaking guides take place aboard an ocean-going craft making catch-and-release fishing for snapper, tuna and wahoo in the choppy coastal waters an alternative to exploring inland canals. Horseback riding and river cruises are available.
Parismina 506 2229 7597
Weekend fishing packages start at US$1,850 per person, week-long packages cost US$3,100

PUERTO VIEJO DE TALAMANCA

ATEC

www.ateccr.org
The not-for-profit Talamanca Association for Ecotourism and Conservation (ATEC) promotes projects in the Puerto Viejo area to encourage Talamanca's cultural and ethnic diversity. Activities include day-trips to the Keköldi indigenous reserve and overnight stays in the Talamanca reserves, including accommodation with local families and canoe trips.
Main street in Old Harbor, Puerto Viejo
506 2750 0191 Half-day from US$20

CACAO TRAILS

www.cacaotrails.com
This multithemed facility opened in 2006 and serves to educate visitors with a demonstration of chocolate production. Other exhibits include displays on chocolate and pre-Columbian culture, snakes in glass cages and a botanical garden. You can glide by canoe through an adjacent lagoon in search of wildlife.
Hone Creek 506 2756 8186
Daily 9–5 US$25

CRAZY MONKEY CANOPY TOUR

www.crazymonkeycanopytour.com
This adrenaline-pumping zipline adventure through the treetops takes place in the coastal mountains and is operated by the owners of Almonds & Corals Lodge. Don't expect to see much wildlife, but the fun factor is huge. You're strapped in harness attached to a wheel-system fixed to a metal cable slung between treetops, and off you go. Wheeeeeeeee!
Punta Uva, 13km (8 miles) south of Puerto Viejo 80 317 4108 Rides daily at 8am and 2pm US$40

FINCA LA ISLA BOTANICAL GARDEN

www.greencoast.com/garden.htm
This abandoned chocolate *finca* has been converted into an experimental farm offering tours and hikes on rain-forest trails. The

finca covers sections of rain forest and areas of crops and spices, including pepper, cinnamon and vanilla. Trails lead through the forest, where various species of poison-dart frogs hop about underfoot.
✉ On the road to Cahuita, just north of Playa Negra, Puerto Viejo ☎ 506 2750 0046 🕑 Fri–Mon 10–4 💰 Entrance: US$5; 2.5-hour tour: US$10

SAMASATI NATURE RETREAT

www.samasati.com
Clinging to a thickly forested mountaintop, with fabulous views over the Caribbean plains and sea, this yoga retreat is a quintessential escape from the bustle of modern life. Made entirely of logs, and with a wall-less lounge-dining room, it exudes a jungle ambience that adds enjoyment to yoga classes and retreats.
✉ Hone Creek, 2km (1.2 miles) north of Puerto Viejo ☎ 506 2756 8015 💰 1-week retreats from US$1,199

SIQUIRRES

BANANERO ESPERANZAS

www.bananatourcostarica.com
Banana plantations swathe the Caribbean lowlands. To learn about production and processing, take a tour at Standard Fruit Co.'s Esperanza packing plant, where guides lead you into the banana fields and packing facility.
✉ Highway 32, Siquirres ☎ 506 2768 8683 🕑 Mon–Sat 9–5 💰 US$10, tours by pre-arrangement

Below *A bare-throated tiger heron in Tortuguero National Park*

TORTUGUERO

BARBARA HARTUNG

www.tinamontours.de
Barbara Hartung, an English-, German- and Spanish-speaking biologist, is frequently recommended for boat tours in Tortuguero, where she has lived for a decade. These independent tours are an antidote to mass tourism. You'll move silently in a dugout canoe on the waterways to observe the prolific wildlife. Barbara, an entomology expert, also takes groups on rain-forest hikes.
✉ Tinamon Tours, Tortuguero ☎ 506 2709 8004 💰 US$5 per person per hour

CAÑO PALMA RESEARCH STATION

www.coterc.org
The Canadian Organization for Tropical Education and Rain-forest Conservation owns the Caño Palma Biological Station, north of town, which provides leadership in education, conservation and research. A volunteer program offers basic rooms and meals. It's a good place for serious naturalists or just for unwinding.
✉ Tortuguero ☎ 506 8381 4116 (in Canada ☎ 905-831-8809) 💰 US$100 per week, 2 weeks minimum

EDDY BROWN SPORTFISHING

Brothers Eddy and Roberto Brown know where the tarpon play and arrange fishing trips in the lagoons and in the rivermouths offshore. Snook, wahoo and tuna are also prime gamefish awaiting your lure. The Browns use 8m (26ft) and 8.5m (28ft) Bimini tops. You will need your own flies and rods, but tackle and lures are provided.
✉ Tortuga Lodge, Tortuguero ☎ 506 2257 0766 💰 US$539 full day, from US$2,140 for 3 nights, including accommodations and meals

SEA TURTLE CONSERVANCY

www.cccturtle.org
This nonprofit organization, formerly the Caribbean Conservation Corps and Turtle Survival League, was founded in 1959 and has improved the survival outlook for several species of sea turtle. Many volunteer opportunities exist to help save rare sea turtles, such as working in information booths. If more hands-on work is what you are looking for, you can sign up for the CCC Participant research program. Check the website for more detailed information. The adopt-a-turtle program allows you to track its migration on the internet.
✉ John H. Phipps Biological Field Station, Tortuguero ☎ 506 2709 8125 🕑 Leatherback turtle project Mar–end Jun; green turtle project Jun–end Nov
💰 1 week from US$1,399; 2 weeks US$1,899

FESTIVALS AND EVENTS

OCTOBER

PUERTO LIMÓN CARNAVAL

Carnival, or *carnaval* as it is known in Puerto Limón, takes place on October 12 with the preceding days building up to the big El Día de la Raza. The town suddenly becomes popular as sedate highlanders flock to the Caribbean to join the music and dancing. The costumes are out in full for Costa Rica's biggest celebration and a moment of genuine unity of Tico and Caribbean influences. Celebrations reach their climax with the Grand Desfile, or great parade, on the Saturday, when Afro-Caribbean culture is revealed in an exuberant tassel-shaking spectacle. Leave your valuables safely at your hotel.
🕑 October

PRICES AND SYMBOLS

The restaurants are listed alphabetically (excluding El, Le, La and Les). The prices given are the average for a two-course lunch (L) and a three-course dinner (D) for one person, without drinks. The wine price is for the least expensive bottle.

For a key to the symbols, ▷ 2.

CAHUITA

CHA CHA CHA

Arguably the finest cooking in Cahuita is served in a refreshingly chic setting one block from the seafront, with fairy lights and flowers set against the crisp white table linen of an open-air dining room. The menu is as varied as it is long, with fusion, Thai, Caribbean and Indian dishes incorporating local ingredients and fresh seafood. Many people come especially from Puerto Viejo to dine at this small restaurant, so reservations are recommended.

✉ Main town road, 100m (110 yards) south from the police station, Cahuita ☎ 506 2755 0476 ⌚ Daily 12–10 ✋ L and D US$18, Wine US$15

MISS EDITH'S

Miss Edith has been a legend in Cahuita since she began serving hearty portions of tasty home cooking from the front porch of her house. While Edith, having established the restaurant, now shares the reins with her sisters and daughters, Miss Edith's remains Cahuita's most popular choice for Caribbean and vegetarian food. Bring your own bottle and be warned that the service is infamously slow. Credit cards are not accepted and reservations are required.

✉ 75m (82 yards) north of police station, Cahuita ☎ 506 2755 0248 ⌚ Mon–Sat 11.30–10, Sun 12–10 ✋ L US$9, D US$15, no wine served

MANZANILLO

RESTAURANTE MAXI

Hit this upstairs open-air beachfront bar-restaurant in its groove and you'll have to squeeze shoulder to shoulder through the party crowd on weekends and holidays. The vibe is funky and unpretentious, with bare-bones furnishings and Bob Marley's reggae riffs the predominant sound. The menu is heavy on seafood, such as roast red snapper and lobster. Meals are served on the beach if the crowd overflows the restaurant. Service can be slow and indifferent. Avoid the *soda* (food stand) which lacks atmosphere and draws flies. Credit cards are not accepted.

✉ At the end of the road in Manzanillo ☎ 506 2759 9086 ⌚ Daily 11.30–10 ✋ L US$8, D US$16, no wine served

PLAYA COCLES

RESTAURANTE MEDITERRANEO

www.totemsite.com

This lovely, two-story, beachfront restaurant exudes a Mediterranean feel. Italian chef Nicolo Baretti is a wizard in the kitchen. Everything is made on-site, including the delicious Romagnola *piadina* flatbread and pastas, which take up a good part of the menu. The spinach and riccota cheese ravioli is delicious. Fresh seafood is a highlight, and there's an oyster bar by day. Pizzas are fired in a traditional oven. Desserts include homemade tropical fruit ice creams and, for a little more decadence, a divine tiramisu. A robust wine list includes a large selection of Italian wines.

✉ Totem Hotel Resort, Playa Cocles ☎ 506 2750 0758 ⌚ Daily 9–10 ✋ B US$8, L US$15, D US$25, Wine US$16

LA PECORA NEGRA

The unpretentious exterior of this Mediterranean restaurant, on the road to Manzanillo, belies its stellar cuisine. The flamboyant character of the Italian chef/owner comes

through in each dish. The fresh pasta and pizzas are superb; daily specials include an inspired selection of fresh fish, seafood and meat dishes, cooked with Italian pizzazz. Credit cards are not accepted.
✉ 2km (1.2 miles) south of Puerto Viejo, Playa Cocles ☎ 506 2750 0490
🕐 Tue–Sun 5.30pm–11; erratic opening hours in the low season, call ahead
✋ D US$22, Wine US$18

PUERTO LIMÓN

BLACK STAR LINE

One of the most popular places in town, the Black Star Line restaurant is housed in a rickety wooden building, formerly the headquarters of the Black Star Line Steamship Company. It is casual and welcoming, drawing the local Afro-Caribbean community for *casados* (set lunches) of local *comida típica*, such as steamed fish in coconut milk, or goat in a piquant pepper sauce, served with rice, beans and fried plantains. The building still serves as a social center, with occasional live music and dancing. Credit cards are not accepted.
✉ Avenida 5, Calle 6 ☎ 506 2798 1948
🕐 Mon–Sat 7.30am–10pm, Sun 11–5
✋ L US$5, D US$10, no wine served

PUERTO VIEJO DE TALAMANCA

CAFÉ RICO

Run with savvy aplomb by Roger, a friendly Englishman, this laid-back cafe is *the* place to breakfast in town. A sand floor, thatch roof and rough-hewn tables and chairs add to the amiably casual setting. Hearty breakfasts include granola with fruit and yoghurt, blackberry pancakes, great omelets and *huevos rancheros*, all at bargain prices. Lunches are heavy on scrambles and wholewheat sandwiches, and the baked desserts are scrumptious. Have your laundry washed here and you'll get free coffee or tea. Credit cards are not accepted.
✉ 50m (55 yards) south of Cabinas Casa Verde, on the northeast side of town
☎ 506 2750 0510 🕐 Fri–Wed 6am–2pm
✋ B US$6, L US$12, no wine served

CAFÉ VIEJO

In the middle of town, this smart Italian restaurant serves homemade pasta, large wood-oven pizzas, fish, seafood and beef dishes. The open-plan design doesn't feel Caribbean, but the atmosphere is relaxed. The food, while a little overpriced, is very good, the presentation artful and the portions generous. Main course dishes include red snapper with capers, tomato and anchovies, and ravioli stuffed with lobster. The vegetarian offerings are limited, but there is a fine antipasti platter. The bar area is good for an early evening drink, with great people-watching.
✉ 75m (82 yards) from ATEC, Puerto Viejo
☎ 506 2750 0817 🕐 Daily 6–10
✋ D US$20, Wine US$12

CHILE ROJO

On Puerto Viejo's main street, this tiny, German-run restaurant is usually packed with lovers of Asian and Middle Eastern food. A list of chalkboard specials complements the lunch and dinner menu, which satisfies all tastes and budgets. With bamboo roofing and clusters of wooden tables, the food, served with expeditious grace, is the star. Appetizers include chicken satay skewers, with coconut rice and peanut sauce, and for main courses there is tuna seared with black bean sauce, sushi, Thai chicken curry and pita (pitta) stuffed with falafel. Credit cards are not accepted.
✉ 100m (110 yards) east of ATEC, Apt 17-7304, Puerto Viejo ☎ 506 2750 0025
🕐 Daily 9am–10pm ✋ L US$12, D US$20, Wine by the glass US$2

PAN PAY CAFÉ

South of town, the Pan Pay is the most popular breakfast stop in town, with its buttery croissants, baguettes, cakes and pastries. A medley of American and Tico breakfasts is served together with freshly baked baguettes topped with tomato and drizzled with olive oil. Inside, the stirring flamenco music, book exchange and notice board keep the atmosphere lively, while outside tables overlooking the sea are more relaxed. With excellent prices it is a convenient place to wait for an onward bus connection. Credit cards are not accepted.
✉ 100m (110 yards) south from the bus stop, overlooking the beach, Puerto Viejo
☎ 506 750 0–081 🕐 Daily 7–5
✋ B and L US$4

TORTUGUERO

DORLING'S BAKERY

Friendly owner-cook Dorling, from Nicaragua, always has a smile for patrons who come to breakfast on granola, yoghurt and fresh fruits, or lunch on pizza and set-meal *casados*. Dorling also makes delicious fresh breads, cheesecakes and raspberry truffle brownies, as well as Nicaraguan *empenadas*.
✉ In the heart of Tortuguero, 100m (110 yards) north of the public dock ☎ 506 2709 8132 🕐 Daily 5am–9pm ✋ B US$5, L US$8, D US$12, no wine served

MISS JUNIE'S RESTAURANT

In the heart of Tortuguero, Miss Junie is renowned in the area for her cheap, abundant and satisfying platters of tasty Caribbean cooking, ranging from jerk chicken to fresh fish in a spicy sauce concoction, served with mounds of rice and beans and fried plantains. Normally, there are just a few meat and fish dishes—it is rare to find a vegetarian choice, but with advance notice, a special dish can usually be prepared. Credit cards are not accepted.
✉ Next to the Natural History Museum, Tortuguero ☎ 506 709 8029 🕐 Daily 7–2, 6–9 ✋ L US$10, D US$14, Wine US$15

TORTUGA LODGE

The most upscale lodgings for miles around (▷ 212) also has the best dining, following an upgrade that has added a romantic outside bar and candlelit tables on the deck. Giant bats swoop past as you dine on gourmet nouvelle cuisine that makes good use of local seafood. Reservations are required.
✉ Tortuga Lodge and Gardens, 4km (2.5 miles) north of the village ☎ 506 2257 0766 🕐 Daily 7–9, 12–2, 7–9 ✋ B US$12, L US$18, D US$25, Wine US$25

PRICES AND SYMBOLS
The prices are for a double room for one night including breakfast, unless otherwise stated. All the hotels listed accept credit cards unless otherwise stated. Note that rates vary widely throughout the year.

For a key to the symbols, ⊳ 2.

CAHUITA

MAGELLAN INN

www.magellaninn.com

The Magellan Inn is among the area's smarter options. Each rather simply appointed, carpeted room has a neat, tiled bathroom, terrace, ceiling fan and wicker furniture. The garden is filled with the perfume of the belladona lily by day and ilan ilan at night, and is filled with masses of birds. The unimposing pool, nestling in leafy gardens where breakfast is served, is set in natural coral surrounds. There is a bar-restaurant, and laundry service is available

2km (1.2 miles) north of Cahuita on Playa Negra 506 2755 0035 US$79–US$99 6 In three rooms only Outdoor

SAMASATI LODGE AND RETREAT CENTER

www.samasati.com

Visitors seeking no-frills calm should follow the signs to the Samasati Lodge, a relaxing place perched on a hill overlooking the Caribbean. The nine hardwood bungalows, with private bathrooms, all have balconies looking across to the ocean or to the rain forest. For a less expensive option, there are five double rooms in the guesthouse set among lush gardens. Private houses are also available for longer stays and groups. The vegetarian restaurant is peaceful and there are walking trails in the forest where over 200 species of birds have been recorded, but the real focus of the retreat is yoga (US$12 per class), meditation (US$5), massage (US$60) and other therapies given in the wonderful setting of the meditation hall, deep within the privacy of the rain forest. A range of packages is available, which include transportation, tours and activities.

Just south of Cahuita, along Highway 36 506 224 1870. Toll free in the US 1-800/563-9643 US$85 per person in the guesthouse (shared bath); US$95 private bath; bungalow US$135 per person 9

PLAYA CHIQUITA

LA COSTA DE PAPITO

www.lacostadepapito.com

On the beach road between Puerto Viejo de Talamanca and Manzanillo, La Costa de Papito is a delightful collection of individually designed bungalows set in a lush tropical garden of 2ha (5 acres) fringed with jungle. The spacious cabins all have cracked-tile bathrooms and a small balcony complete with hammock. The attention to detail extends even to the grain and cut of the wood, which is intrinsic to the design. Breakfast is available, brought to your door if requested, and there are bicycles, surfboards and boogie boards for rent, as well as a massage therapist, hair stylist and laundry service. Phone and internet are available.

Above *Early morning on Cahuita beach*

✉ Playa Chiquita, 1.5km (1 mile) from Puerto Viejo ☎ 506 2750 0704 ✋ US$54–US$78 ⓘ 10 bungalows

SHAWANDHA LODGE
www.shawandhalodge.com
Across the road from the stunning Playa Chiquita, the French-owned Shawandha Lodge is a luxury complex that oozes comfort and refinement while being totally integrated with the beautiful natural setting. Drawing on Polynesia for inspiration, each bungalow, which is designed in a neo-primitive style, is the height of good taste, constructed with exotic hardwoods, vivid ceramics and thatched palm roofs, and well equipped. There is a wonderful atmosphere in the restaurant at night, with dishes created by the French owner/chef. Local tours can be arranged.
✉ Playa Chiquita, 10km (6 miles) south of Puerto Viejo ☎ 506 2750 0018 ✋ US$108–US$147; the seventh night is free during some months ⓘ 12 bungalows

PUERTO VIEJO DE TALAMANCA

CASA VERDE LODGE
www.cabinascasaverde.com
The Swiss owner maintains this heart-of-town lodge with an almost fanatical devotion to neatness and cleanliness. Each year brings an evolution. What was once simple *cabina* lodgings has grown into the town's most appealing and diverse option, with single rooms, doubles, cabins and now two houses for rent. All have ceiling fans and broad balconies with hammocks looking into a lush manicured gardens. A pool with landscaped cascades has now been added.
✉ 200m (220 yards) southeast of the police station, Puerto Viejo ☎ 506 2750 0015 ✋ Rooms US$38–US$50, cabins and houses US$70 ⓘ 7 rooms (some with shared bath), 6 cabins, 2 houses

COCO LOCO LODGE
www.cocolocolodge.com
In a peaceful spot away from the heart of town, five cabins are woven into a blissfully lush setting, just a few hundred meters from the beach. The cabins vary in size, but all are comfortable, spotlessly clean and solidly constructed with hardwood floors, beamed ceilings, bathrooms with hot-water showers, mosquito nets, ceiling fans, and hammocks seductively draped on each porch. German owner Sabine is extremely helpful and informative and the main lodge reception has magazines, books, games and tour information and they can help with tour booking. Free WiFi is available. There are good discounts in the green season and for solo visitors.
✉ 150m (165 yards) from the bus station, Puerto Viejo ☎ 506 2750 0281 ✋ US$35–US$50 depending on size of bungalow ⓘ 5 cabins

PUNTA UVA

ALMONDS AND CORALS TENT CAMP
www.almondsandcorals.com
Some 25km (15.5 miles) south of Cahuita National Park, and just a five-minute walk from the beautiful Punta Uva beach, this is luxury camping on a grand scale. In a magical jungle setting, the 25 screened wooden cabins have private baths, ceiling fans, night lamps and hammocks. The excellent open-air restaurant serves tasty and filling meals of local dishes and seafood. Many activities are available and elevated walkways lead to the beach. Their Jungle Spa offers a full range of pampering treatments. Packages including transportation from San José, accommodations, meals and tours are also available. The hotel will rent out kayaks, bicycles and snorkeling equipment.
✉ Punta Uva ☎ 506 2271 3000 ✋ US$305–US$400 per person, including breakfast, dinner and taxes; 3 nights all inclusive US$432–US$695 per person ⓘ 25 tents

TORTUGUERO

CASA MARBELLA B&B
www.casamarbella.tripod.com
Long-time Tortuguero resident Daryl Loth from Canada runs the nicest bed-and-breakfast accommodations in the village. His waterfront lodge is simply furnished, but Daryl pays close attention to cleanliness. There's a cozy, communal feel to staying here thanks to the common TV lounge and the fact that guests get free use of the kitchen. There's no air-conditioning, but ceiling fans stir the breezes and you can laze outside on hammocks on the deck overhanging the lagoon.Breakfast is served on a riverside patio. You can take a guided water-borne tour of the Tortuguero National Park on the B&B's own craft.
✉ 100m (110 yards) north of the public dock in Tortuguero village ☎ 506 2709 8011 ✋ US$40 ⓘ 5 rooms

TORTUGA LODGE AND GARDENS
www.costaricaexpeditions.com
At the northernmost point of the lagoon, the most fashionable choice in Tortuguero is the Tortuga Lodge and Gardens. Set in 20ha (50 acres), with an awareness of conservation and ecotourism community integration, Costa Rica Expeditions' first lodge has become the most luxurious in their portfolio, following extensive remodeling. Big, bright and breezy rooms are set in a couple of two-floor lodges, each with private bath and a balcony or veranda, complete with hammock overlooking the gardens and the lagoon. The waterside restaurant is à la carte, and there's a wine list worth exploring. On the quiet days you can relax around the free-form pool or wander at will along a couple of trails, viewing poison dart frogs, caiman, monkeys and myriad birds. Be sure to slather on insect repellent, the mosquitos are impossibly aggressive. Expensive, but comfortable, the Lodge has a variety of more economical packages, which include air transportation from San José, accommodations, all meals and tours to the reserve.
✉ Tortuguero ☎ 506 2257 0766 ✋ US$128 standard; US$219 suite per person; inclusive package US$358 for two nights ⓘ 24 Outdoor

PRACTICALITIES

Practicalities gives you all the important practical information you will need during your visit, from money matters to emergency phone numbers.

PUNTARENAS

TEMPERATURE

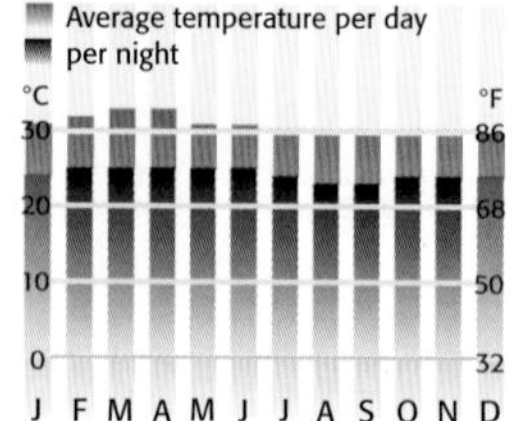

RAINFALL

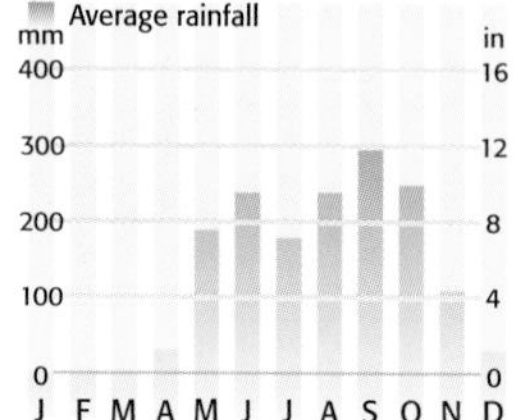

SAN JOSÉ

TEMPERATURE

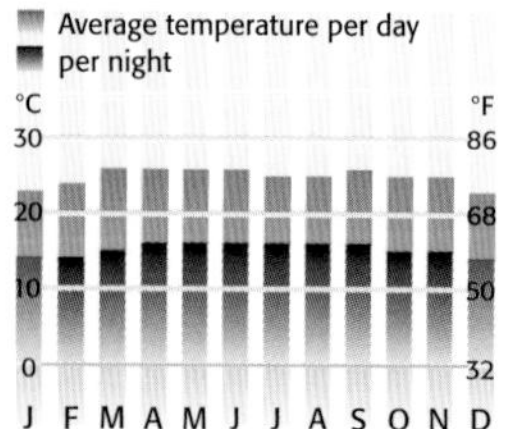

RAINFALL

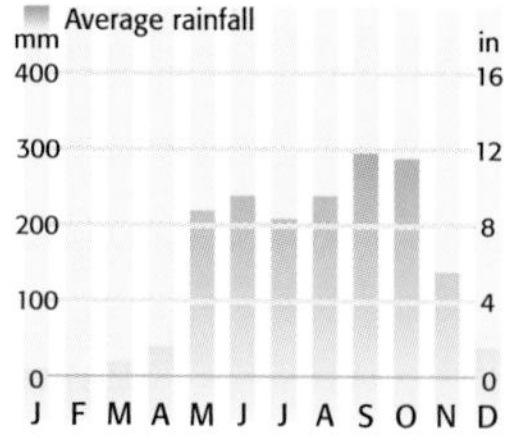

PUERTO LIMÓN

TEMPERATURE

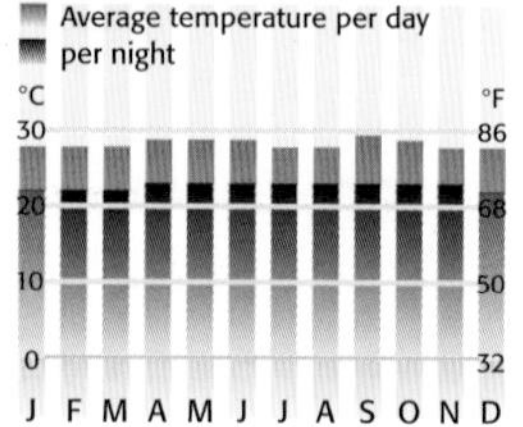

RAINFALL

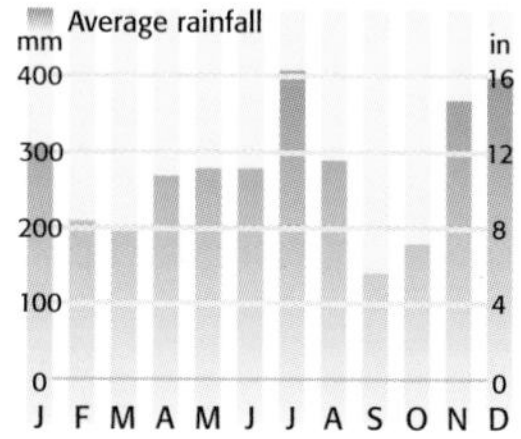

WEATHER

CLIMATE

If your trip is about beaches, blue skies and hot sun, go to the north and central Pacific coast between December and April—the high season. This is a clearly defined time with a marked dry season in the Central Highlands and the Pacific regions where almost no rain falls from mid-December to April. Outside these months rain falls steadily, and is heaviest in September and October. On the Caribbean side, east of the continental divide, rain falls intermittently all year. The drier months are February to June, with a small summer *(veranillo)* in September and October.

Outside the high season, rainfall normally occurs in bursts lasting a couple of hours and travel is possible in most places. This rainy season has been renamed the "green season" by the Costa Rican Tourism Institute and is an increasingly popular time to visit: The country tends to be quieter and discounts are often possible.

TIME ZONES

Costa Rica time is the same as US Central Standard Time, six hours behind Greenwich Mean Time (GMT).

CITY	TIME DIFFERENCE	TIME AT 12 NOON IN COSTA RICA
Amsterdam	+7	7pm
Berlin	+7	7pm
Chicago	0	12 noon
Dublin	+6	6pm
Johannesburg	+8	8pm
Madrid	+7	7pm
Montréal	+1	1pm
New York	+1	1pm
Paris	+7	7pm
Perth, Australia	+11	11pm
Rome	+7	7pm
San Francisco	-2	10am
Sydney	+13	1am
Tokyo	+12	12am

A word of warning: Some places close for a break and a few become inaccessible as many roads are subject to seasonal difficulties such as impassable rivers. Four-wheel-drive vehicles are essential for journeys on unpaved roads. Check road conditions before you set off.

WEATHER REPORTS

The Instituto Meteorológico Nacional in San José provides a five-day weather forecast (in Spanish) on its website: www.imn.ac.cr.

WHAT TO TAKE

Clothes

What to take depends on how long you're staying and what you're doing. Starting at the lower altitudes you'll need beachwear, sunglasses and a sun hat—which you'll probably need everywhere—and sunscreen. If you plan to walk on trails, shorts and a light shirt are ideal. In areas where insects are numerous and aggressive, long-sleeved tops and lightweight long trousers are better. For the Central Highlands you will need to add a light sweater or jacket for the evenings. At higher altitudes pack something warmer. When preparing for rain it's tempting to take a raincoat, but don't bother unless you plan long treks; buy an umbrella or poncho locally or sit the rain out. You will need comfortable shoes appropriate to your activity, as well as a change when they get wet. Buying large size shoes in Costa Rica is not impossible, but the choice will be restricted.

Personal Items

If you have personal medical requirements, take enough to last your trip and seek medical advice before leaving home if you have any reason to be concerned. Items worth taking include a flashlight or headlamp, camera and spare batteries and memory cards, a water bottle, insect repellent and a universal sink plug. If you wear glasses or contact lens, take a spare pair or sufficient supplies for the trip, although it is possible to get most items in Costa Rica. Mosquito repellent is de rigueur once you leave the highlands.

As ever, specialists will want to take items particular to their activity. A good pair of binoculars is essential for birding. Field guides for birders and nature lovers are available in some of the better lodges, but it's better to have your own. Divers and snorkelers might prefer their own mask. It may be cheaper for surfers to rent a board.

Pack in a strong bag, the lighter the better, and ideally one that can be locked with a removable padlock, which could then be used on dodgy doors and lockers if the need arises in cheaper hotels. Most mid- and upper-range hotels have safes.

DOCUMENTS

PASSPORTS AND VISAS

Citizens of the US, Canada, Australia, most Western European nations and Japan are permitted to enter Costa Rica and stay for 90 days if they are carrying a valid passport with at least one blank visa page. Your passport should be valid for at least six months after your travel date. People holding valid passports from most Central American and Caribbean countries are allowed to stay in Costa Rica for 30 days without a visa. Citizens of all countries not listed above must obtain a visa before visiting.

Passport and visa regulations can change at short notice. Always confirm the latest requirements before you travel.

On entering Costa Rica, all visitors should be able to show they have an onward ticket to leave the country or proof of sufficient funds to travel out of the country.

You can extend your stay beyond these limits with a *prórroga de turísmo*, obtained at *migración* in San José, on the road from the capital to the airport. For this you need four passport photos, a copy of your entire passport, an airline or bus ticket out of the country and proof of funds; an extension of one or two months costs US$3 per month. The paperwork can take up to three days but travel agents can arrange all extension and exit formalities for a small fee. Alternatively, leave the country for 72 hours and get a new 30- or 90-day visa when you reenter. If you enter overland, you may be asked for an onward ticket. A bus ticket can be bought close to the border immigration office; you may get the cost refunded in San José.

RESIDENCY

If you want to take up residency, there are a number of options for retirement or investing in Costa Rica. Essentially you need to prove that you have a regular income or that you are going to invest more than US$50,000 to create a regular income. Full details about requirements and the process can be obtained at www.migracion.go.cr. For assistance, contact the Association of Residents of Costa Rica, Casa Canada, Avenida 4 and Calle 40, PO Box 1008-1007, Centro Colón, San José, tel 506 2222 1722; www.casacanada.net/arcr.

TRAVEL INSURANCE

You should take out travel insurance before your trip. Make sure that it covers medical and dental expenses, and repatriation as well as theft and delay. If you are taking items of high value make sure they are covered; some policies do not cover goods over a certain value unless declared in advance. Insurance companies vary in their requirements relating to claims and payments. The bare minimum requirement is a police report. Read the small print in your policy carefully.

CUSTOMS

The duty-free allowance for visitors coming to Costa Rica is 500 cigarettes and three liters of wine or spirits. No customs duties are charged on personal luggage, including items for personal and professional use as long as they are not in sufficient quantities that suggest commercial use. In the case of families, one declaration can be filled out for the whole family. Never bring banned or illegal goods into the country.

EMBASSIES IN COSTA RICA

COUNTRY	ADDRESS	CONTACT DETAILS
Canada	Oficentro Ejecutivo La Sabana, Edificio 5, Sabana Sur, San José	506 2242 4400; www.international.gc.ca/sanjose
Germany	Torre La Sabana, Sabana Norte, San José	506 2290 9091; www.sanjose.diplo.de
Spain	Calle 32, between Paseo Colón and Avenida 2, San José	506 2222 5745; www.mae.es
United Kingdom	Centro Colón, calles 38–40, San José	506 2258 2025; www.britishembassycr.com
United States	Calle 120, Avenida 0, Pavas, San José	506 2519 2000; http://sanjose.usembassy.gov

MONEY

CURRENCY

» The unit of currency in Costa Rica is the colón, consisting of 100 céntimos. Coins are in denominations of 5, 10, 25, 50 and 100 colones. Some public telephones use older silver 5, 10 and 20 colón coins. Notes in use: 1,000, 2,000, 5,000 and 10,000 colones. The colón is colloquially called the peso, cash is called *efectivo*, and loose change is referred to as *menudo*. Note that many shopkeepers will not accept banknotes that are torn.

» Dollars are widely accepted in cities and resorts, but don't rely on being able to use them outside the most popular destinations. Always have some colones as well. Many retail establishments will not accept US$50 and US$100 notes, as there are many counterfeit bills in circulation.

CASH, TRAVELERS' CHECKS OR CREDIT CARDS?

All three is the easy answer. Cash should be taken in dollars; they are by far the easiest to change. It is possible to change other currencies, but the rate is normally reduced and you may have to visit several banks.

Travelers' checks have added security, being replaceable. Take dollar travelers' checks and make sure they are a well-known name like American Express, Citibank or Thomas Cook. Keep the original purchase receipt separate from the checks; for added security photocopy it.

Credit cards are widely accepted in hotels and restaurants in San José and the more established resorts, but may be difficult to use beyond these areas. Check with hotels in advance when making reservations. The real value of a credit card is for easy cash advances from automated teller machines (ATMs) and banks. Visa and MasterCard are accepted, with Visa probably having the edge. American Express and Diners Card are accepted in business hotels, but should not be relied upon outside the business setting. However, many businesses apply a surcharge as high as 15 percent if you pay by credit card.

BANKS AND CHANGING MONEY

Getting some first-day money before departure can be difficult. You may be able to get some in Miami if you are catching a connecting flight. There is a bank, just after customs, at the Juan Santamaría International Airport in San José, which opens to meet arriving flights so you can change money on arrival if you need to.

Banks are the easiest place to change money. Branches of the state banks Banco Nacional and Banco de Costa Rica are found throughout the country. The core opening hours are from 8.30am to 3.30pm, Monday to Friday. However, some branches are opening for longer; occasionally extending to Saturday morning. Service varies wildly. It can be incredibly slow or surprisingly fast. Be prepared to wait. Banks in areas where processing travelers' checks and credit cards is a rare event may take longer, but this isn't always the case.

Commission rates for changing currency generally tend to be around 1 percent.

The black market in Costa Rica has largely disappeared, and the few street money changers that hang around the central area operate illegally. It's best to avoid changing money on the street as scams and robberies are common. Don't flash large amounts of money around.

COST OF LIVING

Budgeting for a trip is always difficult and is dependent on your tastes and mode of travel. Costa Rica is not an expensive country. Income per head of population is around US$11,500.

At the bottom end of the scale you could manage on US$25 to US$40 a day to cover accommodations, meals and travel by bus. As a very rough guideline, bus travel works out at between US$1 and US$1.50 per hour of travel. But this would leave very little for comforts, trips and tours. Comfortable travel is found in the US$45 to US$85 per day range. This should cover reasonable accommodations and pleasant meals based on preference rather than cheapest cost. Beyond US$85 things start to get comfortable, with better service, design and decor.

Renting a vehicle will cost from US$350 a week. Tours range in price from US$45 for a day-trip up to US$250 for a two-day, all-inclusive white-water rafting or Tortuguero wildlife trip.

PRICES OF EVERYDAY ITEMS

ITEM	PRICE (US$)
Bottle of water	0.40–2
Bottle of beer	0.75–3
Packet of 20 cigarettes	1.50
Tico Times newspaper	1
Cup of tea or coffee	0.25–2
Sunscreen	3–10
Sun hat	5–10
Casado (lunch)	2–10

HEALTH

Staying healthy in Costa Rica is straightforward. Most visitors return home having experienced no problems at all, except perhaps an upset stomach. However, the health risks are different from those encountered in Europe or the US. Your health also depends on how you travel, and where. There are clear differences between the risks for the businessperson, who stays in international-class hotels, and the backpacker.

There are English- (or other foreign-language) speaking doctors in most cities who have experience in dealing with locally occurring diseases. Your embassy will often be able to give you the name of a reputable doctor and most of the better hotels have a doctor on standby.

If you fall ill and cannot find a recommended doctor, try the Outpatient Department of a hospital; private hospitals are usually less crowded and offer a more acceptable standard of care.

HEALTHY FLYING

» Visitors to Costa Rica from Europe, the US or as far as Australia or New Zealand may be concerned about the effect of long-haul flights on their health. The most widely publicized concern is Deep Vein Thrombosis, or DVT. Misleadingly called "economy class syndrome," DVT is the forming of a blood clot in the body's deep veins, particularly in the legs. The clot can move around the bloodstream and could be fatal.

» Those most at risk include the elderly, pregnant women and those using the contraceptive pill, smokers and the overweight. If you are at increased risk of DVT see your doctor before departing. Flying increases the likelihood of DVT because passengers are often seated in a cramped position for long periods of time and may become dehydrated.

To minimize risk:

Drink water (not alcohol)

Don't stay immobile for hours at a time

Stretch and exercise your legs periodically

Do wear elastic flight socks, which support veins and reduce the chances of a clot forming

Exercises

Other health hazards for flyers are airborne diseases and bugs spread by the plane's air-conditioning system. These are largely unavoidable, but if you have a serious medical condition seek advice from a doctor before flying.

1 Ankle rotations

Lift feet off the floor. Draw a circle with the toes, moving one foot clockwise and the other counterclockwise

2 Calf stretches

Start with heel on the floor and point foot upward as high as you can. Then lift heels high, keeping balls of feet on the floor

3 Knee lifts

Lift leg with knee bent while contracting your thigh muscle. Then straighten leg pressing foot flat to the floor

BEFORE YOU GO

Take out medical insurance and ensure it covers all eventualities, especially repatriation to your home country.

It is sensible to have a dental checkup, and, if you suffer from a chronic illness, a checkup with your doctor who will be able to provide you with a letter explaining the details of your condition in English and if possible Spanish. Check the current practice for malaria prophylaxis (prevention). Take spare glasses (or a prescription for them), and if you are on regular medication, make sure you have enough to cover the period of your travel.

CHILDREN

More preparation is probably necessary for babies and children than for an adult, and more care should be taken when visiting remote areas. This is because children often become ill more rapidly than adults.

Diarrhea and vomiting are the most common problems, so take the usual precautions. Treatment of diarrhea is the same as it is for adults, except that it should be continued with more persistence. Children get dehydrated quickly in hot countries and can become drowsy unless cajoled to drink fluids. Breastfeeding is best and most convenient for babies, but powdered milk and baby foods are available in Costa Rica. Papaya, bananas and avocados are all nutritious and can be cleanly prepared. Outer ear infections after swimming may be a problem and antibiotic ear drops will help. Wet wipes are extremely useful and sometimes difficult to find, as are diapers in some places.

MEDICINES

There is very little control on the sale of drugs and medicines in Costa Rica. You may be able to buy any drug in pharmacies without a prescription. Be wary of this because pharmacists can be poorly trained and might sell you drugs that are unsuitable, dangerous or old. Many drugs and medicines are manufactured under license from American or European companies, so the trade names may be familiar to you.

Remember that the shelf life of some items, especially antibiotics, is markedly reduced in hot conditions. Buy your supplies at outlets where there are refrigerators and check the expiry date of all drugs. Immigration officials occasionally confiscate scheduled drugs (Lomotil is an example) if they are not accompanied by a doctor's prescription.

VACCINATIONS

Vaccination against the following diseases is recommended. Children should already be properly protected against diphtheria, poliomyelitis, pertussis (whooping cough) and measles. If your child has not had the vaccinations, consider protecting them before you visit Costa Rica. Hepatitis B vaccination for babies is now routine in some countries.

Ask your doctor for advice on tuberculosis: the disease is still widespread in Latin America

Yellow Fever
This is a live vaccination, not to be given to children under nine months or anyone allergic to eggs. Immunity lasts for 10 years; an International Certificate of Yellow Fever Vaccination will be given and should be kept as Costa Rica now requires proof of vaccination against yellow fever for travelers arriving from several South American countries. Yellow fever is very rare in Costa Rica, but the vaccination is usually without side effects and almost totally protective.

Typhoid
A number of new vaccines against this condition are now available: they cause fewer side effects than the old ones, but are more expensive.

Poliomyelitis
Almost everyone in the developed world is vaccinated against this disease as a child. It may be wise to have a booster.

Tetanus
One dose should be given with a booster at six weeks and another at six months, and 10 yearly boosters are recommended.

Infectious Hepatitis
This is less of a problem for visitors than it used to be because of the development of two extremely effective vaccines against the A and B form of the disease. It remains common, however, in Latin America. A combined hepatitis A and B vaccine is now licensed and has been available since 1997; one jab covers both diseases.

OTHER VACCINATIONS

These might be considered in the case of epidemics, for example, meningitis. There is an effective vaccination against rabies, which should be considered by those going through remote areas or if there is a particular occupational risk. You may also wish to be vaccinated against H1N1 (swine flu)—Costa Rican president Oscar Arias famously caught the infection in 2009.

FURTHER INFORMATION

Further information on health risks abroad and vaccinations may be available from a local travel clinic. If you wish to take specific drugs with you, such as antibiotics, these are best prescribed by your own doctor.

In the UK there are hospital departments specializing in tropical diseases in London, Liverpool, Birmingham and Glasgow, and at the London School of Hygiene and Tropical Medicine. In the US the local Public Health Services can give such advice. Information is available centrally from the Center for Disease Control (CDC) in Atlanta, tel 404/639-3534, www.cdc.gov.

The Scottish Centre for Infection and Environmental Health has a website database providing information for visitors at www.fitfortravel.scot.nhs.uk. General advice is also available in the UK in *Health Information for Overseas Travel* (Department of Health), available from HMSO and International Travel and Health (WHO). Handbooks on first aid are produced by the British and American Red Cross.

ON THE WAY

For many visitors, a trip to Costa Rica means a long flight. The best way to get over jetlag is to force yourself into the new time zone as strictly as possible. The symptoms of jetlag may be helped by keeping up your fluid intake on the journey. The hormone melatonin seems to reduce the symptoms of jetlag.

On long-haul flights it is also important to stretch your legs at least every hour to prevent slowing of the circulation and the possible development of blood clots. Drinking plenty of nonalcoholic fluids helps.

STAYING HEALTHY

The thought of catching a stomach bug may worry visitors to Costa Rica, but is rarely a problem and, if you are sensible, intestinal upsets are rare. Diarrhea and vomiting are usually the result of food poisoning, passed on by insanitary food handlers. As a rule, the cleaner and the smarter the restaurant, the less likely you are to suffer.

MEDICAL KIT CHECK LIST

- » Insect repellent containing DEET
- » Mosquito net: preferably permethrin-impregnated
- » Water sterilizing tablets
- » Antimalarial tablets
- » Antiseptic ointment
- » Sachets of rehydration salts
- » Antidiarrhea preparations
- » Painkillers
- » Antibiotics
- » First-aid kit

FOODS TO AVOID

Don't eat uncooked, under-cooked, partially cooked or reheated meat, fish and eggs, especially when they have been left uncovered. Raw vegetables and salads are also possible sources of trouble. Stick to fresh food that has been cooked from raw just before eating and make sure you peel fruit yourself. Wash and dry your hands before eating; disposable wet-wipe tissues are very useful.

Shellfish eaten raw are always risky and at certain times of the year some fish and shellfish concentrate toxins that can cause food poisoning. In that case, the local authorities notify the public not to eat these foods.

Heat treated (UHT), sterilized or pasteurized milk is becoming more available, as is pasteurized cheese. Matured or processed cheeses are safer than the fresh varieties. Fresh unpasteurized milk can be a source of food-poisoning germs. This also applies to ice cream, yoghurt and cheese made from unpasteurized milk.

Tap water is rarely safe outside the major cities, especially in the rainy season. Filtered or bottled water is usually available and safe, although you must make sure that somebody is not filling bottles from the tap and hammering on a new cap. Ice for drinks should be made from boiled water, but it rarely is, so stand your glass on the ice cubes, rather than putting them in the drink. The better hotels have water purifying systems. Drinking water is rarely the culprit in cases of food poisoning. Sea water or river water is more likely to be contaminated by sewage and so swimming can also lead to infection.

The various organisms that give rise to stomach upsets may be viruses, bacteria—for example Escherichia coli (probably the most common cause), salmonella and cholera—or protozoa (such as amoeba and giardia). The diarrhea may come on suddenly or rather slowly. It may be accompanied by vomiting or by abdominal pain; the passage of blood or mucus is a sign of dysentery.

DIAGNOSIS AND TREATMENT

Acute diarrhea is probably due to a virus or a bacterium and/or the onset of dysentery. Treatment, in addition to rehydration, is an antibiotic such as ciprofloxacin; the drug is now widely available and there are many similar ones.

If the diarrhea comes on slowly or intermittently then it is more likely to be caused by an amoeba or giardia. Antibiotics such as ciprofloxacin will have little effect. These cases are best treated by a doctor, as is any outbreak of diarrhea continuing for more than three days. If a doctor is not available then the best treatment is probably tinidazole (Fasigyn). If there are severe stomach cramps, the following drugs may help but are not useful in the management of acute diarrhea: loperamide (Imodium) and diphenoxylate with atropine (Lomotil). They should not be given to children.

Any kind of diarrhea responds well to the replacement of water and salts, taken as frequent sips of some kind of rehydration solution. There are proprietary preparations consisting of sachets of powder which you dissolve in boiled water, or you can make your own by adding half a teaspoonful of salt and two tablespoonfuls of sugar to a liter (1.75 pints) of boiled water. Rehydration is especially important for children.

Paradoxically, constipation is also common, probably induced by dietary change, inadequate fluid intake in hot places and long bus journeys. Simple laxatives are useful in the short-term and bulky foods such as maize, beans and plenty of fruit are also useful.

WATER PURIFICATION

There are a number of ways of purifying water in order to make it safe to drink. Dirty water should first be strained through a filter bag (available in camping shops) and then boiled or treated. Bringing water to a rolling boil at sea level is sufficient to make the water safe for drinking, but at higher altitudes you have to boil the water for a few minutes longer to ensure that all the microbes are killed.

There are proprietary preparations containing chlorine (for example Puritabs) or iodine (such as Pota Aqua) compounds. Chlorine compounds generally do not kill protozoa (for example giardia).

ALTITUDE

Spending time at high altitude in Central America is usually a pleasure but it can cause medical problems. On reaching heights above 3,000m (10,000ft), heart pounding and shortness of breath, especially on exertion, are a normal response to the lack of oxygen in the air; only the mountains of the Chirripó range reach this height in Costa Rica.

HEAT AND COLD

The temperature in Costa Rica rarely exceeds the 30°C mark (86°F), though the humidity may be higher than you are used to. Remember that tepid showers are more cooling than hot or cold ones. Large hats do not cool you down, but do prevent sunburn. There can be a sudden drop in temperature between sun and shade and between night and day, especially in the highlands, so dress accordingly. Warm jackets or woolens are essential after dark at high altitude. Loose cotton is still the best material when the weather is hot.

INSECTS

These are mostly more of a nuisance than a serious hazard and with a bit of preparation you should be able to avoid being bitten.

Some, such as mosquitoes, may be carriers of potentially serious diseases. Sleep off the ground and use an insecticide-impregnated mosquito net or some kind of insecticide. Preparations containing pyrethrum or synthetic pyrethroids are safe. They are available as aerosols or pumps and the best way to use these is to spray the room thoroughly in all areas and then shut the door for a while, reentering when the smell has dispersed. Mosquito coils release insecticide as they burn slowly. Tablets of insecticide that are placed on a heated mat plugged into a wall socket are probably the most effective. They fill the room with insecticidal fumes in the same way as aerosols or coils.

Many insect repellents are effective against a wide range of pests. The most effective is diethyl metatoluamide (DEET). DEET liquid is best for arms and face. Aerosol spray is good for clothes and ankles and liquid DEET can be dissolved in water and used to impregnate cotton clothes and mosquito nets. Some repellents now contain DEET and permethrin, an insecticide. Impregnated wrist and ankle bands can be useful.

If you are bitten or stung, itching may be relieved by taking cool baths or antihistamine tablets. Bites that become infected should be treated with an antiseptic or antibiotic cream, as should any sores or scratches.

TICKS AND MAGGOTS

Ticks usually attach themselves to the lower parts of the body often while you are walking in areas where cattle have grazed. They take a while to attach themselves strongly, but swell up as they start to suck blood. The important thing is to remove them gently, so that they do not leave their head parts in your skin because this can cause infections or an allergic reaction some days later. Do not use petrol, Vaseline, lighted cigarettes, etc, to remove the tick, but, with a pair of tweezers, remove the beast gently by gripping it at the attached (head) end and rocking it out in very much the same way that a tooth is extracted.

Certain tropical flies that lay their eggs under the skin of sheep and cattle also occasionally do the same thing to humans with the unpleasant result that a maggot grows under the skin and pops up as a boil or pimple. The best way to remove these is to cover the boil with oil, Vaseline or nail varnish, thereby stopping the maggot from breathing, and then to squeeze it out gently the next day.

OTHER ANIMAL BITES AND STINGS

It is a very rare event indeed, but if you are unlucky enough to be bitten by a venomous snake, spider, scorpion or sea creature, try to identify it without putting yourself in further danger. Snake bites in particular are very frightening, but in fact rarely life-threatening—even venomous snakes may bite without injecting venom. Victims should be taken to a hospital or a doctor without delay. Commercial snake bite and scorpion kits are available, but are usually only useful for the specific types of snake or scorpion. If someone is bitten, reassure and comfort the victim. Immobilize the limb with a bandage or a splint or by getting the person to lie still. Do not slash the bite area and try to suck out the poison—this does more harm than good. If you know how to use a tourniquet in these circumstances, you will not need advice. If you are not experienced, do not apply a tourniquet.

PRECAUTIONS

Avoid walking in snake territory in bare feet or sandals: wear proper shoes or boots. If you encounter a snake, keep your distance and always look in advance where you put your hands while in the wilderness. Spiders and scorpions may be found in the more basic hotels and wilderness lodges. If bitten or stung, rest, take plenty of fluids and call a doctor. Keep beds away from the walls and look inside your shoes and under the toilet seat every morning.

MARINE BITES AND STINGS

Certain tropical sea fish when trodden upon inject venom into bathers' feet. This can be exceptionally painful. Wear plastic shoes when you go bathing if such creatures are reported. The pain can be relieved by immersing the foot in hot water until the pain fades.

SUNBURN

The burning power of the tropical sun, especially at high altitude, is phenomenal. Always wear a wide-brimmed hat and use some form of sunscreen. Low protection factor sunscreen lotions are not much good; you need protection factor of 15 or above. Glare from the sun and sea can cause conjunctivitis, so wear sunglasses, especially on tropical beaches.

MALARIA

Malaria is theoretically confined to coastal and jungle zones, but is now on the increase again. There are different varieties of malaria parasites, some resistant to the normal drugs. Consult your doctor and make local enquiries if you intend to visit possibly infected zones, and use a prophylactic regime. You can still catch the disease even when sticking to a proper regime, although it is unlikely. If you do develop symptoms (high fever, shivering, headache, sometimes diarrhea), seek medical advice immediately.

All the drugs may have some side effects and it is important to balance the risk of catching the disease against the (albeit rare) side effects. It also makes sense to avoid being bitten (▷ 219, Insects).

DENGUE FEVER

This is transmitted by mosquitoes and, as there is no effective vaccination against it, you should try to avoid being bitten (▷ 219, Insects).

BASICS

CHILDREN

» Remember that a lot of time can be spent waiting for public transport, so make sure you pack some toys. Nothing beats a GameBoy, unless it's two GameBoys and a link cable. Take reading material with you as it is difficult, and expensive, to find.

» Food can be a problem. It is easier to take food and drinks, with you on longer trips than to rely on meal stops where the food may not be to taste. Avocados are safe, easy to eat and nutritious. A small immersion heater and jug for making hot drinks is invaluable, but remember that the electric current varies. Try and get a dual-voltage model (110v and 220v) or an adaptor.

» Discounted fares apply on public transportation, and families will also benefit from reduced fares on sightseeing tours.

» In hotels try to negotiate family rates. If charges are per person, always insist that two children will occupy one bed only, therefore counting as one tariff. If rates are per bed, the same applies. In either case you can almost always get a reduced rate at cheaper hotels. In the better hotels in more commercial resorts, it is quite common for children under 10 or 12 to be allowed to stay for no extra charge if they are sharing a room with their parents.

» Travel with children can bring you into closer contact with local families and generally presents no special problems; in fact the path is often smoother for family groups. Officials tend to be more amenable where children are concerned, and they are pleased if your child knows a little Spanish. Moreover, thieves and pickpockets seem to have some of the traditional respect for families.

» Diapers (nappies) can be difficult to find, so bring a supply with you.

LOCAL CUSTOMS AND LAWS

Costa Rican society is broadly tolerant. The US State Department produce *Tips for Travelers to Central and South America* which

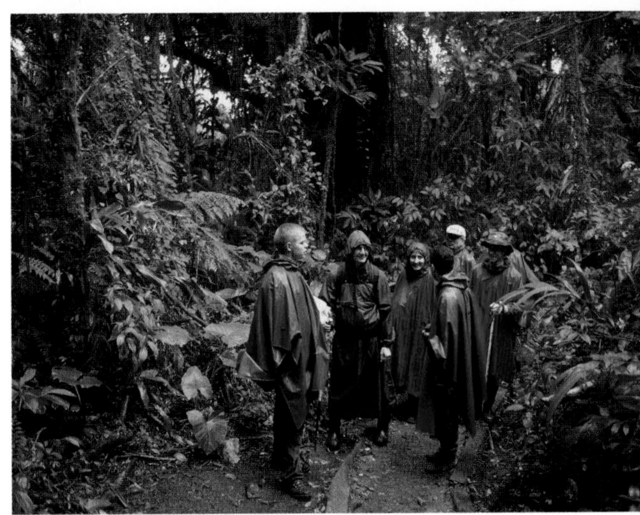

can be obtained through the US Government Printing Office, Washington, DC 20402 or via the Bureau of Consular Affairs at www.travel.state.gov.

CLOTHING

Most Costa Ricans devote a great deal of care to their clothes and appearance. How you dress is how people will judge you, particularly in the business arena. Even on vacation, smart, clean clothes are always appreciated. In beach communities, wear a sarong and a shirt when walking round town or if you're away from the beach.

CONDUCT

Politeness, courtesy and sometimes ceremoniousness prevails in all situations—even the traffic police give tickets in a rather pleasant manner. Being flustered, rushed and hurried simply doesn't fit in with the way of doing things in Costa Rica, a common trait throughout Latin America. Equally common is the sometimes extended process of introductions. Likewise when departing, take the time to say goodbye.

MAÑANA

Visitors should keep to time arrangements or, as it is known, the *hora inglés*. With just a hint of sadness, the *mañana* culture of "tomorrow" is disappearing from many areas. Tours leave on time, bus services tend to leave promptly and restaurant tables should be taken up punctually.

Get involved with the government and bureaucracy and it's a different world: the sheer amount of paperwork required can be frightening. Stay patient and tolerant if dealing with officials.

CONVERSION CHART

FROM	TO	MULTIPLY BY
Inches	Centimeters	2.54
Centimeters	Inches	0.3937
Feet	Meters	0.3048
Meters	Feet	3.2810
Yards	Meters	0.9144
Meters	Yards	1.0940
Miles	Kilometers	1.6090
Kilometres	Miles	0.6214
Acres	Hectares	0.4047
Hectares	Acres	2.4710
Gallons	Liters	4.5460
Liters	Gallons	0.2200
Ounces	Grams	28.35
Grams	Ounces	0.0353
Pounds	Grams	453.6
Grams	Pounds	0.0022
Pounds	Kilograms	0.4536
Kilograms	Pounds	2.205
Tons	Tonnes	1.0160
Tonnes	Tons	0.9842

DRINK AND DRUGS

Drinking is a part of life, but drunkenness is fairly uncommon. Yes, walking through San José, Limón or other cities and popular areas late on a Saturday you will find a few individuals the worse for wear, but nothing excessive.

Although drugs are frowned upon, their presence is increasing as Costa Rica is used as a transhipment port for cocaine coming up from South America. All drugs are illegal in Costa Rica, with a jail term being the likely penalty for possession.

TIPPING

Once a reward for exceptional service, the tendency to tip at the drop of a hat is taking over in Costa Rica. In better restaurants, a 13 percent sales tax and a 10 percent service charge is automatically added to your bill. You are welcome to contest paying the service charge if you wish. The consensus is that bellboys and chambermaids receive tips of between US$0.50 and US$2 per item or day. Generally, taxi drivers are not tipped. Tour guides can be tipped as you see fit—again, the tip should reflect the level of service and attention rather than be an assumed payment.

RELIGION

While 90 percent of Costa Ricans are nominally Roman Catholic, the number that actually attend church on a regular basis is far less. However, respect for the church is still very high.

ELECTRICITY

Costa Rica runs on 110 volts, 60 cycles AC. Plugs are the US flat-pin style.

WEIGHTS AND MEASURES

For customs the metric system is compulsory. Traders use a variety of weights and measures, including imperial and the old Spanish ones.

RESPONSIBLE TRAVEL

Costa Rica has undergone a change in recent decades from slash-and-burn deforestation to be one of the planet's leading exponents of nature tourism and what is currently called ecotourism. This is indisputably one of the world's most popular nature destinations, and tourism, which attracts over a million visitors to the country every year, is the country's leading foreign exchange earner. But while there are clearly benefits for both the host country and visitors—employment and cultural exchange—there can also be a downside. Where visitor pressure is high and poorly regulated, adverse impacts on society and the natural environment may be apparent.

Many national parks are partly funded by receipts from visitors. Similarly, you can promote protection of archaeological sites and heritage through your interest and contributions via entrance fees. You can also support small-scale enterprises by staying in locally run hotels and hostels, eating in local restaurants and by purchasing local goods and services.

Increasingly, visitors are keen to be involved in ecotourism. The Costa Rican Tourist Board (ICT) has introduced an environmentally based classification system—Certified Sustainable Tourism—which could help visitors a lot when choosing between hotels. Currently, the ICT grades hotels with levels from one to five, awarding Green Leaf signs to certified hotels.

FURTHER INFORMATION

In the US contact the International Ecotourism Society, tel 202/347-9203, www.ecotourism.org, for a comprehensive breakdown of the issues. The society has links with several Costa Rican organizations that share an interest in promoting ecotourism.

Organizations like Conservation International in the US (01-703/341-2400, www.ecotour.org) and Tourism Concern in the UK (020 7133 3800, www.tourismconcern.org.uk) have begun to develop and promote ecotourism projects. Additionally, organizations such as Earthwatch (US and Canada on 01-800/ 776-0188, in the UK on 01865 318838, www.earthwatch.org) offer opportunities to participate directly in scientific research and development projects.

While some ecotourism operators' claims need to be interpreted with care, there is clearly demand for this type of activity and opportunities to support worthwhile conservation initiatives.

FINDING HELP

SAFETY

In general, Costa Rica is a very safe country. Nonetheless, crimes against tourists have increased alarmingly in recent years. The majority of crimes can be avoided by being aware of the risks. Government authorities have committed to increasing the police presence with the introduction of a Tourist Police Corps in many popular tourist centers.

Should you require police assistance call 117, in any other emergency call 911.

PROTECTING MONEY AND VALUABLES

» Leave your valuables in a safe box in your hotel, or with reception if you are happy to trust your hotel.
» If you need to carry cash around, keep it in a safe place about your person, preferably somewhere under your clothing so it is concealed.
» Do not walk around wearing a highly visible fanny pack (bumbag) which invites attention.
» If you are carrying a camera, make sure you have your hand on it or the bag at all times.
» Avoid walking through dark areas on your own at night.

DANGEROUS PLACES

» Bus stops are busy places where first-time visitors can become bewildered: perfect conditions for the bag-lifter to relieve you of your belongings. Remain calm at all times. Try not to appear unnecessarily rushed or lost. If you need to get your bearings, sit down and gather your bags together. If you need to ask directions, avoid leaving one person in charge of more bags than they can hold.
» The Coca-Cola Bus Terminal and surrounding area in San José has a reputation for crime. A police office has opened in the terminal area and some locals say that crime is now falling, but nevertheless, take care.
» If you've ever seen a well-organized criminal team work a crowd, you will realize that you have no chance if you have been picked as a victim. Do what you can to avoid being a victim and don't bring anything so precious you can't afford to lose it.

CON TRICKS

To say there is less creative theft in Costa Rica than in other countries is little consolation once you've had your pockets emptied. Be wary of scams that attempt to distract you. One trick is to throw mud or shampoo on you, a helper clears it off while a third relieves you of your possessions. Other tricks involve dropping money and asking if it is yours. In the conversation, with your guard dropped, your pockets are pilfered.

Organized scams operate in major tourist destinations, such as Tamarindo.

DRIVING

Rental cars are commonly the target of theft. The tourist number plates that used to be on rental vehicles, and stuck out like a sore thumb, have now gone. However, your vehicle will still obviously be a rental car.
» Do not park in the street: use hotel parking or find a parking area.
» Do not leave valuables in the car, but if you have no choice, put them out of sight.
» Do not park on the roadside in quiet spots—it will be seen.

WOMEN

The risks for women visitors in Costa Rica are no different to the risks in your home country. In general, Costa Rica is much safer (in terms of violent crime against women) than the US or Europe, and rape and muggings are uncommon. However, there have been some well publicized incidents in which female visitors have been attacked, and you should exercise the normal caution you would anywhere in the world. If the last few years are anything to go by, violent crime with at times fatal consequences is on the increase, but remains extremely rare.
» If you are subject to violent crime do not risk your life defending your possessions.
» Avoid alcohol if you are likely to be on your own, and do not accept alcohol from anyone not in your group.
» Bear in mind that most people who invite you for a stroll on the beach are not motivated by a desire to practice their English.

EMERGENCY PHONE NUMBERS	
All emergencies	911
Police	117
Fire	118
Ambulance	128

SWIMMING AND RIP TIDES

The beauty of some of Costa Rica's beaches hides the very real threat of rip tides—currents that pull you out to sea. If you know what you are looking for, it is possible to see rip currents: They have a noticeable difference in water color, or you may see a gap in the breaking waves or foam and objects floating out to sea. Be sensible and avoid getting caught in a current.

Apart from the beaches at Dominical and Manuel Antonio National Park, there are no lifesaving guards in Costa Rica, so you will have to depend on local advice. Dangerous beaches popular with tourists are Playa Jacó, Playa Esterillos, Playa Dominical, Playa Espadilla, Playa Bonita and Playa Cahuita.

If you get caught in a rip tide, don't panic; many drownings occur in rip tides when people try to fight the current. Swim at a manageable pace parallel to the shore until you are clear of the current; the waves at either side of the rip tide will take you back to the shore. If you cannot break free of the current, let it take you out beyond the breakers, then swim diagonally toward the shore. Trying to swim against the current will result in exhaustion.

TOURIST OFFICES, TICKETS AND OPENING TIMES

TOURIST OFFICES OVERSEAS

The efficient and nationally important Costa Rican Tourism Institute (Instituto Costarricense de Turismo or ICT) has several offices in the US and Europe. The easiest way of getting in touch; the easiest is by visiting www.visitcostarica.com.

Alternatively you can telephone them on 506 2299 5800, or toll free from the US and Canada on 1-800/343-6332, or you can write to PO Box 777-1000, San José, Costa Rica, Central America. Comprehensive sources of information can be found in libraries and in your national press. The country is a popular destination and articles in the press are fairly common.

OPENING TIMES

Generally, shops are open Monday to Saturday from 8am to 6pm. Closing for lunch from 11.30 to 2 is becoming a thing of the past. Opening hours vary between cities and towns. In popular tourist areas, such as the beaches of Guanacaste and the Pacific coastline, shops tend to have more extended opening hours. During the week, and in particular on the weekends, curio and handicraft stalls line the streets of the more developed beach towns.

The post office in San José is open on Monday to Friday from 8am to 5pm and on Saturday from 7.30am to noon.

The core opening hours for banks are from 9am to 3pm, Monday to Friday. However, some branches are open for longer; occasionally extending to Saturday morning. Service varies wildly; it can be incredibly slow or surprisingly fast. Be prepared to wait.

TICKETS

Theater tickets can be bought in advance from the ticket offices (Mon–Sat 10–1, 2–5). Ticket prices range from as little as US$2 for a minor national performance at the Teatro Melico Salazar to around US$12–US$25 at the Teatro Nacional in San José. High profile international performances can vary in price from US$30–US$70 and usually sell out very quickly, so buy tickets as early as possible.

Other theaters often have workshops, especially for children. There are discounts for students at most performances and it is always worth looking in the press listings for two-for-one specials, often on Wednesday. Check out the listings in *La Nación* and the *Tico Times* for information on forthcoming events. Seasons for the Teatro Nacional, Teatro Melico Salazar and many others start in March.

When it comes to live music, Costa Rican groups generally have a low profile outside the country, except for Editus, which won two Grammy awards in collaboration with Panamanian star Rubén Blades. With the exception of pop groups like the Brillianticos there's only a feeding frenzy for tickets when international bands visit.

Cinema is a popular pastime and prices vary from US$3–US$5, often with cheaper tickets before 4pm. Saturday and Sunday afternoon showings are very popular with families and young couples, especially during the rainy season.

ICT TOURIST OFFICES

	CONTACT	OPEN
Next to Museo de Oro Plaza de la Cultura, San José	506 2222 1090 ext. 277	Mon–Fri 9–1, 2–5
Central Post Office Calle 2, avenidas 1–3, San José	506 2258 8762	Mon–Fri 8–4
Juan Santamaría Airport	506 2443 2883	Mon–Fri 9–5
Peñas Blancas border crossing	506 2679 9025	Mon–Fri 8–8
Paso Canoas	506 2732 2035	Mon–Fri 7am–10pm

NATIONAL HOLIDAYS

January 1	New Year's Day
March 19	Feast of St. Joseph
April 11	Juan Santamaría Day
March/April	Easter
May 1	Labor Day
June	Corpus Christi
June 29	St. Peter and St. Paul
July 25	Guanacaste Day
August 2	Feast of the Virgin of Los Angeles
August 15	Assumption and Mother's Day
September 15	Independence Day
October 12	Columbus Day (and Limón carnival)
November 2	All Soul's Day
December 8	Immaculate Conception
December 24	Christmas Eve
December 25	Christmas Day

COMMUNICATION

MAIL

The Costa Rican postal system *(correos)* is seen as dependably slow and unreliable. Post takes about 10 days to North America, and up to three weeks to Europe. Sea mail, which is generally only used for large packages, can take up to three months. Postal rates are affordable. Packing materials are available at post offices in San José and Limón. Opening hours vary between cities and towns. In San José the post office is open Mon–Fri 7.30–6, Sat 7.30–noon. Courier services are available from San José, see contact details, below.

Mail can be sent to you in Costa Rica via the Lista de Correos of a convenient post office. For San José, the address would be Your Name, Correo de Costa Rica, Lista de Correos, San José, Costa Rica, Central America. There is a nominal charge of US$0.15 for each item.

TIPS

» If sending a package, don't seal the bag before you go to the post office as it needs to be cleared by customs first.

» Parcels often go missing, whether being sent or received, so be wary sending anything of value.

TELEPHONE

Costa Rica has the highest number of land and mobile telephone lines per capita in Central America. Even the smallest towns and villages have at least one phone line, and more lines are being installed. This is all very well if you have your own phone, but the majority of visitors will be subjected to hotel telephones, which can attract a hefty surcharge, or unreliable public telephones. A few public telephones still take cash, and accept small change of 5, 10 and 20 colones (old-style, silver-hued coins). Simply dial the number and feed in the money. Rates are cheap but it's a good idea to have plenty of change handy. To get the international operator or to make collect calls dial 116.

PHONE CARDS

Phone or calling cards are very useful. There are three systems. The most useful is Viajera Internacional 199, which permits international and national and calls from any designated public telephone and is available in values of US$10, US$20 and 3,000 colones. After scratching off the security patch, dial 199 and follow the instructions (available in Spanish or English). It can get tedious tapping in the 20-digit security code: To make a follow-on call hit "#". Colibri 197 is for domestic numbers only. The CHIP cards work from blue public phones and are for both domestic and international calls.

FAX AND CREDIT CARD CALLS

In San José you can send and receive faxes (US$0.30 for up to five pages) and make credit card calls from the RACSA Telecommunications Center office at Avenida 5, Calle 1, tel 506 287 0515. They also have a (pricey) internet service. Many hotels, even at the basic end, have fax machines and may allow you to receive faxes for a charge.

INTERNET

Internet access is widely available in Costa Rica and by far the cheapest and easiest way to stay in touch. There is a plethora of internet cafes in San José, and even the smallest towns have at least one cafe, while offices can also be found in out-of-the-way places. Prices vary.

In San José, you should expect to pay around US$1.50 for broadband connection, but in tourist resorts like Tamarindo and Sámara, you may have to pay as much as US$4 an hour. If you intend to use email to keep in touch, make sure you have web-based email such as Yahoo or Hotmail. Some internet companies provide this service already, so you will not need to set up a new account.

If you need to set up an account, most internet cafe owners will happily help. With Skype Hotmail it is possible to make internet telephone calls to the US, Canada and elsewhere which are charged at the internet connection rate—a fraction of the cost of a traditionally routed call.

INTERNATIONAL DIALING CODES

Australia	00 61
Canada	00 1
Germany	00 49
Italy	00 39
New Zealand	00 64
Spain	00 34
UK	00 44
US	00 1

MAILING RATES

FROM COSTA RICA (IN COLONES)

Region	Postcard	Letter	Package up to 2kg
US or Canada	95	115	3,225
Europe	115	180	5,400
Rest of the world	130	200	6,750

INTERNATIONAL COURIERS

COURIER	CONTACT
DHL	Paseo Colón, calles 30–32, San José Tel 506 2209 6000; www.dhl.com
UPS	Paseo Colón, Calle 40, San José Tel 506 2255 4567; www.ups.com

MEDIA, BOOKS AND MAPS

NEWSPAPERS

Of the six daily national newspapers the most popular and oldest is *La Nación* (www.nacion.co.cr) which toes—or creates—the establishment line. It also has the best arts and listings section. *La República* (www.larepublica.net) is the main competition, heavily slanted toward business. Bringing up the rear is *Al Día*, which tends to have a frivolous approach to events but good sports coverage. *La Prensa Libre* (www.prensalibre.co.cr) is a good evening paper. *Rumbo* is the main weekly news magazine of the three available; the others are *Triunfo* and *Perfil*. *La Gaceta* is the official government paper.

English-language readers are treated to the *The Tico Times* (www.ticotimes.net) with a gentle mix of national and international issues. They also publish the densely informative *Exploring Costa Rica*, which stuffs everything you need to know about Costa Rica into a few hundred pages. *Costa Rica Traveler* is a free bimonthly magazine found in better hotels and restaurants. Free regional magazines in Jacó *(Jacó News)*, Quepos *(Quepolandía)* and Tamarindo *(The Howler)* provide local information. Also look out for the bimonthly *Costa Rica Outdoors*, with good information on outdoor activities or visit www.costaricaoutdoors.com).

TELEVISION

There are 13 local television channels, which carry a mix of imported soaps, sport and news. The main station is Channel 7, which competes with cable and satellite services with channels such as the Discovery Channel.

RADIO

Over 100 radio stations are available on the FM band, a few of which broadcast in English. 107.5 FM provides a heady mix of good driving music, and Radio Dos (Doze) on 99.5 FM plays a similar mix of hits.

Once you've had enough of living in the past, explore different wavelengths with the search button. You'll find jazz on Echo 95.7. Outside the Central Highlands reception is patchy.

BOOKS

Natural history

Les Beletsky, *Costa Rica: The Ecotravellers Wildlife Guide* (2002, Academic Press).
» An overview of the natural wealth of the country, with drawings of wildlife—a good all-in-one choice.

Mario Boza, *Costa Rica National Parks* (1999, Incafo).
» Take the small, handy option, or the glossy coffee table one, both filled with good information and pictures compiled by the founder of the national park system.

Archie Carr, *The Windward Road: Adventures of a Naturalist on Remote Caribbean Shores* (1979).
» A collection of tales about Archie Carr's experiences on the north Caribbean shore and the turtle nesting beaches of Tortuguero.

Mike Pariser, *The Surfer's Guide to Costa Rica* (2005, Surf Press).
» Wave-seekers will want to pack this along for the ride.

Erin Van Rheenen, *Moon Living Abroad in Costa Rica* (2007, Avalon Travel Publishing).
» The best of numerous guides to setting up home in Costa Rica.

Gary Stiles and Alexander Skutch, *A Guide to the Birds of Costa Rica* (1989, Cornell University).
» The best guide to the birdlife of Costa Rica—accept no imitations.

Travel guides

Christopher P. Baker, *Moon Costa Rica* (2009, Avalon Travel Publishing).
» A large and detailed guide to every corner of Costa Rica, with detailed maps to both cities and off-the beaten-path drives.

Lee Eudy, *Chasing Jaguars: The Complete Guide to Costa Rican Whitewater* (2003, Earthbound Sports).
» Comprehensive profiles of 40 of the country's best white-water runs, with maps.

Fiction

Barbara Ras, *Costa Rica: A Traveler's Literary Companion* (1994, Whereabouts Press).
» A much loved collection of 26 stories drawn from across the country.

History

Tjabel Daling, *Costa Rica: A Guide to the People, Politics and Culture* (1998, Latin America Bureau).
» A pocket history and overview of the country, picking up on the main themes that make up modern Costa Rica.

Ivan Molina and Steven Palmer, *The Costa Rica Reader: History, Culture, Politics* (2004, Duke University Press).
» A comprehensive background on what makes Costa Rica tick.

Pauline Palmer, *What Happen: A Folk History of Costa Rica's Talamanca Coast* (1977, Ecodesarollos).
» An account of the hardships of life in Costa Rica's southern Caribbean. ("Happen" is a colloquial Creole idiom.)

MAPS

Several companies provide excellent maps of the country. International Travel Maps, published by ITMB in Canada (www.itmb.com), produce an authoritative 1:500,000 travel map which is widely available in stores throughout the country, and internationally in good book stores.

The Instituto Geográfico, Avenida 20, calles 9–11, at the Ministry of Public Works and Transport (MOPT) in San José, sells good 1:50,000 topographical maps, open Monday to Friday 7–12 and 12.45–3.30, from US$2.

Note that even the best maps should not be completely trusted, especially when you're on backroads in remote regions.

USEFUL WEBSITES

The amount of information about Costa Rica on the internet is positively daunting. Most hotels and organizations can be contacted by email; many have their own website.

GOVERNMENT AND CONSERVATION

www.visitcostarica.com
The official Costa Rican Tourist Board site, as good a place as any to start your surfing.

www.ticotimes.net
The *Tico Times* website, very useful for catching up on the latest information. The weekend section has some restaurant reviews.

www.costarica-embassy.org
The Costa Rican embassy site in Washington, with useful information and links.

http://sanjose.usembassy.gov
The US Embassy site in Costa Rica with travel information, and some interesting background including news items relating to US and Costa Rican interaction.

www.rree.go.cr
The Costa Rican Ministry of Foreign Affairs website, with all the information you could need on visas, embassies and residency.

www.sinac.co.cr
The Sistema Nacional de Areas de Conservacion website.

www.inbio.ac.cr
The INBioparques site, with access to the conservation organization's databases.

GENERAL INFORMATION

www.costarica.com
A generic website covering all aspects of the country, from travel to business. It's well worth visiting this site when planning your trip to the country.

www.infocostarica.com
Another good general site.

www.costaricaoutdoors.com
General information and packed with snippets of background information and stories.

www.centralamerica.com/cr
Another good base to start looking around—proclaims itself as the "Oldest & Largest Costa Rican Tourism Site On The Web."

www.costaricaexpeditions.com
The website of one of Costa Rica's best tour operators, but with up-to-date news and weather and which isn't just trying to get you to spend more money.

www.costaricaexpert.net
An excellent media source with a twice-weekly blog.

www.yellow.com/188.html
Costa Rica's Yellow Pages online.

NATIONAL PARKS

www.cct.or.cr
Information on the Reserva Biológica Bosque Nuboso Monteverde.

www.ots.ac.cr
Parque Nacional Palo Verde, La Selva Biological Station and Las Cruces Biological Station. The national park program is described with in-depth information and blogs.

ACCOMMODATIONS

www.turismo-sostenible.co.cr
The Certificate of Sustainable Tourism website lets you compare hotels that have achieved one of five various levels of sustainability.

www.distinctivehotels.com
The website of Costa Rica's foremost hotel group, representing seven luxury boutique hotels that offer a range of experiences, from relaxing and romantic to adventurous and challenging. The hotels are all environmentally conscious.

SHOPPING

Shopping is rarely the main reason for visiting Costa Rica, but if you're on an organized tour there will always be a souvenir-buying stop and there is certainly no shortage of things to buy. Bargaining is not the rule, but you may find occasional opportunities for negotiation. Ambling around general produce markets provides a kaleidoscopic immersion into Costa Rican life, with souvenirs sold alongside foods.

ARTS AND CRAFTS

It's easy to think Costa Rica's shops are only full of mass-produced items. Look a little closer and you'll see the quirky touch and character of the hand-painted souvenirs.

The main place to buy gifts is Sarchí in the Central Highlands. The town has become the artisan capital of the country, churning out vividly hand-decorated *carretas* (oxcarts). The carts have shrunk to become garden ornaments, drinks cabinets and jewellery boxes. They can be flat-packed and shipped if required, as can the sturdy wood and leather rocking chairs. If you can't get to Sarchí, don't worry. You can buy gifts in most towns: wooden carvings are popular, with decorative and functional pieces including bowls and trays, as well as figures and animals.

Jewelry sees semiprecious jade set in gold and silver, and jade, copper and bronze are used to create pre-Columbian replicas. Indigenous pieces are available in a few places, including the deep red ceramics of the Chorotegas in Guaitíl, the masks and woven goods of the Boruca, or the *jícara* (carved gourds) of the Guaymí and Bribrí in the far south.

Don't buy any archaeological artifacts or items made from endangered species including turtles, animal skins and coral.

MUSIC

Music makes a memorable gift. The Costa Rica Pura Vida collection, sold in market squares and record shops, is a broad-based selection of folk sounds. Less manic on the marimbas is the ambient jazz feel of Editus who, with Panamanian Rubén Blades, won a Grammy for their album *Tiempos*. Also look for Costa Rica's very own boy band—the Brillianticos.

TEXTILES

Textiles provide plenty of options beyond the simple T-shirt, with mats, tablecloths and napkins evoking memories of Costa Rica when you're having a meal back home several months later. Although they're from Panama, vivid *molas* (bright appliqués) are available in parts of the south.

Contemporary, traditional and religious art hangs on the walls of galleries dotted around San José and Escazú. Ceramic creations are no more distinctive than in the bright pieces by Cecilia Figueres.

Hammocks are ubiquitous and come in various styles

PHOTOGRAPHY

Capturing wild animals on camera requires patience, a good SLR camera, a zoom lens and a tripod.

For the amateur, a good quality point-and-shoot camera will capture the moment quickly. Fuji (good for slides) has opened up air-conditioned stores all around the country. Take all the photography supplies you need: Memory cards and batteries may not be easy to find. Film is also difficult to get hold of.

ENTERTAINMENT AND NIGHTLIFE

A vibrant dance and theater scene exists in Costa Rica and you'll find everything from opera and ballet productions at the sublime Teatro Nacional to innovative creations like *The Full Monty*. It is not surprising that the capital city, San José, should have a varied nightlife, but from Guanacaste's surf spots to the chilled-out enclaves of the Caribbean, you can find all sorts of nocturnal fun.

Almost all productions will be in Spanish with the exception of those produced by the Little Theatre Group (tel 506 8355 1623 for details or look in listings). Theaters often have workshops, especially for children. Orchestral works, jazz, concerts and dance are common. Seasons for the Teatro Nacional, Teatro Melico Salazar and others start in March.

Modern cinemas show the latest releases and a couple of art movie theaters reminisce on past glories. Films are in English with Spanish subtitles, which can be useful if you're trying to improve your language skills. Most theaters have comfortable seating and air-conditioning. *Viva* in *La Nación* on Thursday will tell you what is showing. Prices vary from US$3 to US$5, often with cheaper tickets before 4pm. Saturday and Sunday afternoon showings are very popular with families and young couples, especially during the rainy season. Live music is also popular, and a cover charge of around US$4 is typical. Music may be a head-thumping rock act, a Tico Brillcream boy band such as the Brillianticos, or something a little more suave. In some bars the tendency is to just turn up and see what happens. Clubs, too, are busy and cover music from techno and garage to reggae, jazz and salsa. Entrance fees are normally between US$5 and US$15.

There are plenty of simple bars where you can hunker down with a beer and a few *bocas* (snacks), and a plethora of tourist magnets, including the ubiquitous American-style sports bars serving Tex-Mex alcohol-mopping fodder with a wide-screen TV backdrop. With laid-back jazz bars, sizzling Latin salsa clubs, rustic beach shacks and dingy hole-in-the-wall, bar-cafe-*sodas*, all tastes are catered to. In the capital, Joséfinos are generally well dressed and usually look smart when hitting the town. In addition to the myriad bars, the greatest concentration of clubs is in El Pueblo.

Smart jeans will get you in to most clubs, but locals will be dressed to impress. Along the coast, surfer culture prevails and nightlife is generally more laissez-faire, with the friendly social scene pivoting around low-key beach bars.

There are a few gay-friendly dance clubs playing a mix of techno and Latin themes and many gentlemen's clubs in the city. Given the number of casinos around San José it seems that gambling is a national sport. Better odds are available at the smart hotels, although the odds are reported to be lower than in North American casinos: the most popular casinos are at the Hotel Costa Rica Morazán, Hotel Gran Costa Rica, Hotel Tryp Corobiel and the top floor of the Hotel Aurora. Out of town the Best Western Irazú, Radisson Herradura, Melía Cariari and Fiesta, near the airport, have popular casinos.

TICKETS

Theater tickets can be bought in advance from the ticket offices (Mon–Sat 10–1, 2–5). Ticket prices range from as little as US$2 to US$12 to US$25. High-profile international performances can vary in price from US$30 to US$70 and usually sell out very quickly.

RESOURCES

La Nación

On Thursdays, the *Viva* section of the national newspaper *La Nación* has comprehensive listings of nightlife venues, theaters, bars and cinema schedules.

The Tico Times

The weekly English-language newspaper often has reviews and lists of forthcoming events.

SPORTS AND ACTIVITIES

When you're bored with relaxing in a beachside hammock, you can take advantage of the enormous range of activities offered by tour operators in Costa Rica, who make the most of the country's natural diversity. Thrill seekers can go white-water rafting, learn to surf or take mountain bike tours through the jungle, while those with more sedate tastes can try birding, wildlife watching (▷ 16–26) or sunset rides on horseback.

BIRDING

Low key it may be, but sooner or later every visitor to Costa Rica will get involved in, maybe even hooked on, wildlife watching. Birdlife is vibrant for the generalist and hypnotic for the specialist. With more species of birds than the whole of North America or Europe—almost 900 at the last count—Costa Rica is undoubtedly a birder's paradise, and thousands of them visit Costa Rica every year, either on their own or as part of a small birding tour group, to see some of the most magnificent birds in the Neotropics; the resplendent quetzal, three-wattled bellbird, bare-necked umbrella bird, violaceous trogon, scarlet macaw, chestnut-bellied heron, turquoise cotinga, sunbittern and hundreds more species.

Birding is good all year round. Of course, rain forests need rain, but you'll seldom miss a day of birding because of the weather. Most places have the highest rainfall between September and November, while Costa Rica's tourist high season is from December to April. If you've already seen many of the North American migrants, you'll be happy to visit Costa Rica later in the year to see the resident bird species. Birds are often easier to spot during the breeding season. Nesting reaches its peak from April to June according to locality and continues on a diminishing scale until August or September.

If you want to experience the raptor migrations between North and South America, then plan your birding trip during March and April or September and October. La Selva Biological Station and Selva Verde Lodge along the route of the Río Sarapiquí, the Siquirres–Guácimo area along the route of the Reventazón, Pacuare and Parismina rivers and several spots along the southern Caribbean are good places to see migrations.

The resplendent quetzal is considered by many to be the most beautiful bird in the world. While Monteverde is famous for quetzals, you can easily see them less than two hours from San José in the Cerro de la Muerte highlands (guided walks can be arranged at Finca Eddie Serrano Mirador de Quetzales, ▷ 189).

Two of the best-known birding spots are La Selva Biological Station (▷ 114)—which runs birding courses—and the world famous Monteverde Cloud Forest (▷ 117–118).

Once out of the towns and cities of the Central Valley you'll find a tremendous diversity of habitats,

Above *A green-breasted mango hummingbird*

from the lush cloud forests of Monteverde, to the dry deciduous forests of Guanacaste, to the rain forests of the Caribbean lowlands and even the subalpine *páramo* in the Cerro de la Muerte highlands. During recent years many new private reserves with comfortable lodges have opened up throughout the country, some bordering national parks. A typical birding trip might include Villa Lapas (bordering Parque Nacional Carara), Tiskita Lodge in the south Pacific coast (near Punta Banco), Monteverde Cloud Forest, Tortuguero National Park on the Caribbean coast, and a visit to La Selva Biological Station.

When planning a birding trip, contact a specialist. While Costa Rica looks small on a map, it's very mountainous and what seems like a short journey might take several hours to drive. Always allow yourself at least three nights at each place to give you two full days to see the birds. The Birding Club of Costa Rica has monthly outings that you can join with a temporary membership (fee US$10); get details and an up-to-date Costa Rica bird list by emailing costaricabirding@ hotmail.com. More general tours can be arranged through tour operators in San José. From the US you can organize tours with Cheeseman's Ecology Safari Tours, Field Guides or Wings.

Resources

A Guide to the Birds of Costa Rica (by Gary Stiles and Alexander Skutch, published by Cornell University Press). Serious birders will need this bible.

The Birds of Costa Rica: A Field Guide (by Richard Gariguez and Robert Dean, published by Cornell University Press) is another indispensable guide.

La Selva is part of the Organization for Tropical Studies (www.ots.ac.cr).

Birdwatch Costa Rica, Apdo 7911, 1000 San José, Costa Rica, tel 506 2228 4768; www.birdwatchcostarica.com.

Field Guides, 9433 Bee Cave Road, Building 1, Suite 150, Austin, TX 78733, USA, tel 800/728-4953 or 512/263-7295; www.fieldguides.com.

Wings, 1643 N. Alvernon, Suite 105, Tucson, AZ 85712, tel 888/293-6443 or 520/320-9868; www.wingsbirds.com.

Cheeseman's Ecology Safari Tours, 20800 Kittredge Road, Saratoga, CA 95070, tel 800/527-5330 (USA) or 408/741-5330; www.cheesemans.com.

BUNGEE JUMPING

Probably the biggest buzz in Costa Rica, Tropical Bungee will attach you to a big elastic band outside an inflatable raft and let you freefall to the Río Colorado some 80m (262ft) below. Since they started in 1991, Tropical Bungee have had more than 10,000 jumps to their name. They are based on the Pan-American Highway close to Grecia, tel 506 2248 2212; www.bungee.co.cr.

CANOPY TOURS

The rain forest canopy is where most of the wildlife action takes places and there are now a multitude of ways of getting you up there. The calmest is probably exploring on a suspension bridge, strung out along the trees where you are free to walk at leisure, or with a guide, in complete silence if you wish. The main suspension tours are in Santa Elena, close to Puerto Viejo de Sarapiquí, and La Fortuna Rainmaker near to Quepos.

An equally calm way through the canopy is on an aerial tour, using adapted ski lifts. The most well known (and expensive) is on the eastern fringes of Braulio Carrillo National Park, with a similar operation near Jacó.

The best way to get an adrenaline rush is the zipline, which whizzes you down high-tension steel cables strung out between giant forest trees. You won't see much as you fly through the air, but it is good fun and you do get close to the forest canopy. It's a popular option, but be wary, there have been several fatal accidents on ziplines in Costa Rica. If you do not receive sufficient reassurance of the safety of the equipment, don't do the ride. The advent of licensing should ensure that every operator has properly considered safety.

Finally, there is the good old-fashioned option of climbing a tree. Hacienda Barú (▷ 155), let you use tree-climbing grappling and ropes. Prices vary greatly, starting at US$15, rising to around US$75.

Below *Setting off on a Sky Trek Canopy Tour, north of Santa Elena*

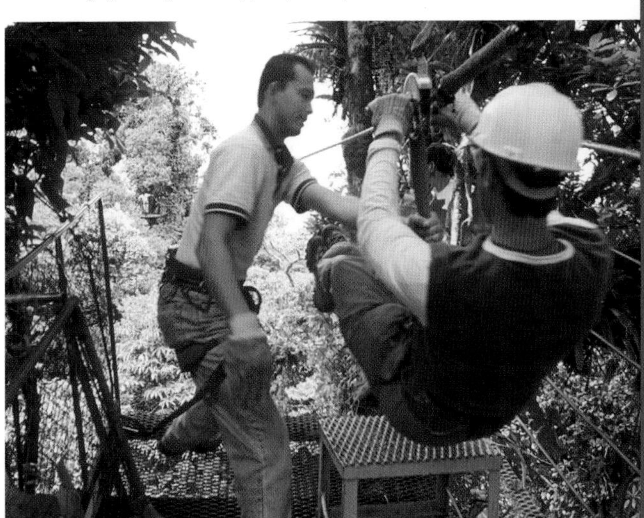

DIVING

Costa Rica suffers on the diving front primarily because of occasional poor visibility in the 9–15m (30–50ft) range in the wet season. Go when there is less rain and you can enjoy the warm waters.

The northern Pacific coast around Playas del Coco is a local diving hotspot with trips out to nearby islands. Farther south, Drake, on the northern coast of the peninsula, is a popular base to visit Isla del Caño where you're almost guaranteed sightings of sharks and rays. On the Caribbean side, the dive action is in the coral waters off the coast of Cahuita National Park and farther south around Gandoca-Manzanillo National Wildlife Refuge. Each region has specialist dive shops that can arrange diving—although it might be a good idea to make advance reservations at Drake if you're planning to visit. The best diving happens far away in the clear waters around the Cocos Islands, 500km (310 miles) southwest of Costa Rica in the Pacific. Undisturbed corals and hammerhead and white-tipped sharks await visitors on the live-aboard dive boats sailing from Puntarenas.

The cost of diving starts at around US$45 for a beach dive on the south Caribbean, rising to around US$90 for a two-tank dive. A PADI Open Water Course out of Playas del Coco is about US$400. Diving trips out to the Cocos Islands on live-aboard boats start at around US$2,495 for an eight-day trip, with five full days' diving and equipment rental.

GOLF

In Costa Rica the Pacific Coast has seen a spate of 18-hole championship links courses come to fruition, including Los Sueños Marriott in the Central Pacific. Farther north, close to Playa Conchal and Papagayo, are the Garra de León and Four Seasons courses, or just south of Tamarindo is Hacienda Pinilla. In the Central Highlands you'll find the opportunity to swing your clubs at the Cariari Country Park outside San José or a short distance west of Santa Ana at the Valle del Sol. Green fees tend to range from US$45 to US$140 at the country clubs, but operators may offer deals.

Above *Hammerhead sharks off the Cocos Isands*

HOT-AIR BALLOONING

Serendipity Adventures, based in Turrialba (▷ 104), has trips over the Central Highlands and the Lake Arenal area.

MOUNTAIN BIKING

As befits the host of the world's toughest mountain bike race (La Ruta de los Conquistadores, ▷ 31), pedal power has made a big impression in parts of Costa Rica, with operators renting bicycles by the hour, the day or the week. You can strike out on your own and just see where your instincts take you, but if you're really into the idea of mountain biking, joining a tour is the best way to get to some of the off-road trails.

Possibilities vary greatly. According to Brenda Kelly at Coast to Coast, Guanacaste is ideal for hugging the coastline, getting fantastic views and a challenging ride. Several two-day trips out of San José give you the chance to get seriously muddy, ending up in places like Manuel Antonio, or mixing the biking with paddling down white water. The ultimate adventure is a coast-to-coast ride that takes 14 days, lots of muscle and determination—there are some serious uphill sections—but it's ultimately rewarded with views from the continental divide and down the Orosí Valley.

Coast-to-Coast Adventures (tel 506 280 8054, www.ctocadventures.com) can provide bespoke bicycling tours, or you can fit in with their busy schedule. They provide all the gear, including bike, water bottle and helmet. Mountain bike rental from a general rental company works out at around US$5 an hour. A four-day trip with Coast-to-Coast is US$940 all inclusive. For serious adventure sports fans, Coast to Coast offers several trips that combine bicycling, hiking and rafting.

RAFTING

Rafting in Costa Rica takes you through some of the most spectacular scenery in the country. One moment you're drifting through valleys that merge the highlights of the Hanging Gardens of Babylon with the Garden of Eden, the next you're being forced head-first through a wall of water. It isn't everyone's idea of fun, but it is certainly exciting.

White-water rafting needs mountains (or at least hills) and water. "Costa Rica has an abundance of water," according to Michael Mayfield and Rafael Gallo in *The Rivers of Costa Rica: A canoeing, kayaking and rafting guide*. It is this surfeit of water that fills the channels of the Reventazón, Pacuare and Sarapiquí rivers on the Caribbean slope, and the General and Corobicí on the Pacific, creating a fantastic array of aquadventure.

White-water rafting in Costa Rica started in the 1980s. From early pioneer days of struggling with equipment to remote put-ins, the popular rivers and routes are now well established, with fairly easy access. Most trips in Costa Rica start from San José and head out to the chosen river. All-inclusive trips remove the need to think about food and refreshment. You will need a change of clothes for the night if you are on a two- or three-day trip, and some dry clothes for the end of the trip.

As with all adventure sports, safety is paramount—fatal accidents have occurred in Costa Rica. Good commercial outfits like Costa Rica Expeditions or Rios Tropicales will assess your experience and suitability before taking your reservation. You receive a complete safety briefing before beginning rafting and if you're not up to standard you will be asked to leave. Likewise, if you are not satisfied with the level of safety, seek reassurance and if still not satisfied, ask to leave.

You don't have to be an adrenaline junky for white-water rafting, or even be incredibly fit. Rafting assesses rivers in terms of difficulty. A simple trip or float down parts of the Corobicí or Sarapiquí is a Class I or II; gentle and relaxing, it's a great way to see wildlife. Class III marks the beginning of white-water rafting, with Classes IV and above requiring previous experience. The most popular Class III and IV rivers are sections of the Pacuare and Reventazón, near Turrialba, the Sarapiquí and General. Class V requires experience and expert knowledge.

You can raft all year, although conditions vary. If you want to go down a particular river it is worth planning in advance with a specialist tour operator. Costs vary considerably depending on the number of days, with a one-day trip starting at around US$75, a couple of days costing US$250 and three days US$300, including all meals and transport to and from San José.

SOCCER

The national sport in Costa Rica is soccer and it's a great experience to join the migrating fans to a Sunday morning match. The quality may not be fantastic, but soccer lovers know that the game is more about loyalty. And in Costa Rica, of that there is no doubt. The 12 teams of the national league play on Sunday mornings, and sometimes on Wednesday, and tickets are rarely sold out. The two dominant sides are Saprissa, who play in Tibas, north of San José, and La Liga in Alajuela. By all accounts the country went mad in 1990 when the national squad qualified for the World Cup, and every time Paulo Wanchope touched the ball for the UK's Manchester City team, Costa Rican newspapers plastered the sports pages with reports.

SPORTFISHING

Fishing just doesn't get any better than you will find in Costa Rica, with tarpon and snook on the Caribbean; marlin, sailfish, dorado, tuna and other species on the Pacific; and trout, rainbow bass *(guapote)*, bobo, machaca and more in lakes and rivers inland. According to Jerry Ruhlow—who has been living, fishing and writing about it in Costa Rica since 1983—it is essential to plan ahead. Peak fishing varies with the time of year, and beach accommodations and the top boats are often hard to find when fishing is at its best, so make reservations in advance. The best seasons in the different parts of Costa Rica vary from year to year, depending on weather, water temperatures and other factors.

On the southernmost Pacific coast, in the Golfito, Puerto Jiménez

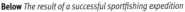

Below *The result of a successful sportfishing expedition*

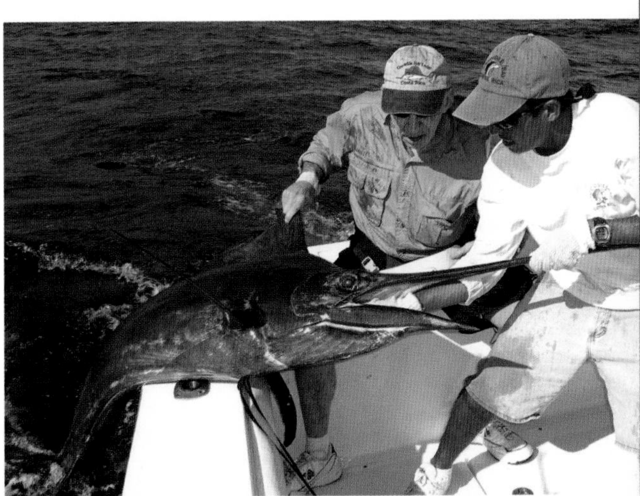

and Drake Bay region, marlin action is best from August to December. There are sailfish year round, but the peak is from late November to March. It may slow from April into June, then pick up again in July. If nonstop action is your preference and you don't have to hang a billfish to be happy, the Golfito region is your best bet. More than 40 International Game Fish Association (IGFA) certified world records have been established here, and the species you can expect to catch at almost any time of year include tuna (sometimes to 180kg/400lb), wahoo, amberjack, jack crevalle, grouper, cubera, barracuda, big roosterfish, corbina and snook.

The next major fishing area, heading north, is Quepos, where December to end of April is the best season for billfish, although some marlin and sailfish are taken year round. Dorado and small tuna are nearly always plentiful, and they often get giant yellowfin tuna too.

Mid-December to April are the best months for boats based in Playa Carrillo and the Sámara region as the main body of fish continue moving north. They often get there earlier and stay longer, depending on water temperature and other factors. Dorado and tuna are also plentiful in these months.

A northerly wind blows from December into May in the northernmost region, but once the calm has returned, the fishing is little short of sensational from late May or June into early September, with marlin peaking in August and September. There are two major tournaments in March and July—a few years ago one of those tournaments posted a record 1,696 billfish in a four-day competition out of Flamingo Marina (currently closed). Charter boats operate out of Tamarindo, Portrero, Ocotal and Playas de Coco. There's always plenty of dorado and tuna in the area, and anglers working the nearby Catalina and Murcielago (Bat) islands also score wahoo, amberjack, cubera and roosters.

On the northern Caribbean coast, tarpon and snook are around most of the year, with slumps from May to mid-July when the rains are at their heaviest. The peak season is from about September through April, although late July during the *veranillo* (little summer), when rains usually stop for two or three weeks, is also excellent most years. Rainbow bass and other freshwater species can be caught here year round in the rivers and lagoons. The most consistent fishing is out of the lodges near the mouth of the Río Colorado, but some are also caught at Tortuguero and Parismina. The northern Caribbean coast does not offer much in the way of sportfishing.

For inland waters, Lake Arenal offers year-round fishing, but the quality will vary depending on wind and water level. It is a beautiful 35km-long (22-mile) lake about three hours' drive from San José. The *Rain Goddess,* a dedicated fishing boat, operates here and offers multiday packages. Rainbow bass is the species most anglers go for. A beautiful fish in shades of pink, green and blue, with a vicious set of teeth, it is found only in Costa Rica and a few inland waters of southern Nicaragua. The IGFA record is 5.7kg (12.5 lb), taken here. Rainbow bass, bobo, machaca, tepemechin and other tropical species are also found in rivers throughout the country, along with rainbow trout in some high mountain rivers.

Caño Negro Lagoon is a huge inland waterway that offers all of the above, plus tarpon and snook. Some waters are seasonal, and regulations often change from year to year, so check in advance.

SURFING

Costa Rica offers the surfer world-class waves in beautiful surroundings, with air and water temperatures averaging in the high 20°sC (82°F). Most breaks work better at the end of the wet season, supposedly when the rivers have had time to form the sand bars properly. The tidal range for the Pacific coast is quite large, being up to 3.5m (12ft), and this can affect the size of the waves. If surfing on the Pacific coast, you'll need a tide chart—freely available in most surf centers or printed in the free regional magazines. On the Caribbean coast the variation is not a problem, with daily fluctuations of around 0.5m (1.5ft).

A four-wheel-drive vehicle is a necessity if traveling along much of the Costa Rican coast as many waves are only accessible along dirt tracks, and these can be inaccessible during the wet season. Check at a local surf shop before leaving. Also, a number of breaks are only accessible by boat. You may need to check how to access these waves before leaving to avoid being disappointed.

One of the resorts most associated with surfing in Costa Rica is Tamarindo. Located 450km (280 miles) northwest of San José, Tamarindo is an excellent place from which to access the quality breaks that lie along the north Pacific coast. The best surfing conditions are from December to June. Tamarindo itself has lots of attractive hotels and three good breaks; El Estero, a long right-hander; Pico Pequeño; and Langosta, a strong point wave. Just north of Tamarindo lies Potrero Grande. Known as Ollie's Point (supposedly after Oliver North who had a secret base nearby), Potrero Grande is a fast right-hander breaking over a reef. A southerly swell can give a wave of up to 2m (7ft). Access is by boat. Playa Grande is the most westerly point of Costa Rica and as a result can get swells from north, south and west.

To the far north is Santa Rosa National Park and Playa Naranjo, home of Peña Bruja, mistakenly translated in the 1980s as "Witches Rock." The name has stuck and the beach provides a high-quality and picturesque beach break. Access is by four-wheel drive (boat during the wet season) and camping is available at the rangers' station.

South from Tamarindo, around the coastline of the Nicoya Peninsula lie Avellanas, Playa Negra, Callejones and Junquillal. Playa Negra is 10 minutes' south of Avellanas and a popular spot. This solid right-hand wave can be busy and dangerously shallow at low tide. Farther south lies Callejones, which can be much less crowded than Playa Negra.

Toward the end of the peninsula and the Cabo Blanco Reserve are a number of beautiful and uncrowded beach breaks, including Nosara, Sámara and Punta Guiones. After this spot, the waves become more of a challenge to get to, with many only accessible by four-wheel drive.

Boca Barranca, just north of Jacó, has a long left-hander that breaks over a sand bottom and into the river mouth. The best time to surf here is early in the morning, and on a good day it can hold up to 3m (10ft).

Playa Escondida lies at the mouth of the Gulf of Nicoya and is accessible only by boat. A number of quality breaks can be found close to Jacó. Roca Loca is five minutes' walk south of Jacó and is accessible only by climbing down the cliffs—but has a good-quality wave that is not for the fainthearted. Ten minutes south of Jacó lies Playa Hermosa, a high-quality break that is the setting for Coast Rica's annual surf championship.

On the journey south toward Quepos is Esterillos, some 40 minutes' drive from Jacó. It is a quiet, uncrowded beach break with entertainment provided by the nearby town. Between Esterillos and Quepos lies the town of Parrita, offering both reef and beach breaks, and Playa El Rey, which is accessed via a palm tree plantation. Just north of Quepos is Boca Damas. Next to the mouth of the Río Damas, this spot can hold a sizeable swell. Quepos itself offers lively nightlife and a beach break with strong lefts.

Farther south again is the town of Dominical. This laid-back surfer's haven offers some of the best beach breaks in Costa Rica. It also has a left and right reef break and the area is often frequented by pods of dolphins.

The south Pacific coastline is dominated by the Osa Peninsula. At the north end close to the mainland is Bahía Drake. Only accessible by boat, Drake is a beautiful spot for surfing. At the southern tip of the peninsula is Matapalo, which can be reached by car from Puerto Jiménez or by boat from Pavones, just across the mouth of the Golfo Dulce. The best waves are a 20-minute walk through jungle teeming with native fauna. The three spots worth checking out in the area are Back Wash; Pan Dulce, a small white sand bay with a hollow right-hander; and powerful Matapalo.

SURFING BEACHES IN COSTA RICA

1 Potrero Grande
2 Playa Naranjo (Roca de la Bruja)
3 Playa Grande
4 Playa Tamarindo
5 Langosta
6 Avellanas
7 Playa Negra
8 Nosara
9 Playa Coyote
10 Malpaís
11 Cabuya
12 Boca Barranca
13 Puerto Caldera
14 Playa Tivives & Valor
15 Playa Escondida
16 Playa Jacó
17 Roca Loca
18 Playa Hermosa
19 Playa Esterillos Oeste
20 Playa Esterillos Este
21 Playa El Rey
22 Boca Damas
23 Quepos
24 Playa Espadilla
25 Playa Dominicav
26 Bahía Drake
27 Matapalo
28 Pavones
29 Punta Burica
30 Manzanillo
31 Puerto Viejo
32 Playa Negra, Cahuita
33 Westfalia
34 Isla Uvita
35 Playa Bonitaa

NI
0 50 km
0 30 miles
Upala
Liberia
Santa Cruz
Nosara
Guácimo
Puntarenas
Heredia
Alajuela
SAN JOSÉ
Puerto Limón
Bribrí
Malpaís
Jacó
Parrita
Quepos
San Isidro de El General
Dominical
Palmar Norte
PA
Golfito

Across the Gulf lies Pavones, the longest ride in Costa Rica. On a large swell the left-hander can give a ride for 800m (0.5 miles) as the different sections connect. Pavones is a five-hour drive from south of Dominical, or a short boat taxi from Golfito, but its quality can lead to a crowded line up.

Toward the border with Panama is Punta Banco, 3km (2 miles) south of Pavones. It's a good place to go if the waves at Pavones are too crowded. Punta Burica is the last beach on the Costa Rican Pacific coast before Panama, which shares this headland with Costa Rica. This beach is only accessible by boat.

Storms in the Caribbean Sea produce swells which break on the coral reefs close to Costa Rica's coast. The best waves are found from November to March. The coastline is shorter than the Pacific coast, with most of the breaks to the south of Limón. The three quality breaks in Limón are Playa Bonita, breaking over a coral reef which can be a challenging drop; Portete, which is a hollow right-hander breaking over coral; and Isla Uvita, only accessible by a dawn boat out of Limón, with a wave that breaks in three sections over a shallow coral reef. On a good day this can produce a wave of up to 3m (10ft).

South from Limón toward the Panamanian border lies Cahuita, a beautiful National Park with great beaches and waves. Farther south still is Puerto Viejo. Known as "Salsa Brava," Puerto Viejo has an extremely powerful wave breaking over coral—you may need to pack a spare board for this one. Ten minutes farther down the coast is the fun beach break of Playa Cocles, which can have strong currents, and Manzanillo, which has uncrowded waves.

If your appetite has been whetted, you can rent boards and arrange tuition at most major surf spots, such as Dominical (▷ 155).

TREKKING AND HIKING

Short treks ranging from 20 minutes to multiday trips can be found throughout the country, but with so many competing activities, hiking and trekking often take a bit of a back seat. As well as short guided walks lasting a few hours, there are some very good hiking opportunities: just examine a topographical map.

The most popular hike has to be up Cerro Chirripó, the country's highest peak at 3,820m (12,533ft). The shortest route is a steady trudge up and down, but there are many variations on that theme that add to the two- or three-day hike. Second on the list is hiking through the tropical wet forest of Corcovado National Park on the Osa Peninsula: hot, sweaty, hard work, but very rewarding.

Less common walks head from the cloud forests of Monteverde down the Caribbean slope to Arenal, and farther north trails lead through the national parks of Rincón de la Vieja and Tenorio.

The ultimate trek is to cross the continental divide following ancient indigenous trails from Puerto Viejo de Talamanca west to the Pacific. Several tough days, carrying all your own gear, through an altitude gain of over 3,000m (9800ft)—scenic, arduous and, hopefully, satisfying.

WINDSURFING

Westerly trade winds blow across the north between December and April. The air picks up speed as it channels through the corridor where Lake Arenal is situated. The most reliable winds in the northern hemisphere provide the western end of the lake and Bahía Salinas on the Pacific to the north with world-class windsurfing destinations.

Beginner courses are provided by a couple of lodges in the area, with boards, wetsuits and even money-back guarantees. For the experts, if you fancy a change you can try out the latest watersport developments, including kite-surfing.

Below *Cameras at the ready near the San Pedrillo River in Corcovado National Park*

FOR CHILDREN

For both tots and teens, Costa Rica teems with life, bombarding the senses on all sides with shades of green and cacophonous noise.

In general, organized activities are not as necessary as in other Latin American countries.

In San José, theaters, including the Eugene O'Neil Cultural Center, organize special workshops for children, and the Teatro Melico Salazar often has performances which may be suitable for them. Children will generally pay reduced rates for tickets.

Along the coast, especially in family-friendly resorts like Tamarindo, children are welcomed in restaurants and travel with kids can often bring you into closer contact with local families and usually presents no problems—in fact the path is often smoother for family groups.

Shopping for arts and crafts can also be an enjoyable pastime for children, with places like Sarchí providing plenty of objects to stir a child's curiosity, and cafes for respite.

A lot of time can be spent waiting for buses, so remember to pack toys. Also, take children's reading material with you as it is difficult, and expensive, to buy.

In San José, the Children's Museum and Parque de Diversiones amusement park will keep kids entertained.

FESTIVALS AND EVENTS

Public holidays are normally a cause for celebration and Costa Rica is no different. Large festivals tend to go big on processions, costumes and marching bands, but find a small town and you'll find bull-friendly bull fighting (where the lucky beast leaves the ring exhausted but alive), horse-racing, and a chance to rub shoulders with the townsfolk at any minor gathering.

The main holiday periods of the year are Christmas, New Year and Easter, when much of San José decamps to the beaches. Reserve in advance.

On national holidays, banks, government offices and stores close down.

National holidays are listed here; regional and local festivals are listed in the relevant chapters.

CALENDAR

1 January New Year's Day.

March (second Sunday) National Oxcart Day, with music and vibrant processions in Escazú.

March–April Maundy Thursday and Good Friday, Easter Week.

11 April Juan Santamaría Day, celebrating the victorious Battle of Rivas against William Walker in 1856.

1 May Labor Day, which heralds the President's State of the Nation address, cricket matches and a day off.

25 July Annexation of Guanacaste, celebrating Guanacaste's decision to stay with Costa Rica rather than join Nicaragua in 1824.

2 August Virgin Mary, Queen of Angels, Patron of Costa Rica, celebrated with pilgrimages to Cartago's Basilica.

15 August Day of the Virgin marks Mary's Assumption to Heaven and also Mother's Day in Costa Rica.

15 September Independence Day, with parades and marching bands through the streets of San José.

12 October Spanish discovery of the New World celebrated with particular energy in Limón and the Caribbean.

2 November All Soul's Day or the Day of the Dead, showing respect to those who have died.

25 December Christmas celebrations build before and continue in the week after, particularly in San José, but also on a smaller scale throughout much of the country.

31 December, 1 and 2 January *La Danza de los Diabolitos* is a lively festival with traditional masks, costumes, music and country dancing in the Indian village of Boruca.

Tour operators in San José offer trips throughout the country, ranging in length from half a day to all-inclusive packages for up to a week or longer. It is possible to do most of the activities independently by public transportation or using a rented vehicle, but rarely within the same time frames. The disadvantage is having to adhere to a structured itinerary.

Companies listed here organize tours and create custom tours.

COSTA RICA EXPEDITIONS
www.costaricaexpeditions.com
Costa Rica's first travel company offers upscale wildlife adventures and owns Tortuga Lodge on the Caribbean coast, Corcovado Lodge Tent Camp on the Osa Peninsula and Monteverde Lodge near Santa Elena. Options include rafting.
Avenida 3, Calle Central–2 506 2257 0766 Daily 5.30am–9pm

COSTA RICA TEMPTATIONS
www.crtinfo.com
This reputable tour operator offers tours and a reservation service.
Apdo 1199–1200 San José 506 2508 5000

EXPEDICIONES TROPICALES
www.expedicionestropicales.com
Range of one- and two-day tours. One of their most popular tours is The Best of Costa Rica.
Avenidas 11–13, Calle 3, San José 506 2257 4171 Daily 6am–10pm

HORIZONTES
www.horizontes.com
Good tour operator offering services from car rentals to trips focusing on natural history, birding, culture, photography and adventure.
Avenidas 1–3, Calle 28 506 2222 2022 Mon–Fri 8–5.30, Sat 9–12

SWISS TRAVEL SERVICE
www.swisstravelcr.com
These outlets will arrange almost anything. Their Birdwatcher's Paradise day-trip is popular.
Branches in all major hotels 506 2282 4898

TAM TRAVEL
www.tamtravel.com
Local tours such as the Poás Volcano Tour, combined with a visit to the Doka Coffee Estate.
Branch in Daniel Oduber International Airport, Liberia 506 2527 9700

SPECIAL INTERESTS

AGUAS BRAVAS
www.aguas-bravas.co.cr
Specializes in white-water rafting. Other activities include horseback riding and mountain biking.
506 2292 2072

ARMO TOURS
www.armotours.com
Highly recommended for national tours; German, French, English and Italian spoken.
Avenida 6, Calle 9, San José 506 2257 0202

AVENTURAS NATURALES
www.adventurecostarica.com
This respected tour operator specializes in white-water rafting. For rafters with an interest in natural history, this is the best company.
Avenida Central, calles 33–35, San José 506 2225 3939

CALYPSO TOURS
www.calypsocruises.com
Calypso are the originators of the Isla Tortuga Cruise.
Avenida 7, Calle 36, San José 506 2256 2727 Day-trips from US$109

CENTRAL AMERICAN TOURS
www.catours.net
Will help with full trip planning service and day tours.Specializes in tours of Guanacaste.
Pavas 506 2257 3529

COOPRENA TOURS
www.turismoruralcr.com
The reservations arm of a network of community-owned lodges.
Apdo 6939-1000, San José 506 2290 8646

COSTA RICA OUTDOORS
www.costaricaoutdoors.com
Specialists in outdoor activities, notably fishing.
Apdo 5094, San José 1000 506 2231 0306

COSTA RICA SUN TOURS
www.crsuntours.com
Departures on many usual tours.
Apdo 1195–1250, Escazú 506 2296 7757

ECOLE TRAVEL
www.ecoletravel.com
Tours and tailor-made excursions.
Avenida Central, calles 5–7, San José 506 2253 8884

GREEN TROPICAL TOURS
www.greentropical.com
Specializing in tailor-made itineraries.
Calle El Rodeo, Apdo 675-2200, Coronado 506 2229 4192

ORIGINAL CANOPY TOUR
www.canopytour.com
Installations at Monteverde, Mahogany Park by Orotina and Drake Bay.
Avenida 9, Calle 3a, San José 506 2291 4465 From US$45 per person

RÍOS TROPICALES
www.riostropicales.com
Specialists in white-water rafting and sea kayaking.
Calle 38, between avenidas 3 and 5, San José 506 2233 6455

EATING

Thanks to the influx of nationalities from around the world, dining in Costa Rica is a form of culinary globe-trotting. With such a variety of cuisines, especially in larger towns, you can try national delights one day, and familiar dishes from around the world the next. Tastes vary in Costa Rica from the spicy cuisine of the Caribbean to plainer dishes in the highlands. One thing is certain: you won't taste better coffee anywhere.

RESTAURANTS

Restaurants in Costa Rica meet the needs of locals and visitors. Local restaurants tend to do most of their business at lunchtime when *comida típica* (typical food) is served at a cost of a few dollars: a salad starter, rice and beans served with chicken or beef for the main course, and a filling dessert, such as *tres leches,* a light sponge cake drenched in condensed milk.

More trendy restaurants improve the level of service, setting, food and, naturally, the price. You'll find almost anything your palate desires in San José and in the more popular locations around the country, including French, Italian, Asian, Pacific fusion and superb locally caught seafood.

In less tourist-oriented places, you will find regional dishes and more limited menus.

At food stands, called *sodas*, in markets, basic, but very often tasty, food is available.

REGIONAL DISHES

Many people return from Costa Rica enthusing about *gallo pinto*, the ubiquitous staple dish of rice and beans. However, each region yields a variety of gastronomic treats. In the Central Highlands for example, blackberries and strawberries flourish and in the *sabanero* heartland of Guanacaste, *tamales*—corn maize-based pasties mixed with chicken, meat or vegetables—fuel the rural worker and visitor alike.

The oceans teem with marlin, dorado, yellowfin tuna, snapper and wahoo. Along the Caribbean coast you'll find spicy chicken and desserts prepared in coconut milk.

To start the day, rice and beans come with eggs, sour cream and tortillas, and tropical fruits to try include *pejibaye*, a palm fruit with a soft spiky exterior.

Cajetas is a sweet spread, which is added to everything from slabs of bread to tortillas.

LOCAL DRINKS

Costa Ricans don't indulge heavily in drinking. On Friday and Saturday nights the streets are not filled with people moving from one bar to another—but the bars are lively. Once you've tapped into the local happening bar, beer is the drink of choice, with Imperial and Pilsen being the most popular lagers and Bavaria a darker malty option. Fruit juices, either straight or with water, are also popular, as are *refrescos* (soft drinks) by day.

The spirit of choice is *ron*—the Spanish for rum. Other spirits and good quality wines find their way to the tables of bars and restaurants as the price rises.

The sugar-cane-based, falling-over juice found in dive-bars is *guaro*, guaranteed to provide a night you won't forget, even if it is only for the headache the following day.

Cafe Rica is a coffee-based liquor, true to the country's coffee-producing origins.

MENU READER

Although you're not going to rhapsodize about the country's traditional cuisine in a postcard home, local food can be very tasty. The best dishes are often the simplest, with fresh fish and fruit being Costa Rican cuisine's greatest strengths. The national diet is based on combinations of rice, beans and meat or fish. This menu reader describes some of the local dishes and foods that you will find in restaurants. Menus in tourist areas will usually have a description of the dishes in English alongside the Spanish name.

MEAT DISHES

Arroz con pollo rice with chicken
Carne/bistek meat/steak
Casados standard national lunchtime dish of rice and beans with meat, chicken or fish and a bit of salad
Cerdo pork
Chicharrón deep-fried pork skin cooked until crispy
Cordero lamb
Empanadas deep-fried tortilla stuffed with meat or chicken
Pato duck
Pavo turkey
Perdiz partridge
Pollo chicken
Ternera veal

FISH AND SEAFOOD

Those who go out on a game-fishing trip will often bring back some of the catch, such as tuna or swordfish, to be cooked for the evening meal.
Atún tuna
Camarón prawn
Ceviche raw fish marinated in lemon and coriander
Corvina sea bass
Langosta lobster
Mariscos seafood
Pescado fish
Pez espada swordfish
Pulpo octopus

SIDE DISHES

Arroz rice
Bocas small dishes for nibbling, which may be meat, chicken or fish in various forms
Gallo pinto rice and black beans, which in the Caribbean has the distinctly pleasurable addition of coconut milk
Patacones mashed plantain deep fried and normally served with beans
Plátano plantains, or savory banana, often fried
Tamales a cornstarch/corn flour-based pasty mixed with chicken, meat or vegetables served in a plantain leaf
Tortillas cornflour pancake

DESSERTS

Cajeta de leche thick, fudge-like milk pudding
Cajetas a delightful, tooth-achingly sweet spread
Dulce de leche baked sweet milk
Helados ice cream
Miel de abeja glorious Costa Rican honey
Tres leches sponge cake soaked in sweet milk

FRUIT

In addition to the usual tropical fruits—in particular several different types of mango—Costa Rica supplies some unusual ones you may not have met before.
Aguacate avocado
Cas bitter tasting straight from the fruit, but when mixed with honey or sugar it makes a great *refresco* (soft drink)
Fresa strawberry
Limón lemon
Manzana apple
Naranja orange
Pejibaye almost unique to Costa Rica, it's a popular fruit from a palm tree with a soft spiky outside. Sold by the bag-load along the roadside, some people love it, for others it's more effort than it's worth
Platano banana
Tamarindo a date-like fruit that is refreshing to the core when pulped and mixed with ice-cold water
Uva grape

VEGETABLES

Ajo garlic
Judías beans
Patata potato
Pimientos red/green peppers

DRINKS

Agua water
Cafe coffee
Cerveza beer
Leche milk
Vino wine

Above *Try some of the local dishes while you are in Costa Rica*

From sumptuous hotels to basic cabins, accommodation options cover all styles and budgets. It is hardly surprising that in Costa Rica the variety and diversity is spectacular. Eccentric and purist designs perched on hillsides providing respite for mind and body; quiet hotels tucked away in secluded private reserves; beachfront properties amid nonstop action; and glorious romantic hideaways—the choice is yours.

HOTELS

The high season runs from December to April, with the two weeks around Christmas and the New Year constituting an extra-high high season. Easter week (*Semana Santa* or Holy Week) is a major holiday period and everything at the beach fills up fast; if you're planning a trip at this time, make reservations early. Outside of these months it is the green season, when discounts are common and can be up to 50 percent. They vary greatly according to location, and some places prefer to close for the low season.

The good hotels fill up in the high season (and some in the green season as well) and reservations are advisable. Mid- and upper-range hotels may require a deposit. Lower budget hotels will also accept reservations, and while you may not be able to secure the room, do what you can to check the reservation is being taken seriously. Hotels in almost every price range (except the lowest) offer confirmed reservations via websites and email in addition to telephone. If you plan to arrive late in the evening, let the hotel know.

Service levels vary considerably in Costa Rican hotels; price can be a good indicator of standards.

A few chains have several hotels in the country: Best Western has hotels in many tourist areas, and the Barcelo group has half a dozen all-inclusive resorts open and more pending. Marriot and Melia are two other chains with properties throughout the country. Several hotels have grouped together into marketing consortia. One of particular note is the Small Distinctive Hotels of Costa Rica (tel 506 2258 0150, www.distinctivehotels.com), with eight hotels, including gorgeous Florablanca in Santa Teresa (▷ 171) and the charming Grano de Oro (▷ 81) in San José, that are small, individual and provide excellent service.

COSTS

Hotels are subject to a 16 percent tax (13.39 sales and 3 percent room tax). Many hotels don't include this tax in the quoted price; check whether it is included in the price you are given. Tax is included in the prices in this guide, unless stated otherwise. Some mid-range hotels and above allow children under 12 to stay in their parents' room for free or at a lower rate. Ask when making reservations. Many hotels charge an additional 5 to 15 percent for using a credit card.

BED-AND-BREAKFAST

Bed-and-breakfast has made relatively little impact in Costa Rica. Those you may find tend to operate in the mid- to high price range.

YOUTH HOSTELS AND SURF CAMPS

Hostelling International, the international arm of the Youth Hostel Association, represents four hostels in Costa Rica. Visit www.hihostels.com for details. You'll have to be a member of the YHA to take advantage of the low prices. There are many additional hostels unaffiliated with YHA, and surfers' hostels and camps have blossomed at beach resorts.

HOME STAYS

Cooprena (www.turismoruralcr.com), a national ecotourism cooperative, organizes courses and represents lodges in rural communities.

NATURE LODGES

Nature lodges have become hugely successful in recent years. Often located in remote areas in or close to national parks and reserves, they may take time and effort to reach: a multiday stay is preferable. Many offer outdoor activities.

Above *Veranda of the Bijagua Heliconia, Parque Nacional Volcán Tenorio*

WORDS AND PHRASES

A little Spanish will make a difference to your visit. Once you have learned a few basic rules, it's an easy language to speak: It is phonetic and, unlike English, particular combinations of letters are always pronounced the same way. When a word ends in a vowel, an n or an s, the stress is usually on the penultimate syllable; otherwise, its on the last syllable. If a word has an accent, this is where the stress falls.

a	as in	pat
e	as in	set
i	as **e** in	be
o	as in	hot
u	as in	flute
ai, ay	as **i** in	side
au	as **ou** in	out
ei, ey	as **ey** in	they
oi, oy	as **oy** in	boy

Consonants as in English except:
c before **i** and **e** as **th**, *although some pronounce it as* **s**
ch as **ch** in church
d at the end of a word becomes **th**
g before **i** or **e** becomes **ch** as in loch
h is silent
j as **ch** in loch
ll as **lli** in million
ñ as **ny** in canyon
qu is hard like a k
r usually rolled
v is a **b**
z is a **th**, *but sometimes pronounced as s*

MAP PHRASES
Ranger Station
Estacíon Guardabosque
Park Entrance
Parque Entrada
National Park
Parque Nacional
Protected Area
Zona Protectora
Wildlife Reserve
Refugio de Vida Silvestre
Biological Reserve
Reserva Biológica
Cloud Forest
Bosque Nuboso
Hot Springs
Fuente Caliente

CONVERSATION
What is the time?
¿Qué hora es?
I don't speak Spanish
No hablo español
Do you speak English?
¿Habla inglés?
I don't understand
No entiendo
Please repeat that
Por favor repita eso
Please speak more slowly
Por favor hable más despacio
What does this mean?
¿Qué significa esto?
Can you write that for me?
¿Me lo puede escribir?
My name is...
Me llamo...
What's your name?
¿Como se llama?
Hello, pleased to meet you
Hola, encantado(a)
I'm from...
Soy de...
Good morning/afternoon
Buenos días/buenas tardes
Good evening/night
Buenas noches
Goodbye
Adiós
This is my wife/husband/son/daughter/friend
Esta es mi mujer/marido/hijo/hija/amigo
See you later
Hasta luego
That's all right
Está bien
I don't know
No lo sé
You're welcome
De nada
How are you?
¿Cómo está?

USEFUL WORDS
yes .... sí
no .... no
please .... por favor
thank you .... gracias
there .... allí
where .... dónde
here .... aquí
when .... cuándo
who .... quién
how .... cómo
why .... por qué
free .... gratis
I'm sorry .... Lo siento
excuse me .... perdone
large .... grande
small .... pequeño
good .... bueno
bad .... malo

TIMES/DAYS/MONTHS/HOLIDAYS
morning
la mañana
afternoon
la tarde
evening
la tarde/noche
day
el día
night
la noche
today
hoy
yesterday
ayer
tomorrow
mañana
now
ahora
later
más tarde
spring
primavera
summer
verano
autumn
otoño
winter
invierno
Monday
lunes
Tuesday
martes

Wednesday
miércoles
Thursday
jueves
Friday
viernes
Saturday
sábado
Sunday
domingo
month
el mes
year
el año
January
enero
February
febrero
March
marzo
April
abril
May
mayo
June
junio
July
julio
August
agosto
September
septiembre
October
octubre
November
noviembre
December
diciembre
Easter
Pascua
Christmas
Navidad
New Year
El Año Nuevo
All Saints' Day
Todos los Santos
vacation (holiday)
las vacaciones
pilgrimage
una romería

MONEY

Is there a bank/bureau de change nearby?
Hay un banco/una oficina de cambio cerca?
Can I cash this here?
¿Puedo cobrar esto aquí?
I'd like to change dollars/sterling into colones
Quisiera cambiar dólares libras para colonnes
Can I use my credit card to withdraw cash?
¿Puedo usar la tarjeta de crédito para sacar dinero?
What is the exchange rate?
¿Cómo está el cambio?

GETTING AROUND

Where is the information desk?
¿Dónde está el mostrador de información?
Where is the timetable?
¿Dónde está el horario?
Does this train/bus go to...?
¿Va este tren/autobús a...?
Does this train/bus stop at...?
¿Para este tren/autobús en...?
Do I have to get off here?
¿Me tengo que bajar aquí?
Do you have a subway/bus map?
¿Tiene un mapa del metro/de los autobuses?
Can I have a single/return ticket to...
¿Me da un boleto sencillo/de ida y vuelta para...?
Can I have a standard/first-class ticket to...
¿Quisiera un boleto de segunda/primera clase para...?
I'd like to rent a car
Quiero alquilar un coche
Where are we?
¿Dónde estamos?
I'm lost
Estoy perdido
Is this the way to...?
¿Es esto el camino para ir a...?
I am in a hurry
Tengo prisa
Where can I find a taxi?
¿Dónde puedo encontrar un taxi?
Please take me to...
Me lleva a..., por favor
Please slow down
Vaya más despacio por favor
Can you turn on the meter
Podría poner el metro
How much is the journey?
¿Cuánto cuesta el viaje?

POST AND TELEPHONES

Where is the nearest post office?
¿Dónde está la oficina de correos más cercana?
What is the postage to...
¿Cuánto vale mandarlo a...?
I'd like to send this by air mail
Quiero mandar esto por correo aéreo
Hello, this is...
Bueno, habla...?
I'd like to speak to...
Podría hablar con...
Who is speaking?
¿Con quién hablo?
What is the number for...
¿Cuál es el número de...?
Please put me through to...
Comuníqueme con..., por favor
Where can I buy a phone card?
¿Dónde puedo comprar una tarjeta de teléfono?
Extension..., please
La extensión..., por favor

SHOPPING

Could you help me please?
¿Me podría atender por favor?
How much is this?
¿Cuánto vale esto?
I'm looking for...
Estoy buscando...
When does the shop open/close?
¿A qué hora abre/cierra la tienda?
I'm just looking
Sólo estoy viendo
Do you have anything less expensive/smaller/larger
¿Tiene algo más barato/pequeño/grande?
Do you have this in...?
¿Tienen esto en...?
This is the right size
Esta talla está bien
I'll take this
Me llevo esto
Do you have a bag for this?
¿Tiene una bolsa para esto?
Can you gift wrap this?
¿Me lo envuelve para regalo?
Do you accept credit cards?
¿Aceptan tarjetas de crédito?
I'd like...grams
Me pone...gramos, por favor
I'd like a kilo of...
Me da un kilo de...

I'd like...slices of that
Me pone ... pedazos de eso
This isn't what I want
Esto no es lo que quiero
Can I help myself?
¿Puedo servirme?
bakery
la panadería
bookshop
la librería
pharmacy
la farmacia
supermarket
el supermercado
market
el mercado
sale
las rebajas

NUMBERS

1 ... uno
2 ... dos
3 ... tres
4 ... cuatro
5 ... cinco
6 ... seis
7 ... siete
8 ... ocho
9 ... nueve
10 ... diez
11 ... once
12 ... doce
13 ... trece
14 ... catorce
15 ... quince
16 ... dieciséis
17 ... diecisiete
18 ... dieciocho
19 ... diecinueve
20 ... veinte
21 ... veintiuno
30 ... treinta
40 ... cuarenta
50 ... cincuenta
60 ... sesenta
70 ... setente
80 ... ochenta
90 ... noventa
100 ... cien
1,000 ... mil

HOTELS

Do you have a room?
¿Tiene una habitación?
I have a reservation for...nights
Tengo una reservación para... noches
How much per night?
¿Cuánto es por noche?
Double room
Habitación doble con cama de matrimonio
Single room
Habitación sencilla
Twin room
Habitación doble con dos camas
With bath/shower
Con baño/ducha
Swimming pool
La alberca
Air conditioning
Aire acondicionado
Non smoking
Se prohibe fumar
Is breakfast included?
¿Está el desayuno incluido?
When is breakfast served?
¿A qué hora se sirve el desayuno?
May I see the room?
¿Puedo ver la habitación?
Is there an elevator?
¿Hay elevador?
I'll take this room
Me quedo con la esta habitación
The room is dirty
La habitación está sucia
The room is too hot/cold
Hace demasiado calor/frío en la habitación
Can I pay my bill?
La cuenta por favor
Could you order a taxi for me?
¿Me pide un taxi por favor?

RESTAURANTS

See also the menu reader on page 240.
I'd like to reserve a table for .... people at...
Quisiera reservar una mesa para ... personas para las...
A table for ..., please
Una mesa para ..., por favor
We have/haven't booked
Tenemos una/no tenemos reservación
What time does the restaurant open?
¿A qué hora se abre el restaurante?
We'd like to wait for a table
Queremos esperar a que haya una mesa
Could we sit here?
¿Nos podemos sentar aquí?
Is this table free?
¿Queda libre esta mesa?
Are there tables outside?
¿Hay mesas afuera?
Is there a car park?
¿Hay aparcamiento?
Where are the lavatories?
¿Dónde están los baños?
Can I have an ashtray?
¿Me da un cenicero?
I prefer non-smoking
Prefiero no fumadores
Could you warm this up for me?
¿Me podria calentar esto?
Could we see the menu/wine list?
¿Podemos ver la carta/carta de vinos?
We would like something to drink
Quisiéramos algo a beber
What do you recommend?
¿Qué nos recomienda?
Can you recommend a local wine?
¿Puede usted recomendar un vino de la región?
Is there a dish of the day?
¿Hay un plato del día?
I am a vegetarian
Soy vegetariano
I am diabetic
Soy diabético(a)
I can't eat wheat/sugar/salt/pork/beef/dairy/nuts
No puedo tomar trigo/azúcar/sal/cerdo/carne (de res)/productos lácteos/nueces
Could I have a bottle of still/sparkling water?
¿Me podría traer una botella de agua mineral sin/con gas?
Could we have some more bread?
¿Nos podría traer más pan?
Could we have salt and pepper?
¿Nos podría traer sal y pimienta?
How much is this dish?
¿Cuánto es este plato?
This is not what I ordered
Esto no es lo que había pedido
I ordered...
Habia pedido...
I'd like...
Quisiera...
May I change my order
¿Puedo cambiar la orden?
I'd prefer a salad
Prefiero una ensalada
How is it cooked?
¿Cómo está hecho?

Is it very spicy?
¿Esta muy picante?
The food is cold
La comida está fría
... is too rare/overcooked
... está demasiado crudo/demasiado hecho
We would like a coffee
Quisieramos tomar cafe
May I have the bill, please?
¿Me trae la cuenta, por favor?
Is service included?
¿Está incluido el servicio?
What is this charge?
¿Qué es esta cantidad?
The bill is not right
La cuenta no está bien
We didn't have this
No tomamos esto
Do you accept this credit card (travelers' checks)?
¿Acepta usted esta tarjeta de crédito (cheques de viajero)?
I'd like to speak to the manager
Quisiera hablar con el jefe
The food was excellent
La comida fue excelente
We enjoyed it, thank you
Nos ha gustado, muchas gracias
breakfast
el desayuno
lunch
la comida
dinner
la cena
starters
los antojitos/botanas
main course
el plato principal
dessert
el postre
bread
el pan
sugar
el azúcar
wine list
la carta de vinos
knife/fork/spoon
el cuchillo/el tenedor/ la cuchara
waiter/waitress
El mesero/la mesara

TOURIST INFORMATION

Where is the tourist information office?
¿Dónde está la oficina de turismo?
Do you have a city map?
¿Tiene un mapa de la ciudad?
Can you give me some information about...?
¿Me podría dar información sobre...?
What sights/hotels/restaurants can you recommend?
¿Qué lugares de interés/hoteles/restaurantes nos recomienda?
Can you point them out on the map?
¿Me los podría señalar en el mapa?
What time does it open/close?
¿A qué hora se abre/cierra?
Are there guided tours?
¿Hay visitas con guía?
Is there an English-speaking guide?
¿Hay algún guía que hable inglés?
Can we make reservations here?
¿Podemos hacer las reservaciones aquí?
What is the admission price?
¿Cuánto es la entrada?
Is photography allowed?
¿Se permite tomar fotos?
Is there a discount for senior citizens/students?
¿Hay descuento para los mayores/los estudiantes?
Do you have a brochure in English?
¿Tiene un folleto en inglés?
What time does the show start?
¿A qué hora empieza la función?
How much is a ticket?
¿Cuánto vale una entrada?

IN THE TOWN

church .... la iglesia
castle .... el castillo
museum .... el museo
park .... el parque
cathedral .... la catedral
bridge .... el puente
gallery .... la galería de arte
river .... el río
no entry .... prohibido el paso
entrance .... entrada
exit .... salida
lavatories .... los baños
men/women .... caballeros/señoras
open .... abierto
closed .... cerrado

ILLNESS AND EMERGENCIES

I don't feel well
No me siento bien
Could you call a doctor?
¿Podría llamar a un médico?
I feel nauseous
Tengo ganas de vomitar
I have a headache
Tengo dolor de cabeza
I am allergic to...
Soy alérgico a...
I am on medication
Estoy tomando medicamentos
I am diabetic
Soy diabético(a)
I have asthma
Soy asmático
hospital
el hospital
How long will I have to stay in bed/hospital?
¿Cuánto tiempo tendré que quedarme en la cama/ el hospital?
How many tablets a day should I take?
¿Cuántas pastillas debéna de tomar diario?
Can I have a painkiller?
¿Me da un analgésico?
I need to see a doctor/dentist
Necesito ver un médico/dentista
I have bad toothache
Tengo un dolor de muelas horrible
Help!
Socorro
Stop thief!
Al ladrón
Call the fire brigade/police/ambulance
Llame a los bomberos/la policía/una ambulancia
I have lost my passport/wallet/purse/handbag
He perdido me pasaporte/la cartera/el monedero/la bolsa
Is there a lost property office?
¿Hay una oficina de objetos perdidos?
I have had an accident
Tuve un accidente
I have been robbed
Me han robado
Where is the police station?
¿Dónde está la comisaría?

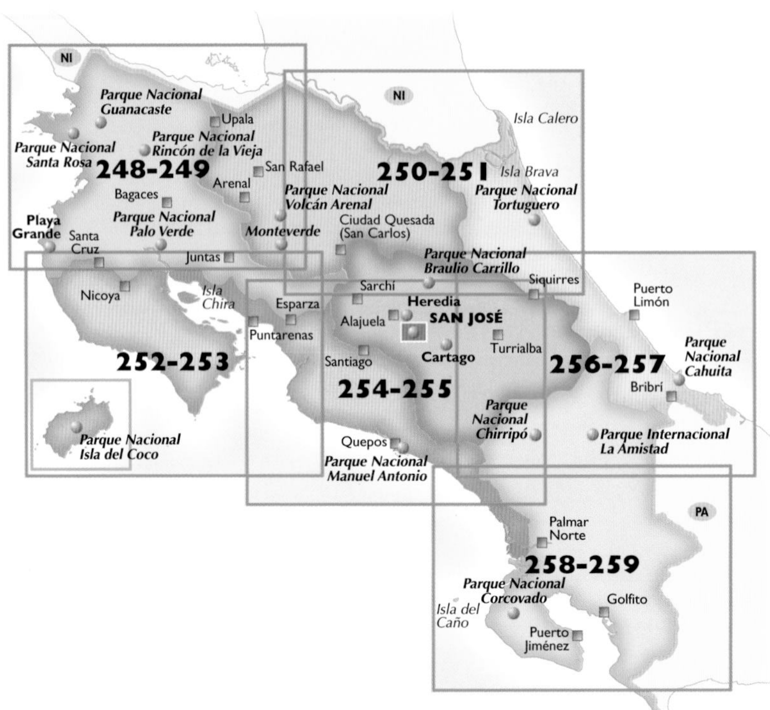

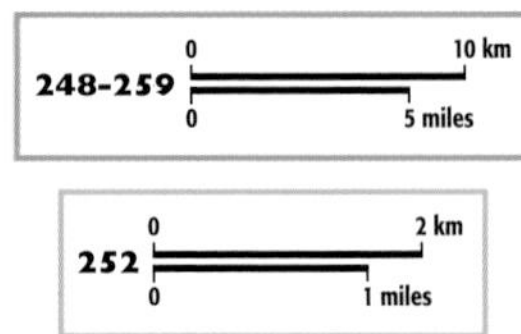

	Motorway		Featured place of interest
	Interamericana / Pan-American Highway		City / Town
	National road		Built-up area
	Regional road		National park
	Main road		Indian reserve
	Local Road		Airport
	Untarred road	621	Height in metres
	Railway		Port / Ferry route
	International boundary		Border crossing
	Administrative region boundary		Viewpoint

MAPS

Map references for the sights refer to the atlas pages within this section or to the the individual town plans within the chapters. For example, Parque Nacional Manuel Antonio has the reference ✚ 255 J8, indicating the page on which the national park is found (255) and the grid square in which it sits (J8).

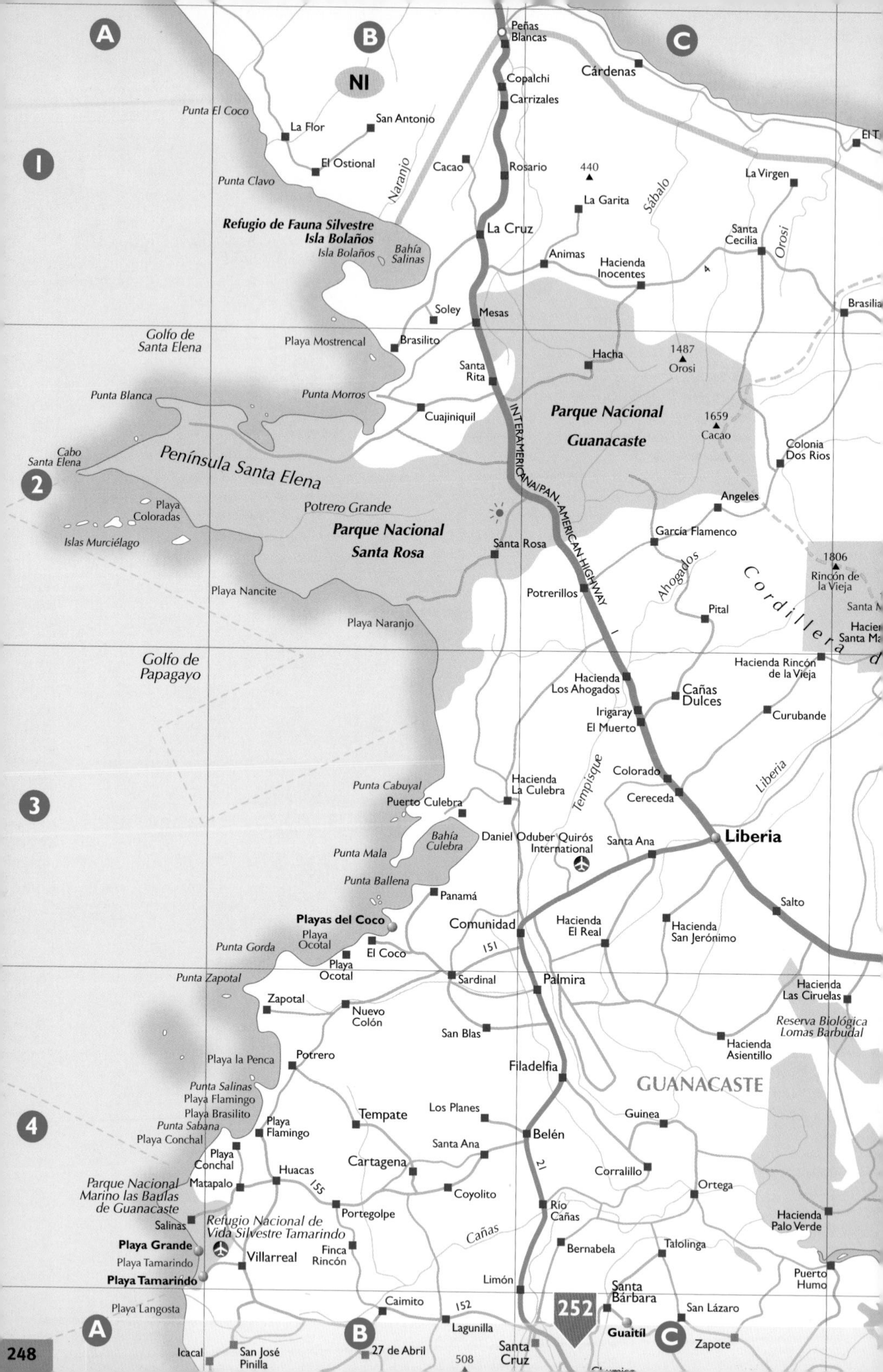
A
B
C
1
2
3
4
NI
Peñas Blancas
Copalchi
Carrizales
Cárdenas
Punta El Coco
La Flor
San Antonio
El Ostional
Naranjo
Cacao
Rosario
440
La Garita
Sábalo
La Virgen
Punta Clavo
Refugio de Fauna Silvestre Isla Bolaños
Isla Bolaños
Bahía Salinas
La Cruz
Animas
Hacienda Inocentes
Santa Cecilia
Orosi
Soley
Mesas
Brasilia
Golfo de Santa Elena
Playa Mostrencal
Brasilito
Hacha
1487
Orosi
Santa Rita
Punta Blanca
Punta Morros
Cuajiniquil
Parque Nacional Guanacaste
1659
Cacao
Cabo Santa Elena
Península Santa Elena
INTERAMERICANA/PAN-AMERICAN HIGHWAY
Colonia Dos Rios
Playa Coloradas
Potrero Grande
Angeles
Islas Murciélago
Parque Nacional Santa Rosa
Santa Rosa
García Flamenco
1806
Rincón de la Vieja
Ahogados
Cordillera
Playa Nancite
Potrerillos
Pital
Playa Naranjo
Golfo de Papagayo
Hacienda Rincón de la Vieja
Hacienda Los Ahogados
Cañas Dulces
Irigaray
El Muerto
Curubande
Tempisque
Colorado
Liberia
Punta Cabuyal
Hacienda La Culebra
Cereceda
Puerto Culebra
Bahía Culebra
Daniel Oduber Quirós International
Santa Ana
Liberia
Punta Mala
Punta Ballena
Panamá
Salto
Playas del Coco
Playa Ocotal
Comunidad
Hacienda El Real
Hacienda San Jerónimo
Punta Gorda
El Coco
151
Playa Ocotal
Punta Zapotal
Sardinal
Palmira
Hacienda Las Ciruelas
Zapotal
Nuevo Colón
Reserva Biológica Lomas Barbudal
San Blas
Hacienda Asientillo
Playa la Penca
Potrero
Filadelfia
GUANACASTE
Punta Salinas
Playa Flamingo
Playa Brasilito
Punta Sabana
Playa Conchal
Playa Flamingo
Tempate
Los Planes
Guinea
Belén
Santa Ana
Cartagena
Playa Conchal
Huacas
Corralillo
21
Parque Nacional Marino las Baulas de Guanacaste
Matapalo
155
Coyolito
Ortega
Salinas
Refugio Nacional de Vida Silvestre Tamarindo
Portegolpe
Río Cañas
Hacienda Palo Verde
Cañas
Playa Grande
Bernabela
Talolinga
Playa Tamarindo
Villarreal
Finca Rincón
Playa Tamarindo
Puerto Humo
Limón
Santa Bárbara
Playa Langosta
Caimito
152
252
San Lázaro
Lagunilla
Guaitíl
Icacal
San José Pinilla
27 de Abril
508
Santa Cruz
Zapote

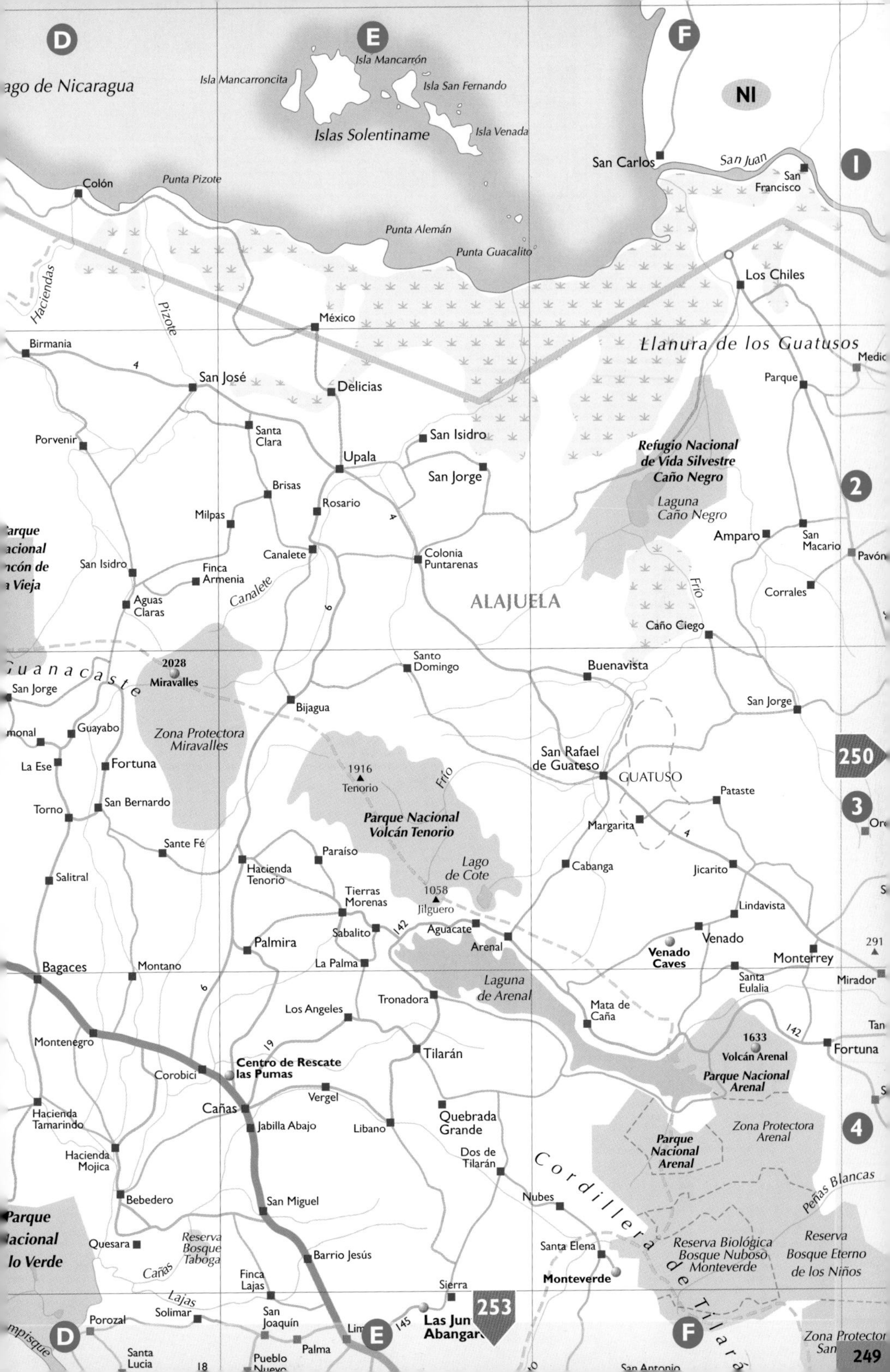
Lago de Nicaragua
Isla Mancarroncita
Isla Mancarrón
Isla San Fernando
Islas Solentiname
Isla Venada
San Carlos
San Juan
San Francisco
NI
Colón
Punta Pizote
Punta Alemán
Punta Guacalito
Los Chiles
Haciendas
Pizote
México
Llanura de los Guatusos
Birmania
San José
Delicias
Parque
Porvenir
Santa Clara
San Isidro
Upala
San Jorge
Refugio Nacional de Vida Silvestre Caño Negro
Laguna Caño Negro
Brisas
Rosario
Milpas
Parque Nacional Rincón de la Vieja
San Isidro
Canalete
Finca Armenia
Colonia Puntarenas
Amparo
San Macario
Pavón
Aguas Claras
Canalete
ALAJUELA
Frío
Corrales
Caño Ciego
Guanacaste
2028 Miravalles
Santo Domingo
Buenavista
San Jorge
Bijagua
San Jorge
Guayabo
Zona Protectora Miravalles
La Ese
Fortuna
1916 Tenorio
Frío
San Rafael de Guateso
GUATUSO
Pataste
Torno
San Bernardo
Parque Nacional Volcán Tenorio
Margarita
Sante Fé
Paraíso
Hacienda Tenorio
Lago de Cote
Cabanga
Jicarito
Salitral
Tierras Morenas
1058 Jilguero
Lindavista
Sabalito
Aguacate
Arenal
Venado Caves
Venado
Monterrey
291
Palmira
Bagaces
Montano
La Palma
Laguna de Arenal
Santa Eulalia
Mirador
Tronadora
Mata de Caña
Los Angeles
Montenegro
1633 Volcán Arenal
Fortuna
Tilarán
Centro de Rescate las Pumas
Parque Nacional Arenal
Corobici
Vergel
Cañas
Quebrada Grande
Hacienda Tamarindo
Jabilla Abajo
Libano
Zona Protectora Arenal
Hacienda Mojica
Dos de Tilarán
Parque Nacional Arenal
Cordillera de Tilarán
Peñas Blancas
Bebedero
San Miguel
Nubes
Parque Nacional Palo Verde
Quesara
Reserva Bosque Taboga
Santa Elena
Reserva Biológica Bosque Nuboso Monteverde
Reserva Bosque Eterno de los Niños
Cañas
Barrio Jesús
Monteverde
Finca Lajas
Lajas
Sierra
Solimar
San Joaquín
Las Juntas de Abangares
Porozal
Palma
Zona Protectora
Santa Lucia
Pueblo Nuevo
San Antonio
Tempisque
4
6
19
142
145
18
D
E
F
I
2
3
4

250
253

San
cisco
G
H
J
I
Sábalo
Santa Cruz
Sábalo
hiles
Guatusos
Medio Queso
que
Coquital
Pocosol
NI
Pocosol
Guaria
Llano Verde
Crucitas
2
Cristo Rey
San
Macario
Pavón
Concho
Chamorro
Infernito
rrales
35
Pocosol
Carmen
Boca San
Carlos
Ceiba
Llanura de San Carlos
ge
Paraíso
Patastillo
249
San Joaquin
Betania
Acapulco
Plomo
Boca
Tapada
Tambor
San Carlos
Laurel
Galán
3
Orquidea
Toro
San Marcos
Boca Sahíno
Las
Medias
Santa Rosa
Santa Delia
San Andrés
Amigos
Sahíno
Pangola
Buenos
Aires
Chaparrón
Terrón
Colorado
291
Chambacú
Ahogadas
Santa
Teresa
onterrey
Pitahaya
Mirador
Boca
Arenal
San Rafael
Bellavista
Veracruz
Altamira
Muelle
Tanque
Pinar
Sardinal
Puerto Vie
de Sarapiq
142
Bijagual
Muelle
Fortuna
Toro
Chilamate
Angeles
Pital
4
Varablanca
Bajos de
Chilamate
Zona Protectora
La Selva
San Francisco
Josefina
Vega
Estación
Biológica
La Selva
Palmera
Platanar
Tabla
Santa
Rita
4
Corte
La Virgen
Chiles
Jabillos
4
Peñas Blancas
Santa
Clara
Aguas
Zarcas
Centro
Neotrópico
Sarapiquís
San Isidro
Florencia
Venecia
Río
Cuarto
La Tigra
San Ramón
Reserva
Bosque Eterno
de los Niños
Ciudad Quesada
(San Carlos)
San Miguel
Rara A
Sucre
Cordiller
Parque Nacional
Juan Castro Blanco
Reserva Bosque
Cordillera
Volcánica
San Lorenzo
Buena
Vista
Cariblanco
Zona Protectora
San Ramón
Cinchona
Zapote
Laguna
Bajos del Toro
Parque Nacional
Volcan Poás
La Paz Waterfall
Gardens
2150
Cacho Negro
5
2704
Poás
Zarcero
Zona
Protectora
Chayote
Parque Naciona
Zapotal
Finca Paz
Alto
Villegas
Poasito
120
Vara Blanca
Braulio Carrillo
254
cional
vestre
Reserva Bosque
Grecia
2906
Barva
15
Fraijanes
Piedades Sur
Volio
9
Sacramento

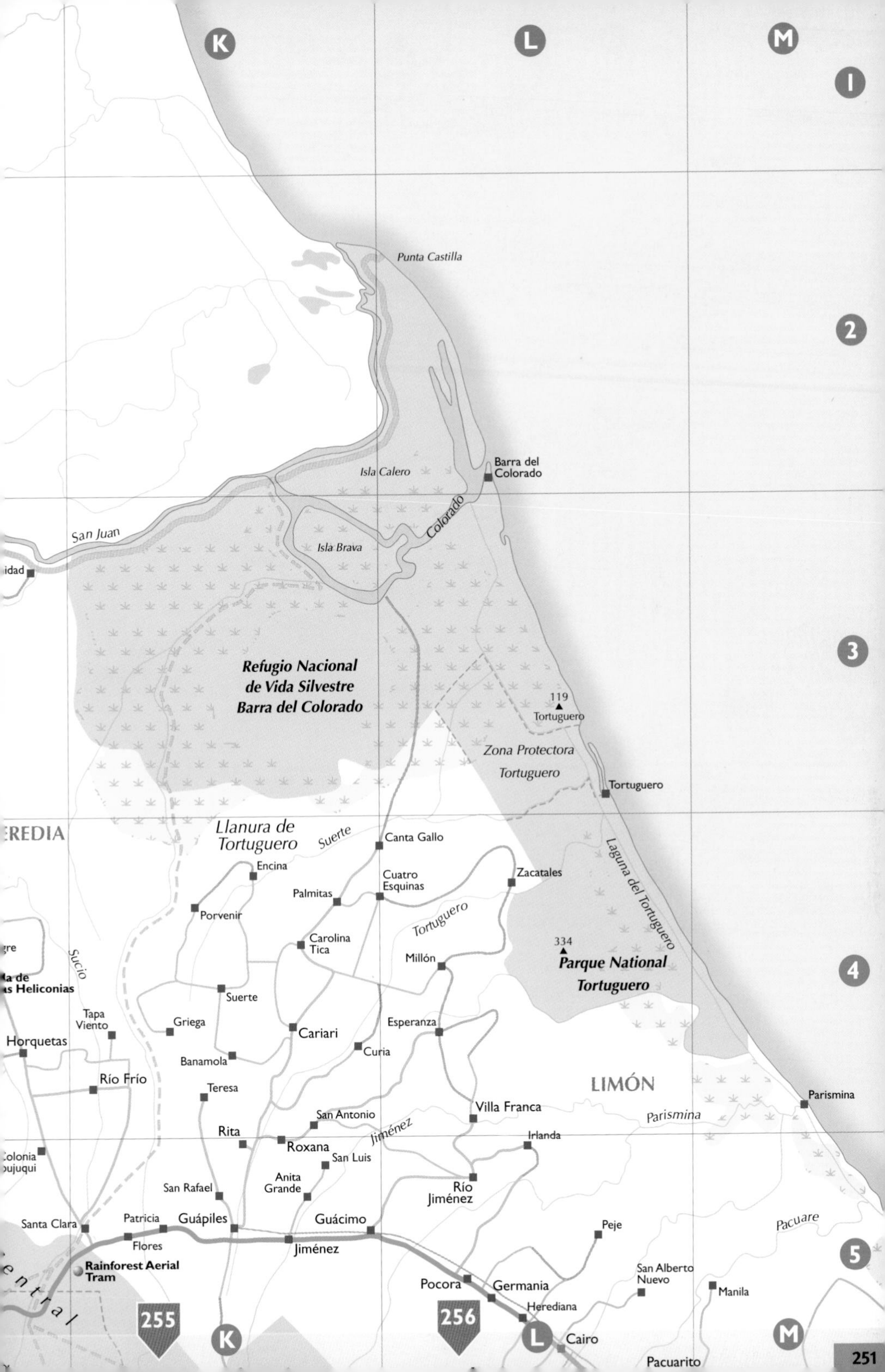
K
L
M
1
2
3
4
5
Punta Castilla
Isla Calero
Barra del Colorado
Colorado
San Juan
Isla Brava
Refugio Nacional de Vida Silvestre Barra del Colorado
119
Tortuguero
Zona Protectora Tortuguero
Tortuguero
Llanura de Tortuguero
Suerte
Canta Gallo
Encina
Cuatro Esquinas
Palmitas
Zacatales
Porvenir
Tortuguero
Laguna del Tortuguero
Carolina Tica
Millón
334
Parque National Tortuguero
Sucio
Suerte
Tapa Viento
Griega
Esperanza
Horquetas
Cariari
Banamola
Curia
Río Frío
LIMÓN
Teresa
Villa Franca
San Antonio
Parismina
Parismina
Rita
Roxana
Jiménez
Irlanda
San Luis
Anita Grande
San Rafael
Río Jiménez
Santa Clara
Patricia
Guápiles
Guácimo
Peje
Pacuare
Flores
Jiménez
Rainforest Aerial Tram
San Alberto Nuevo
Pocora
Germania
Manila
Herediana
255
256
Cairo
Pacuarito

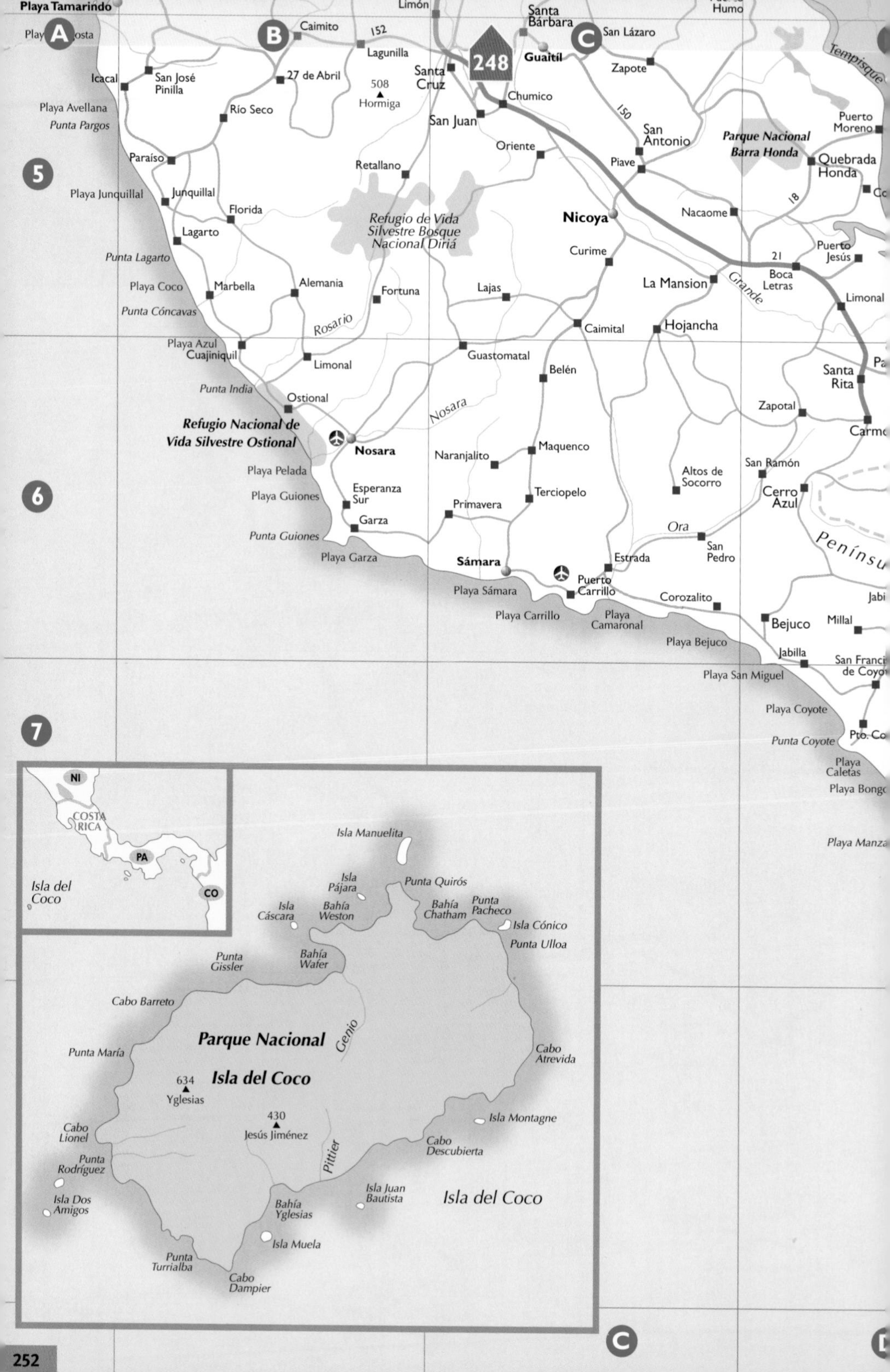

Playa Tamarindo
Limón
Santa Bárbara
Humo
A
B
C
Caimito
152
San Lázaro
Lagunilla
248
Guaitil
Tempisque
Icacal
San José Pinilla
27 de Abril
Santa Cruz
Zapote
508
Hormiga
Chumico
Playa Avellana
Punta Pargos
Río Seco
San Juan
150
Puerto Moreno
San Antonio
Parque Nacional Barra Honda
Oriente
5
Paraíso
Retallano
Piave
Quebrada Honda
Playa Junquillal
Junquillal
18
Florida
Nicoya
Nacaome
Refugio de Vida Silvestre Bosque Nacional Diriá
Lagarto
Punta Lagarto
Curime
Puerto Jesús
21
Alemania
Boca Letras
Playa Coco
Marbella
La Mansion
Grande
Fortuna
Lajas
Limonal
Punta Cóncavas
Rosario
Caimital
Hojancha
Playa Azul
Cuajiniquil
Limonal
Guastomatal
Santa Rita
Belén
Punta India
Ostional
Zapotal
Nosara
Refugio Nacional de Vida Silvestre Ostional
Nosara
Maquenco
Naranjalito
Playa Pelada
San Ramón
Altos de Socorro
6
Esperanza Sur
Terciopelo
Cerro Azul
Playa Guiones
Primavera
Garza
Ora
Punta Guiones
San Pedro
Playa Garza
Estrada
Sámara
Puerto Carrillo
Playa Sámara
Corozalito
Playa Carrillo
Playa Camaronal
Bejuco
Millal
Playa Bejuco
Jabilla
Playa San Miguel
Playa Coyote
7
Punta Coyote
Playa Caletas
NI
COSTA RICA
PA
Isla del Coco
CO
Isla Manuelita
Isla Pájara
Punta Quirós
Isla Cáscara
Bahía Weston
Bahía Chatham
Punta Pacheco
Isla Cónico
Punta Ulloa
Punta Gissler
Bahía Wafer
Cabo Barreto
Parque Nacional
Isla del Coco
Genio
Punta María
Cabo Atrevida
634
Yglesias
430
Jesús Jiménez
Isla Montagne
Cabo Lionel
Cabo Descubierta
Pittier
Punta Rodríguez
Isla Juan Bautista
Isla del Coco
Isla Dos Amigos
Bahía Yglesias
Isla Muela
Punta Turrialba
Cabo Dampier
C

Finca Lajas
Sierra
Monteverde
de los Niños
Lajas
Solimar
San Joaquín
Limonal
145
Las Junt
Abanga
249
E
F
G
Lorenzo
Palma
Santa Lucia
18
Pueblo Nuevo
Huacas
Zona Protectora San Ramón
San Antonio
Lagarto
Pozo Azul
Guacimal
San Buenaventura
Colorado
Aranjuez
Tortugal
Yomale
Zapotal
Finca Paz
5
Coyolito
Refugio Nacional de Vida Silvestre Peñas Blancas
Coyolar
Manzanillo
Cabuyal
Peñas Blancas
Piedades Sur
Playa Camerita
Pajaros
San Gerardo
Miramar
Salvador
Isla Chira
Morales
247
Rancho Grande
Barbudal
144
San Isidro
Cerrillo
Reserva Biológica Isla Pájaros
San Agustín
Ciruelas
Barranca
Golfo de Nicoya
Chomes
San Jerónimo
INTERAMERICANA/ PAN-AMERICAN HIGHWAY
Isla Bejuco
Pitahaya
Barranca
Macacona
Corazal
Isla Venado
Isla Caballo
Esparza
San Rafael
161
Puntarenas
17
Chacarita
San Juan Grande
131
San Mateo
Canjel
Playa Doña Ana
Jesús María
Jicaral
Lepanto
Playa Naranjo
Caldera
6
Cuajiniquil
Isla San Lucas
Reserva Biológica Isla Guayabo
Puerto Caldera
Montaña Grande
Zona Protectora Tivives
Ceiba
Esperanza
Gigante
27
Coyolar
Corralillo
Quebrada Bonita
San Jerónimo
Nicoya
Río Grande
Isla Cedros
Tárcoles
755
Guadalupe
254
Río Seco
Reserva Biológica Islas Negritos
Paquera
Guaria
Curú
Refugio Nacional de Vida Silvestre Curú
Río Frío
PUNTARENAS
Playa Tárcoles
Parque Nacional Carara
Isla Tortuga
Pachanga
Tárcoles
Pochote
Quebrada Ganado
Playa Pochote
Santa Fé
Tambor
Bahía Ballena
Tacotales
Playa Tambor
7
Cóbano
34
Playa Cocalito
Santiago
Playa Cocal
Herradura
Montezuma
Punta Leona
Playa Montezuma
Playa Herradura
Playa Teresa
Jacó
Malpaís
Playa de Jacó
Cabuya
Reserva Natural Absoluta Cabo Blanco
Pochotal
Quebrada Amarilla
Playa Balsitas
Playa Hermosa
Cabo Blanco
Esterillo Oeste
Isla Cabo Blanco
8
E
F

F
G
H
5
6
7
8
9
Zapotal
Finca Paz
Alto Villegas
Protectora Chayote
Poasito
Reserva Bosque Grecia
Coyolar
Cabuyal
Refugio Nacional de Vida Silvestre Peñas Blancas
Peñas Blancas
250
Piedades Sur
Volio
San Juan
Miramar
Salvador
San Ramón
Naranjo
Sarchí
Rancho Grande
Barbudal
144
San Isidro
Cerrillo
Grecia
San Pedro de Poás
Puente de Piedra
Ciruelas
Palmares
Barranca
Constancia
San Jerónimo
Zona Protectora Río Grande
Tacares
INTERAMERICANA/ PAN-AMERICAN HIGHWAY
1
Cambronero
Santiago
135
Alajuela
Zoo Ave
Pitahaya
Macacona
Berlin
Alto López
Barranca
Esparza
Mercedes
17
Chacarita
San Rafael
Cuajiniquil
Atenas
La Garita
San Juan Grande
131
Concepción
La Guácima
Playa Doña Ana
Jesús María
San Mateo
3
Zona Protectora Cerro Atenas
Turrúcares
Caldera
Hacienda Vieja
Balsa
Vueltas
Mastate
Puerto Caldera
San Pablo de Turrubares
Piedras Negras
Colón
Santa Ana
Zona Protectora Tivives
Ceiba
Orotina
Zona Protectora El Rodeo
27
Coyolar
Corralillo
Grifo Alto
137
Desamparaditos
San Jerónimo
Guayabo
Zona Protectora Cerros de Escazú
San Juan de Mata
San Luis
Barbacoas
Tárcoles
San Antonio
Tabarcia
253
Zona Protectora Cerros de Turrubares
Mercedes Sur
Santiago
Reserva Biológica Islas Negritos
Palmichal
Floralia
1756
Turrubares
Jilgueral
Candelarita
Playa Tárcoles
Parque Nacional Carara
Carara
Candelaria
Tárcoles
Túfares
Teruel
Sabanillas
Quebrada Ganado
Tulín
Zona Protectora La Cangreja
Delicias
Concepción
34
San Gabriel
239
ZAPATON
Caspirola
Herradura
Punta Leona
Gloria
San Vicente
Playa Herradura
San Isidro
Gamalotillo
Jacó
Mesas
Playa de Jacó
Fila Surubres
Pochotal
Finca Rancho Nuevo
Porvenir
Quebrada Amarilla
Playa Hermosa
Finca La Palma
Esterillos Oeste
Esterillos Este
239
Playa Esterillos Oeste
Playa Esterillos Este
Julieta
Parrita
Damas
Playa Palma
Rios
Punta Quepos

Braulio Carrillo
J
2906
Barva
251
K
L
Herediana
Cairo
5
Siquirres
Sacramento
San Valentín
Florida
Alegría
Lomas
Moravia
Reventazón
San José de
la Montaña
Reserva Bosque Central
Cordillera Volcánica
32
10
Barva
Alto Palma
3328
Turrialba
Bonilla
Arriba
Café
Britt
San Isidro
San Rafael
SAN JOSÉ
Parque Nacional
Volcán Irazú
3432
Irazú
Santo
Domingo
INBio
San Isidro
Lajas
Peralta
Santa
Cruz
SAN
JOSÉ
Guadalupe
Monumento
Nacional
Guayabo
San Pedro
Llano
Grande
Tierra
Blanca
Santa Rosa
6
Curridabat
Tres Ríos
Pacayas
Turrialba
Pavones
Alajuelita
Desamparados
Cipreses
Juan Viñas
Eslabón
Cabeza
de Buey
Zona Protectora
Carpintera
Cervantes
Cartago
San Rafael
La Suiza
Aserrí
Tobosi
Tejar
Tucurrique
Atirro
Tuis
Paraíso
Cachí
Tarbaca
San Isidro
Jardín
Botánico
Lankester
Ujarrás
1865
Pejibaye
Corralillo
2
San Gabriel
Orosi
Zona Protectora
Cuenca del Río Tuis
Zona Protectora
Río Navarro y
Río Sombrero
Tapantí
Monterrey
San Cristóbal
Norte
202
San Andrés
Santa
Cruz
Empalme
CARTAGO
Jardín
Parque Nacional
Tapantí-Macizo de la Muerte
San Pablo de
León Cortés
Cañon
7
Reserva Bosque
Río Macho
Santa
María
Tres de Junio
San Marcos
12
256
Copey
San Carlos
San Lorenzo
3156
Vueltas
Guaria
3491
Villa Mills
La Muerte
San Gerardo
de Dota
Siberia
Cordille
Reserva Bosque
Los Santos
3333
Urán
Piedra
Naranjo
Río Blanco
Cerritos
Esquipulas
Savegre
División
3820
Chirripó
Santo
Tomás
Santa
Eduviges
Herradura
Zona
Protectora
Cerro Nara
Londres
San Gerardo
de Rivas
8
Santo
Domingo
La Ese
Chimirol
Parque Nacional
Chirripó
22
Finca Bartolo
División
Savegre
Abajo
3295
Amí
Viento
Fresco
San Rafael
Norte
Rivas
Parque Nacional
Manuel Antonio
Pastora
Santa Rosa
SAN JOSÉ
Savegre
San Isidro de
El General
Chiles
Santa Elena
Cedral
Esperanza
22
Playa Savegre
22
Matapalo
Guabo
Palmares
Santa María
Playa Matapalo
Platanillo
Tinamaste
Cajón
Hatillo
Barú
Platanillo
Angostura
Hacienda
Barú
Juntas
San Pedro
Playa Barú
Cordoncillo
Dominical
San Luis
9
Cacao
258
1223
Uvita
Cambutal
244
Mesas
San
Rafael
Santa Ana
China
Kicha
J
K
L
Playa Hermosa
Pejibaye

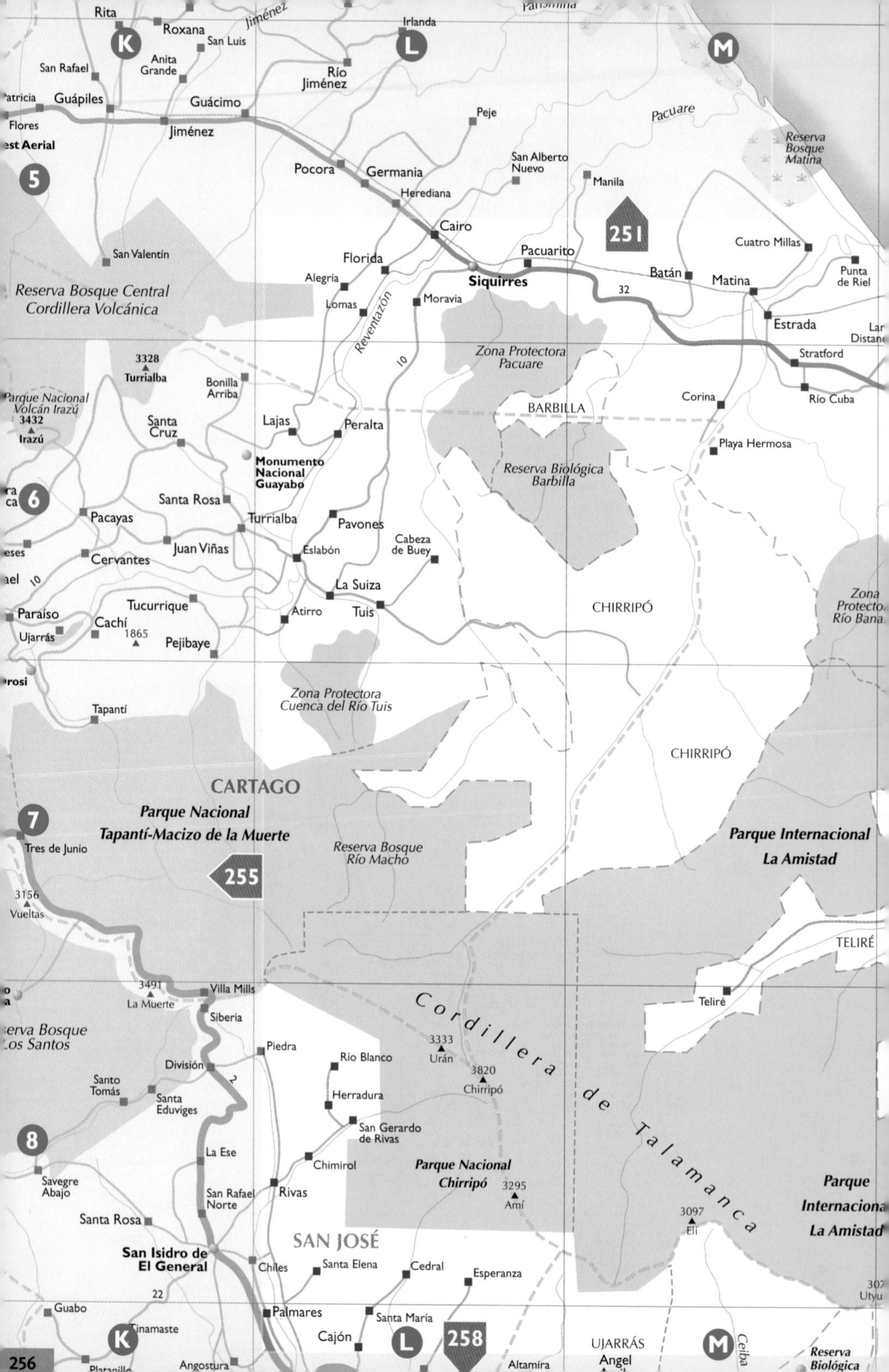
Rita
Roxana
San Luis
Jiménez
Irlanda
K
L
M
San Rafael
Anita Grande
Río Jiménez
Guápiles
Flores
Guácimo
Jiménez
Peje
Pacuare
Reserva Bosque Matina
5
Pocora
Germania
San Alberto Nuevo
Manila
Herediana
251
Cairo
San Valentín
Florida
Pacuarito
Cuatro Millas
Alegría
Siquirres
Batán
Matina
Punta de Riel
Reserva Bosque Central Cordillera Volcánica
Lomas
Moravia
32
Estrada
Reventazón
10
Zona Protectora Pacuare
Stratford
3328
Turrialba
Bonilla Arriba
Parque Nacional Volcán Irazú
3432
Irazú
BARBILLA
Corina
Río Cuba
Lajas
Peralta
Santa Cruz
Playa Hermosa
Monumento Nacional Guayabo
Reserva Biológica Barbilla
6
Santa Rosa
Pacayas
Turrialba
Pavones
Juan Viñas
Eslabón
Cabeza de Buey
Cervantes
10
La Suiza
Tucurrique
Tuis
CHIRRIPÓ
Zona Protectora Río Banano
Paraíso
Cachí
Atirro
Ujarrás
1865
Pejibaye
Tapantí
Zona Protectora Cuenca del Río Tuis
CHIRRIPÓ
CARTAGO
7
Parque Nacional Tapantí-Macizo de la Muerte
Parque Internacional La Amistad
Tres de Junio
Reserva Bosque Río Macho
255
3156
Vueltas
TELIRÉ
3491
La Muerte
Villa Mills
Telirė
Siberia
Cordillera de Talamanca
Reserva Bosque Los Santos
Piedra
3333
Urán
Río Blanco
División
3820
Chirripó
Santo Tomás
Santa Eduviges
Herradura
2
San Gerardo de Rivas
8
La Ese
Chimirol
Parque Nacional Chirripó
Savegre Abajo
Rivas
San Rafael Norte
3295
Amí
Parque Internacional La Amistad
3097
Eli
Santa Rosa
SAN JOSÉ
San Isidro de El General
Chiles
Santa Elena
Cedral
Esperanza
22
Guabo
Palmares
Tinamaste
Santa María
Cajón
258
UJARRÁS
Angel
Ceiba
Reserva Biológica
Angostura
Altamira
Utyu

N
P
Q
5
6
7
8
Puerto Limón
Isla Uvita
Portete
Moín
Liverpool
Cieneguita
Río Blanco
Veragua Rainforest Research & Adventure Park
Westfalia
Trébol
Beverly
Banano
María Luisa
Bananito Norte
Finca Banaga
San Clemente
Penshurst
Playa Cahuita
Punta Cahuita
Limonal
Cahuita
Pandora
Vesta
Dindiri
Carbón Dos
Parque Nacional Cahuita
Valle de la Estrella
36
Reserva Biológica Hitoy Cerere
Valle de las Rosas
Hotel Creek
Puerto Viejo de Talamanca
Bribrí
COCLES
Manzanillo
Refugio Nacional de Vida Silvestre Gandoca-Manzanillo
Olivia
Margarita
Teliré
Shiroles
Sibube
Paraíso
Elena
Sixaola
Sepeque
Bratsi
TALAMANCA
Katsi
Valle de Talamanca
Bris
Guabito
Yorkin
PA
Parque Internacional La Amistad
Alto Lari
Sukut
Guachalaba
259

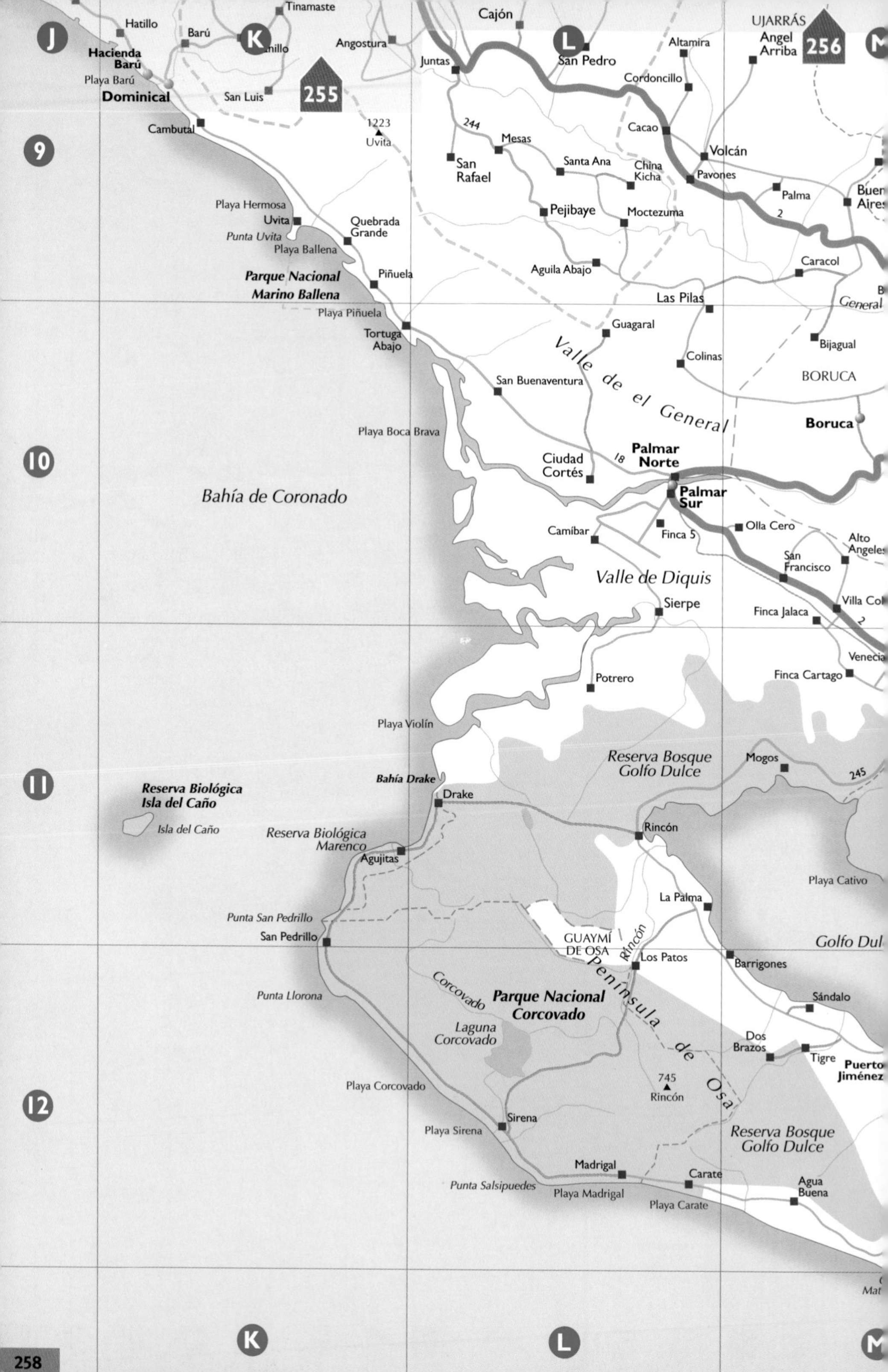

Tinamaste
Hatillo
Barú
Hacienda Barú
Playa Barú
Dominical
San Luis
Angostura
255
Cajón
Juntas
San Pedro
Altamira
UJARRÁS
Angel Arriba
256
Cordoncillo
Cambutal
1223
Uvita
244
Mesas
San Rafael
Santa Ana
China Kicha
Cacao
Volcán
Pavones
Palma
Pejibaye
Moctezuma
Playa Hermosa
Uvita
Punta Uvita
Quebrada Grande
Playa Ballena
Parque Nacional Marino Ballena
Piñuela
Aguila Abajo
Caracol
Las Pilas
Playa Piñuela
Tortuga Abajo
Guagaral
Valle de el General
Colinas
Bijagual
BORUCA
San Buenaventura
Boruca
Playa Boca Brava
Ciudad Cortés
18
Palmar Norte
Palmar Sur
Bahía de Coronado
Camíbar
Finca 5
Olla Cero
San Francisco
Valle de Diquis
Sierpe
Finca Jalaca
Potrero
Finca Cartago
Playa Violín
Reserva Bosque Golfo Dulce
Mogos
245
Bahía Drake
Drake
Reserva Biológica Isla del Caño
Isla del Caño
Reserva Biológica Marenco
Agujitas
Rincón
Playa Cativo
La Palma
Punta San Pedrillo
San Pedrillo
GUAYMÍ DE OSA
Rincón
Los Patos
Barrigones
Península de Osa
Punta Llorona
Corcovado
Parque Nacional Corcovado
Sándalo
Laguna Corcovado
Dos Brazos
Tigre
745
Rincón
Playa Corcovado
Sirena
Playa Sirena
Reserva Bosque Golfo Dulce
Madrigal
Carate
Punta Salsipuedes
Playa Madrigal
Playa Carate
Agua Buena
9
10
11
12
J
K
L
M

257
N
P
Q
Reserva Biológica Durika
ALITRE
CABAGRA
3122
Naí
Parque Internacional La Amistad
9
Cabagra
Cabagra
3335
Cerro Fábrega
3204
Bine
Helechales
Potrero Grande
Finca Colorado
Alto Cacao
Vueltas
Zona Protectora Las Tablas
Agua Caliente
10
237
Guácimo
Coto Brus
Palmira
Alturas
Santa Fé
2468
Pando
Jabillo
Bonanza
Fila Guinea
Flor del Roble
Poma
Mellizas
2874
Picacho
Santa Lucia
Valle de Coto Brus
La Lucha
Río Negro
PUNTARENAS
Paraíso
Sabanillo
237
Limoncito
Sabalito
Río Sereno
GUAYMÍ COTO-BRUS
San Vito
Linda Vista
Chacarita
Chirriquí Viejo
Copal
La Navidad
Jardín Botánico Wilson
Cañas Gordas
Volcán
Guaria
Parque Nacional Piedras Blancas
Agua Buena
PA
11
INTERAMERICANA/PAN-AMERICAN HIGHWAY
Briceño
16
Los Planes
Gamba
Dominical
Refugio Nacional de Fauna Silvestre Golfito
Río Claro
2
Caracol
Ciudad Neily
GUAYMÍ ABROJOS-MONTEZUMA
Esperanza
Bajo Mansito
Golfito
Finca 58
Abrojo
Playa Gallardo
14
Coto 47
San Andrés
Coloradito
Portón
Coto Colorado
Pueblo Nuevo
Gloria
Canoas
La Concepción
Zancudo
Playa Platanares
Sábalos
Valle de Coto Colorado
La Cuesta
Gariche
12
Playa Zapote
Puerto Pilón
Progreso
Playa Tamales
Punta Ojo de Agua
Conte
Bella Luz
Laurel
La Esperanza
Playa Sombrero
Finca Cañaza
Pavones
Nicaragua
Blanca Arriba
Colorado
GUAYMÍ CONTE-BURICA
Palo Blanco

MAPS | INDEX

MAPS INDEX

A

B

C

D

PICTURES

The Automobile Association wishes to thank the following photographers and organisations for their assistance in the preparation of this book.

Abbreviations for the picture credits are as follows – (t) top; (b) bottom; (l) left; (r) right; (c) centre; (AA) AA World Travel Library

2 AA/Clive Sawyer;
3(i) AA/Nicholas Sumner;
3(ii) AA/Nicholas Sumner;
3(iii) AA/Nicholas Sumner;
3(iv) AA/Clive Sawyer;
4 AA/Clive Sawyer;
5 AA/Steve Watkins;
6 AA/Nicholas Sumner;
7 Danita Delimont/Alamy;
9 Purestock/Alamy;
10 AA/Clive Sawyer;
11bl AA/Clive Sawyer;
11tr AA/Clive Sawyer;
12 AA/Clive Sawyer;
13t Instituto Costarricense de Turismo;
13b AA/Clive Sawyer;
16 Kevin Schafer/NHPA;
17 Kevin Schafer/NHPA;
18 Michael & Patricia Fogden;
19bl Robin Chittenden/Alamy;
19br George Bernard/NHPA;
20 Tom Vezo/Nature Picture Library;
21 Jack Ewing/Hacienda Baru National Wildlife Refuge;
23tl Michael & Patricia Fogden;
23tr AA/Nicholas Sumner;
24 Ted Miller/Still Pictures;
25bl AA/Nicholas Sumner;
25br Michael & Patricia Fogden;
26bl Carlos Villoch - MagicSea.com/Alamy;
26br Michael & Patricia Fogden;
27 Didi/Alamy;
28 AA/Nicholas Sumner;
29bl Instituto Costarricense de Turismo;
29tr Michael & Patricia Fogden;
30 www.jjphoto.dk;
31bl AA/Nicholas Sumner;
31br AA/Nicholas Sumner;
32 Thornton Cohen/Alamy;
33t AA/Clive Sawyer;
33b AA/Clive Sawyer;
34 Chris Fredriksson/Alamy;
35 AA/Nicholas Sumner;
36 Hemis/Alamy;
37bl Carver Mostardi/Alamy;
37tr AA/Clive Sawyer;
38 AKG Images;
39t AA;
39b AA;
40 Bettmann/Corbis;
41bl Kent Gilbert/AP/Press Association Images;
41tr AA/Nicholas Sumner;
42 AA/Clive Sawyer;
43 AA/Nicholas Sumner;
44 AA/Nicholas Sumner;
45 Christopher P Baker;
46 Pixtal Images/Photolibrary.com;
47 AA/Clive Sawyer;
48 AA/Clive Sawyer;
49 AA/Nicholas Sumner;
51 AA/Nicholas Sumner;
52 AA/Clive Sawyer;
54 AA/Clive Sawyer;
56 AA/Steve Watkins;
57 AA/Nicholas Sumner;
58 AA/Nicholas Sumner;
59 Radius Images/Photolibrary;
60 AA/Clive Sawyer;
64 AA/Nicholas Sumner;
65 AA/Nicholas Sumner;
66 AA/Nicholas Sumner;
67 AA/Nicholas Sumner;
68 AA/Clive Sawyer;
69bl Michel Renaudeau/Photolibrary;
69br AA/Nicholas Sumner;
70 AA/Nicholas Sumner;
71 AA/Nicholas Sumner;
72 AA/Nicholas Sumner;
73 AA/Nicholas Sumner;
74 AA/Clive Sawyer;
75 Mayela Lopez/AFP/Getty Images;
76 Oliver Gerhard/Alamy;
78 AA/Nicholas Sumner;
80 Christopher P Baker;
82 Johnny Haglund/Lonely Planet Images;
84 AA/Nicholas Sumner;
85 AA/Nicholas Sumner;
86 travelib costa rica/Alamy;
87 AA/Clive Sawyer;
88 AA/Nicholas Sumner;
89 AA/Nicholas Sumner;
90 AA/Clive Sawyer;
91br Instituto Costarricense de Turismo;
92 AA/Clive Sawyer;
93 AA/Clive Sawyer;
94 AA/Nicholas Sumner;
95 Instituto Costarricense de Turismo;
96 AA/Nicholas Sumner;
97tl AA/Clive Sawyer;
97tr AA/Clive Sawyer;
98 AA/Nicholas Sumner;
99 AA/Nicholas Sumner;
100 AA/Nicholas Sumner;
101tl AA/Nicholas Sumner;
101tr AA/Nicholas Sumner;
102 AA/Nicholas Sumner;
104 Kevin Schafer/Alamy;
105 First Light/Alamy;
107 AA/Nicholas Sumner;
108 Jon Arnold Images Ltd/Alamy;
110 AA/Clive Sawyer;
112 AA/Steve Watkins;
113 Instituto Costarricense de Turismo;
114 AA/Clive Sawyer;
116 AA/Nicholas Sumner;
119 AA/Nicholas Sumner;
120 Bruce Coleman Inc./Alamy;
121t AA/Nicholas Sumner;
121b AA/Nicholas Sumner;
122 AA/Nicholas Sumner;
123bl AA/Nicholas Sumner;
123br AA/Nicholas Sumner;
124 imagebroker/Alamy;
126 Danita Delimont/Alamy;
127 Photodisc;
128 Hemis/Alamy;
130 David Noton Photography/Alamy;
132 AA/Nicholas Sumner;
133 AA/Clive Sawyer;
134 AA/Nicholas Sumner;
135 AA/Nicholas Sumner;
136 AA/Nicholas Sumner;

137 AA/Nicholas Sumner;
138 AA/Nicholas Sumner;
139t AA/Nicholas Sumner;
139b AA/Nicholas Sumner;
140 AA/Nicholas Sumner;
141 AA/Clive Sawyer;
142 AA/Nicholas Sumner;
144 Carver Mostardi/Alamy;
146 Christopher P Baker;
148 James Tims;
150 AA/Nicholas Sumner;
152 AA/Nicholas Sumner;
154 AA/Clive Sawyer;
155 AA/Nicholas Sumner;
157 Norbert Probst/Photolibrary;
158 AA/Clive Sawyer;
159 Instituto Costarricense de Turismo;
160 Instituto Costarricense de Turismo;
161 AA/Clive Sawyer;
162 Ian Woolcock/Alamy;
164 Calypso Cruises;
166 AA/Nicholas Sumner;
167 Hotel Makanda by the Sea;
169 Robert Harding Picture Library Ltd/Alamy;
171 Florblanca Resort;
172 Mauritius Images GmbH/Alamy;
174 AA/Clive Sawyer;
175 AA/Clive Sawyer;
176 AA/Clive Sawyer;
177 AA/Clive Sawyer;
178 Jan Csernoch;
179 AA/Nicholas Sumner;
180 AA/Nicholas Sumner;
181 AA/Clive Sawyer;
182 AA/Steve Watkins;
183bl Inger Hogstrom/Photolibrary;
183br Instituto Costarricense de Turismo;
184 Instituto Costarricense de Turismo;
185 AA/Clive Sawyer;
187 AA/Nicholas Sumner;
188 WaterFrame/Alamy;
189 AA/Steve Watkins;
190 travelib costa rica/Alamy;
191 Nicholas Gill/Alamy;
192 Christopher P Baker;
194 Chris Fredriksson/Alamy;
196 Stuart Pearce/Alamy;
197 AA/Clive Sawyer;
198 AA/Clive Sawyer;
199 AA/Steve Watkins;
200t AA/Steve Watkins;
200b AA/Clive Sawyer;
201bl AA/Clive Sawyer;
201br Stuart Pearce/Alamy;
202 Stuart Pearce/Alamy;
203 AA/Nicholas Sumner;
204 AA/Clive Sawyer;
206 travelib prime/Alamy;
208 Danita Delimont/Alamy;
209 travelib costa rica/Alamy;
211 David South/Alamy;
213 AA/Nicholas Sumner;
216 AA/Nicholas Sumner;
220 Michael & Patricia Fogden;
221 AA/Clive Sawyer;
222 AA/Nicholas Sumner;
224 AA/Nicholas Sumner;
226 AA/Clive Sawyer;
228 AA/Clive Sawyer;
229 AA/Clive Sawyer;
230 Michael & Patricia Fogden;
231 AA/Nicholas Sumner;
232 Instituto Costarricense de Turismo;
233 Kelly Shannon Kelly/Alamy;
235 AA/Clive Sawyer;
236 AA/Steve Watkins;
237 AA/Clive Sawyer;
239 AA/Clive Sawyer;
240 AA/Nicholas Sumner;
241 AA/Nicholas Sumner;
247 Zach Holmes/Alamy.

Every effort has been made to trace the copyright holders, and we apologise in advance for any accidental errors. We would be happy to apply any corrections in the following edition of this publication.

CREDITS

Series editor
Sheila Hawkins

Project editor
Bookwork Creative Associates Ltd

Design
Low Sky Design Ltd

Cover design
Chie Ushio

Picture research
Alice Earle

Image retouching and repro
Jackie Street

Mapping
Maps produced by the Mapping Services Department of AA Publishing

Main contributors
Christopher P Baker, Peter Hutchison, Caroline Lascom

Updater
Christopher P Baker

Indexer
Marie Lorimer

Production
Lorraine Taylor

See It Costa Rica
ISBN 978-1-4000-0549-9
Third Edition

Published in the United States by Fodor's Travel and simultaneously in Canada by Random House of Canada Limited, Toronto.
Published in the United Kingdom by AA Publishing.
Fodor's is a registered trademark of Random House, Inc., and Fodor's See It is a trademark of Random House, Inc.
Fodor's Travel is a division of Random House, Inc.

Color separation by AA Digital Department
Printed and bound by Leo Paper Products, China
10 9 8 7 6 5 4 3 2

Special Sales: This book is available for special discounts for bulk purchases for sales promotions or premiums. Special editions, including personalized covers, excerpts of existing books, and corporate imprints, can be created in large quantities for special needs.
For more information, write to Special Markets/Premium Sales, 1745 Broadway, 3–2, New York, NY 10019
or e-mail specialmarkets@randomhouse.com
Important Note: Time inevitably brings changes, so always confirm prices, travel facts, and other perishable information when it matters. Although Fodor's cannot accept responsibility for errors, you can use this guide in the confidence that we have taken every care to ensure its accuracy.

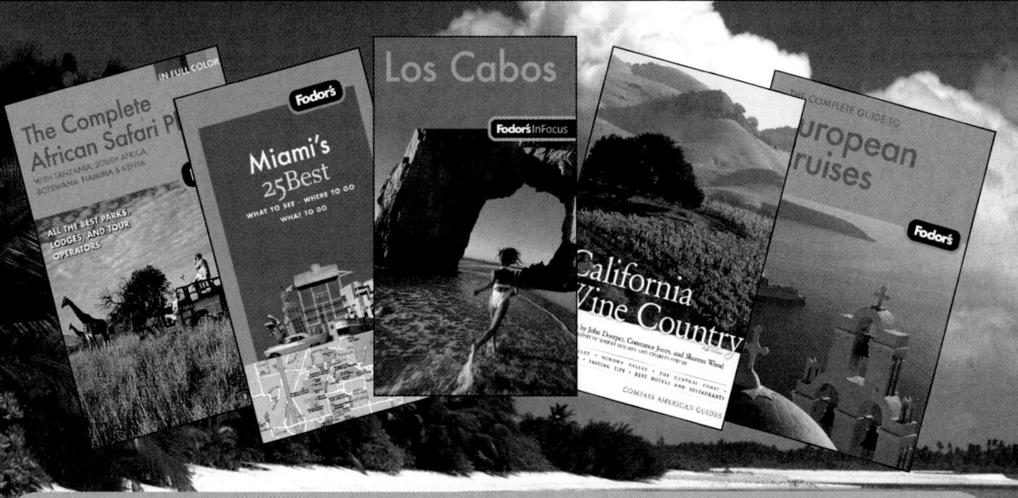
IN FULL COLOR
The Complete African Safari Pl
WITH TANZANIA, SOUTH AFRICA, BOTSWANA, NAMIBIA & KENYA
ALL THE BEST PARKS, LODGES, AND TOUR OPERATORS
Fodor's
Miami's 25Best
WHAT TO SEE · WHERE TO GO WHAT TO DO
Los Cabos
Fodor's InFocus
California Wine Country
COMPASS AMERICAN GUIDES
THE COMPLETE GUIDE TO
uropean ruises
Fodor's